To my friend Jean-Francois Remy Neris

NAPOLEON'S IMPERIAL GUARD UNIFORMS AND EQUIPMENT

THE CAVALRY

PAUL L. DAWSON

COLOUR PLATES BY KEITH ROCCO

FRONTLINE
BOOKS

Napoleon's Imperial Guard Uniforms and Equipment
THE CAVALRY

First published in Great Britain in 2019 by Frontline Books,
an imprint of Pen & Sword Books Ltd, Yorkshire - Philadelphia

ISBN: 978-152670-896-0

Typeset in Sabon by Gill Sans

Printed and bound in India by Replika Press Pvt. Ltd.

Pen & Sword Books Ltd incorporates the imprints of Pen & Sword Archaeology, Air World Books, Atlas, Aviation, Battleground, Discovery, Family History, History, Maritime, Military, Naval, Politics, Social History, Transport, True Crime, Claymore Press, Frontline Books, Praetorian Press, Seaforth Publishing and White Owl

For a complete list of Pen & Sword titles please contact:

PEN & SWORD BOOKS LTD
47 Church Street, Barnsley, South Yorkshire, S70 2AS, England
E-mail: enquiries@pen-and-sword.co.uk
Website: www.pen-and-sword.co.uk
Or
PEN AND SWORD BOOKS,
1950 Lawrence Roadd, Havertown, PA 19083, USA
E-mail: Uspen-and-sword@casematepublishers.com
Website: www.penandswordbooks.com

CONTENTS

ACKNOWLEDGEMENTS

In the preparation of this book I would like to thank all those who have offered advice, support and who have helped me with my research.

I am indebted to M. Yves Martin, Ian James Smith, John Lubomski and Sally Fairweather for their assistance with, and photographing of, archival material during many visits to the Archives Nationales and Service Historique de la Défence Armée du Tére, in Paris. Without their help this book could not have been written.

Ronald Pawly is also to be thanked for digital media copies of documents at the Archives Nationales. Without this most generous support the book would have taken far longer to complete.

George Lubomski provided copious material on the history and organisation of the Polish lancers, for which I am very grateful. I am indebted to M. Pierre de Witt, M. Jean-Marc Largeaud, Mr Terry Crowdy, Miss Rachael Cresswell BSc PGCE and Mrs Emily Lancaster BSc MSc for their help in the preparation of the text. Jerome Croyet must be thanked for his permission to reproduce the photographs I have taken of the former Brunon collection. Isabelle Artaud, of the Musée de l'Armée, Paris, is also to be heartily thanked for also providing me with permission to use images of the collections of the Musée de l'Armée.

INTRODUCTION

The most famous military organisation of the Napoleonic Wars was Napoleon's Imperial Guard. The story of the Guard in France spans many centuries. Almost all the kings and queens in French history had a guard in one form or other. The Imperial Guard owes it origins to three distinct body guards, moulded into a single force under the eyes of First Consul Bonaparte between December 1799 and January 1800.

The oldest formation to become part of the Consular Guard was the *Guardes de la Prévôté Hotel*, which had been formed in 1789. With the creation of the national assembly, their title changed to the *Garde de l'Assemblée Nationales* on 20 June 1789, but two years later, on 10 May 1791, the name changed yet again to the *Compagnie de la Prévôté*. The title quickly changed to *Gendarmes Nationaux*, but this lasted only five days before the unit was re-titled once again, becoming the *Grenadiers-Gendarmes pres de la Representation Nationales* on 15 May 1791. The organisation was expanded on 22 July 1795 and it was renamed the *Grenadiers pres la Representation Nationales*, shortened to the *Gardes de la Convention*. With the dissolution of the Convention on 26 October 1795 and the introduction of the *Corps Legislatif*, the *Garde de la Convention* became the *Garde du Corps Legislatif* (28 October 1795) and comprised 1,200 men nominated by the directory. In the same year, the directory formed a guard to act as an honour guard and provide protection to its members. The final element of the Guard came from Napoleon's Guides raised in 1796 in Italy.

In 1799, all three organisations were amalgamated into a new *Gardes de Consuls*. The Guards of the Legislature became the *grenadiers-à-pied*, while the Guides became the *chasseurs-à-cheval*. The directory provided a smattering of men, non-commissioned officers and officers to the new Consular Guard, its influence upon the latter being limited as it was the smallest of all three guards, mustering no more than 240 officers and men.

The cavalry of the Guard of the Consuls was to have a staff under the decree of 3 January 1800:[1] one *chef du brigade*, five squadron heads (three for the grenadiers), one staff captain, one quartermaster treasurer, one captain instructor, five adjutants, five standard bearers, two surgeons, one trumpet major, one corporal trumpeter and six master workmen.[2]

The master smith, tailor and saddler ranked as sergeants and wore the badges of rank and trade, while the other master workmen were ranked as corporals.[3]

Each squadron was to be composed of: one captain, one first-lieutenant, one second-lieutenant, one sub-lieutenant, one sergeant-major, four sergeants, one fourrier, eight corporals, one blacksmith, ninety-six grenadiers and two trumpeters.[4]

On 15 February 1800, Napoleon decreed that the Guard of the Consuls was to have a band of seventy-five musicians. Of these, twenty-five were mounted to act as a band for the *grenadiers* and *chasseurs*. The band was dressed in the same manner as the trumpeters of the *chasseurs-à-cheval*. On 18 May 1804, the French senate announced that the governance of the French Republic was to be handed over to Napoleon, who was to be Emperor of the French. He would be crowned by the pope at Notre Dame, Paris, on 5 December 1804.

By the decree of 28 *Floréal*, Year XII (18 May 1804), the Consular Guard became the Imperial Guard.[5]

The decree of 10 *Thermidor*, Year XII (29 July 1804) directed a massive expansion of the Guard and formed a general staff, the *Regiment de Grenadiers-à-Pied*, the *grenadiers-velites*, the *Regiment de Chasseurs-à-Pied*, the *chasseurs-velites*, a veteran company, the marine battalion, the *Regiment de Grenadiers-à-Cheval*, the *Regiment de Chasseurs-à-Cheval*, the *mamelukes*, the *gendarmes d'elite*, a force of light artillery and artisans and a medical staff. By the end of 1804 the Guard had an authorised strength of 9,798 men. For the most part, the Guard was an elite formation. The decree of 30 *Fructidor*, Year XIII (17 September 1805) added two squadrons of mounted *velites*, which were intended to complete the number of squadrons in case of need.[6]

The *velite* squadrons were to become essential elements of the Guard. They were formed from physically fit men who aspired to be the officers of the future, and were willing to pay 200 *francs* a year for this privilege, payable very four months. If the payments stopped, in the absence of extenuating circumstances, the *velite* would be sent to the line.[7] They were to be at least 18 years old and 170 cm tall,[8] to be conscripted for three years, with each department of France to provide six conscripts of suitable condition to enter the corps.[9] When joining the corps, the *velites* had to supply their own uniform, having to have with them on admission a pair of doeskin breeches, a pair of boots and a pair of regimental gloves.[10]

The formation of these units was a deliberate means of wooing and binding various elements of French society to the emperor and thereby strengthening his grip on the French throne. The key to the reason the *velites* were raised is found in the stipend demanded of the parents of the *velites*. Aside from the size requirements, which simply implied that they would be bigger and stronger than the average Frenchman, it was required that the parents provided financial support of their sons in the service. Napoleon began a process of binding himself to the politically influential and financially important middle class of France. The organisation changed again in April 1806. The decree of 15 April 1806 stated that, when on campaign and times of war, the *velite* squadrons were distributed among the Old Guard companies to make them up to 250 men, and that any surplus *velites* would be used to form a fifth squadron. The regimental staff was reduced by a squadron head and two adjutants.[11]

The decree also expanded the Guard with a newly formed regiment of dragoons. The following year, in 1807, the Polish light horses added to the Guard, while 1811 witnessed the creation of a second light horses regiment, this time Dutch, which became the famous Red Lancers. The *velites* in the *grenadiers*, *chasseurs* and dragoons were formed into a single war squadron in August 1811. Only the Red Lancers retained their *velites*. In 1812 a regiment of Lithuanian lancers were formed and 1813 witnessed the expansion of the Guard with the creation of four regiments of Guards of Honour, and the breaking of the *grenadiers*, *chasseurs*, dragoons and Red Lancers into Old Guard and Young Guard regiments. Three regiments of *èclaireurs* were created in December 1813. The cavalry of the Guard was dissolved in July 1814.

CHAPTER 1

ADMINISTRATION OF THE REGIMENT

The officers and senior sub-officers were responsible for the day-to-day running of the regiment, overseen by the regimental staff (*etat major*).

From 15 March 1794, each battalion was administered by a council of administration (*conseil d'administration*). At battalion level it was responsible for discipline, expenses incurred by the battalion, detailing the number of men and horses on a daily basis, and noting those on leave, on detachment or in hospital. It was to comprise of the battalion commander, who would act as president, an officer, a sub-officer (a sergeant-major, sergeant or corporal-quartermaster) and two troopers. The officer was to be nominated by their fellow officers from the battalion and then elected by drawing lots if more than one candidate was put forward. The sub-officer was to be nominated in the same manner. It was the duty of the sub-officer to report those men of the battalion absent, on leave or in hospital. In the absence of the battalion commander, his duties were to be replaced by the senior captain.

Each company of the battalion was to present two troopers to the council. These men had to be elected to the position by a majority vote. Of the four troopers presented, the two most senior were to be elected to the council. All members of the council were to be elected for a period of six months, and could only continue to be members if returned there by election. If for any length of time the battalion was detached from the regiment over a distance of 13½ miles, it was to act for the council of the regiment.

The council of the regiment was to comprise the regimental colonel, who was to act as president of the regiment, three officers, three sub-officers and six privates. These men were to be drawn from the battalion councils. In the absence of the regimental colonel, his place was to be taken by the senior battalion commander.

Election to the regimental council was for six months. In the first half of the year, the members were to come from the 1st Battalion and in the second half of the year from the 2nd Battalion. The sub-officers had to be nominated after election through majority from the members of the battalion council. Of the privates, the longest serving was elected. In addition, the battalion commander quartermaster-treasurer was an ex-officio member and carried out the function of secretary.

According to the decree of 20 July 1794, the regimental council was attached to the regimental staff. The council was responsible for authorising the purchase of clothing, equipment, horses, forage, discipline of the regiment, promotions, the discharge of horses, men and disposal of worn-out items of clothing. The council oversaw the payment of the regiment and docking of pay to pay for consumables when in barracks or lodgings. This was to be overseen by a commissioner for war.

Provision of rations for the men, clothing and equipment was vested in specific officers on the regimental staff. They had to ensure that the correct quantity of feeds was purchased according to government guidelines, and that all purchases were fully accounted for.

The lieutenant clothing officer had to oversee the purchase of all items of equipment and clothing for the sub-officers and troopers. Officers provided their own uniforms and equipment. The regimental council oversaw that the items purchased on the regiment's behalf were of good quality, that they matched the regiment's specification and that the cost of purchase was as agreed in the contract. All receipts had to be lodged in separate account books that were overseen by a commissioner for war. This was to ensure that officers did not pocket money from the regiment obtaining contracts. The specification for each item of uniform was recorded in a register of uniforms (*registre de tenues*). The commissioner for war was to ensure that items purchased matched this register. All deliberations of the council in obtaining contracts for clothing and equipment from contractors were to be recorded so that the commissioner for war could see how and why a regiment chose a certain contractor.

The clothing officer also had to ensure that all regimental property held in the regimental magazines at the depot were in good condition and all accounted for. The clothing and equipment of men in hospital was also the responsibility of the clothing officer, who had to ensure it was stored in good condition while the member of the regiment was hospitalised. Each company commander had to keep a report of the items of clothing and equipment issued to their company and note which items needed repairing, what was beyond use and which items were new. These reports were submitted to the clothing officer, who then collated the information. The magazines and regiment were to be inspected every year by a commissioner for war to ensure that the paperwork of the regiment matched reality and to agree to the disposal of warn-out clothing and equipment.

Purchase of items

The council of administration each year, acting with the clothing officers, drew up a store's inventory of the regiment, as well as gathered the parade states of the items of equipment and clothing issued. Items of clothing had a specific lifespan. Each time an item was inspected it was classed as new, in need of repair, due to expire or expired and in need of replacement. From this data the clothing officer was able to report the total number of items needing to be replaced or repaired.

The contracts for repair of clothing do not survive, but the minutes drawn up by the council of administration do. The council of administration prepared paperwork for the total purchase of cloth, buttons, leather items, etc, needed to replace worn-out items and needed to equip new entrants to a regiment. These discussion documents were classed as *exercise* – basically an expression of obtaining formal quotes to tender for the provision of items. These items were then purchased through *marches*, which in essence are bills of sale. They list what items were ordered, from which supplier and their address, when the order was placed, when the bill was paid and also when the items were delivered. It is from these *exercise*, *marche* and store reports that we are able to comment upon the uniform and equipment of the various regiments in this study.

Items were either ordered from suppliers as complete items, or the material was obtained with which to make them. Each regiment had up to six master workmen. Their workshops were located in the regimental depot. Each workman would take on at least two of the regiment's children as apprentices. The workmen included:

- Master tailor. He ranked as a sergeant and was responsible for manufacturing uniforms for his regiment, as well as making repairs to the uniforms. Every man who joined the regiment would be measured and have a uniform altered to fit. Uniforms came in three sizes. In the Guard, especially the Old Guard, the uniforms were custom-made for each man. The master tailor charged the regiment for his time to make items at an established rate of pay before the work commenced. In addition, from 1810 it seems each company had at least one tailor, and company funds were used to pay his wages.
- Master armourer. He ranked as a corporal and it was his duty to ensure weapons were kept in good repair and repaired as needed.
- Master cordwainer. The master shoe-maker ranked as a corporal and was responsible for the manufacture and repair of shoes and boots.
- Master gaiter-maker. The gaiters of a regiment had, prior to 9 September 1799, been made by the master tailor. After that date, the duties were passed to the gaiter-maker.

For clothing, in many cases the regiment bought cloth and paid for the items to be made in-house by the regiment's tailors. Items such as shoes were often bought in bulk from factories rather than made in-house. Leather items were ordered from manufacturers, as were metal fittings like buttons. Headdress was also out-sourced. If made in-house or bought in *marches*, they would be prepared for agreement by the regiment's administrative council, who would oversee the work and inspect the quality of the workmanship or materials. Each regiment, it seems, kept a sealed pattern for each item of equipment which was the established model to be copied by suppliers.

Limitations of sources used

The archive materials presented in the following chapters are transcripts of the original material used by the author. We must note that the archive material for all regiments in this study is incomplete. The lack of material means we will never know for sure what some regiments actually wore. Lucian Rousselot attempted to fill the gaps in the archive material using period iconography. However, these images are open to a great deal of speculation and artistic license. Rousselot used the Hoffmann image and David's painting of the distribution of the eagles to reconstruct the uniform of the *sapeurs* of the *grenadiers-à-pied*. This is a laudable approach, but what Rousselot presented as fact, and copied by more modern illustrators, is guesswork. The total absence of paperwork for the *chasseurs-à-pied* means any reconstruction of the uniform of the *sapeurs* and drummers is total guesswork – we simply do not have any archive material to reconstruct the clothing. Neither can we say that what Hoffmann and Potrelle show *circa* 1804 is anything like what was worn in 1804, or in later years. Artists show the band of the 3rd Grenadiers with yellow facings, yet archive material makes no mention of yellow wool cloth. Therefore, there is no primary evidence to support this idea. The earliest representation of the band with yellow facings is by Noirmont and Marbot from the mid-nineteenth century. We do not know what source they used to obtain the information for the facing colours. Based on the regiment's archive, the band is likely to have had not *bleu de ciel* coats, but mid-blue faced in crimson. Therefore, we cannot say beyond reasonable doubt that the yellow facings are correct. Some records list the amount of a specific lace destined for drummers or *sapeurs* or similar troops. The writer of the documents 200 years ago would know exactly how this lace was sewn on to a uniform coat. For the modern researcher, we have no idea how the lace was sewn on to a garment or how much lace was issued per man. This absence of evidence has allowed for the creation of a large quantity of material presenting so-called *de facto* uniform guides for regiments, based on little more than guesswork, the vagueness of the sources being used to give the modern interpreter free rein in how they reconstruct a uniform. We cannot say, however, that what they show is correct. Therefore, we have limited ourselves to offering the original source data and some suggestions of what the original uniform may have been like based on the analysis of extant items and period iconography. But even then, we cannot be sure that what we suggest is a true reflection of what was actually used.

We must acknowledge, therefore, that the vast majority of the archive material relating to the dress of the Imperial Guard is now lost and we will never be able to reconstruct the uniform in any degree of completeness. A lot of artists and historians in the last 200 years have used period images as their starting point in reconstructing the dress of the Guard, rather than starting with the archive sources, which do not give all, or in some cases any, answers to our questions.

The archive documents can be brought to life by the analysis of original garments, regulations and period iconography to show us what an item described in the documents may have looked like. The *marche* accounts and similar documents do not go into great detail about the appearance of items, as the officers creating the documents knew exactly what items looked like, therefore had no need to describe them. This is where inference on the part of the interpreter is needed, as noted before. In creating this narrative, has endeavoured to let the primary sources speak for themselves without fitting what they say into a superficial construct created by others. This approach has allowed a fresh and revisionary narrative to be produced on the uniform of the Imperial Guard. We must also stress the role of the interpreter in the creation of the narrative. We all have pre-conceived ideas and personal biases towards historical events based on political, economic, sociological and ideological grounds. These will impact on the way the interpreter interprets the source material. No historian is free from bias. Interpretation of source material to construct a narrative is thereby affected by the response, desire and needs of different interpreters.

We will never know exactly what some regiments wore.

Cloth and colours

Before we look at the clothing of the soldier, we need to define the type of cloth fabric used in the construction of the clothing and also something about the colour of the cloth used.

Cloth

In general terms, the French Army of Napoleon I used flax or hemp fibres to be woven into linens, or wool fibre to be made into wool cloth. The army used two types of wool cloth:

- Broadcloth – a dense, plain-woven wool cloth
- Twill – woven with a pattern of diagonal parallel ribs

Above left: Sample of Aurore cloth dated 1823. Aurore has been shown by many artists to be a shade of yellow, when in fact it is a vivid shade of dark orange. (Collection KM)

Above right: This cloth sample from 1823 is *bleu de ciel*, the colour of cloth used by the trumpeters of the Imperial Guard. It is much darker than the colour shown by modern artists. (Collection KM)

Above left: This cloth sample from 1823 shows Imperial Blue wool cloth as used by the *grenadiers-à-cheval* and *Elite Gendarmes* for their *habits*. In 1815 the name of the cloth changed to *bleu de roi*. (Collection KM)

Above right: We are left in no doubt as to the colour of the facings of the Polish lancers and of trumpeters of the Guard cavalry with this cloth sample of 1823. (Collection KM)

The defining characteristic of broadcloth is not its finished width, but the fact that it was woven much wider (typically fifty to seventy-five percent) than its finished width and then heavily milled (traditionally the cloth was worked by heavy wooden trip hammers in hot soapy water in order to shrink it) in order to reduce it to the required width. The effect of the milling process is to draw the yarns much closer together than could be achieved in the loom and allow the individual fibres of the wool to bind together in a felting process. This results in a dense, blind face cloth with a stiff drape that is highly weather-resistant, hard-wearing and capable of taking a cut edge without the need for being hemmed. For the lower classes and the soldiers of the line, the cloth was dyed once it was made. This cloth is known as 'dyed in the piece'. The wool would be made at a mill and the resulting 'white cloth' sold onto a dye works for the cloth to be dyed. This meant that a clothier could readily supply large lengths of cloth of different colours. Cloth woven with dyed thread had a longer production time. This method produced a much stronger and more consistent shade through the cloth. It was noticeably far costlier than cloth dyed in the piece, as the clothier had to buy the cloth ready dyed in far longer lengths than the cloth dyed once woven – it was, and is, easier to buy 1,000 m of cloth and dye 10 m blue and the rest another colour, than having to buy 1,000 m of cloth and only needing 10 m initially in the chosen colour.

The yarn used in this high-grade fabric contained a percentage of imported Spanish *merino* wool, mixed with high-quality French-produced yarn. This high-grade cloth was produced in the Elbeuf region. Dyeing the yarn before weaving gave a better quality of colour, but it meant that a mill had to produce minimum quantities of cloths of different colours, whereas the mills producing cloth that was dyed later could produce a cheaper product, as the looms produced a natural cloth using yarn that was not as well sorted or selected as the higher-grade fabric. This coarser fabric was known as *drap de lodeve* and was, it seems, the 'bog standard' army cloth. The better-quality yarn and finish on the cloth would also reflect the way in which the dye was taken up into the yarn fibres, so the same dye on a high-grade superfine would look different to the same dye on a much lower grade and coarser fabric.

In a twill weave, each weft or filling yarn floats across the warp yarns in a progression of interlacings to the right or left, forming a distinct diagonal line. This diagonal line is also known as a wale. A float is the portion of a yarn that crosses over two or more yarns from the opposite direction.

A twill weave requires three or more harnesses, depending on its complexity. A twill weave is the second most basic weave that can be made on a fairly simple loom. The army used different qualities of twill:

- *Cadis* – milled *serge*
- *Serge*
- *Tricot*
- *Blicourt* – a superfine milled *serge*

Above left: The scarlet facings of the *grenadiers-à-cheval*, Empress Dragoons and other regiments that had scarlet facings was in this rich bright scarlet cloth. (Collection KM)

Above right: This sample of iron-grey wool cloth from 1823 leaves in no doubt as to the colour used by the artillery and equipment trains. (Collection KM)

Above left: This sample of dark green cloth is the same colour as used by the Guard light cavalry from 1800 to 1815. (Collection KM)

Above right: This sample of chamois cloth is the same colour as used by the *voltigeurs* of the Line and Light Infantry and *flanqueur* regiments of the Guard in 1815. (Collection KM)

For *pantalons*, gaiters and fronts of *vestes, tricot* was used. This is akin to an English milled kersey. *Tricot* was a lighter weight cloth than broadcloth.

For linings of *vestes* and *habits, cadis* was used. It was often known by the province or town it was made. For example, *blicourt* is a type of milled *serge* made at Blicourt. For the back of *vestes* an un-milled *serge* was used, known as *serge*.

Linen was woven from hemp or flax. It would either be a very fine weave for shirts and *calceon* (underwear) or a coarse canvas-type fabric to line haversacks and to act as interlinings for buttonholes. Linen is laborious to manufacture, but the fibre is very absorbent and garments made of linen are valued for their exceptional coolness and freshness in hot weather. Linen fabrics have a high natural lustre. Their natural colour ranges between shades of ivory, ecru, tan or grey. Pure white linen is created by heavy bleaching. Linen fabric typically varies somewhat in thickness and is crisp and textured, but it can in some cases feel stiff and rough and in other cases feel soft and smooth. When properly prepared, linen fabric has the ability to absorb and lose water rapidly. Linen can absorb a fair amount of moisture without feeling unpleasantly damp to the skin, unlike cotton. Linen is a very durable, strong fabric, and one of the few that are stronger wet than dry. The fibres do not stretch and are resistant to damage from abrasion. However, because linen fibres have a very low elasticity, the fabric eventually breaks if it is folded and ironed at the same place repeatedly over time. Linen could also be woven in a herringbone weave. In a coarse weave, often made from hemp, the cloth was called *treillis*. With a very tight weave from flax fibres the cloth was called *coutil*.

Above left: This sample of yellow cloth *(janquille)* is from 1823. (Collection KM)

Above right: This sample of rose (pink) is from 1823. (Collection KM)

Colours

All the varying shades of blue used during the First Empire were indigo-derived. In the First Empire, woad (*pastel* in French) was mixed with a percentage of indigo of a ratio of 256 g of indigo to 100 kg of woad. Woad contains indigotin, but at a weaker concentration to that derived from other plants. A variety of plants have provided indigo throughout history, but most natural indigo was obtained from those in the genus *Indigofera*. In Napoleonic France, woad was primarily grown around Albi, Turin and Florence, selling the dye at 18 to 20 *francs* per kilogram under a set tariff introduced in 1791. The cost of obtaining indigo dye is why the French Army became dressed in undyed cloth uniforms for a period in 1806 and 1807. For red colours, cochineal, kermes and galle were used. For yellows, *gaude* wood and *sumac fustet* were used. A dye book printed in 1811 says that the rose colour for facings was obtained by mixing *sumac fustet* and cochineal to make rose, capucine and aurore. Clearly, rose facings for some units was not pink as some artists and re-enactors would have us believe.

The French war ministry laid down clear regulations on cloth colour and quality. This was introduced on 23 September 1807. Each mill/cloth supplier had to provide to the war ministry a length of cloth 1 *aune* wide (which varied from 112 cm to 119 cm) by 19 *aunes* (20 m) for the cloth quality to be checked and quality of dyed colour to be checked over the entire length of the fabric

Above left: This sample of madder red or garance cloth is from 1823. (Collection KM)

Above right: This sample of light green cloth is from 1823. (Collection KM)

before the war ministry would order the cloth. The war ministry had a list of approved contractors and set prices for cloth type and colour. This was adhered to throughout the empire. The colours of uniforms were confirmed again with the Bardin regulations of 1812. Some colours were obtained by mixes, notably beige, which was made from brown and white fibres, and iron-grey from blue and white fibres. Napoleon's famous greatcoat is not grey, but actually a very fine quality beige. Beige in 1815 was not a natural wool colour, but brown was.

Checking cloth quality was the role of inspectors of review and war commissioners. Yes, colour could vary between batches of dye and mills, but overall the colour of cloth was very well regulated. With blue cloth and scarlet, the colours dyed in, say 1811, are the same in 2018. Quality of finish of the cloth, the selection of wool fibres and the way the cloth was dyed affects colour. A lot of factors to consider when trying to recreate the colours of the period. But the shade of blue an item is now can be taken pretty much to be the colour it was when new.

The colour blue was created by the length of time the cloth or yarn was in the vat and how old the vat of dye was.

We need to make comment here on the colour of lace and braid used by the Imperial Guard. The *grenadiers-à-cheval* and Empress Dragoons had dark yellow lace, and the *chasseurs-à-cheval* had aurore. Aurore in the First Empire was an almost scarlet orange.

CHAPTER 2

GRENADIERS-À-CHEVAL

The directory decided in November 1795 to form a guard, its function being to act as *garde d'honneur* to the directory and provide protection for its members. Each director was to have two guards to protect him. For this duty, men were drafted from the 3rd Regiment of Dragoons. The title given to this force was *Garde du Directoire* and it was formally established on 4 October 1796. The force was to consist of 120 infantry and 120 cavalry. Under this law of 4 October 1796, the cavalry was to form two companies of fifty-five men, to comprise a staff of a squadron commander and standard bearer, with each company to have one captain, one lieutenant, one sub-lieutenant, one sergeant-major, one *fourrier*, four corporals, two trumpeters, one farrier and forty-one *grenadiers*.

With the coup of 11 November 1799, it was decided to merge the *Garde du Directoire* with the *Garde du Corps Legislatif* and to reinforce it where necessary. Its title was to be the *Garde des Consuls*.[1]

Clothing and equipment

Very few documents for the dress of the regiment for the period 1799-1808 can be found in the regiment's archive in Paris. The officer in charge of clothing the regiment from 1806 to 1814 was Jean Varnout.[2] He was born on 11 March 1773 at Avalon. He enlisted into the 16th Cavalry Regiment on 17 October 1793 and passed to the *grenadiers-à-cheval* of the Directory Guard on 1 January 1797. Promoted to quartermaster-corporal in 1799 and sergeant in 1801 in the *grenadiers-à-cheval* of the Guard of the Consuls, he was promoted to second-lieutenant in December 1802 and was serving in May 1804 in the 6th Company of the 2nd Squadron. Following Austerlitz, he was promoted to first-lieutenant in December 1805 and was passed to 8th Company, which was part of 4th Squadron. On 15 April 1806, he was made lieutenant-adjutant for clothing, a post he held until 1812. Upon his return from the Russian campaign, he was promoted to *captain d'administration* on 9 February 1813, in charge of clothing. On 3 April 1814, he was appointed captain-adjutant-major. He passed to the Royal Corps of Cuirassiers of France in July 1814. Awarded the brevet rank of squadron commander, he was discharged in November 1815.

The team of master workmen in charge of the production of boots, clothing and equipment were as follows:[3]

Jean Fabritzius was born on 10 August 1754. He was master saddler of Grey. He married Marie Jacquemon and stood 1.72 m tall, had an oval face, grey eyes and black hair and eyebrows. He was admitted as boot-maker into the 10th Regiment of

Above left: Image of a trumpeter of the regiment by the German artist Otto. The uniform matches in many respects the archive documents for the dress of the trumpeters. The *bleu de ciel housse* shown here was replaced by crimson from 1809, giving a *terminus antiquem* for the image. Otto, however, gives red and gold lace to the collar and *contre-epaulettes*. This is likely an artist's error as no such lace was ever purchased by the regiment.

Above right: Colonel of the regiment in a painting by Nicolas Hoffmann. This shows Colonel Ordener. The gold lace to the collar is unexpected, as is the gilt base to the plume.

Chasseurs-à-Cheval on 31 July 1782. Admitted to the *grenadiers-à-cheval* as master boot-maker in 1803, he was discharged on 15 September 1815. His two sons, Jean-Pierre and Casimir, were in the regiment as workmen.

Jean-Pierre Fabritzius was born on 11 June 1786. He stood 1.62 m tall, had a round face, low forehead, blue eyes and narrow nose. Admitted as boot-maker to the regiment in 1803, he was promoted to chief boot-maker on 23 July 1814 and was discharged on 23 November 1815.

Casimir Jean Francois Fabritzius was born on 29 March 1791 and married Marie Antoinette, a native of Paris, on 13 September 1820 at Devaux. Casimir was of slight build and stood 1.66 m tall, had a round face with a high forehead,

Trooper by Nicolas Hoffmann c. 1806. The uniform shown is exactly as we believe the regiment to have been dressed, even down to the trooper's moustache. One oddity is the lace cross on the *portmanteau*. In all other respects, Hoffmann has captured very accurately the appearance of the regiment.

grey eyes, a large nose and mouth, round chin and stone-coloured hair. He entered the *grenadiers-à-cheval* on 17 August 1811, not as a conscript, but as one of the few direct entrants to the regiment as a regimental saddler. His skills appear to have been of more value to the regiment than his lack of service history and height. By 27 January 1814, Fabritzius was made master saddler of the regiment and was transferred to the Royal Corps of Cuirassiers of France on 23 July 1814, and back to the *grenadiers-à-cheval* of the Imperial Guard on 1 April 1815. He was dismissed on 25 November 1815, but enlisted voluntarily into the 2nd Regiment of *Grenadiers-à-Cheval* of the Royal Guard on 13 January 1819. The Royal Guard was disbanded on 11 August 1830 and he passed to the 1st Regiment of Cuirassiers as master saddler on 21 June 1831. He retired on 31 December 1845. He served in the campaigns of 1812, 1813 and 1814.

Antoine Louis Aubry was the regiment's master armourer. He was born in Paris on 14 February 1792. Admitted to the regiment on 16 April 1813, he passed to the Royal Corps of Cuirassiers of France on 23 July 1814, was admitted back to the *grenadiers-à-cheval* of the Imperial Guard on 1 April 1815, and was discharged from the regiment on 25 November 1815.

Jean Francois Gerel was the regimental master breeches-maker. He was born on 15 March 1751 at Lignitz, the son of Francois Gerel and Marie Hoffmann. He stood 1.76 m tall, had an oval face, brown eyes and blond hair and eyebrows. He was admitted to the regiment on 3 January 1800 and passed to the Royal Corps of Cuirassiers of France on 23 July 1814, was admitted back to the *grenadiers-à-cheval* of the Imperial Guard on 1 April 1815, and discharged on 25 November 1815.

Michel Hubert Bosquet was the regiment's master tailor. Admitted to the regiment in 1804, he was discharged on 25 November 1815. He was born in Paris on 3 February 1778.

1799

The *grenadiers-à-cheval* of the Guard of the Consul was in effect the old Guard of the directors, with a new title. The new regiment at its formation was dressed in its existing clothing. The regiment underwent a shakedown inspection by General

Kellermann, Duke of Valmy, on 15 April 1799, which tells us a great deal about the regiment as it was when Bonaparte came to power.[4]

The staff of the squadron comprised thirty-eight officers and men, of which thirty-two were musicians, headed up by an adjutant and riding instructor. These men were all equipped with clothing that comprised thirty-eight *habits*, thirty-eight *gilets*, three pairs of sheep hide breeches, one *manteau*, thirty-nine *surtouts* and two bearskins for the adjutants.[5]

The 1st Company was commanded by Captain Augé and mustered one sergeant-major, two sergeants, one *fourrier*, four corporals, thirty-nine *grenadiers* and two trumpeters. These men had the following items of clothing and equipment:[6]

ITEM	*TOTAL ITEMS*	*ITEMS NEEDED*	*IN GOOD CONDITION*	*NEEDING REPAIR*	*NEEDING TO BE REPLACED*
Habits	52	0	9	43	0
Gilets	52	0	9	39	4
Culottes de peau de mouton	52	0	48	0	4
Manteaux	52	1	45	0	6
Surtouts	52	0	9	39	4
Gilets d'ecurie	52	0	20	28	4
Chapeaux	52	0	3	4	45
Casques	52	0	52	0	0
Bonnets de police	52	0	48	0	4
Pantalons de treillis	52	0	4	0	48
Ceinturons	52	0	52	0	0
Gibernes	46	0	46	0	0
Giberne belts	46	0	46	0	0
Mousqueton slings	46	0	46	0	0
Porte-manteaux	52	0	52	0	0
Boots	52	0	4	48	0
Saddles	52	0	52	0	0
Bridles	52	0	52	0	0
Head collars	52	0	52	0	0
Saddle blankets	52	0	37	0	15
Musketoons	46	0	46	0	0
Sabres	52	0	48	0	4
Pistols	52	7	45	0	0

The 2nd Company was commanded by Captain Guillotin and mustered one sergeant-major, two sergeants, one *fourrier*, four corporals, forty *grenadiers* and two trumpeters. These men had the following items of clothing and equipment:[7]

ITEM	*TOTAL ITEMS*	*ITEMS NEEDED*	*IN GOOD CONDITION*	*NEEDING REPAIR*	*NEEDING TO BE REPLACED*
Habits	51	0	9	40	2
Gilets	51	0	9	40	2
Culottes de peau de mouton	51	0	40	0	11
Manteaux	51	0	73	0	8
Surtouts	51	0	0	41	10
Gilets d'ecurie	51	0	30	21	0
Chapeaux	51	0	6	0	43
Casques	51	0	49	0	2
Bonnets de police	51	0	49	0	2
Pantalons de treillis	51	0	0	4	47
Ceinturons	51	0	51	0	0
Gibernes	45	0	45	0	0
Giberne belts	45	0	45	0	0
Mousqueton slings	46	0	46	0	0
Porte-manteaux	51	0	51	0	0
Boots	51	0	45	6	0
Saddles	51	0	51	0	0
Bridles	51		51		
Head collars	51		51		
Saddle blankets	51		39		12
Musketoons	45		45		
Sabres	51		51		
Pistols	51		48		3

We assume the word *casque* is an error on the document. The document is a French army pre-printed pro-forma. The clothing part of the document is formatted for cavalry and dragoons, and thus the word *casque* we assume must be in this case representing bearskin, as the regiment never wore helmets, only ever *chapeaux* and bearskins. Later in the document where a summary of items is presented, the *casques* are clearly re-labelled as *bonnets a poil*, i.e. bearskins. Kellermann noted the dress of the regiment was good, but cloth was needed to buy replacement clothing. Cloth in the magazine was as follows:[8]

For *habits*:

- 80 m of red milled *serge*
- 6 m of white wool cloth
- 2 m of scarlet wool cloth
- 20 m of linen

For *gilets*:

- 79 m of white milled *serge*

For *surtouts*:

- 80 m of milled blue *serge*
- 18 m of linen

For stable coats:

- 18 m of blue wool cloth
- 49 m of milled blue *serge*

The tariff for making items of uniform tells us a great deal about how the regiment was dressed and no doubt appeared during the Battle of Marengo, which was pivotal in the career of Bonaparte and in the history of the regiment:[9]

Habit:

- 1.47 m of blue wool cloth, costing 21.50 *francs* a metre
- 2.40 m of red milled *serge* for lining the *habit* at 4 *francs* a metre
- 0.50 m of scarlet wool cloth for collar and cuffs at 25 *francs* a metre
- 0.50 m of white wool cloth for *revers* and cuff flaps at 18 *francs* a metre
- Twelve large buttons at 25 *centimes* a dozen
- Twenty-four small buttons at 65 *centimes* a dozen
- 0.70 m of linen for lining of the sleeves at 1.70 *francs* a metre
- 0.40 m of linen pockets at 1.70 *francs* a metre
- One set of four embroidered grenades at 2.50 *francs*
- One *aiguillette* and trefoil in wool, costing 9.50 *francs*
- Hooks and eyes at 10 *centimes*
- Labour: 3.50 *francs*
- Total 56.29 *francs*

Veste:

- 0.40 m of white wool cloth
- 0.60 m of white *tricot* for back of the *veste* at 2.60 *francs* a metre
- 0.90 m of white milled *serge* for lining at 1.20 *francs* a metre
- Twelve small buttons at 65 *centimes* a dozen
- 0.25 m of linen for interlining at 1.70 *francs* a metre
- Labour: 1.50 *francs*
- Total: 10.47 *francs*

Surtout:

- 1.47 m of blue wool cloth, costing 21.50 *francs* a metre
- 2.40 m of blue milled *serge* for lining the *habit* at 4 *francs* a metre
- 0.50 m of scarlet wool cloth for collar and cut out grenades at 25 *francs* a metre
- Thirteen large buttons at 25 *centimes* a dozen
- 0.70 m of linen for lining of the back and sleeves at 1.70 *francs* a metre
- Labour: 3 *francs*
- Total: 28.26 *francs*

Stable coat:

- 1.20 m of blue wool, costing 14 *francs* a metre
- 1.80 m of linen for lining at 1.70 *francs* a metre
- Fourteen small buttons at 65 *centimes* a metre
- Labour: 1.50 *francs*
- Total: 18.80 *francs*

Pantalons-à-cheval:

- 1.10 m of blue wool, costing 14 *francs* a metre
- 0.40 m of linen for lining at 1.70 *francs* a metre
- One *basin* hide for exterior of *pantaloons* at 1.25 *francs*
- Thirty-six bone buttons, costing 10 *centimes* a dozen
- Labour: 1.75 *francs*
- Total: 16.80 *francs*

Bonnet de police:

- 0.40 m of blue wool at 14 *francs* a metre
- 0.10 m of scarlet wool cloth for piping at 25 *francs* a metre
- 0.20 m of linen for lining at 1.70 *francs* a metre
- Yellow wool lace, yellow round cord and yellow tassel, costing 1.20 *francs*
- Labour: 1.50 *francs*
- Total: 6.38 *francs*

Manteau:

- 5.30 m of *blanc picque de bleu* wool cloth at 15 *francs* a metre
- 1.50 m of red milled *serge* for lining at 2 *francs* a metre
- Six brandenburgs in yellow wool lace at 50 *centimes*
- One large copper hook and eye at 25 *centimes*
- Labour: 2.75 *francs*
- Total: 76 *francs*

Gaiters:

- 0.80 m of black worsted twill, costing 3.60 *francs* a metre
- 0.30 m of linen for lining at 1.70 *francs* a metre

- Twenty-four copper buttons at 60 *centimes* a dozen
- Labour: 75 *centimes*
- Total: 5.80 *francs*

Of interest, the *surtout* was entirely blue with a scarlet collar. It was closed by thirteen large buttons – if eight buttons were on the back, it means the front was closed by just five buttons. A portrait of a member of the squadron gives

Above left: Trumpeter in parade dress by Nicolas Hoffmann. The parade *housse* and chaperons were made once in 1801 and seemingly never replaced, no doubt due to cost, during the life of the regiment. The parade coat is also clearly the consular period item with horizontal pockets. Again, the parade *habits* were made in 1804 and infrequently replaced, so it would be perfectly acceptable for a coat that was four years old to still be in service when this painting was made. Hoffmann correctly shows a black bearskin.

Above right: Kettledrummer in full dress. Archive documents show this uniform and elaborate harness was created in 1801 and was never replaced, no doubt due to the huge cost of doing so. A new *dolman* was made in 1811, and by 1814 the kettledrummer was wearing a trumpeter's coat. Hoffmann is the only source for the appearance of the kettledrummers clothing and equipment beyond the purchase accounts for these items which, alas, do not tell us what they looked like.

the *surtout* a scarlet collar and the front closed by seven buttons, with two at the shoulder, which leaves three buttons spare. The closure of the cuffs was by a minimum of one button, leaving a pair of buttons to appear on the back. The tails were decorated with red cut-out cloth grenades. Other items included the white wool breeches, a linen fatigue smock, stable trousers, *culottes de peau* made from sheep hide and *bottes a l'écuyer* (i.e. fully-soft knee boots). Other items were:[10]

To be replaced every four months:

- *Manchette du botte*

To be replaced every six months:

- Shirt, costing 5.15 *francs*
- A pair of woollen socks, costing 2.25 *francs*
- A black stock, costing 3.25 *francs*
- Cockade, costing 20 *centimes*
- Pair of shoes, costing 4.50 *francs*

To be replaced every twelve months:

- Red plume in cockerel feathers
- Sword knot in yellow wool
- Pair of gauntlets

To be replaced every eighteen months:

- *Chapeaux* with yellow stays and *ganse*
- *Chapeaux* for sub-officers
- A pompom
- *Chapeaux marrons* to last eighteen months

To be replaced every two years:

- *Aiguillette* in red and gold for sub-officers
- *Aiguillette* in yellow wool for *grenadiers*
- Gold lace for decoration of *habits* and *surtouts* of sergeant-majors, sergeants and trumpeters

To be replaced every three years:

- Bearskin cords and tassel in yellow wool
- Bearskin cords and tassel in red wool and gold thread for sub-officers

To be replaced every four years:

- Trumpet
- Trumpet cords in yellow wool with large tassels and *tosards*

Lieutenant Noel painting in 1814. Pierre Alexander Noel was born on 14 July 1785. He was admitted into the 1st *chasseurs-à-cheval* in November 1803 and admitted to the *grenadiers-à-cheval* on 8 July 1807. Promoted to corporal on 9 May 1808, and sergeant on 1 July 1809. On 1 May 1811, he was promoted to sergeant major. He returned from the Russian campaign and was awarded the Legion of Honour on 4 April 1813. He served in the 1813 campaign, and the opening stages of the 1814 campaign as sergeant-major. He was wounded at the affair of Mery-sur-Seine on 20 March 1814 with a lance wound to the left side of his chest. He was incapacitated and captured by the Cossacks, but escaped on 25 March 1814. He was re-admitted to his old regiment on 3 April 1814 and promoted to 2nd lieutenant-sub-adjutant-major. Promoted to 2nd lieutenant on 23 July 1814. He served at Waterloo and later travelled to America in 1815. (Musée de l'Empéri, Collections du Musée de l'armée, Anciennes collections Jean et Raoul Brunon)

To be replaced every six years:

- Bearskin without plate
- Rigid parade boots

Leather equipment comprised a cavalry-model *giberne* with grenade plate in copper. This is clearly the 1786 model *giberne* as issued to the cavalry regiments (i.e. the precursors to the *cuirassiers*), which was suspended from a *chasseur*-pattern *giberne* belt, with copper buckle, slide and tip. The belt also had *surpicquer* stitching on the edges. *Gibernes* and belts were to last ten years. The waist belts were made from buff leather with two rings, a long and short sling and grenade plate in copper. As with the *giberne* belt it had *surpicquer* stitching and was to last ten years. These items when bought new in 1799 would still have been in service at Wagram.

The *porte-manteaux* were made from blue wool cloth decorated with yellow lace 119 cm long. It was lined in heavyweight hemp canvas and was, in theory, to last for six years. The ends of the *porte-manteaux* were reinforced with leather to make it more robust and to endeavour to keep it square. The *housse* and *chaperons* were to last, in theory, four years. Even in 1799, these items had an oil cloth interlining. The *housse* and *chaperons* only had a single row of lace in 1799. The two rows were introduced, it seems, at some point in 1800. In concluding the report, Kellermann authorised the issuing of funds to re-clothe the squadron entirely, and to issue new equipment.

Trooper of the regiment painted in August 1813, part of a series of images of the Guard made in 1813, which also include a Marin, Lithuanian Tatar, *aide-de-camp*, elite company of the headquarters staff. The trooper's uniform is depicted very accurately, although the bearskin cord *raquettes* seem to be hung from the cockade rather than from a length of knotted cording. (Musée de l'Empéri, Collections du Musée de l'armée, Anciennes collections Jean et Raoul Brunon)

1800

The next oldest document relating to the dress of the regiment was compiled on 17 September 1800 and lists the following items that had all been distributed up to that date, no doubt re-dressing the regiment after Marengo:[11]

- 6,596 m of dark yellow wool lace, 22 mm, for back patch of bearskins and stays of *chapeaux*
- 10,027 m of round wool cord for *bonnets de police* (for *grenadiers-à-pied*, *chasseurs-à-pied*, *grenadiers-à-cheval*)
- 4,553 grenades embroidered in dark yellow wool (for *grenadiers-à-cheval*, *grenadiers-à-pied*, *chasseurs-à-pied*)
- 1,350 *aiguillettes* in yellow wool at 7.75 *francs* each (for *grenadiers-à-cheval* and *chasseurs-à-cheval*)
- 182 *aiguillettes* in red wool and gold thread at 42 *francs* each (for *grenadiers-à-cheval* and *artillerie-à-cheval*)
- 300 sets of bearskin cords in yellow wool, costing 6 *francs* each
- 240 sets of bearskin cords in red wool and gold thread, costing 18 *francs* each
- 707 grenades for *schabraques* at 2.80 *francs* a pair
- 118 sets of grenades embroidered in gold thread for sub-officers at 6 *francs* a set
- Fifty-three pairs of *marrons* in red wool and gold thread for *chapeaux* of sub-officers at 8 *francs* a pair
- Twenty sets of trumpet cords in red wool and gold thread at 96 *francs* each
- Sixty-four *aiguillettes* in crimson and gold thread for trumpeters at 36 *francs* each
- 780 *culottes de daim* (doe hide breeches) at 42 *francs* each
- 825 pairs of chin scales at 4 *francs* a pair
- 1,045 pairs of fully soft knee boots at 20 *francs* a pair
- 2,700 pairs of *manchette du botte* at 2 *francs* a pair
- 1,005 pairs of gauntlets at 7 *francs* a pair
- Seventy-five pairs of semi-soft boots at 30 *francs* a pair
- 630 pairs of rigid boots for parade dress at 30 *francs* a pair
- 500 bearskins at 22.25 *francs* each
- 720 *gibernes* at 6.50 *francs* each
- 720 *giberne* belts at 7 *francs* each
- 400 grenade plates for *gibernes* at 1 *franc* each
- 794 *musketoon* buckets and straps at 3 *francs* a set
- 433 waist belts at 8 *francs* each
- 1,152 saddles, costing 80 *francs* each
- Forty-one *housses* and pairs of *chaperons* in crimson wool cloth, costing 96 *francs* each
- Thirty-eight *housses* and pairs of *chaperons* in blue wool cloth, costing 130 *francs* each

When we look at the cloth purchased in September 1800 for the regiment, blue of two qualities were obtained, the same for white cloth for *habit revers* and waistcoats, along with scarlet wool cloth and milled *serge* in scarlet and white. Crimson cloth was purchased for the trumpeter. Clearly, the trumpeter's *habit* in 1800 was imperial blue faced in crimson.

1803

A stores inventory of 23 September 1803 lists the following materials:[12]

MATERIALS		*QUANTITIES (AUNES)*	*PRICE PER AUNE (FRANCS)*
Blue wool cloth	First quality	312 13/24	28.50
	Second quality	359 5/24	25
	Third quality	315 7/24	23
	Fourth quality	0	
White		158.75	22
Scarlet	First quality	24.75	26
	Second quality	46 15/32	22.50
Crimson	First quality	19/30	26
	Second quality	0	
Bleu-celeste	First quality	22 5/12	23.50
	Second quality	37	20
	Third quality		
Blanc picque de bleu		222 5/6	9
Tricot	Blue	1,011 13/24	5
	Bleu celeste	54 7/8	4.50
	White	343 5/12	2.75
Milled *serge*	Scarlet	800.50	3
	Crimson	17	3
	White	383.50	1.65
Linen	White	375 11/12	2.40
	Blondine	852.50	1.875
	Ecru	1149 1/6	1.74
	Yellow	33.50	2.20
White *coutil*		829 1/6	2.80
Treillis	d'Alençon	751	1.90

The *bleu celeste* cloth was clearly for the manufacture of clothing for the trumpeters. This is the first reference to this cloth being obtained, so clearly in 1803 the colour of the trumpeter's *habits* changed from imperial blue to a much lighter shade.

This plate by Vernet, published in 1810, shows a trumpeter in campaign dress, wearing the parade *chapeau*. Assuming the *bleu de ciel housse* and *chaperons* are not artist's error, the print shows the uniform pre-1809, after which date *crimson housse* and *chaperons* were adopted.

The yellow cloth was presumably nankeen. Clothing and equipment in the depot comprised the following items:[13]

- Thirteen *grenadier's habits*
- Two trumpeter's *habits*
- Twelve *grenadier's surtouts*
- Two trumpeter's *surtouts*
- Twenty-eight white *gilets*
- Five pairs of blue wool knee breeches
- One *bleu celeste* waistcoat
- One pair of *bleu celeste* woollen knee breeches
- 188 white *vestes*
- Ninety-two *grenadier's bonnets de police*
- One trumpeters *bonnet de police*
- Eleven sub-officer's *manteaux*
- Seventeen *grenadier's manteaux*
- Thirteen *grenadier's porte-manteaux*

same letter complained that the regiment had to buy 107 remounts in Poland, being mostly Saxon or Prussian cavalry mounts, which 'were nothing more than miserable beasts that did live up the expectations of the *grenadiers-à-cheval*'.[20] General Walther followed up the missive asking for funds to replace the 107 horses obtained in Poland with a second missive asking for funds to cover the horses lost in the previous campaigns:

- Forty-two horses lost at the Battle of Austerlitz, total value 25,200 *francs*
- Fifty-seven horses lost in the campaign from the fatigues of war, total value 34,200 *francs*
- 143 horses lost at the Battle of Eylau, total value 80,000 *francs*
- 100 horses lost in the campaign from the fatigues of war, value 60,000 *francs*

Furthermore, Walther complained the regiment had to replace, out of its own funds, forty-six horses that the *velites* had taken with them when they were passed to new regiments: an outlay of 69,000 *francs*. Walther added that seventy-seven horses had died of illness, eighteen had been killed, fourteen had been sold as unsuitable during the campaign in Germany, a further sixty-two died of disease, and fifty-six sold during the course of the campaign in Poland. Stores held on 1 January 1808 were:[21]

MATERIALS		*IN DEPOT ON 1 JANUARY (METRES)*	*AMOUNT PURCHASED (METRES)*	*AMOUNT ISSUED (METRES)*
Blue wool cloth	First quality	63.39	653.92	523.07
	Second quality	239.60	974.97	1,175.37
	Third quality	341.80	1,156.05	1,014.09
	Fourth quality	1,378.57	1,563.08	2,864.27
White		111.65	302.41	402.135
Scarlet	First quality	16.32	91.20	88.38
	Second quality	12.57	57.87	36.21
Crimson	First quality	16.19		2.17
	Second quality	0.45	5.94	3.27
Bleu de ciel	First quality	43.16		7.3
	Second quality	112.67	63.82	94.53
	Third quality	100.44		26.58
Blanc picque de bleu			336.91	318.41
Tricot	White	457.60	485.3	530.44

MATERIALS		*IN DEPOT ON 1 JANUARY (METRES)*	*AMOUNT PURCHASED (METRES)*	*AMOUNT ISSUED (METRES)*
Milled *serge*	Scarlet	841.34	3,458.11	2,605.81
	Crimson	60.74	30	56.75
	White	356.70	766.86	1,060.80
Linen	Blondine	143.02	2,349.9	1,789.72
	Ecru	608.34	3,618.8	4,046.89
White *coutil*		125.35	481.57	633. 93
Treillis	d'Alençon	55.18	2,108.19	1,809.12
Oil cloth		322.68	47.57	244.83

Items of *passamenteries* were as follows:[22]

MATERIALS		*IN DEPOT ON 1 JANUARY*	*AMOUNT PURCHASED*	*AMOUNT ISSUED*
Gold Lace	54 mm			
	34 mm			
	28 mm		14.26 m	14.26 m
	22 mm	14.25 m	129.75 m	135.76 m
	18 mm			
	14 mm		64.40 m	9.50 m
Brandenburgs for trumpeter's *habit*		4		4
Embroidered crowns in gold for *housse*, pairs				
Embroidered crowns in wool for *grenadier's housse*, pairs			1,066	80
Wool lace	54 mm	24.28 m	3,752.05 m	912.03 m
	34 mm	435.13 m	469.21 m	843.48 m
	28 mm	125.36 m	3,302.70 m	1,599.15 m
	14 mm	11.43 m	387.90 m	210.07 m
Grenades embroidered in wool	For *housse*	14	20	23
	For *habit*	13	1,462	1,231
Cording for *bonnet de police*		757 m	1,283.26 m	1,687.67 m
Tassels for *bonnet de police*		516	240	710

MATERIALS	*IN DEPOT ON 1 JANUARY*	*AMOUNT PURCHASED*	*AMOUNT ISSUED*
34 mm-wide silver lace		75.26 m	47.52 m
Brandenburgs in silver		48	48
Soutache in silver		24	24

Leather work in the depot was as follows:[23]

ITEMS		*IN DEPOT ON 1 JANUARY*	*AMOUNT PURCHASED*	*AMOUNT ISSUED*
Culottes	Doe hide	217	195	409
	Sheepskin	65	609	672
Gauntlets		80	592	620
Sword knots in buff		291	149	406
Chapeaux	Trumpeters			
	Sub-officers		75	75
	Grenadiers	44	445	486
Bearskins		292	156	431
Chin scales		489	291	482
Bearskin covers		158		
Plumes and covers		546	140	304
Boots	Rigid	17	902	602
	Semi-soft		72	72
Spurs		605		602
Spur straps		716		72
Aiguillettes	Sub-officers	16	8	23
	Trumpeter's full dress	14	1	7
	Trumpeter's undress			
	Grenadiers	284	500	418
Bearskin cords	Sub-officers	28		10
	Trumpeters	12		3
	Grenadiers	261	500	415
Farrier's horse shoe arm badges		27		18

ITEMS		*IN DEPOT ON 1 JANUARY*	*AMOUNT PURCHASED*	*AMOUNT ISSUED*
Sword knots	Sub-officers	34		27
	Trumpeters	16	1	9
Grenades in gold, pairs of for *housse*		12	172	173
Trumpets		4	12	16
Trumpet cords	Undress		25	25
Shakos for couriers			4	4

Items of equipment were as follows:[24]

ITEM			*IN DEPOT ON 1 JANUARY*	*AMOUNT PURCHASED*	*AMOUNT ISSUED*
Fusils and bayonets			340	159	183
Bearskin cockades	Sub-officers				
	grenadiers				
Musket slings			150	500	260
Lock covers			12	500	285
Gibernes			115	245	242
Banderoles			245	146	232
Giberne plates			191	250	239
Fittings for *banderoles*			259		132
Bayonets					13
Sword slings	Long		172	217	186
	Short		389	456	177
Epinglettes					33
Saddles	Sub-officers (lacquered)				
	Grenadiers		94	259	191
Housse	Trumpeters	Full dress	6		1
		Undress	23	3	26
	Grenadiers	Full dress		100	100
		Undress			780

Above and opposite: Three bearskins exist for the regiment. One is housed in the collection of Vincent Bourgeot. Another in the Musée de l'armée was overly restored in the 1960s when new fur was fitted to the original leather carcass, along with a new cockade and copper chinscales. This example shown here is the only example in seemingly 100 percent original condition. (Collection de l'Office du Tourisme de Pontarlier. Dépôt au Musée municipal de Pontarlier, France)

Above and opposite: Housed in the Musée de l'armée is this ensemble of items from the former collection of the artist Detaille. This mannequin has very few 1st Empire items on show. The *contre-epaulettes* and *aiguillette* are undoubtedly of the period, as is the waistcoat. The *habit* is a reconstruction made for Detaille, the breeches, boots and leather-work are all much later items from the end of the nineteenth century. The *giberne* is a modern reconstruction using an original plate. The bearskin cords are also from the 1st Empire. Overall, the mannequin gives a good impression of how the regiment appeared. (Musée de l'armée)

- 100 m of 12 mm wide wool lace, total 27 *francs*
- 834 pairs of embroidered crowns for *housse* at 6 *francs* each
- 700 sets of four embroidered grenades for *habits* at 1.25 *francs* a set
- 1,000 m of round wool lace for *bonnets de police*, total 50 *francs*
- 400 dark yellow wool tassels for *bonnets de police* at 28 *centimes* each
- Thirty *aiguillettes* for sub-officers at 44.20 *francs* each
- 400 *aiguillettes* for *grenadiers* at 8 *francs* each
- 300 sets of bearskin cords for *grenadiers* at 2.25 *francs* each

Here in this purchase account we have epees and waist belts for sub-officers, along with *aiguillettes* for sub-officers. It seems that sub-officers had the same *bonnet de police* as other ranks. The contract for the *chapeaux* was awarded to Maillard. The *chapeaux* were strung with red and gold *soutache* instead of dark yellow wool used by other ranks and had red and gold *marrons*. The *chapeaux* for *grenadiers* were strung with dark yellow *soutache*, had a wool *ganse* and had red wool *marrons*.[30]

We also see that sub-officers, and presumably trumpeters, used saddles that were lacquered and made from white leather, so were very much in imitation of officer's saddles. The contract for their production was dated 26 January. It states that the trooper's saddles came complete with breastplate, crupper, pillion saddle (*coussinet*), bridle, head collar, pistol holsters, *musketoon* bucket and straps. The sub-officer's saddles came with a leather cover and the pads under the saddle were in white *serge*.[31]

In addition, a contract with M. Herbert, *passementer*, of Paris, gives us more detail about sub-officer's and trumpeter's distinctions:[32]

- Thirty *aiguillettes* for sub-officers at 44.20 *francs* each
- 400 *aiguillettes* for *grenadiers* at 8 *francs* each
- 300 bearskin cords for *grenadiers* at 2.50 *francs* each
- *Aiguillettes* for sergeant-majors costing 53 *francs* each
- *Aiguillettes* for trumpeter's undress uniform costing 30 *francs* each
- Embroidered horseshoe badges for farriers at 3.80 *francs* a pair
- Embroidered grenades in gold for *habits*, set of four at 3.80 *francs* a set

The sergeant-major's *aiguillette* was of a different pattern to those of the sergeants and *fourriers*. Presumably the ratio of red to gold in those of sergeants and *fourriers* was one gold to two red, and for the sergeant-major two gold to one red.

The contract for the bearskins was awarded to M. Koenig, furrier, of 14 rue bone enfants, Paris. It states that the 200 bearskins were to be furnished with a *calotte* (top patch) in scarlet wool, ornamented with a cross made from 22 mm wide dark yellow wool lace. The chin scales and cords were not supplied by Koenig.

Portrait of Jacques Guillaume Frederic la Bachellerie. He was born at Brive in the Correze on 30 December 1782. He entered the 10th Dragoons on 17 July 1803 and was promoted to corporal on 11 November 1804. He was then promoted to sergeant on 1 February 1806, 3rd lieutenant on 7 April 1807 and thence 2nd lieutenant on 31 August 1810. He passed to the *grenadiers-à-cheval* on 18 February 1812 as 2nd lieutenant in 3rd company of 3rd squadron. He was one of the 127 members of the regiment to return from the Russian campaign and was appointed 1st lieutenant-adjutant on 1 April 1813. Promoted to squadron head captain-adjutant-major on 3 April 1814. With the formation of the *Cuirassiers de France* in July 1814, he was appointed to captain adjutant, and in this capacity, he appears to have served at Waterloo. He passed to the 16th *Chasseurs* as a major on 6 March 1816. (Private collection)

The new bearskins cost 38 *francs* each. Koenig was also asked to repair bearskins at a cost of 9 *francs* each, as well as providing new *calottes* (bearskin back patch made from leather, covered in scarlet wool broadcloth decorated with a yellow lace cross) and covers for 3.50 *francs* each.[33]

The chin scales were supplied by M. Munir, of 10 rue Jacob, Paris. The chinstraps were to be large scales in copper, with a ribbon to tie them together.[34]

The tailoring charges for each item of uniform were as follows:[35]

- One trumpeter's *habit*, full dress, at 12 *francs* each
- 238 *grenadier's habits*, full dress, at 2.75 *francs* each
- 696 *grenadier's habits*, undress, at 2.75 *francs* each
- Six trumpeter's undress *habits* at 3.25 *francs* each
- Fourteen *surtouts* for drummers and trumpeters at 2.75 *francs* each
- Seventy-four *surtouts* for *grenadiers* and farriers at 2.25 *francs* each
- 612 white *vestes* at 1.20 *francs* each
- Three *redingotes* for sub-officers at 2.75 *francs* each
- Ten *bleu de ciel gilets* at 1.50 *francs* each
- Ten *bleu de ciel culottes* at 1.40 *francs* each
- Laced *habit veste* at 2.75 *francs* each
- *Habit-veste* at 2.50 *francs* each
- Forty-nine pairs of blue *pantalons* at 1.75 *francs* each
- 436 *bonnets de police* at 50 *centimes* each
- Ten trumpeter's *bonnets de police* at 50 *centimes* each
- 277 *blanc picque de bleu manteaux-trois-quatre* at 1.75 *francs* each
- Four blue *manteaux* for sub-officers at 1.75 *francs* each
- Five trumpeter's *manteaux* at 1.75 *francs* each
- 763 stable coats at 1.40 *francs* each
- 932 pairs of stable trousers at 1.40 *francs* each
- *Habit revers* at 75 *centimes* a pair

The laced *habit-vestes* may be courier's coats, or perhaps to mark out a groom. The *habit-vestes* with no lace were made for grooms, the laced *habit-vestes*, which according to the store's inventory were not made in 1811, is a resolved question as to its ownership.

1808-14

The regiment's preserved paper archive is the most complete and extensive of any regiment of the Imperial Guard. The wealth of paperwork preserved was thankfully condensed, and is presented below, in 1814. When the regiment was disbanded a summary of all items purchased from 1 January 1808 to 24 July was created, which is an incredible source in reconstructing the dress of the regiment in these six years:[36]

YEAR		In magazine	1808	1809	1810	1811	1812	1813	1814	Total
HABITS	Parade	26	321	757	223	238	109	0	0	1,674
	Undress	0	0	430	521	696	990	724	634	3,995
SURTOUTS	Sub-officer	21	0	0	0	0	0	0	0	21
	Other ranks	18	719	73	48	74	40	110	23	1,105
VESTES		275	853	1,414	825	612	1,595	3,010	0	8,584
REDINGOTES		3	55	64	36	3	11	15	3	190
SURCLOTTES		554	356	330	565	342	283	0	0	2,430
BONNETS DE POLICE		19	710	662	518	436	640	1,360	310	4,655
MANTEAUX	White	97	41	371	0	277	213	120	0	1,119
	Blue	0	34	2	1	4	48	0	0	89
STABLE COATS		102	1,430	1,031	849	763	1,550	1,473	315	7,513
BLUE WOOL STABLE TROUSERS		0	1,369	469	59	49	2	2	0	1,950
STABLE TROUSERS		0	585	540	1,382	932	468	100	20	4,027
GREY PANTALONS		0	0	0	0	0	0	880	535	1,415
CAPOTE MANTEAUX		0	0	0	0	0	0	1,522	83	1,605
PORTE-MANTEAUX		293	376	602	380	412	464	1,442	178	4,147

Trooper in full dress in a print by Aaron Martinet, published in Paris in 1808. The *portmanteau* has a double row of lace to the ends, which was formally removed from the uniform on 1 January 1808 for a single row. Rather than *contre-epaulettes*, also adopted in 1808, he retains trefoils, which dates the print to pre-1808. Otto shows the correct single row of lace on the *portmanteau* and *contre-epaulettes* for the uniform after 1 January 1808 until the adoption of the undress *habit* on 1 January 1809. The Martinet print shows the uniform much as it was from 1800 to 1808 and is worth comparing to the print by Hoffmann.

From the table, we can see that after 1812 the parade *habit* was discontinued. The undress *habit* introduced in 1809 was the same cut as the parade *habit*, but made from cheaper materials. The scarlet cuff facings were replaced with blue. The table below shows the amount of materials required:[37]

CLOTH	*PARADE* HABIT	*UNDRESS* HABIT
Blue wool cloth of first quality	148.6 cm 115 cm	
Blue wool cloth, third quality		148 cm 115 cm
White wool cloth	14 cm 119 cm	14 cm 119 cm
Scarlet wool cloth for cuffs and piping, first quality	9.90 cm 119 cm	
Scarlet wool cloth for piping, second quality		3.70 cm 119 cm

Belt plate of officers of *grenadiers-à-cheval* of the Consular Guard. (Musée de l'Empéri, Collections du Musée de l'armée, Anciennes collections Jean et Raoul Brunon)

CLOTH	*PARADE* HABIT	*UNDRESS* HABIT
Serge scarlet for lining and facing of tails	237.70 cm 50 cm	237.70 cm 50 cm
Linen for lining sleeves, jacket body and pockets	148.60 cm 104 cm	148.60 cm 104 cm
Undyed linen for *doit fils*	29 cm 104 cm	29 cm 104 cm
Grenades (set of four)	1	1
Large buttons	12	12
Medium buttons	24	24
Lace	19 cm	19 cm

It also seems that sub-officer's *surtouts* were discontinued from 1808. The *surtouts* issued, however, were destined to clothe the farriers and workmen, their examples being entirely blue with no pockets on the tails. The *surtouts* issued in 1813 were distributed to sub-officers as well as to the farriers, who received 122 *surtouts*. The *surtouts* made in 1813 were made of cheaper materials than before. The farrier's *surtouts* were entirely blue. The *surtout* was in use by 1799, if not earlier. A report made by the future Marshal Kellermann conducted July to August 1799 lists the *surtout* as having a red collar, blue *serge* turnbacks to the tails with red cut-out cloth grenades decorating them. The front was closed with nine buttons, two appearing on the *taille* (small of the back). The collars were changed to blue on 23 March 1800, when ten tailors were ordered to change the collars in twenty-four hours. We assume the turnbacks remained blue *serge*, as there is no reference to them being changed.[38] Indeed, the *surtout* was not authorised as a regulation uniform under the orders of 3 January 1800, confirming the use of the old directory items. Between 1800 and 1802, the *surtout* was used for riding practice and a second *habit* distributed. New *surtouts* were introduced in 1802. By 1 January 1808, the turnbacks were in scarlet *serge*, if not from August 1804. Two *grenadier's surtouts*, which cost 48.92 *francs* each, and a trumpeter's *surtout* are listed in stores for 23 September 1804.[39] No *surtouts* are mentioned in an inspection report of 23 July 1814, although 100 *surtouts* were fitted as *habits* in 1815.[40] No *surtouts* are listed in the dress regulations of 8 April 1815.[41]

The white *coutil surclottes* were discontinued in 1813 in favour of grey *pantalons*. These had the inner seat reinforced with a second layer of wool cloth, and two patches on each thigh where the *musketoon* and sabre would rub. Both the old *manteaux* and the new *capote manteaux* were used side-by-side. Sub-officers no longer wore blue *manteaux* following the Russian campaign. In addition, sub-officers were also issued blue *vestes* and breeches to be worn with the *surtout*. The blue stable trousers were issued to sub-officers and corporals, the other ranks having theirs made from *treillis*. Items of headdress, leather breeches issued and other items of clothing were as follows:[42]

YEAR	*CULOTTES*		GAUNTLETS	*CHAPEAUX*		BEARSKINS	BEARSKIN COVERS	PLUMES AND COVERS	BOOTS		SPURS	*AIGUILLETTES*		BEARSKIN CORDS	
	DAIM	*MOUTON*		*SUB-OFFICERS*	*OTHER RANKS*				*RIGID*	*SEMI-SOFT*		*SUB-OFFICERS*	*OTHER RANKS*	*SUB-OFFICERS*	*OTHER RANKS*
In magazine	217	65	80	0	44	292	158	546	17	0	605	16	284	28	261
1808	195	609	592	75	445	156	0	140	902	72		8	500	0	200
1809	432	594	311	39	207	400	0	450	498	26	210	82	1,062	60	1,30
1810	400	566	658	106	948	350	400	400	946	0	260	60	845	0	200
1811	351	609	613	79	673	195	150	200	552	30	650	40	200	22	100
1812	400	450	510	51	368	347	0	595	992	32	350	8	625	6	300
1813	476	1,173	1,194	26	95	1,589	0	1,135	1,080	796	1,790	92	738	80	1,32
1814	222	38	344	14	17	172	0	340	384	0	350	0	0	0	200
Total	2,693	4,104	4,302	390	2,797	3,501	708	3,806	5,371	956	4,215	306	4,254	196	3,88

Arms and equipment was as follows:[43]

YEAR	*FUSIL* AND BAYONETS	COCKADES FOR BEARSKINS		MUSKET SLINGS	LOCK COVERS	*GIBERNES*	*BANDEROLES*	*GIBERNE* PLATES	GAITERS	*CONTRE EPAULETTES*			SABRE *BRIQUETS*	AXES
		SUB-OFFICERS	*OTHER RANKS*							*IN CLOTH*	*IN LACE*	*DRUMMERS*		
In magazine	340	0	0	150	12	115	245	191	10	0	0	0	0	0
1808	159	0	0	257	500	356	146	250	1	0	0	9	12	0
1809	118	0	0	250	450	250	250	150	0	0	0	0	0	0
1810	66	0	0	150	250	150	110	0	0	0	0	8	0	0
1811	0	144	2,000	0	200	0	0	0	0	0	0	0	0	0
1812	29	0	0	150	250	150	150	200	0	0	0	0	0	0
1813	1,522	0	1,310	1,300	1,292	1,706	1,750	1,670	0	927	0	0	0	0
1814	100	0	0	0	0	0	0	0	0	0	483	0	0	100
Total	2,334	144	3,310	2,257	2,954	2,727	2,651	2,461	11	927	483	17	12	100

The matter of firearms issued to the regiment is not particularly clear. At first it seems the regiment was armed with long *musketoons* under the directory. In 1798, General Kellermann lists the *grenadiers* being issued with *porte-musketoons* and *musketoons* with protection covers. These *musketoons* did not have bayonets, as not one listed in the inspection returns. The equipment of the *grenadiers* was described as incomplete and defective.[44] These *musketoons* were of the 1777 cavalry model, as issued in February 1797, when 150 were issued with copper fittings and leather cover. They were 1.17 m long.[45]

It is little wonder, therefore, that new *porte-musketoons* were issued by the decree of 2 January 1800[46] as part of the trooper's buff hide belting. These new belts did not last long. They were replaced yet again with a new pattern, as on 12 March 1801 the *grenadiers* were ordered to hand in their old *musketoons* and be issued new ones. The company commanders were authorised to supply carrying straps for the *musketoons*, [47]which is shown clearly on the plate of the Guard cavalry in the Augsbilder series.[48] What pattern the new *musketoon* was in 1801 is unknown. It could simply be an issue of the Year IX correction of the 1777 type.[49]

These cavalry muskets can only have been in service for a few years, as it is indisputable that the mounted *grenadiers* were armed with a cavalry musket and bayonet from April 1803. These firearms were introduced by order of the first consul, who announced his intention on 14 April 1803 to introduce for use by the mounted *grenadiers* 'a distinctive model of cavalry musket, the handsomest possible, and being of the length of a dragoon musket with a bayonet, which would permit manoeuvres involving three ranks'.[50]

The bayonets were issued in June 1803.[51] A stores inventory of September 1803 lists 160 cavalry muskets. A year later, 150 muskets with bayonets are listed as being in stores.[52] The same stores list also mentions two musket butt holders, two straps for these items and four support straps for the musket, plus 106 pairs of pistols were also in stores.[53]

This *musketoon* is shown in the works of Otto, Martinet, Hoffman and Beyer. We assume this to be the same pattern as carried by the dragoons, as no mention is made of a specific pattern for the *grenadiers* in the list of muskets and *musketoons* compiled by Gassendi in 1809.[54] The total length of the *musketoon* was 1.44 m, with a barrel length of 1.06 m, and having the characteristics of the firearms of the Guard, that is to say with all brass fittings, a distinctive upper band, the heel plate with grenade, square sling rings and the special screw-piece. In January 1812, 714 new *musketoons* were issued. In 1813 infantry muskets were issued. All the different types of *musketoon* and musket were carried at the side of the saddle in a musket, but on the right-hand side of the saddle. In 1815, Year XI *cuirassier's* carbines were used.

Two patterns of *housse* and *chaperons* were issued: a parade dress with scarlet piping and an undress with no piping. One hundred new parade *housses* were issued in 1808, 1,070 in 1811 and 200 in 1812. None was made in 1813. The undress *housse* was introduced in 1809, with 954 being issued that year. Furthermore, sixteen were issued in 1810, forty-eight in 1811, thirty-seven in 1812, 419 in 1813 and 196 in 1814 – 1,650 examples. The number of *housses* issued in 1813 is far less than the regimental strength. Were the parade *housses* kept in store and out of need issued for field use in 1813, with the new undress examples being issued to the Young Guard companies? This seems probable. It is possible, though, that the Young Guard squadrons had no *housse* and the examples made in 1813 were destined for the Old Guard squadrons. Either scenario is possible and cannot be resolved as no documentation exists to state to which squadrons the different *housses* were issued in 1813. The specification for the *housse* was established on 5 January 1807:[55]

Housses for *grenadiers*:

- 1.09 m of blue wool cloth, third quality, at 20.19 *francs* a metre
- 0.22 m of scarlet wool cloth, second quality, at 20.19 *francs* a metre

- 2.37 m of *treillis*, Alençon quality, at 1.85 *francs* a metre
- 8.91 m of dark yellow wool lace, 54 mm wide, at 1.30 *francs* a metre
- 8.91 m of dark yellow wool lace, 23 mm wide, at 63 *centimes* a metre
- One pair of grenades at 1.85 *francs*
- 2.37 m of oil cloth at 1.05 *francs* a metre
- Labour: 9 *francs*
- Total: 61.49 *francs*

The drummer's equipment is most interesting. For foot duties, the regiment had eight drummers and a drum corporal. They wore a trumpeter's *surtout*, with their own pattern contre-epaulettes but no *aiguillette*. The drummer's equipment was the same as for the infantry and comprised a sabre and bayonet with its sabre belt, drum carriage with stick holders, waist belts and apron, and drum with slings. The headdress was either the bearskin or a *chapeau*. The gaiters, we assume, were for the drummers also.

An idea of the cloth used by the regiment can be garnered from a *marche* of 16 April 1813:[56]

- 515.70 m of blue wool cloth, Elbeuf second quality, costing 24 *francs* a metre
- 916.95 m of blue wool cloth, *de berry* third quality, costing 23.50 *francs* a metre
- 1,268.64 m of blue wool cloth, fourth quality, costing 12 *francs* a metre
- 408.12 m of white wool cloth, costing 20.25 *francs* a metre
- 56 m of scarlet wool cloth, first quality, costing 28 *francs* a metre
- 64.70 m of scarlet wool cloth, second quality, costing 18.50 *francs* a metre
- 38.58 m of crimson wool cloth, second quality, costing 18.50 *francs* a metre
- 110 m of *bleu de ciel* cool cloth, second quality, costing 20.25 *francs*
- 1,972.60 m of *blanc de picque bleu* wool cloth for *manteaux*, costing 11.50 *francs* a metre
- 456.70 m of white *tricot*, costing 2.36 *francs* a metre
- 1,549.58 m of scarlet milled *serge*, costing 2.90 *francs* a metre
- 141.90 m of crimson *serge*, costing 2.90 *francs*
- Total: 91,783.56 *francs*

Clearly, by 1813 the expensive Elbeuf first quality cloth was no longer purchased and the inferior *de berry* cloth was used in its place. Not even the *grenadiers-à-cheval* were immune from cost cutting as the empire drew to a close.

Disbandment

On 12 May 1814, the king decreed that the regiment was to be renamed the Royal Corps of Cuirassiers of France (*Corps Royal des Cuirassiers de France*). The title of *grenadiers-à-cheval* was to pass to a new organisation as part of the king's military household on 15 July 1814, re-establishing the old monarchy regiment formed in 1676. Marshal Ney was placed in charge of the Royal Corps of Cavalry. General Dupont was made minister for war, until December when he was replaced with Marshal Soult. The regiment had vast quantities of clothing and equipment that were passed to the successor formation:[57]

ITEM	*1813*		*1814*		*IN MAGAZINE ON 23 JULY 1814*
	NUMBER MADE	*NUMBER ISSUED*	*NUMBER MADE*	*NUMBER ISSUED*	
Habit Grand Uniforme	0	0	0	43 (from magazine)	0
Habit Petit Uniforme	724	850 (126 from magazine)	634	787 (153 from magazine)	0
Habit Trompette Grand Uniform	0	0	0	0	0
Habit Trompette Petit Uniform	37	30	3	10 (7 from magazine)	0
Surtout for sub-officers	0	0	0	0	0
Surtout for *grenadiers*	110	106	23	13	14
Surtout de trompettes	11	13 (2 from magazine)	7	7	0
Veste blanche	3,010	2630	0	640	0
Redingote bleu	2	15 (13 from magazine)	0	3 (from magazine)	0
Gilets bleu de ciel	12	12	7	7	0
Redingote trompette	0	2 (from magazine)	0	0	0
Surclotte	0	0	0	0	381
Culottes bleu de ciel	12	12	7	7	0
Bonnet de police	1,360	1,308	41	439 (398 from magazine)	111
Bonnet de police trompette	41	30	0	11 (from magazine)	0
Manteaux for sub-officers	0	0	0	0	0

ITEM	*1813*		*1814*		*IN MAGAZINE ON 23 JULY 1814*
	NUMBER MADE	*NUMBER ISSUED*	*NUMBER MADE*	*NUMBER ISSUED*	
Manteaux blanc	0	180 (from magazine)	0	0	0
Manteaux trompette	25	24	6	11 (5 from magazine)	0
Porte-manteaux bleu	1,442	1,415	178	402 (241 from magazine)	6
Porte-manteaux trompette	36	23	0	11 (from magazine)	12
Veste d'ecurie	1,473	1,509 (36 from magazine)	315	518 (203 from magazine)	377
Pantalons d'ecurie drap bleu	0	0	0	0	0
Pantalons de treillis	100	142 (42 from magazine)	20	10	16
Pantalons gris	880	870	535	545 (10 from magazine)	0
Capote manteaux	1,522	1,246	83	354 (271 from Magazine)	5
Brandenburgs for *manteaux*	1,548	1,522	231	83	174
Grenades en laine pour housse (paire)	615	570	105	150	11
Grenades en laine pour garniture d'habit (par 4)	1,809	1,195.25	843	741.50	567
Culottes du daim	476	411	222	415	40
Culottes du mouton	1,773	1,768	38	195	0
Gants a crispin	1,194	1,342	344	439	71
Dragonnes	1,750	1,281	0	350	192
Chapeaux de trompette	0	0	0	0	0
Chapeaux for sub-officers	26	26	14	14	0
Chapeaux for grenadiers	95	96 (1 from magazine)	17	14	3

ITEM	*1813*		*1814*		*IN MAGAZINE ON 23 JULY 1814*
	NUMBER MADE	*NUMBER ISSUED*	*NUMBER MADE*	*NUMBER ISSUED*	
Bonnets d'ourson	1,589	1,411	172	301	61
Mentonnieres	1,675	1,413	277	314	251
Etuis de bonnet	0	0	0	0	158
Plumets de bonnet	1,135	1,102	340	357	180
Etuis de plumets	1,135	1,105	340	357	180
Bottes fortes (paires)	1,080	1,572	384	711	38
Bottes molles (paires)	796	796	0	0	0
Eperons (paires)	1,790	1,468	350	660	139
Laniers d'eperons (paires)	0	0	0	0	816
Shoes	0	0	0	0	54
Aiguillettes for sub-officers	92	75	0	17	0
Aiguillettes trompette grand uniforme	0	0	0	0	0
Aiguillettes trompette petit uniforme	31	29	12	19	0
Aiguillettes for *grenadiers*	738	536	0	409	180
Cordons du bonnet of sub-officers	80	58	0	25	0
Cordons du bonnet de trompette	30	24	0	6 (from magazine)	0
Cordons du bonnet de grenadiers	1,320	1,305	200	332 (132 from magazine)	0
Fers-à-cheval (paires)	30	32	12	13	8
Dragonne for sub-officers	0	11 (from magazine)	0	0	2
Dragonne de trompette	0	1 (from magazine)	0	0	9
Garnitures en or (paires de)	144	157	0	35 (from magazine)	4
Trompettes	20	19	3	6 (3 from magazine)	3

ITEM	*1813*		*1814*		*IN MAGAZINE ON 23 JULY 1814*
	NUMBER MADE	*NUMBER ISSUED*	*NUMBER MADE*	*NUMBER ISSUED*	
Cordons du trompette grand uniforme	0	0	0	0	0
Cordons du trompette petit uniforme	21	19	0	6 (3 from magazine)	0
Shirts	0	0	400	344	56

Equipment of the *grenadiers-à-cheval* then in use passed to the *Cuirassiers de France*:

ITEM	*1813*		*1814*		*IN MAGAZINE ON 23 JULY 1814*	*COMMENTS*
	NUMBER MADE	*NUMBER ISSUED*	*NUMBER MADE*	*NUMBER ISSUED*		
Boutes de sabre	12	18	0	0	0	
Bois de sabre	0	6	0	0	0	
Moutiers de sabre	0	44	0	100	0	
Haches de campement	0	0	100	0	100	
Ceinturons d'epee	0	0	0	0	5	
Pistolets (paires)	1,184	1,057.50	100	335.50	0	
Fusils et baionettes	1,522	1,255	100	559		
Cocarde du bonnet de sub-officers	0	0	0	0	0	144 made in 1810
Cocarde du bonnet de troupe	1,310	1,310	0	0	0	
Bretelles de fusil	1,300	1,243	0	110	99	
Couvre platines	1,292	1,251	0	0	267	
Gibernes	1,706	1,362	0	343	92	
Banderolles	1,750	1,294	0	324	198	
Plaques du gibernes	1,670	1,364	0	328	137	
Agremens de banderolles	0	0	0	0	42	
Belieres de ceinturon grandes	0	40 (from magazine)	0	0	88	
Belieres de ceinturon petit	0	38 (from magazine)	0	0	42	

ITEM	*1813*		*1814*		*IN MAGAZINE ON 23 JULY 1814*	*COMMENTS*
	NUMBER MADE	*NUMBER ISSUED*	*NUMBER MADE*	*NUMBER ISSUED*		
Epinglettes	0	0	0	0	20	
Sabre *briquets*	0	0	0	0	3	
Guetres (paires)	0	0	0	0	0	
Contre-epaulettes for 2nd *Grenadiers en drap (paires)*	927	927	0	0	0	
Contre-epaulettes for 2nd *Grenadiers en galon (paires)*	0	0	483	483	0	
Boutons en cuivre pour giberne	850	850	0	0	0	
Musettes	904	897	350	357	0	
Sacs a distribution	890	887	350	353	0	
Contre-epaulettes *de tambour (paires)*	0	0	0	0	5	
Shako *pour* courier	0	0	0	0	4	Made in 1809
Habit pour courier	0	0	0	0	4	Made in 1808
Dolman *pour timbalier*	0	0	0	0	1	Made in 1811
Capote de guimbardier	0	0	0	0	4	Made in 1808

Harnesses and saddles of the *grenadiers-à-cheval* then in use passed to the *Cuirassiers de France*:

ITEM	*1813*		*1814*		*IN MAGAZINE ON 23 JULY 1814*
	NUMBER MADE	*NUMBER ISSUED*	*NUMBER MADE*	*NUMBER ISSUED*	
Saddles for sub-officers	3	4 (1 from magazine)	0	0	1
Saddles *de troupe*	1,514	1,540	60	72	0
Tetieres de bride	0	18	0	294	0
Reins (pairs)	0	19	150	269	0
Filets en cuir noir	0	15	150	175	0

ITEM	1813		1814		IN MAGAZINE ON 23 JULY 1814
	NUMBER MADE	NUMBER ISSUED	NUMBER MADE	NUMBER ISSUED	
Filets en fil dark yellow	0	0	0	0	0
Housse de trompette grand unif.	0	0	0	0	0
Housse de trompette petit unif.	30	28	4	6 (2 from magazine)	0
Housse for *grenadier grand unif.*	0	0	0	0	0
Housse for *grenadier petit unif.*	540	419	150	196	75
Cocardes-à-cheval grande	0	0	0	0	0
Cocardes-à-cheval petit	0	0	0	0	0
Rubons a natter	0	0	0	0	0
Potrails	0	0	0	106	70
Croupiers	0	1	0	209	83
Etrierivier	0	6	0	144	12
Dragonnes	0	1	0	250	204
Chainettes de tetiere	0	0	0	0	0
Sangles	0	200	0	243	0
Martingales	0	1	0	0	37
Licols de force	0	0	0	0	0
Licols de parade	0	27	150	209	0
Licols d'ecurie	0	65	0	0	118
Longe en corde	0	0	0	0	0
Longe en cuir noir	0	8	0	129	190
Longe en cuir blanc		60	0	0	219
Bridons d'abrevoir	0	65	0	0	101
Porte-crosse	0	35	0	185	0
Courroies de porte-crosse	0	0	0	0	0
Courroies de charge	0	10	0	98	58
Courroies de milieu	0	8	0	159	33
Mors de bride	1,631	1,648	3,148	395	0

ITEM	1813		1814		IN MAGAZINE ON 23 JULY 1814
	NUMBER MADE	NUMBER ISSUED	NUMBER MADE	NUMBER ISSUED	
Filet	24	38	0	0	140
Bridon	0	0	0	0	81
Etriers (paire)	150	40	0	96	14
Gourmettes	0	0	40	40	18

Clothing of the *grenadiers-à-cheval* then in use passed to the *Cuirassiers de France*:

ITEM	GOOD CONDITION	NEED REPAIRS	NEEDING TO BE REPLACED	NEED TO BE REPLACED	ITEMS SHORT
Habits	282	167	80	18	28
Vestes blanche	392	27	95	21	41
Bonnets de police	452	26	39	6	252
Capote manteaux	101	392	12	10	60
Veste d'ecurie	114	243	91	10	117
Pantalons gris	125	28	142	0	280
Culottes de daim	378	12	0	0	185
Culottes de mouton	95	2	21	0	0
Pairs de gants	357	52	0	0	166
Dragonne de sabre	559	8	0	0	8
Bonnets a Poil	356	4	51	14	150
Bottes fortes (paires)	222	132	16	43	156
Eperons (paires)	447	5	0	0	123
Aiguillettes	296	69	111	0	99
Ceinturons et plaques	514	77	0	0	0
Gibernes et banderolle	483	88	0	0	4
Fusils et bayonets	0	0	0	0	0
Sabres	198	441	0	0	0
Pistolets (paires)	336.50	64.50	0	0	0
Selles	59	497	38	0	0
Brides	211	431	0	0	0
Bridons	296	195	39	0	0

ITEM	*GOOD CONDITION*	*NEED REPAIRS*	*NEEDING TO BE REPLACED*	*NEED TO BE REPLACED*	*ITEMS SHORT*
Bridons d'ecurie	0	0	0	0	0
Licols et longe	0	0	0	0	0
Licols de parade	210	355	24	0	0
Sangles et surfaix	0	0	0	0	0
Housse et chaperons	88	467	29	0	0
Porte-manteaux	147	322	68	9	98
Mors de bride	268	411	0	0	0
Scarlet cloth	21.03 m	0	0	0	0
Shirts	1,565	0	0	0	0
Pantalons de toile	0	0	0	0	0
Cols noir	1,036	0	0	0	0
Cols blanche	1,532	0	0	0	0
Paires de souliers	475	0	0	0	0
Paires de guetres grises	364	0	0	0	0
Sacs a toile	0	0	0	0	0
Mouchoires de poche	1,494	0	0	0	0
Manchettes du bottes, paires	832	0	0	0	0
Cocardes	477	0	0	0	0
Epinglettes	0	0	0	0	0
Tournvis	347	0	0	0	0
Trousse bompletes	325	0	0	0	0
Sacs a avoine	440	0	0	0	0
Musettes	457	0	0	0	0
Paires de ciseax	457	0	0	0	0
Eponges	457	0	0	0	0
Brosses	457	0	0	0	0
Etrilles	457	0	0	0	0
Cords a fourrages	348	0	0	0	0
Livret	480	0	0	0	0

ITEM	GOOD CONDITION	NEED REPAIRS	NEEDING TO BE REPLACED	NEED TO BE REPLACED	ITEMS SHORT
Boutielles clisses	0	0	0	0	0
Boies a graise	327	0	0	0	0
Brosse a graise	353	0	0	0	0

Items in the magazine of the *grenadiers-à-cheval* passed to the *Cuirassiers de France*:

ITEM	NEW	GOOD CONDITION	NEED REPAIRS	WORN-OUT
Capote manteaux	50	0	0	45
Habits	0	0	0	57
Vestes blanche	0	0	0	56
Culottes de daim	0	0	0	7
Culottes de mouton	0	0	0	14
Bonnet a poil	0	0	0	59
Plumet et etuis	0	0	0	25
Bottes (paires)	0	0	0	25
Eperons (paires)	0	0	0	3
Ceinturon du sabre	0	28	4	15
Gibernes	0	50	44	32
Banderolles	30	10	46	34
Fusils	0	0	20	0
Selles	0	0	0	180
Brides	0	0	0	58
Housses et chaperones	36	0	0	100
Mors de bride	38	0	0	21
Harnais de chevaux de bat	0	6	0	0

The *Cuirassiers de France* throughout their ten-month existence wore the clothing and equipment of the *grenadiers-à-cheval*. In theory, the regiment was to be dressed as *cuirassiers*. Only three *cuirassier habits* were ever made, no doubt as samples, in the three regulation sizes. No armour was ever made or issued. At Waterloo, the re-activated *grenadiers-à-cheval* were dressed as in previous years.

Trumpeters

The trumpeter-major served the regiment from 1798 to 1815. He was Jean Joseph Eggere, born at Cambrai on 19 March 1779. He stood 1.64 m tall, had an oval face, high forehead, blue eyes, a long nose, medium sized mouth, round chin and blond hair and eyebrows. He was admitted into the 17th Cavalry Regiment in 1792 and passed as trumpeter of the *grenadiers-à-cheval* of the Directory Guard in 1798, promoted to corporal-trumpeter in 1804 and then to trumpet-major on 3 April 1814. After fighting with the *grenadiers* at Waterloo, he passed as sergeant-major trumpeter to the *chasseurs-à-cheval* of the Royal Guard on 1 November 1815.[58] Some of his fellow trumpeters were:[59]

Pierre Laurent Benoist, born in Paris on 20 July 1795, was the son of Jean Pierre Benoist and Rose Dore. He stood 1.60 m tall, had an oval face, blue eyes, round chin and blond hair and eyebrows. Admitted as cadet trumpeter on 16 November 1811, he was promoted to trumpeter on 8 February 1813. He deserted on 23 July 1814.

Antoine Burthez was born on 30 November 1777 and was the legitimate son of Jean Leonard Burthez and Madeleine. He stood 1.62 m tall, had an oval face, grey eyes and dark blond hair and eyebrows. He enlisted in the 2nd Horse Artillery Regiment on 1 August 1793 and became the corporal-trumpeter for the regiment in 1798. He passed to the *grenadiers-à-cheval* as a trumpeter on 21 February 1811. He was promoted to corporal-trumpeter on 21 February 1813. With the fall of Napoleon and the restoration of the monarchy, rather than join the *Cuirassiers* of France and serve a king, Burthez deserted on 1 June 1814. However, his desire not to serve the Bourbons seems to have waned compared to the need to earn money to support him and his son, as two weeks later he entered the army once again and was admitted as trumpet-major of the *grenadiers-à-cheval* of the king's military household on 16 June 1814. With the disbandment of that regiment in 1815, he passed back into the *grenadiers-à-cheval* on 1 April 1815 with the rank of corporal-trumpeter and served as captain's trumpeter in 1st Company, which was part of 1st Squadron. Following the debacle at Waterloo, he deserted again on 6 July 1815 with uniform, baggage and horse. He was re-admitted into the *grenadiers-à-cheval* of the Imperial Guard on 1 November 1815 as sergeant-trumpeter, and passed on 25 November 1815 to the 1st Regiment of *grenadiers-à-cheval* of the Royal Guard. He left the army on 3 December 1822. His service records state that he took no part in any campaigns after 1810. Therefore, we must assume he took a role in the depot company or was able to get out of any campaigning. He was awarded the Legion of Honour on 19 August 1823. Clearly, he was something of a bad character and a fair-weather friend, hedging his bets with the turning tide of Napoleon's political fortunes.

Guilaumme Antoine Burthez was born on 28 December 1801, the son of Antoine Burthez and Marie Decruge. He passed to the *grenadiers-à-cheval* as *enfant de troupe* in 1803 and appointed as *timbalier trompette* on 13 December 1811.

Charles Marie Dubray was born on 1 May 1780. He was the son of Claude Alexander, toymaker, and Frances Adelaide Gattelier, and brother of Lieutenant Claude Marie Leonor, 2nd Infantry of the Royal Guard. He stood 1.59 m tall had an oval face, grey eyes and dark blond hair and eyebrows. He joined as a trumpeter in the 4th Dragoons in November 1796. He passed as a trumpeter to the *grenadiers-à-cheval* on 12 February 1809, remaining in the post throughout the course of the empire and First Restoration. At Waterloo he was a trumpeter in 5th Company, part of 1st Squadron. He was discharged from the regiment with the proposal of retirement on 25 November 1815. In 1816, he was appointed as corporal trumpeter of the 2nd Regiment of *Cuirassiers* of the Royal Guard. He was awarded the Legion of Honour on 27 February 1814. He died on 17 November 1835.

Jacques Francois Grossin was born on 25 December 1793. Admitted to the *grenadiers-à-cheval* as a cadet trumpeter on 30 July 1808, he was promoted to trumpeter in February 1813 and passed to the Royal Corps of *Cuirassiers* of France on 23 July 1814, passing back to the *grenadiers-à-cheval* on 1 April 1815, serving in 8th Company as a trumpeter.

Jean Baptiste Guiochet was one of the characters of the regiment. He was born in 1770 and joined the army in 1780 as a fifer in an infantry regiment. He transferred to the 15th Cavalry Regiment as a child of the regiment (*enfant de troupe*) in 1783. When he reached the age of 18 in 1788, he signed on as a full member of the regiment. He joined the *grenadiers-à-cheval* as a trumpeter in 1802, was promoted to corporal-trumpeter in 1804 and was awarded the Cross of the Legion of Honour in 1806. He came back from the Russian campaign and remained in his post as corporal-trumpeter in the *grenadiers-à-cheval* charge at Hanau on 30 October 1813. He was wounded with a bullet to his right shoulder. He took no part in the 1814 campaign. He was transferred to the *Cuirassiers* of France on 23 July 1814 and left the regiment 16 March 1815.

Jude Poinsignon was born on 12 December 1794 in Paris, the son of Henry Poinsignon and Marie Delpierre. He stood 1.64 m tall, had an oval face, low forehead, grey eyes, small nose, medium sized mouth, round chin and dark blond hair and eyebrows. Admitted as a cadet trumpeter on 28 October 1811, he was promoted to trumpeter on 2 February 1813. He passed as a trumpeter to the Royal Corps of *Cuirassiers* of France on 23 November 1814, and passed as a trumpeter of 2nd Company *grenadiers-à-cheval* of the Imperial Guard on 1 April 1815.

Under the directory, the trumpeters wore the uniform coat of a *grenadier*, which, from 17 January 1797, had a row of gold lace 20 mm wide on the cuffs. Lace was officially applied to the collar from 19 June 1798.[60] The *arête* of 22 June confirmed this lace to the collar, and then to the *revers* after 22 June 1797 for musicians. Upon the formation of the 2nd Squadron, new cloth was purchased for the trumpeters between 21 April and 22 September 1800. However, only crimson cloth was purchased along with *aiguillettes* of crimson and gold, gold brandenburgs for the *habit*, trumpets in silvered copper and copper with blue and gold trumpet cords. The saddle cloth and pistol holsters were in crimson wool cloth laced in gold for 96 *francs* each.[61]

Can we, therefore, assume that for the Consular Guard the *habit* was laced as before (collar, *revers*, cuffs) with brandenburgs to the buttonholes, and the coat being dark blue faced in crimson? Certainly, by the time, Hoffman was working, the *habits* had become *bleu de ciel*.

The first inventory to list sky blue cloth for trumpeters dates from September 1804.[62] The stores held 29 m of first quality *bleu de celeste* cloth, 47 m of second quality *bleu celeste*, along with 10 m each of first and second quality crimson, 141 m of *bleu celeste tricot*, and 112 m of crimson *serge* all destined for the trumpeters.[63] By 1809 the clothing colour had changed to the darker *bleu de ciel*.

The clothing for the trumpeters made between 1808 and 1814 was as follows:[64]

YEAR	*HABITS*		*SURTOUTS*	*REDINGOTES*	*GILETS*	*CULOTTES*	*BONNETS DE POLICE*	*MANTEAUX*	*STABLE COATS*	*PORTE-MANTEAUX*	*CHAPEAUX*	*AIGUILLETTES*		*BEARSKIN CORDS*	*SWORD KNOTS*	*TRUMPET CORDS*	
	PARADE	*UNDRESS*	*PARADE*									*PARADE*	*UNDRESS*			*PARADE*	*UNDRESS*
In magazine	0	0	5	0	0	0	33	5	0	25	0	14	0	12	16	0	0
1808	0	4	13	3	0	1	0	11	0	0	0	1	0	0	1	0	25
1809	25	23	2	1	0	0	23	5	0	10	30	29	24	22	0	0	42
1810	0	29	10	4	0	0	26	1	0	0	0	0	21	1	22	0	4
1811	1	6	14	0	10	10	10	5	0	21	0	0	15	2	11	0	12
1812	0	10	20	2	16	16	40	27	0	18	0	0	17	6	0	0	30
1813	0	37	11	2	12	12	41	25	0	36	0	0	31	30	0	0	27
1814	0	3	7	0	7	7	0	6	0	0	0	0	12	0	0	0	0
Total	26	112	82	12	45	46	173	85	0	110	30	44	120	73	50	0	140

Of the trumpeter's *surtouts*, twenty-five were made for the cadet trumpeters, along with the *gilets* and *culottes*. The specification for the dress *habits* was as follows:

CLOTH	*COATS NEEDED*	*DRESS* HABIT	*UNDRESS* HABIT
Bleu de ciel wool cloth, first quality		148.60 cm 115 cm	148.60 cm 115 cm
Crimson wool cloth, first quality		22 cm 119 cm	148.60 cm 115 cm
Serge crimson for lining		237.70 cm 50 cm	144 cm 115 cm
Linen for lining sleeves, jacket body and pockets		148.60 cm 104 cm	22 cm 119 cm

CLOTH	*COATS NEEDED*	*DRESS* HABIT	*UNDRESS* HABIT
Undyed linen for *doit fils*		29 cm 97 cm	22 cm 119 cm
Grenades (set of four)		1	237.70 cm 50 cm
Large buttons		12	148.60 cm 104 cm
Medium buttons		24	29 cm 97 cm
Gold lace six *lignes*/12 mm wide	25	29 cm	1 m
Eight *lignes*/18 mm wide	4 (corporal trumpet)	148 cm	120 cm
	1 (trumpet-major)	356 cm	240 cm
Fifteen *lignes*/34 mm wide	25	623 cm	290 cm
	1 (trumpet-major)	214 cm	445 cm
Brandenburg in gold		5 m	5 m

The undress coat had a substantially reduced amount of gold lace. No parade coats for trumpeters were made from 1812. They were presumably kept in store for parade purposes only and the habitual wear of the trumpeters was either the *surtout* or undress *habit*.

The headdress of the trumpeters was the *chapeaux* or bearskin. The full dress headgear was a black felt hat, edged with crested braid in white, red and blue, furnished with cords and a cockade strap and gold terminals at the corners. Braided trumpeter's hats cost 103 *francs* in 1804. The stores held twenty-five of these items. A white-over-red plume was worn, it seems, after 1804, as no plumes are specifically listed for trumpeters in 1804. Hoffman and Vernet both agree on the appearance of the hat and the colouring of the plume. However, only scarlet plumes were purchased.

The archive paperwork lists thirty new hats being purchased at the end of 1809, the same time that new dress coats were made. The hats were to be 'the same quality, as for general officers'. They no longer had cords and were ornamented with a 54 mm wide braid in front and 27 mm on the inside, crested with crowns and grenades, and a 61 mm strap also in gold. Each hat with scarlet plume cost 138 *francs*.[65] It is likely that the hat was the parade dress item, as Garnier's painting shows 'the marriage procession of Napoleon and Marie Louise in the Tuilleries Gardens'.[66] Garnier shows, in the distance, the head of the horse *grenadiers'* column.

The trumpeters shown are marching in fours and mounted on white horses, and are wearing the gold braided hat with a large white plume. They have the parade harness without the *valise* and they precede the kettle drummer clothed hussar-style and flanked by two *grenadiers*. Unfortunately, the reduced dimensions of this group prevent our discerning all the details.

The bearskin was also worn by the trumpeters. The first image of a trumpeter sporting this headgear is by Hoffmann. The bearskin is black with what appear to be gold cords. The *raquettes* were worn on the left side of the bearskin rather than the more typical right for the *grenadiers*, so we may assume this was a particular style adopted by the trumpeters. The stores inventories for 1804 list the *chapeau* being the only specific item for the trumpeter, along with bearskin cords. The stores do not list bearskins specifically for the trumpeters between 1804 and 1814, so we assume they wore a standard black bearskin as shown by Hoffmann and Otto.[67]

Otto shows the bearskin having dark yellow and crimson, or gold and crimson, cords and *raquettes* and a *bleu de ciel* plume.[68] The bearskin also has chin scales. The Strasbourg collection, created in the late 1820s, shows a black bearskin with dark yellow cords and a *bleu de ciel* plume tipped in crimson.[69] The Alsatian collection shows a black bearskin, as does Lejeune for 1805.

Detaille, Marbot and others show the trumpeters wearing a white bearskin. Indeed, Marbot is the earliest reference to this and may well be the progenitor of the white bearskin. Boisselier and Knoetel copy Marbot's error. The *marche* accounts do not list any white bearskins being purchased from 1808 to 1814, which is also confirmed by the stores inventories, which do not list these items.

The Brunswick manuscript is the only source from the period to show a trumpeter ascribed to the *grenadiers* sporting a white bearskin, though it more closely resembles a colpack. The uniform worn is naively depicted, so no great reliability can be place on the illustration.[70] Therefore, we can be fairly certain that the white bearskin is an invention of the mid-nineteenth century.

The trumpeter's parade *schabraque* was crimson from 1804, as shown by Hoffman[71] and confirmed in the *marche* accounts from 1808.[72] No grenades were purchased for parade *schabraques* from 1809, and they appear to have been replaced with crowns. Grenades were listed under items purchased for undress *schabraques* after 1808. The specification for the *housse* was established on 5 January 1807:[73]

Housses de trompette:

- 1.09 m of crimson wool cloth, third quality, at 20.19 *francs* a metre
- 0.22 m of *bleu de ciel* wool cloth, second quality, at 20.19 *francs* a metre
- 2.37 m of *treillis*, Alençon quality, at 1.85 *francs* a metre
- 8.91 m of dark yellow wool lace, 54 mm wide, at 1.30 *francs* a metre
- 8.91 m of aurore wool lace, 23 mm wide, at 63 *centimes* a metre
- One pair of grenades at 1.85 *francs*

- 2.37 m of oil cloth at 1.05 *francs*
- Labour: 9 *francs*
- Total: 61.49 *francs*

The *porte-manteau* was also *bleu de ciel*, of which eighty were purchased from 1808. A single *bleu de ciel* example was in store on 23 September 1804, which cost 22 *francs*, along with seven full-laced *schabraques*, which cost 262 *francs* each. Gold grenades are listed for *schabraques* in the same stores return.[74] The dress *schabraque* was ornamented with crowns with 950 cm of 52 mm wide gold lace. Between 1808 and 1814, only twenty-five parade *schabraques* were purchased, all in 1810.[75] Seventy-three undress *schabraques* were purchased for campaign use of at least two specifications. Twenty-nine were ordered in 1813 for the trumpeters.[76] Like the dress *schabraque*, it was crimson by 1808. However, prior to this date it appears to have been *bleu de ciel* (the Strasbourg collection shows *bleu de ciel*,[77] as does Otto[78] and Vernet), laced in gold, with grenades in the rear corners, as shown by Vernet and Otto.[79]

Of the ten *schabraques* made from 1804 to 1814 ornamented with crowns, we assume they were the same item as those made from the first quality cloth, perhaps for the trumpet-major and corporal-trumpeters. Only thirteen were piped with *bleu de ciel* wool. Those laced with narrow 22 mm lace we assume to be for the cadet-trumpeters. There appears to have been three different styles of lacing to the *schabraques*:

1. Thirty-four with an outer row of 30 mm lace and inner row of 22 mm lace
2. Thirteen with an outer row of 30 mm lace and inner row of 22 mm lace and edged in *bleu de ciel*
3. Twenty-six with a single row of 30 mm lace

We note that twenty-eight undress *schabraques* were purchased in 1813. Clearly, from 1813 the undress *schabraque* was used for full dress. These items were also used in full dress by the cadet-trumpeters as no parade items were purchased for them. Indeed, on 23 July 1814 an inspection return lists only one *schabraque* model for the trumpeters. Based on the regiment's accounts these were the undress variety.[80] The trumpeter's *porte-manteau* was made from second quality *bleu de ciel* wool cloth, piped in scarlet as opposed to crimson. Eighty-five of these were purchased from 1808. Otto,[81] Vernet and the Alsatian[82] collection both show this as square, *bleu de ciel* and laced in dark yellow with a single row of lace, which matches those purchased from 1808. Hoffmann's trumpeters do not have a *portemanteau*.[83] In 1815, twenty-four new *schabraques* for trumpeters, along with twenty-four *bleu de ciel portemanteaux* were held in stores. The colour of the *schabraque* is not known. The lace on the *schabraque* was in yellow wool.

Kettledrummers

From 1800, the regiment had a kettledrummer. The accounts of 17 September 1800 lists the following items:[84]

- Two *legendre* embroidered in silver for kettledrummers, costing 90.50 *francs* each
- 1,803.73 m of fringing in gold at 12 *francs* a metre
- 7,062 m of gold lace, 104 for *legendre*, at 12 *francs* a metre
- Four kettledrums at 1,350 *francs* each
- One plume for kettledrummer, costing 40 *centimes*
- Two head collars and lead ropes for kettledrummers at 4.50 *francs* each
- Four pairs of straps for kettledrums at 3.50 *francs* each
- Two *coussinets* (pad saddles) for kettledrums at 18 *francs* each
- One sabre for kettledrummer costing 75 *francs*.

The kettledrummers in the regiment were:[85]

> MAT No. 9 Antoine Jean Bruneau Lemoine, son of Antoine Marcel Lemoine and Aime Ameleot, born in Paris, joined the regiment on 3 January 1800. He passed to the *chasseurs-à-cheval* on 2 February 1803.
>
> MAT No. 1264 Hypolite Cailles, son of Claude Cailles and Anne Barbara Gauthier, born on 14 September 1788. He joined the Guides of Bonaparte as a trumpeter on 22 September 1797 and joined the *grenadiers* on 3 February 1803. He was named as a *fourrier* in the *mamelukes* on 1 July 1806.
>
> MAT No. 1614 Jean Baptiste Victor Boireaux was born on 7 December 1793 at Lille, the son of Louis-August Boireaux and Anne Oudette Muselier. Admitted as a kettledrummer on 30 June 1806, he was named as a trumpeter on 13 December 1811. He was last seen on 14 December 1812, presumed prisoner-of-war.
>
> MAT No. 354 Guillaume Antoine Burthez. Passed to the *grenadiers-à-cheval* as *enfant de troupe* in 1803 and appointed on 13 December 1811 as *timbalier trompette*. Following the Russian campaign, he was appointed as cadet-trumpeter in February 1813, but he deserted with his father in 1814. He was admitted back to the *grenadiers-à-cheval* as a trumpeter-kettledrummer on 1 April 1815. He deserted with his father on 6 July.

We know in August 1811 a new set of uniform was made for the kettledrummer, perhaps for young Burthez. The uniform was made from the following items: a new scarlet cloth dolman with blue collar and cuffs, ornamented with 12.50 m of square gold braid and 91.50 m of gold embroidery. As the specification does not show flat braid, it is the closed-up embroidery, forming complicated ornaments, that which took its place.[86] How long this uniform was worn is not clear, as it may have been replaced with a *habit* a year later. The regiment only ever purchased two kettledrums and a set of harnesses. This was repaired in 1815.[87] Only two uniforms were ever made for the kettledrummer, both being hussar in style. Hoffmann shows the uniform. His hussar-type clothing seems to have remained unchanged until 1811. It was still the imperial blue dolman, crimson *pelisse* and breeches, braided and ornamented with gold embroidery, crimson *sabretache* bearing the imperial arms, the shako without a peak, crimson with gold braid and cord, crimson plume, crimson hussar-type *schabraque* braided with gold, as well as the drum aprons, head harness with gilded buckles and ornaments and crimson plume with small sky blue and white plumes at the base.[88]

A print by Chataignier and Poisson shows a blue hussar dolman with scarlet collar and presumably cuffs, with gold braiding and lace. The *pelisse* is scarlet with gold lace and braid and grey fur trim. The breeches are also scarlet laced in gold. The drum banners and *schabraque* are scarlet edged in gold lace with gold fringing, for which the purchase accounts mention. The print also shows a *sabretache* and sabre. The sabre and belt cost 75 *francs*. Hoffmann shows ostensibly the same uniform.

Garnier's painting,[89] of which we have already mentioned concerning the description of the parade uniform of the trumpeters, shows, for 1810, the kettledrummer clad in a hussar style. Unfortunately, the small size does not allow us to see the detail of the costume, made even vaguer by an unfortunate fountain of water that partly hides it. In 1811, the kettledrummer received a new scarlet cloth dolman with blue collar and cuffs, ornamented with 12.50 m of square gold braid and 91.51 m of gold embroidery. However, the Strasbourg collection shows the kettledrummer wearing fanciful *mameluke*-style dress in crimson and sky blue,[90] the band being turned out in sky blue dolmans laced in dark yellow and crimson *pelisse*. This was set off with a white *chasseur*-style colpack and crimson *schabraques*.[91]

What date must we give to the kettledrummer reproduced in 1902 by Job, in *Tenues de Troupes de France*, after a painting kept in the Musée de l'Armée? It is likely to be 1814 and shows the kettledrummer wearing a trumpeter's *habit*. This makes sense given the duel function of the kettledrummer as trumpeter-kettledrummer.

Drivers

Regimental drivers were authorised from 15 April 1806, but do not seem to have appeared until the new year of 1807. They were discontinued with the imperial decree of 24 August 1811. Henceforth, the duties of regimental drivers were passed to the equipment train of the Guard.

Between 1 January 1808 and 24 August 1811, the regimental baggage drivers were issued with twenty-one capes, twenty-one all blue *habit-vestes* and thirty-one waistcoats. Clearly, to equip all fifty-one personnel charged with moving baggage, this can only have been a partial re-equipping of the drivers, and older stocks of clothing must have remained in service since 1807.[92]

Their uniform coat is described in the *marche* accounts as *habit-vestes*. Perhaps short-tailed *habit-longes* with the square lapels like the *grenadiers* and used by the Guard equipment train. The *habit-vestes* were made from fourth quality blue cloth. They were closed by twenty-four medium buttons, presumably a version of the *grenadiers* in style, with the lapels being closed with fourteen buttons, each cuff with three: two at the collar and two at the *taille*. Based on the cloth purchased, the *revers*, cuffs, tail lining and turnbacks were in blue cloth.

Headgear was likely to be a *chapeau* and leg wear perhaps the thirty-five pairs of blue *pantalons* mentioned earlier, if not leather breeches and long boots as well. These men drove the regiment's vehicles, consisting primarily of artillery caissons and field forges.

The harness for the horses was of the German style. The horses were harnessed in pairs. The only complete description of artillery harness for the Napoleonic era is that of the French harness. The French used the German or French system of harnessing, which used the same basic elements, described below, after Bardin 1812 and Gassendi 1819. The German-style full harness for four horses comprised two front traces and two rear traces. The harness of the drivers comprised dragoon-pattern saddle and accessories, i.e. holsters, straps, loading straps, stirrup irons and leathers, bridle, bit and reins. The harness was in the regiment's depot in 1814 and 1815.

Grooms

Officers and sergeants were allowed their own grooms or domestics only with the permission of the commanding colonel from 1803, and with a certificate of reference. The uniform prescribed for the *chasseurs-à-cheval* domestics was a green sleeved waistcoat, cut round at the front, in green cloth with a yellow collar, the cuffs and front being closed with domed, white, metal buttons. The headgear was to be a *chapeau* with a *ganse* in white wool and no lacing or *marrons*. The waistcoat and leg wear to be in grey or green cloth.[93]

The grooms of the *grenadiers-à-cheval* were equipped with *habits*. The regimental archive lists the purchase of 113 *habit-vestes*: fifty in 1808, twenty in 1809, seventeen in 1810, twenty-three in 1811 and three in 1812. Of these, ninety-six are listed as being for grooms. The *habits* needed twenty-four large buttons and six medium buttons. We assume the medium buttons closed the cuffs, leaving eight large buttons for the tails and fourteen buttons for the front of the coat, and two at the shoulder. They were made from third quality blue cloth, and of the ninety-two, sixty-nine had white cuffs and white piping to the collars, cuff flaps and long pockets, as the amount of white cloth purchased matches the amount of scarlet cloth purchased for the cuffs, facings and pipings of the *grenadier's habits*.

CHAPTER 3

CHASSEURS-À-CHEVAL

Napoleon ordered the formation of his personal bodyguard, the *guides-à-cheval*, on 11 *Prairial*, Year IV (30 May 1796), after nearly being captured by a force of raiding Austrian hussars at Valeggio. These men became his personal escort and bodyguard while commander-in-chief of the army of Italy, and would accompany him for the next twenty years. In 1799, the Guides accompanied Napoleon to Egypt, some returning to France at the close of the year. These men became the nucleus of the *chasseurs-à-cheval* of the Consular Guard in the new year of 1800.

The *chasseurs-à-cheval*, following Marengo, was increased in size progressively so that by the end of the empire it had ten squadrons. On 18 January 1813, an 8th squadron was formed to contain 250 men – the regiment to contain 2,000 men in total.

A few months later, on 6 March 1813, a 9th Squadron was formed which, as with the 5th, 6th, 7th and 8th Squadrons, ranked as part of the Young Guard. The *mamelukes* were likewise formed into to a squadron of two companies, and received the number 10th.

The organisation of the regiment in March 1813 was as follows:

SQUADRON	COMPANY	STATUS
1st	1st and 6th	Old Guard
2nd	2nd and 7th	Old Guard
3rd	3rd and 8th	Old Guard
4th	4th and 9th	Old Guard
5th	5th and 10th	Young Guard
6th	11th and 15th	Young Guard
7th	12th and 16th	Young Guard
8th	13th and 17th	Young Guard
9th	14th and 18th	Young Guard
10th	1st and 2nd	*Mameluke*, Old and Young Guard

The squadrons of the Old Guard were under the command of Colonel-Major Lion, those of the Young Guard stood under the command of Colonel-Major Meuziau. The squadrons of the Young Guard were re-christened at the end of December as the *Deuxième Régiment de Chasseurs-à-Cheval de la Jeune Guarde*, but when the *èclaireurs* of the Guard were formed, the *Hussards Èclaireurs de la*

Engraving by Vernet of a senior officer of *chasseurs-à-cheval* in the hussar-style parade dress (Peter Harrington)

Jeune Garde was used in its place. The origin of the somewhat strange designation *Hussards Èclaireurs* is not completely clear. A possible explanation could be that in 1813 three *èclaireurs* regiments of the Guard were set up and assigned to the *grenadiers-à-cheval*, dragoons and *chevau-légèrs-lanciers* of the Guard, for the *chasseurs* there was no intended supporting unit. This deficiency can perhaps explain the strange naming.

Clothing and equipment

The *chasseurs* had two uniforms: the showy and flamboyant hussar uniform and the more sombre *chasseur* uniform. From the preserved archive sources, we know nothing about clothing and equipment between 1800 and 1809, a gap of nine years in the historical record. The dolman was always dark green with scarlet cuffs. The front, the waist, the collar, the cuffs and the false pockets were edged with a flat, aurore braid. The same braid covered the seams of the back and adorned the projecting *sabots* at the rear waist. An aurore wool piping cord ran alongside the cuff braid forming a trefoil. It also extended on each side of the braid of the back-forming loops and a Hungarian knot. The dolman was adorned with square braiding, which formed buttonhole decorations and, according to the

Colpack pompom cockade and *raquettes*. These were worn on the opposite side of the colpack to the flame. They were worn with the plume in full dress. (Private collection, Switzerland)

period, had three or five rows of eighteen buttons, those in the centre being large and the others of medium size.

The *pelisse* of scarlet cloth was lined with white flannel and edged with curly lamb's wool. It was decorated in the same manner as the dolman, with the same flat face, square cord braid, piping cord and buttons. Twenty-six large buttons went into its manufacture, of which eighteen were in front and eight in the waist *sabots*. In addition, it was fitted with a suspension cord and toggle in aurore wool. The barrel sash was made up of a double skein of dark green wool cord, which passed through nine movable runners of scarlet braiding. The ends were fastened by two cockled, flat, fixed knots of scarlet wool. Finally, at one end of the sash was a scarlet toggle held by a strong cord of the same colour, while the other end was fitted with a double scarlet cord with securing knots in green wool, which ended in a scarlet tassel with green fringes. The coat (*habit*) in use from 1800 to 1815, a relic of the old Guides of Italy and Egypt, did not change in its composition. It was always made of dark green cloth with collar, pointed cuffs, lapel edges and the pleat patches in scarlet. Epaulette loops were aurore. Horns in aurore wool were embroidered on scarlet patches sewn to the turnbacks. The coat had eighteen large, yellow, buttons, of which there were seven on each *revers* and two on each pleat patch, and six small, of which two were on each cuff and one on each shoulder. An *aiguillette* of aurore wool, mounted in trefoil on green cloth ending in two brass ferrules, was placed on the left, while the right shoulder had an aurore braid trefoil backed onto green cloth. The cloth Hungarian breeches had their side seams covered with a flat aurore wool braid stripe. The same braid formed the Hungarian knots at the

Issued in 1804 was the first type of *sabretache* for the regiment. The eagle in the centre of the *sabretache* was embroidered but was replaced by a copper stamping for the 2nd type. The quality of embroidery on the eagle is of a very high standard indeed. (Private collection, Switzerland).

opening of the small fly flap. On the march, or on campaign, the *chasseurs* used decorated trousers, the composition of which changed several times. In 1808, they were made from green cloth with leather reinforcement to the seat and bottom of the leg, with an aurore side stripe. At the end of 1813, the trousers changed colour and were made of a Marengo-grey cloth. They were closed at the sides, reinforced in grey cloth or calfskin, and decorated on each side with a double stripe of red cloth.

The *sabretache*, mark of the light cavalryman, adopted at the end of 1800, was larger and of a more elegant shape than that of the empire. Based on the Hoffmann prints and an extant original item, the scarlet cloth face was decorated with the badge of the republic and a hunting horn, encircled with foliage and embroidered in their natural colours. On the upper part was stitched a scroll bearing the words '*Garde des Consuls*'. The surrounding lace-stripe, woven in diagonal bars, and the accompanying piping were of aurore wool.

The *sabretache* of the empire had a green base and was surrounded by an aurore *soubise* stripe, slightly wavy along the edges. It had, in the centre, the imperial mantling bearing an eagle and surmounted by a crown. It was accompanied by blue, red and green *guidons*.

The oldest known model (Musée de l'Armée, Detaille collection) has the imperial crown, the mantle, the eagle and the *guidons* cut out of cloth and sewn to the green base. The seams are largely hidden by gold-yellow cords with the pikes, staffs, cravats, fringes and butts of the flags embroidered in coloured wool. The outer lace stripe has an inner lining of aurore piping. On the second model, only the white base of the mantle is of cloth and the rest of the ornamentation is embroidered in coloured wools underlined with aurore cord, and the eagle on it is of embossed brass. The pattern at the end of the empire is identical and its price unchanged, though the outer lace stripe had lost its accompanying piping. Plain leather examples are listed in use in 1814 by the Corps Royale.

The *sabretache* flap was almost always covered with a varnished black oilskin *sabretache* cover. This accessory, initially without ornament, was decorated in 1812 with a crowned eagle painted on in yellow.

The distinctions of the sub-officers were a little more complicated as, in addition to having rank and service stripes of gold lace, the lace and cording that went into the manufacture of their uniforms were of wool mixed with one-third gold.

In addition, the specification showed a greater quantity of lacing in the manufacture of their dolman, *pelisse*, laced waistcoat and green Hungarian trousers. The braid, piping, cord and 'olive' of the *pelisse*, the braid and piping of the waistcoat, the boot fittings, the piping and tassel of the colpack bag, the flounders and tassels and the stop-knots of the sash cord were a mixture of gold and green wool. Also, the *pelisse* was edged with marmot fur, the waistcoat was fitted with five rows of buttons and the *sabretache* had its outer lace in gold with accompanying green and gold piping. The braid used in making the riding trousers used from 1809 to 1813 was gold and red, the lace and horn on the base of the forage cap was gold, while the Hungarian knot on the cloth breeches was accompanied by piping that formed loops and trefoils.

The coat was fitted with epaulette straps of gold and green braid, and its turnbacks were decorated with gold horns embroidered onto a red background. An *aiguillette* and a trefoil, mixed half gold and half green wool, completed the ensemble, an extant item being found in the Brunon collection.

Painting of *chasseur* wearing the *chasseur*-style uniform as observed by the German artist Otto.

1800

The oldest document relating to the dress of the regiment is dated 8 September 1800:[1]

- One shako and plume, 24 *francs*
- One *pelisse* in scarlet cloth, 45 *francs*
- One dolman in green cloth, 30 *francs*
- One *bonnet de police*, 8.84 *francs*
- One pair of shoes, 4.75 *francs*
- One pair of black gaiters, 5 *francs*
- One shirt, 5 *francs*
- One black stock in silk, 2 *francs*
- One *chapeau*, with *marrons* and cockade, 8.75 *francs*
- One pair of stockings, 2.50 *francs*
- One pair of *pantalons* in scarlet wool, 25 *francs*
- One *sabretache*, 24 *francs*
- One *schabraque* in green cloth, laced in scarlet, with tassel and embroidered hunting horn in scarlet wool on green backing, 50 *francs*.

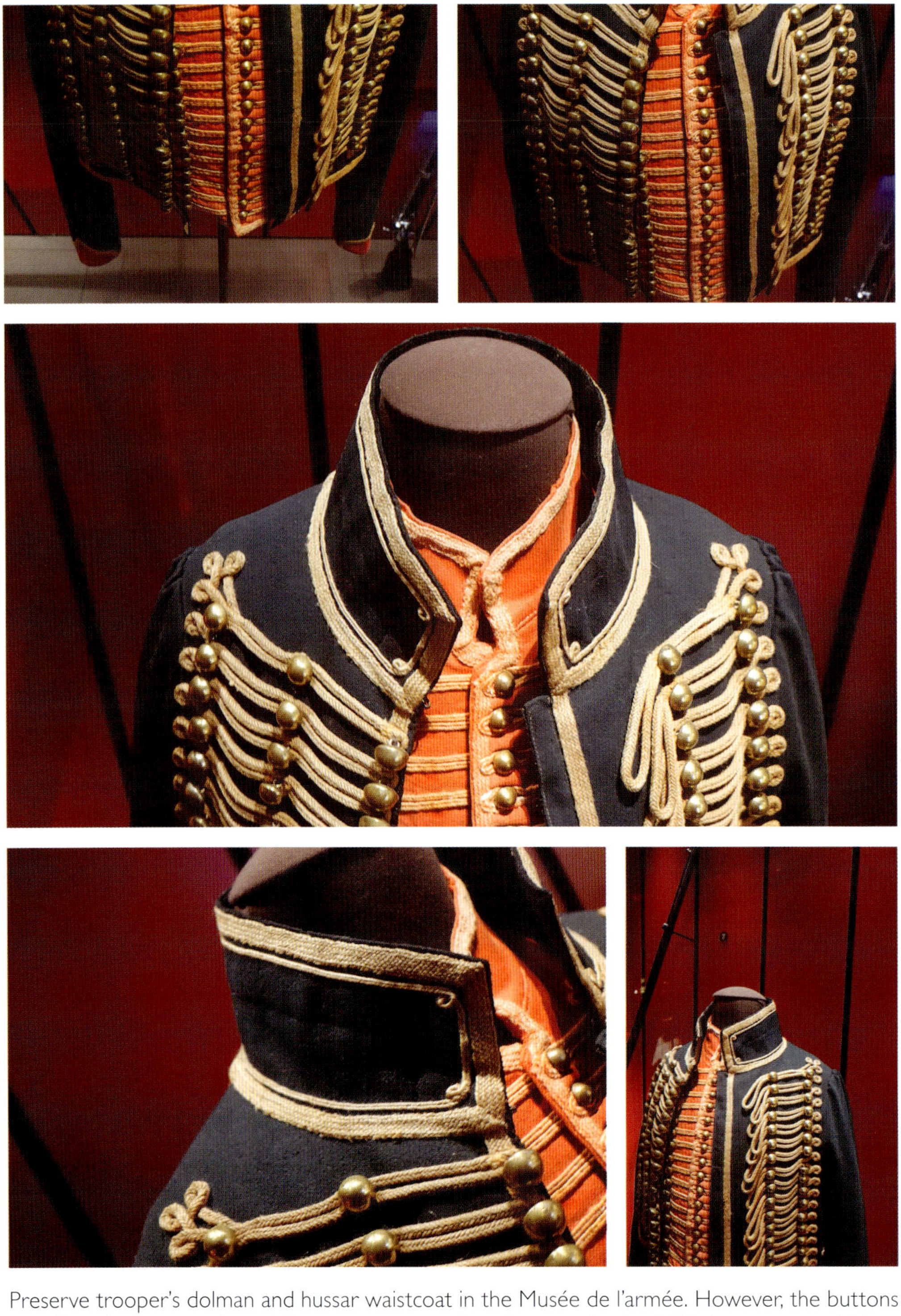

Preserve trooper's dolman and hussar waistcoat in the Musée de l'armée. However, the buttons are all made post-epoch, and the garments were heavily re-cut in the 1960s in an over-ambitious restoration. (Musée de l'armée)

The characteristic aurore lace and green *pantalons* were not adopted until 1804, based upon the series of plates by Hoffmann. We have no definite documents giving the date for the changeover. A more comprehensive list of items for the dress of the regiment was compiled on 17 September:[2]

Cloth:

- 1,299.04 m of green wool cloth, first quality, at 26 *francs* a metre
- 880.04 m of green wool cloth, second quality, at 19 *francs* a metre
- 547.09 m of green *tricot* at 3.75 *francs* a metre

Passamenteries:

- 7,888.68 m of aurore wool *soutache* at 25 *centimes* a metre
- 3,604.86 m of aurore wool flat braid, 10 mm wide, at 70 *centimes* a metre
- 1,344.98 m of aurore wool square braid at 55 *centimes* a metre
- 1,514 hunting horns embroidered in aurore wool at 2 *francs* a set (*chasseurs-à-cheval* and *chasseurs-à-pied*)
- 249 barrel sashes in wool, costing 30 *francs* each
- 1,350 *aiguillettes* in yellow wool at 7.75 *francs* each (*grenadiers-à-cheval* and *chasseurs-à-cheval*)
- Sixty-three *aiguillettes* in green wool and gold thread, costing 42 *francs* each
- 172 sets of colpack cords in green wool and gold thread, costing 18 *francs* each
- 52 sets of shako cords in green wool and gold thread, costing 18 *francs* each
- 26 sets of shako cords in crimson wool and gold thread, costing 18 *francs* each
- 263 aurore wool tassels for boots at 60 *centimes* a pair
- 575 aurore wool tassels for *schabraques* at 2 *francs* a pair
- 650 hunting horns for *schabraques*, costing 2.50 *francs* a pair
- 11,884.72 m of *soutache* in green wool and gold thread, costing 11.50 *francs* a metre
- 3,359.05 m of narrow *soutache* in green wool and gold thread, costing 11.50 *francs* a metre
- 4,260.93 m of crimson and gold *soutache*, costing 11.50 *francs* a metre
- 3,359.05 m of crimson wool and gold thread square braid at 11.50 *francs* a metre
- 7,735.90 m of crimson wool and gold thread flat braid, 10 mm wide, at 11.50 *francs* a metre
- Sixty hunting horns embroidered in gold, costing 5.50 *francs* a set

- Sixteen trumpet cords in green wool and gold thread, costing 96 *francs* each
- 100 sets of stays for *chapeaux* in green wool and gold thread at 8 *francs* a metre
- 242 *sabretache* at 18.25 *francs* each
- Sixteen s*abretache* for sub-officers at 50.50 *francs* each
- Seventeen trumpeter's *sabretache*, costing 50.50 *francs* each

Buttons:

- 2,350 dozen large hussar buttons at 90 *centimes* a dozen
- 2,523 dozen small hussar buttons at 45 *centimes* a dozen
- 120 dozen gilded large hussar buttons for sub-officers at 3 *francs* a dozen
- 240 dozen gilded small hussar buttons for sub-officers at 1.50 *francs* a dozen

Equipment:

- Fifteen trumpets at 160 *francs* each
- 1,226 hunting horns stamped in copper at 1.80 *francs* each
- 400 *porte-mousquetons* at 4.50 *francs* each
- 513 pairs of hussar boots at 14 *francs* a pair
- 160 *gibernes*, costing 7 *francs* each
- 160 *giberne* belts, costing 7 *francs* each
- 120 *porte-carabines* at 6 *francs* each
- 794 carbine slings at 3 *francs* each
- 700 waist belts, costing 8 *francs* each
- 1,200 sets of *sabretache* slings at 95 *centimes* each
- Twenty-four trumpeter's *gibernes* and belts in red morrow leather and gold embroidery at 36 *francs* each
- Thirty-four trumpeter's waist belts in red morrow leather with gold embroidery at 47.50 *francs* each

Headdress:

- 1,390 plumes, costing 5.50 *francs* each
- 501 hussar shakos at 25.50 *francs* each

Harness:

- 390 saddles, costing 80 *francs* each

From this document we see that sub-officers had green and gold distinctions to their dolman, *pelisse* and braided waistcoat and no doubt Hungarian breeches. The trumpeters had crimson and gold distinctions. The headdress at this date was a shako covered in fur. The colpack we think was introduced with the formation of the Imperial Guard, when the trumpeters received *bleu celeste* clothing instead of green and crimson.

1803

The first detailed document for the clothing of the regiment is from 23 September 1803:[3]

ITEM	*TYPE*	*NUMBER OF*	*PRICE PER GARMENT (FRANCS)*
Pelisse	Sub-officer	1	112.50
	Trumpeter	0	112.50
	Chasseur	0	59.02
Dolman	Sub-officer	2	61.82
	Trumpeter	0	61.82
	Chasseur	10	43.15
Habits	Sub-officer	2	67
	Trumpeter	2	67
	Chasseur	8	58
Redingotes	Sub-officer	0	
Gilets	Scarlet	0	
	Crimson	2	19
Gilet tresse	Sub-officer	2	42
	Trumpeter	0	
	Chasseur	1	18
Hungarian breeches in wool	Sub-officer	0	
	Trumpeter	1	31
	Chasseur	17	36
Culottes de daim		0	
Pantalons-à-cheval		0	
Stable coats	*Chasseur*	0	
	Trumpeter, *bleu de ciel*	0	
Bonnets de police	Sub-officer	0	
	Trumpeter	0	
	Chasseur	50	7
Manteaux		1	70
Stable trousers		9	12
Shoes		0	
Gaiters		0	

Above left: The German artist Henschel worked between 1806 and 1807. Here we see his depiction of a *chasseur* wearing the sombre *chasseur*-style uniform of *habit*, breeches and scarlet braided waistcoat.

Above right: Nicolas Hoffmann painted several series of images of the Consular and Imperial Armies. Here he shows an officer of the regiment in the sombre undress uniform.

1804

The next document for the clothing of the regiment is from 23 September 1804:[4]

ITEM	*TYPE*	*NUMBER OF*	*PRICE PER GARMENT* (FRANCS)
Pelisse	Sub-officer	5	112.50
	Trumpeter	0	
	Chasseur	0	
Dolman	Sub-officer	4	61.82
	Trumpeter	0	
	Chasseur	0	

ITEM	*TYPE*	*NUMBER OF*	*PRICE PER GARMENT* (FRANCS)
Habits	Sub-officer	3	75.15
	Trumpeter	3	77.89
	Chasseur	6	63.59
Redingotes	Sub-officer	0	
Gilets	Scarlet	145	18.44
	Crimson	0	
Gilet tresse	Sub-officer	0	
	Trumpeter	0	
	Chasseur	48	19.57
Hungarian breeches in wool	Sub-officer	3	32.56
	Trumpeter	0	
	Chasseur	9	19.57
Culottes de daim		0	
Pantalons-à-cheval		176	32.25
Stable coats	*Chasseur*	94	14.45
	Trumpeter, *bleu de ciel*	5	13.91
Bonnets de police	*Chasseur*	64	7.79
	Trumpeter, *bleu de ciel*	1	7.79
Manteaux		53	75.74
Rotondes		64	21.56
Stable trousers		58	5.20
Shoes		961 pairs	5
Gaiters		961	2.25

The *rotonde* was a shoulder cape with collar that could be worn over the dolman or *habit*, or as an additional layer to the *manteau*. These items were issued, it seems, solely in 1804 and 1805, as none appears in later (or indeed earlier) stores returns.

1805

On 23 September 1805, the depot held the following items:[5]

ITEM	*TYPE*	*NUMBER OF*	*PRICE PER GARMENT* (FRANCS)
Pelisse	Sub-officer	11	112.50
	Trumpeter	5	112.50
	Chasseur	130	59.02

ITEM	*TYPE*	*NUMBER OF*	*PRICE PER GARMENT* (FRANCS)
Dolman	Sub-officer	8	61.82
	Trumpeter	6	61.82
	Chasseur	162	43.15
Habits	Sub-officer	3	75.15
	Trumpeter	5	77.89
	Chasseur	38	63.59
Redingotes	Sub-officer	0	
Gilets	Scarlet	47	18.44
	Crimson	2	18.44
Gilet tresse	Sub-officer	0	
	Trumpeter	2	29
	Chasseur	144	19.57
Hungarian breeches in wool	Sub-officer	4	32.56
	Trumpeter	3	32.56
	Chasseur	27	19.57
Culottes de daim		110	40
Pantalons-à-cheval	Sub-officer and *chasseur*	166	32.25
	Trumpeter	7	32.25
Stable coats	*Chasseur*	202	14.45
	Trumpeter, *bleu de ciel*	22	13.91
Bonnets de police	*Chasseur*	85	7.79
	Trumpeter, *bleu de ciel*	14	7.79
Manteaux		89	75.74
Rotondes		61	21.51
Stable trousers		484	5.20
Shoes		616	5
Gaiters		925	2.25

1806

At the end of 1806, the regiment's staff drew up the following list of items in stores as of 1 January 1807:[6]

ITEM	*TYPE*	*NUMBER OF*	*PRICE PER GARMENT* (FRANCS)
Pelisse	Sub-officer	8	112.50
	Trumpeter	4	112.50
	Chasseur	214	59.02

ITEM	*TYPE*	*NUMBER OF*	*PRICE PER GARMENT* (FRANCS)
Dolman	Sub-officer	4	61.82
	Trumpeter	3	61.82
	Chasseur	201	43.15
Habits	Sub-officer	4	75.15
	Trumpeter	4	77.89
	Chasseur	118	63.59
Redingotes	Sub-officer	1	70.50
Gilets	Scarlet	134	18.44
	Crimson	2	18.44
Gilet tresse	Sub-officer	1	29
	Trumpeter	2	29
	Chasseur	145	19.57
Hungarian breeches in wool	Sub-officer	4	32.56
	Trumpeter	3	32.56
	Chasseur	145	19.57
Culottes de daim		6	40
Pantalons-à-cheval		327	32.25
Stable coats	*Chasseur*	368	14.45
	Trumpeter, *bleu de ciel*	19	13.91
Bonnets de police	*Chasseur*	595	7.79
	Trumpeter, *bleu de ciel*	12	7.79
Manteaux		75	75.74
Stable trousers		307	5.20
Shoes		259 pairs	5
Gaiters		643 pairs	2.25

1807

At the end of 1807, the regiment's staff drew up the following list of items in stores as of 1 January 1808:[7]

ITEM	*TYPE*	*NUMBER OF*	*PRICE PER GARMENT* (FRANCS)
Pelisse	Sub-officer	1	112.50
	Trumpeter	1	112.50
	Chasseur	12	59.02

ITEM	*TYPE*	*NUMBER OF*	*PRICE PER GARMENT* (FRANCS)
Dolman	Sub-officer	1	61.82
	Trumpeter	1	61.82
	Chasseur	11	43.15
Habits	Sub-officer	16	75.15
	Trumpeter	18	77.89
	Chasseur	73	63.59
Redingotes	Sub-officer	0	70.50
Gilets	Scarlet	190	18.44
	Crimson	0	18.44
Gilet tresse	Sub-officer	15	29
	Trumpeter	15	29
	Chasseur	117	19.57
Hungarian breeches in wool	Sub-officer	21	32.56
	Trumpeter	21	32.56
	Chasseur	117	19.57
Culottes de daim		60	40
Pantalons-à-cheval		70	32.25
Stable coats	*Chasseur*	230	14.45
	Trumpeter, *bleu de ciel*	0	13.91
Bonnets de police	Chasseur	30	7.79
	Trumpeter, *bleu de ciel*	0	7.79
Manteaux		20	75.74
Stable trousers		112	5.20
Shoes		140	5
Gaiters		523	2.25

Other items in the depot included seven white trumpeter's colpacks for parades costing 32 *francs* each and one black colpack for trumpeters costing 24 *francs*, six for sub-officers costing 24 *francs* and twelve for *chasseurs* costing 22 *francs*. Sub-officers and trumpeters share a common pattern *aiguillette* and sabre waist belt, as well as *sabretache*. Sub-officers and trumpeters also share a common pattern *chapeau*, boots, *giberne* and *porte-giberne*. Thirty-two trumpeter's parade *schabraques* costing 183.35 *francs* each were in the depot, along with twenty-five for troopers and sub-officers, which cost a fraction of those for the trumpeters at 22 *francs* each.[8]

Above left: Trooper by Hoffmann wearing the hussar-style full dress uniform.

Above right: Hoffmann shows the trooper wearing the more sombre undress uniform. He still retains the sheepskin *schabraque* from the former Guides of Bonaparte.

1809

The most important document from 1809 is a stores inventory prepared on 1 January. The items of clothing and equipment in the depot at the time comprised:[9]

ITEM	*TYPE*	*NUMBER OF*	*PRICE PER GARMENT* (FRANCS)
Pelisse	Sub-officer	0	112.50
	Trumpeter	2	112.50
	Chasseur	13	59.02
Dolman	Sub-officer	1	61.82
	Trumpeter	2	61.82
	Chasseur	20	43.15
Habits	Sub-officer	14	75.15
	Trumpeter	10	77.89
	Chasseur	14	63.59

ITEM	*TYPE*	*NUMBER OF*	*PRICE PER GARMENT* (FRANCS)
Redingotes	Sub-officer	0	70.50
Gilets	Scarlet	10	18.44
	Crimson	17	18.44
Gilet tresse	Sub-officer	0	29
	Trumpeter	8	29
	Chasseur	14	19.57
Hungarian breeches in wool	Sub-officer	4	32.56
	Trumpeter	1	32.56
	Chasseur	1	19.57
Culottes de daim		5	40
Pantalons-à-cheval		117	32.25
Stable coats	*Chasseur*	13	14.45
	Trumpeter, *bleu de ciel*	2	13.91
Bonnets de police	Sub-officer	4	7.79
	Trumpeter	9	
	Chasseur	81	7.79
Manteaux		6	75.74
Stable trousers		179	5.20
Shoes		89	5
Gaiters		472	2.25

Other items in the depot comprised:[10]

- Green *porte-manteaux* 49
- *Bleu de ciel porte-manteaux* 3
- Pairs of boots for *chasseurs* 113
- Trumpeter's parade colpack 7
- Trumpeter's undress colpack 0
- *Chasseur's* colpack 129
- Plumes for colpack 120
- Pompoms 6
- Plumes for sub-officer's *chapeau* 16
- *Porte-giberne* with copper fittings 77
- Sub-officer's colpack cords 1
- Trumpeter's colpack cords 23
- *Chasseur's* colpack cords 38

- Sub-officer's *aiguillette* 8
- Trumpeter's *aiguillette* 2
- *Chasseur's aiguillette* 139
- Sword knots 38

The inventory also describes thousands of metres of cloth, lace and thousands of buttons held for the production of new items of clothing.

In terms of equipment, the inventory shows that three types of sabre waist belt were in use and at least three models of *gibernes*. The waist belts are described as sub-officer, trumpeter or *chasseur*, with no clear definition of what the differences actually were. Three patterns of *sabretache* were used: sub-officer with red green and gold lace edging; *chasseur* with aurore lace edging; and trumpeters, presumably with a crimson ground to the embroidery, but we cannot be sure. Around 23 leather *sabretache* covers were in stores. These were used on campaign to protect the costly and easily damaged and soiled embroidery and lace on the front face. The stores also held six *gibernes* for sub-officers and trumpeters, which presumably had brass flanks and not leather to the body of the *giberne*, seventy five *gibernes* for *chasseurs* and eighty-three *gibernes* of the 'new model' for *chasseurs*. We are at a loss as to the differences between the old and new models.[11]

New items of clothing and saddlery made in August 1809 were as follows:[12]

- 238 *porte-manteaux*
- 358 *schabraques*
- 469 *sabretache* covers
- 705 sets of *sabretache* slings
- 238 sabre waist belts, costing 10 *francs* each
- 235 *gibernes* for *chasseurs,* costing 7.50 *francs* each
- 235 *gibernes* belts, costing 9.50 *francs* each
- 215 carbine shoulder belts, complete with hook, costing 14 *francs* each
- 235 saddles, costing 63 *francs* each
- 235 bridles, costing 6.50 *francs* each
- 235 pairs of reins, costing 2.15 *francs* each
- 235 *bradoons* costing 3 *francs* each
- 235 *surcingles,* costing 6 *francs* each
- 235 head collars, costing 3 *francs* each
- 235 lead ropes, costing 1.50 *francs*
- 700 stable head collars, costing 4.50 *francs* each
- 700 watering bridles, costing 3.50 *francs* each
- 400 lock covers for carbines, costing 3 *francs* each
- 300 bayonet frogs, costing 2.50 *francs* each
- Fifty axe cases, costing 1 *franc* each

Above left: Hoffmann is the only source to show a kettledrummer. We know the regiment purchased kettledrums, but we know virtually nothing else about the dress and clothing of the kettledrummer, so we have to rely upon Hoffmann as the primary source of information.

Above right: Trooper in full dress wearing the hussar-style uniform, as envisioned by the Parisian print maker Aaron Martinet.

The axes were carried on the saddles of sub-officers and corporals in place of a pistol. It meant that each *peleton* could cut its own firewood on campaign.

During 1808, the regiment had been on campaign in Spain. It returned to France in the new year of 1809 and headed off to Germany to fight the famous Austria campaign. While the regiment marched from one theatre of war to the other, the regiment's depot had been busy ordering new clothing, listed below:[13]

- Forty-seven sub-officer's *habits*, total cost 5,179.40 *francs*
- Four *habits* for trumpet-corporals, total cost 553.30 *francs*
- One *habit* for trumpet-major, less lace, total cost 29.04 *francs*
- (Illegible) *habits* for trumpeters, total cost 1,306.20 *francs*
- 504 *habits* for *chasseurs*, total cost 36,706.32 *francs*
- Thirteen braided waistcoats for sub-officers and trumpeters, total cost 478.27 *francs*

- 248 braided waistcoats for *chasseurs*, total cost 5,029.44 *francs*
- 584 scarlet waistcoats, total cost 11,014.24 *francs*
- 434 *pantalons-à-cheval* with cow hide seat, total cost 15,589.29 *francs*
- 307 *pantalons-à-cheval* with basane seat, total cost 10,106.44 *francs*
- 274 *bonnets de police*, total cost 2,216.66 *francs*

On the reverse of the same document is a list for the following items:[14]

- Thirty *habits* and *aiguillettes* for *chasseurs*, total cost 2,186.98 *francs*
- Ten braided waistcoats for *chasseurs*, total cost 202.27 *francs*
- Thirty waistcoats, total cost 188.50 *francs*
- 150 *pantalons-à-cheval*, total cost 4,939.66 *francs*
- Fifty-four stable coats, total cost 990.03 *francs*
- Twenty-five *manteaux*, total cost 1,913.72 *francs*
- Twenty-five *porte-manteaux*, total cost 390.20 *francs*
- Five *habits* for farriers, total cost 197.13 *francs*
- Two pairs of stable trousers, total cost 12.85 *francs*
- Two pairs of *pantalons*, total cost 71.86 *francs*
- Six driver's *capotes*, total cost 381.13 *francs*
- 122 *schabraques*, total cost 6,507.99 *francs*
- Saddle blankets, total cost 790 *francs*

The regiment also purchased new colpacks in 1809 from M. Koenig. The purchase account is very interesting, as it gives the specification for the item. They were to be made from leather and covered in bear hide. They were to measure 9.25 *pouce* (23.50 cm) tall at the front, 10.25 *pouce* (26 cm) at the back and be 9.25 *pouce* (23.50 cm) in diameter. The headband was to be made from linen and basane, both to measure three *pouce* (7.60 cm) in height. The *flamme* (bag) pompom, cockade and cords were included in the final price of 30 *francs* apiece. Koenig was also contracted to supply marmoset fur for the *pelisse* of sub-officers, costing 30 *francs*, black lambskin for *chasseurs* at 10 *francs*, and colpack covers made from waterproofed silk taffeta costing 1.25 *francs*. He was also charged to repair nine colpacks at the cost of 12 *francs*, and provide new *flammes* and covers for these colpacks, costing 8 *francs*.[15] The order for the purchase of the items was confirmed on 29 August 1809 and was for twenty-seven marmoset pelts at 30 *francs* each, 442 black lambskins at 10 *francs* a piece, 469 colpacks with covers for 31.25 *francs* and 100 Canadian fox pelts costing 120 *francs* each for officer's *pelisses*. The lining of the officer's *pelisse* was to be in grey fur, the pelts costing 50 *francs* each. A single officer's parade *schabraque* was purchased from M. Koenig in the same order. It was to be made from a complete panther hide, lined in stripped linen ticking, with a 34 mm wide gold lace edging, costing 350 *francs*.[16] Officers had to provide their own clothing at their own cost. The fact that officers' furs and the ostentatious *schabraque*

Above left: Officer in parade dress by Martinet.

Above right: Officer as envisioned by Martinet wearing the sombre *chasseur*-style undress uniform.

were ordered and paid for with the troopers clothing allowance does smack somewhat of the regiment 'fiddling their expenses'.

Chapeaux for sub-officers, trumpeters and *chasseurs* were ordered in August 1809. Ninety examples with gold lace costing 25 *francs* each were obtained for sub-officers and trumpeters, and 864 with yellow wool lace for the *chasseurs*, costing 12 *francs* each, were purchased.[17]

Made new in 1809 were 469 pairs of Hungarian breeches in doe hide, 1,432 pairs of gloves in doe hide and 716 sword knots in buff, along with 137 pairs of boots for sub-officers and trumpeters, costing 24 *francs* a pair, and 1,295 pairs of boots for other ranks, costing 21 *francs* a pair.[18] Also made in 1809 were:[19]

- 469 *pelisses* for sub-officers, trumpeters and *chasseurs*
- 918 *habits* for sub-officers and *chasseurs*
- Twenty-five trumpeter's *habits*
- Forty-nine *redingotes* for sub-officers
- One *redingote* for trumpet-major
- 953 braided waistcoats

Above left: Trumpeter of the chasseurs wearing the fantastically elaborate parade dress. After 1809 the white colpack was not used.

Above right: Trooper shown dismounted wearing the *chasseur*-style undress uniform.

- 953 pairs of Hungarian breeches
- 953 pairs of *pantalons-à-cheval*
- 665 stable coats
- Fifty *bonnets de police* for sub-officers
- 665 *bonnets de police* for *chasseurs*
- 238 *manteaux*
- 716 pairs of stable trousers

1812-4

When the regiment was wound up in summer 1814, it prepared a list of all items of clothing, equipment, material, etc, that had been purchased by the regiment between January 1812 and August 1814. This remarkable resource of information is presented below. It means we can exactly reconstruct the dress of the regiment in these years using extant items in museum collections and this incredible document.

Clothing made and issued 1812 to 1814 was as follows:[20]

Items for sub-officers

YEAR	*PELISSE*		DOLMAN		*HABITS*		*SURTOUTS*		*GILETS*		*REDINGOTES*		*GILET TRESSE*		*CULOTTES*		*BONNETS DE POLICE*	
	MADE	*ISSUED*	*MADE*	*ISSUED*	*MADE*	*ISSUED*	*MADE*	*ISSUED*	*MADE*	*ISSUED*	*MADE*	*ISSUED*	*MADE*	*ISSUED*	*MADE*	*ISSUED*	*MADE*	*ISSUED*
In magazine	6	0	28	0	5	0	0	0	3	0	6	0	14	0	0	0	13	0
1812	6	0	26	10	9	9	2	2	0	1	30	18	10	12	39	15	21	12
1813	0	2	221	160	3	8	3	3	0	0	144	112	151	113	128	92	158	11
1814	0	10	0	52	1	1	0	0	0	2	0	16	0	50	0	60	0	46
Total	12	12	275	222	18	18	5	5	3	3	180	146	175	175	167	167	192	69
In depot 1814	0	0	0	53	0	0	0	0	0	0	0	34	0	0	0	0	0	23

The sub-officers also had eighty-nine pairs of cloth-braided *pantalons* made in green cloth issued in 1812. The 167 pairs of *culottes* issued needed 5.46 m of flat braid in wool and gold. These are likely to be Hungarian breeches rather than *culottes*, i.e. knee breeches.[21] It is clear that, from 1812, sub-officers rarely wore the *pelisse* and *habit* or *surtout*. The number of *pelisses* tallies with their issue to senior sub-officers only. The sub-officers clearly wore the dolman with braided hussar-style waistcoat (*gilet tresse*) as their habitual wear. Neither did they have the grey cloth *pantalons*. Only eighteen *habits* were issued for sub-officers. A tariff from 1 January 1813 states the following materials were needed in its manufacture:[22]

- 1.80 m of green wool cloth, first quality, costing 26.50 *francs* a metre
- 0.20 m of scarlet wool cloth, first quality, costing 33.50 *francs* a metre
- 0.59 m of white milled *serge* for lining, costing 1.50 *francs* a metre
- 1.18 m of linen, blondine quality, costing 1.64 *francs* a metre
- 0.30 m of ecru linen, costing 1.54 *francs* a metre
- 0.84 m of lace in wool, 10 mm wide
- 0.20 m of strong linen, costing 1 *franc* a metre
- Twenty-four large buttons, costing 30 *centimes* a dozen
- Six small buttons, costing 20 *centimes* a dozen
- Four embroidered hunting horns, costing 1.10 *francs*
- Labour: 3 *francs*
- Total: 62.76 *francs*

The same tariff lists that *habits* of sub-officers needed 1.90 m of green cloth, and the lace was to be flat braid in gold and wool, as used on the dolman, *pelisse* and braided waistcoat. For trumpeters, 1.80 m of *bleu de ciel* cloth was needed, and a total of 33 m of crimson wool cloth was purchased from 1812 to 1814 for the trumpeter's *habit*. The trumpet-major had first quality cloth, and the trumpeters had second quality.

Portrait of a surgeon of the regiment. He carries an officer's *aiguillette* on the right shoulder and wears an officer's braided waistcoat. The collar has the buttonhole loop embroidery for surgeons as ascribed by the 1801 regulations. (Musée de l'Empéri, Collections du Musée de l'armée, Anciennes collections Jean et Raoul Brunon)

Other ranks

YEAR	*PELISSE*		DOLMAN		*HABITS*		*GILET TRESSE*		*CULOTTES*		*CULOTTES DE DAIM*		STABLE COATS		*BONNETS DE POLICE*		*CAPOTE MANTEAUX*	
	MADE	*ISSUED*	*MADE*	*ISSUED*	*MADE*	*ISSUED*	*MADE*	*ISSUED*	*MADE*	*ISSUED*	*MADE*	*ISSUED*	*MADE*	*ISSUED*	*MADE*	*ISSUED*	*MADE*	*ISSUED*
In magazine	190	0	464	0	164	0	308	0	109	0	69	0	288	0	293	0	135	0
1812	12	35	561	325	171	322	405	288	511	449	60	35	582	372	598	358	363	667
1813	0	0	2,633	2,869	12	12	2,445	2,404	2,141	1,340	1	0	2,776	2,965	2,490	2,807	2,248	2,433
1814	1	168	745	1,161	0	13	3	467	0	972	0	95	371	697	465	697	357	3
Total	203	203	4,403	4,355	347	347	3,161	3,159	2,761	2,761	130	130	4,017	4,034	3,846	3,862	3,103	3,103
In depot 1814	0	0	0	44	0	0	0	2	0	0	0	0	0	1	0	2	0	0

This ensemble of items is preserved at the Musée Emperi in the South of France. It comprises an original dolman for a *sous-officier*. We know this as the flat braid is scarlet and gold, and the braiding between the buttons is red, green and gold. The scarlet waistcoat is also braided with scarlet and gold flat braid. So too is the scarlet pelisse. The waist belt, sabre and *sabretache* are all original items. The breeches are modern reproductions. The vignette gives an excellent impression of a *sous-officier* in barracks. (Musée de l'Empéri, Collections du Musée de l'armée, Anciennes collections Jean et Raoul Brunon)

As with the sub-officers, only corporals were issued the *pelisse* Sub-officers alone were issued the *culottes de daim*, it seems. Corporals were the only other ranks issued *habits*. Around 1,570 pairs of green *pantalons* were issued, the depot holding 491 sets on 1 January 1812, 1,063 pairs being made in 1812, of which 492 were issued in 1812, a meagre nineteen were made in 1813, and 1,081 were issued in 1813. Issued alongside were *pantalons-à-cheval* made from Marengo grey wool cloth, reinforced with leather. For these garments, 771.71 m of wool cloth was purchased in 1813, of which 731.60 m was used in that year, and 824.46 m was purchased in 1814, of which 864.57 m was used. Furthermore, 2,761 pairs of Hungarian breeches were issued, needing 5.46 m of yellow wool flat braid. These are likely to be Hungarian breeches rather than *culottes*.[23]

Some 2,784 sets were made in 1813, of which 2,386 were issued in the same year, and a further 638 made in 1814, of which 1,128 were issued. The green cloth breeches listed under *culottes* are noteworthy, as they are clearly not the Hungarian breeches. Also issued were 789 pairs of grey gaiters. The regimental depot held, on 1 January 1812, some 299 pairs, and a further 490 pairs were made in 1813, of which 789 pairs were issued in 1814. Clearly, the *chasseurs* did some form of foot duty wearing, we assume, the breeches and gaiters. Traditionally under the *habit* the *chasseurs* had worn a double-breasted scarlet *gilet*. For the other ranks, none was in the depot in 1812 and none was made. Clearly, therefore, the braided waistcoat was worn under the *habit*. In 1814, 770 green double-breasted *gilets* were made and all were issued. By 1812, the scarlet *veste* of the *chasseurs* was no longer in use. Furthermore, 1,075 sets of stable trousers were made, 288 sets being issued in 1812, 681 in 1813 and 106 in 1814. Also, 897 pairs of shoes were purchased in 1813, all issued the same year.

Disbandment

At the end of the 1814 campaign, and thus also at (provisionally) the end of the empire, the strength of the regiment amounted to eighty-nine officers and 1,357 sub-officer's men. During the First Restoration, the regiment was reduced in size. The commanders remained as General Lefèbvre Desnoëttes and Major-General Lion. The 2nd Regiment of *Chasseurs-à-Cheval* of the Imperial Guard, on 6 June 1814, had 367 men, of which twenty-six were on leave and eighty in hospital. Eighty-two men were classed as Old Guard.

On 8 June 1814, the 2nd Regiment of *Chasseurs-à-Cheval* of the Imperial Guard was to be disbanded and taken into the line.[24] The former 6th Squadron, comprising 11th and 15th Companies, along with 12th Company, comprising some eighty-nine men, were transferred to the 2nd Regiment of *Chasseurs-à-Cheval*. The former 8th Squadron comprised the 13th and 17th Companies as well as the 16th Company, comprising 113 men, were transferred to the 3rd Regiment of *Chasseurs-à-Cheval*. The 14th and 18th Companies along with the *mamelukes*, 102 men, were transferred to the 7th *Chasseurs-à-Cheval*. The men sent to the 3rd *Chasseurs-à-Cheval* were commanded by Captain Salmon. Also taken into the regiment was 4th Squadron of the 4th Regiment of Scouts of the Imperial Guard, headed by Major Toussain.[25]

Some Young Guardsmen were transferred into the Royal *Chasseurs* and stationed at Saumur. The regiment was again organised with a strength of four squadrons of two companies each, with a total strength of forty-four officers and 641 men. The staff of the new corps was formed at Beauvais on 10 June 1814, overseeing the formation of the corps. Officers, sub-officers and troopers retained or passed to new regiments in June 1814 were as follows from the 2nd Regiment of *Chasseurs-à-Cheval* of the Imperial Guard:[26]

CLASS	GRADE	2ND CHASSEURS	3RD CHASSEURS	7TH CHASSEURS	ROYAL CORPS
Old Guard	Officer	4	0	0	12
	Sub-officer	10	4	3	4
	Trooper	12	17	11	78
Young Guard	Officer	0	5	0	0
	Sub-officer	1	6	7	0
	Trooper	66	86	82	0
Total		93	118	103	94

The royal ordinance of 26 June 1814 fixed the corps composition and was organised by Marshal Ney on 30 July. At this point the regiment had eighty-nine officers with 262 horses, and 1,357 sub-officers and troopers with 1,088 horses. In addition were twenty-four draught horses for moving the regiment's baggage. The organisation of the corps was as follows:[27] one colonel with three horses, one major with three horses, two squadron commanders each with two horses, two adjutant majors each with two horses, one lieutenant-quartermaster with one horse, one standard-bearer with one horse, one surgeon major with one horse, one assistant surgeon with one horse, two adjutant-sub-officers each with one horse, one master veterinarian with one horse, one second-class veterinarian with one horse, one corporal-trumpeter, one tailor, one saddler, one boot-maker and one armourer.

Each company was to comprise:[28] one captain, one first-lieutenant, two second-lieutenants, one sergeant-major, four sergeants, one quartermaster-corporal, eight corporals, two trumpeters, forty mounted troopers, sixteen dismounted troopers and two farriers.

In order to affect the reduction in size of the regiment, the following troops were retained or dismissed from the new corps:[29]

Troopers:

- Fifty-four sub-officers, sixty-four corporals, seven cadet trumpeters and 516 troopers placed in the new corps
- Thirty-nine sub-officers attached to the corps
- 175 on leave
- 203 sub-officers and troopers of Italian, German or Belgian origin returned home
- Thirty-seven *mamelukes* returned home
- Seventy-one placed on half-pay
- Fourteen reformed
- Twelve sent to the colonial battalions
- Three sent to the veterans
- Nine *chasseurs* and three *mamelukes* sent to the *invalides*

- Thirty-two discharged due to wounds or infirmity
- Thirty-one sent to the military police under observation as being suspect
- Ninety-nine troopers sent to other regiments

Troop horses:
- 1,287 retained by the new corps
- Fifteen removed
- Eighty-seven sold

Of the officers retained by the regiment were:[30]

Staff:
Colonel: Lefèbvre-Desnoëttes
Major: Lion
Squadron commanders: Kirmann, Rabusson
Squadron commander quartermaster: Pistre
Squadron commander adjutant-major: Blanquefort
Captain-adjutant-major: Assant, Brice
Lieutenant standard-bearer: Boireau
Surgeon-major: Lachaume
Assistant surgeon-major: Pergot
Lieutenant-adjutant-major: Vazilier, Moutard

Company officers:[31]
Captains: Barbenegre, Decoux, Gay, Kleinberg, Louis, Maziau, Maysant, Rocourt
First-lieutenants: Bayard, Bugat, Darmagnac, Durand, Dupont, Helson, Mey de Chaales, Stephanopoloy
Second-lieutenants: Bailleu, Beller, Chapelle, Caillet, Dackweiller, Devascourt, Francois Jallot, Kaper, Lagaume, Laquarte, Macheret, Oswald, Pecheur, Sprerriere, Vanheulle

Officers attached to the new corps were:[32]

Squadron commander: Bayern
Captain-quartermaster: Bellancourt
Lieutenant-adjutant-major: Briu
Captains: Larriviere, Ladroite
First-lieutenants: Foullon, Toulongeon
Second-lieutenants: Desey, Le Blanc, Pelissier, Pellion

Officers who were placed into the depot of the new corps were:[33]

Squadron commanders: Bellebaux, Cayre
Captain: Chahm

First-lieutenants: Bonnet, Garnier, Perrier
Surgeon: Ferrus

Officers placed into new regiments were as follows:[34]

Squadron Commander Lafitte was promoted to major of the King's Hussar Regiment
Squadron Commander Quartermaster Guiot was posted to the Royal Corps of *Cuirassiers* of France
Captains Abdallah, Renno and Villa were posted to the Royal Corps of Light Horse Lancers of France
First-Lieutenants Allamant, Cabarat, Enubeault, Gutschenritter, Kerval, Lambert and Rolin were posted to the Royal Corps of Light Horse Lancers of France
Second-Lieutenants Billard, Blandin, Deleventi, Fischer, Mirza and Tonnade were posted to Royal Corps of Light Horse Lancers of France

Officers placed directly on half pay were:[35]

Major: Dautancourt, Meuziau
Squadron commander: Haraiby
Captains: Delaroche, Lemercier
First-lieutenants: Blot, Decalonge, Donchery, Ellisa, Limbourg, Massac, Soliman
Second-lieutenants: Mertens, Velay
Surgeon first class: Bockemheimer, Charmel, Giradot
Surgeon second class: Bouley, Demerlot, Faure, Sorlin

No new officers were admitted to the corps in 1814. It was in essence the nucleus of the old *chasseurs-à-cheval* of the Imperial Guard, which were reformed in 1813 around the survivors of the 1812 campaign.

Uniforms

On 30 July 1814, the new Royal Corps mustered fifty-five officers and 774 sub-officers and troopers. Marshal Ney noted that same day that the trooper's manoeuvres were exact and prompt, the equitation was of a high standard, but would improve with lessons in the riding school, discipline was perfect, the dress of the corps was very good and regular, and the horses were of a good sort and type. His praise of the corps was unstinting. The sub-officers were all old soldiers with excellent instruction and theory. The same was true of the officers in Ney's report. Ney further adds:[36]

> I beg you Monsieur le Comte to garrison the *Chasseurs* of France at Saumur. The civil authorities have asked this as a favour … the spirit of the regiment is excellent. Its discipline and obedience have earned it the

admiration and affection of the inhabitants. The soldiers know their duties and are handsome in build and appearance. The clothing is practically new and perfectly maintained. The tack and equipment are complete, in good condition and very well kept. The barracks and stables are excellent. Only the beds are mediocre. The horses are beautiful and of a good type.

On 30 July 1814 the regiment had the following items of uniform and equipment:[37]

ITEM	*ITEMS IN SERVICE*	*NEW*	*NEED REPAIR*	*NEED REPLACING*
Pelisses for sub-officers	0	0	0	0
Pelisses for troopers	609	0	153	0
Dolmans for troopers	835	149	102	0
Dolmans for trumpet-major	0	0	0	0
Habits	36	3	3	0
Braided waistcoats	601	0	0	0
Hungarian breeches	881	0	14	0
Barrel sashes	889	0	145	0
Stable coats for sub-officers and troopers	717	0	0	0
Stable coats for trumpet-major	0	0	0	0
Riding trousers	272	0	46	0
Stable caps for trumpet-major	0	0	0	0
Stable caps for sub-officers and troopers	833	0	0	0
Sleeved overcoats	687	0	149	0
Colpacks	906	128	127	28
Plumes	15	0	0	0
Hussar boots	353	0	0	0
Spurs	899	0	0	0
Ammunition boxes	1,042	0	0	0
Ammunition box belts	1,042	0	0	0
Sabretache in leather	52	0	0	0
Sabretache, embroidered in wool, for troopers	638	0	32	0
Sabretache covers	90	0	0	0

ITEM	*ITEMS IN SERVICE*	*NEW*	*NEED REPAIR*	*NEED REPLACING*
Waist belt	995	0	0	0
Trumpets and trumpet cords	Illegible	0	0	0
Musket slings	871	0	0	0
Schabraques	664	0	0	0
Porte-manteaux	690	0	0	0
Parade head collars	787	0	0	0
Parade lead ropes	787	0	0	0
Carbine buckets	760	0	0	0
Gauntlets	753	0	0	0
Sword knots	724	0	0	0
Carbines	786	0	0	0
Sabres	1,001	0	0	0
Pistols	872	0	0	0

Between 30 July 1814 and 1 March 1815, the following items were delivered to the corps:[38]

ITEM	*ITEMS MADE*	*TOTAL IN SERVICE*
Pelisses for sub-officers	0	Illegible
Pelisses for troopers	0	609
Dolmans for troopers	141	976
Dolmans for trumpet-major	Illegible	Illegible
Habits	4	40
Braided waistcoats	406	1,007
Hungarian breeches	881	0
Barrel sashes	889	0
Stable coats for sub-officers and troopers	60	777
Stable coats for trumpet-major	0	0
Riding trousers	452	724
Stable caps for trumpet-major	0	0
Stable caps for sub-officers and troopers	136	969
Sleeved overcoats	136	823

ITEM	*ITEMS MADE*	*TOTAL IN SERVICE*
Redingotes for sub-officers	70	70
Colpacks	245	1,151
Plumes	1,001	1,016
Hussar boots	353	0
Spurs	899	0
Ammunition boxes	91	1,133
Ammunition box belts	110	2,152
Sabretache in leather	52	0
Sabretache, embroidered in wool, for troopers	130	768
Waist belts	142	1,135
Trumpets and trumpet cords	Illegible	Illegible
Musket slings	85	956
Schabraques	307	971
Porte-manteaux	91	781
Parade head collars	144	931
Parade lead ropes	144	931
Carbine buckets	0	760
Gauntlets	302	1,055
Sword knots	152	876
Carbines	177	963
Sabres	118	1,119
Pistols	236	1,108

Clearly, therefore, the corps was dressed identically as before under Napoleon, but with the absence of both the traditional hussar barrel sash with the dolman, and the costly second, or undress, uniform of braided waistcoat and *habit* were dispensed with, clearly on the grounds of cost.

Trumpeters

At its creation in November 1799, the modest company of mounted *chasseurs* of the Consular Guard only had two trumpeters, but the changes made in the composition of the corps and the successive augmentations of its strength soon gave it more.

In September 1800, the *chasseurs* formed a squadron of two companies with four trumpeters, and then in August 1800, they were brought up to two squadrons (four companies) with eight trumpeters.

Above left: Otto's rendering of the trumpeter of the regiment wearing the *chasseur*-style uniform. Overall, he captures the uniform very well. He is the only source for the *bleu de ciel* waistcoat for the trumpeter.

Above right: Naïve impression of an officer of the regiment by Chataignier and Poisson, Parisian Print makers.

The organisation of 1802 fixed their number at three per company, their effective strength was twelve and they were controlled by a trumpet-major and two *brigadiers-trompettes* (corporal-trumpeters). At the end of the same year, the regiment was made up of four squadrons and there were twenty-four trumpeters, excluding the trumpet-major and the two brigadiers. After the formation of the 5th Squadron in 1811, there were thirty trumpeters with the regiment and, in 1813, the four squadrons of the Young Guard, newly created, only had twenty-four of them.

The *habit* issued was cut from *bleu de ciel* cloth with collar and pointed cuffs, and the lapel edging, pockets and turnbacks in crimson. The collar and cuffs were edged with gold lace 22 mm wide and 15 mm for the lapels. The turnback ornaments were hunting horns embroidered in gold on crimson cloth. In addition, the left shoulder of the coat had an *aiguillette* of crimson wool mixed with one-third gold by length, mounted in a trefoil. On the right shoulder was a gold lace trefoil mounted on crimson and with the centre of the loops sky blue. The waistcoat, furnished with five rows of small buttons, was crimson with flat braid and piping of sky blue and gold. The breeches were of yellow skin and the boots were edged with piping and a tassel of mixed sky blue and gold. The *pelisse* was of crimson cloth, lined with white flannel

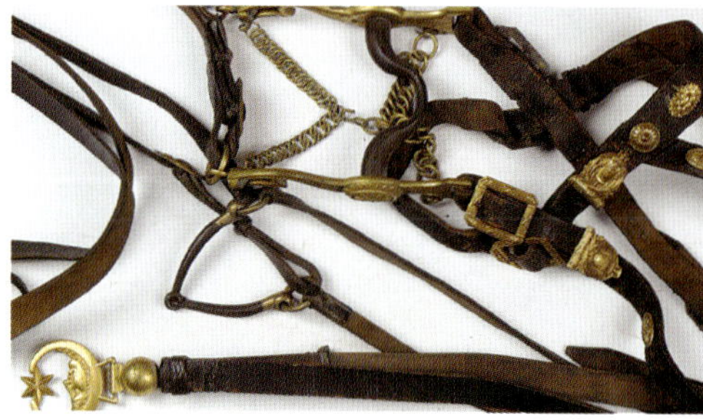

Two views of the *schabraque* for the regiment preserved in the Musée de l'armée, Paris. The embroidered eagle is noticeably in a different colour to the lace around the edge of the *schabraque*. The *schabraque* lace and that on the *portmanteaux* is aurore, the lace on the *sabretache* is yellow, and is a reproduction. The eagles may be more modern replacements. Much of this display is not what it seems, as the *pelisse* is actually from the 4th Hussars as well as the dolman, and the *sabretache* is a modern item. Despite the display being composite with a mix of modern and original items from different regiments, it gives an excellent overall impression of the regiment's hussar-style uniform. (Musée de l'armée)

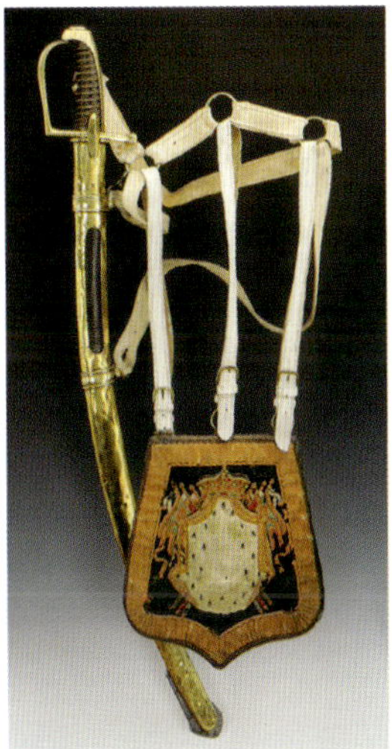
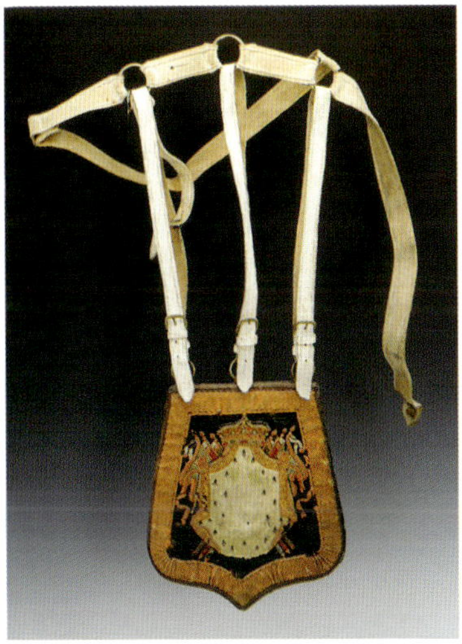

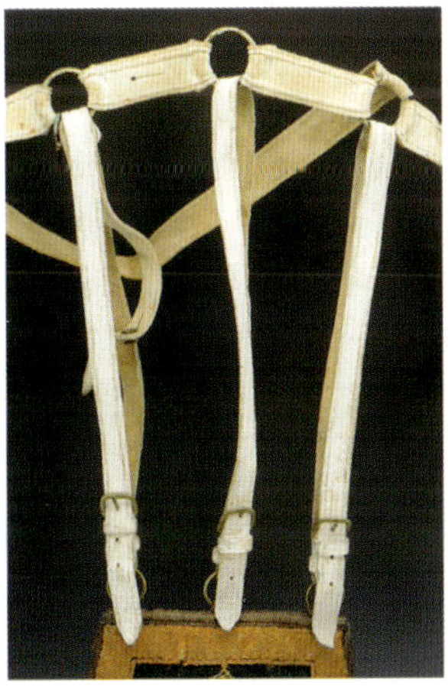
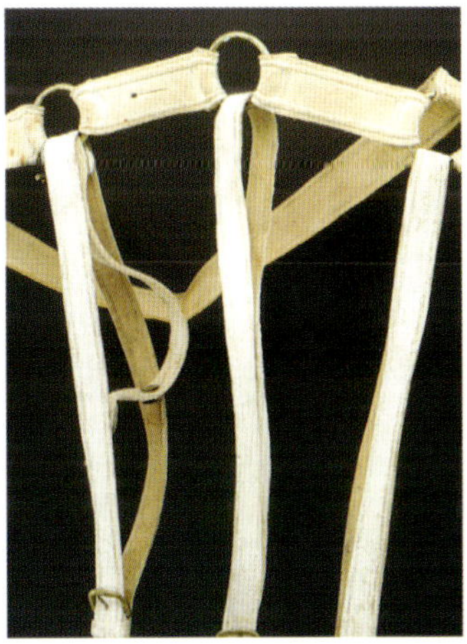
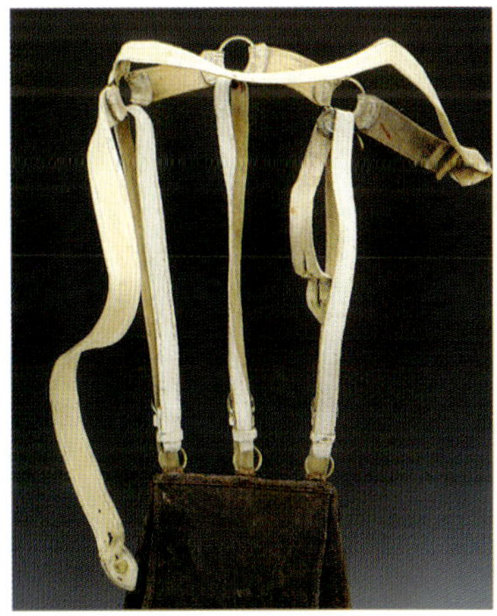

Two views of the *schabraque* for the regiment preserved in the Musée de Emperi. The embroidered eagle is noticeably in a different colour to the lace around the edge of the *schabraque*. The *schabraque* lace is aurore. This is a good example of the contrasting colour of aurore and yellow, and that the two colours are not interchangeable. The lace on the *portmanteaux* is yellow, and the item is clearly a reproduction. The eagles may be more modern replacements. Much of this display is not what it seems, as the braid waistcoat belongs to the 7th Hussars. Despite the display being composite with a mix of modern and original items from different regiments, it does give an excellent overall impression of the regiment's hussar-style uniform. (Musée de l'Empéri, Collections du Musée de l'armée, Anciennes collections Jean et Raoul Brunon)

and edged with black fur. Buttons were as for the dolman with eight large ones for the waist extensions (*sabots*). Flat braid, square braid, piping braid, suspension cord and toggle were of sky blue mixed with one-third gold. As for the dolman, it had 12.68 m of ornamented piping braid. The dolman was cut from *bleu de ciel* cloth with crimson cuffs and collar, five rows of eighteen copper buttons, square branding forming brandenburg loops, flat braid for the edges and ornamental piping braid in crimson wool mixed with one-third gold. The trumpeter published in 1803 by Jean, rue de Beauvais, had a sky blue dolman collar and it is probable that this was the case from 1801-11 as a crimson collar, and the manufacturing specification of 1813 shows cloth of this colour for the collar and the cuffs. The specification of 1813 also shows a large quantity of piping braid (*soutache*): 12.68 m for the trumpeters and the sub-officers, rather than the 8.90 m for the troopers. This extra served to double with the flat braid of the collar and the chest.[39]

Under the *habit* a double-breasted waistcoat of crimson with five rows of buttons, initially with fifteen, then sixteen, and finally eighteen in 1813, was worn. From 1814, it buttoned down the front with a single row of fifteen buttons.[40] Cloth Hungarian breeches adopted at the end of 1800 and made of crimson cloth with decorations of flat braid and piping braid in sky blue and gold were the full dress garments. In 1803, they became sky blue with decorations in crimson and gold and were worn for normal use and for undress. In addition to the 5.34 m of flat, mixed braid necessary for their Hungarian knots and lacing, the specifications for 1813 show 8.91 m of piping braid, mixed, to go around and augment the Hungarian knots and the side lacing. This was for the trumpeters and sub-officers only.[41]

YEAR	*PELISSE*		DOLMAN		*HABITS*		*GILET TRESSE*		*CULOTTES*		STABLE COATS		*BONNETS DE POLICE*		HUNGARIAN BREECHES		*PANTALONS-À-CHEVAL*	
	MADE	*ISSUED*	*MADE*	*ISSUED*	*MADE*	*ISSUED*	*MADE*	*ISSUED*	*MADE*	*ISSUED*	*MADE*	*ISSUED*	*MADE*	*ISSUED*	*MADE*	*ISSUED*	*MADE*	*ISSUED*
In magazine	0	0	13	0	2	0	11	0	0	0	0	0	9	0	3	0	4	0
1812	4	4	5	6	6	4	31	3	0	6	27	10	23	9	36	9	0	0
1813	0	0	101	72	63	60	47	86	8	63	134	93	128	82	3	33	96	69
1814	0	0	33	25	0	1	1	1	77	76	0	22	0	18	0	0	15	52
Total	4	4	152	103	71	65	90	90	85	145	161	125	160	109	42	42	115	121
In depot 1814	0	0	0	48	0	6	0	0	0	0	0	36	0	51	0	0	0	0

From 1812, it seems the trumpeters no longer wore the *pelisse*, neither were they issued crimson double-breasted *gilets* for use with the *habit*, as was the custom in previous years. Trumpeters wore both the *habit* and dolman with the braided hussar *gilet*. A single *redingote* for the trumpet-major was made in 1812 and issued the following year. Trumpeters clearly wore green *manteaux-capote*, and on campaign from 1813, *bleu de ciel pantalons-à-cheval*. Campaign leg wear in previous years seem very likely to be the same as the others ranks, i.e. green reinforced in black leather with a scarlet side stripe for the button stand. Only eighty-five sets of Hungarian breeches were made. These required 1.50 m of *bleu de ciel* wool cloth, 0.59 m of linen, 5.46 m of flat braid in wool and gold and 89 cm of *soutache* in wool and gold.[42]

No trumpeter's colpacks were made from 1812, so we assume they wore the same item as the other ranks. Colpack cords were issued in 1813, with 188 sets of sub-officer and trumpeter types being made, of which twenty-seven were issued in 1812, 127 in 1813 and thirty-eight in 1814. Sub-officers and trumpeters were also issued *chapeaux*, seventy-eight being purchased between 1812 and 1814, of which eighteen were issued in 1812, fifty-six in 1813 and four in 1814. A total of 112 trumpeter's *porte-manteaux* were made, of which six were issued in 1812, fifty-five in 1813 and forty-nine in 1814, with two examples left in the depot. Trumpeters and sub-officers shared the same pattern boots and *aiguillettes* with sixty-four sets being made, all being issued. This number is far less than the number of *habits* in use, so the shoulder decoration for the majority of the trumpeters and sub-officers is in question. From 1812, trumpeters and sub-officers had the same pattern *sabretache*, with 131 examples being made, of which nine were issued in 1812, eighty-five in 1813 and thirty-seven in 1814. Hussars traditionally wore a barrel sash, for the trumpeters and sub-officers 181 examples were made, eight being issued in 1812, 135 in 1813 and thirty-eight in 1814. The *giberne* and belt used by the sub-officers was the same pattern issued to trumpeters. Some 177 examples were made in 1812, seven were drawn from the stores, of which eleven were issued in 1812, 127 in 1813 and thirty-nine in 1814.

For the Young Guard squadrons raised in 1813, the document provides detail on the appearance of the shako. Some 1,726 shakos were purchased in spring 1813, 1,694 being issued that year, and 281 in the following year. For the shakos, 157 covers were purchased, ninety-three being issued in 1813 and sixty-four in 1814. Clearly, it seems these were destined for sub-officers and trumpeters based on the very low numbers issued. The shako for sub-officers and trumpeters rather than having copper chin scales had in their place a gilded chain, hung from lion's head bosses, of which twenty-four sets were issued in 1813 and forty-eight in 1814.

Another interesting and important document detailing the clothing of the regiment was prepared in 1813 and set out detailed specifications for items of clothing as follows:[43]

Dolman:

- 1.10 m of green wool cloth, third quality, at 18.70 *francs* a metre
- 0.75 m of scarlet wool cloth at 24 *francs* a metre
- 1.75 m of ecru linen at 1.54 *francs* a metre
- 0.20 m of strong linen at 1 *franc* a metre
- Eighteen medium buttons at 30 *centimes* a dozen
- Seventy-two small buttons at 20 *centimes* a dozen
- 15.25 m of aurore square wool braid at 15 *centimes* a metre
- 8.91 m of wool *soutache* at 8 *centimes* a metre
- 8.91 m of flat wool braid at 20 *centimes* a metre
- 1.34 m of red basane, costing 1.50 *francs*
- Labour: 3.25 *francs*
- Total: 37.44 *francs*

Gilet:

- 0.35 m of scarlet wool cloth, costing 24 *francs* a metre
- 0.59 m of ecru *tricot,* costing 2.60 *francs* a metre
- 0.45 m of ecru linen, costing 1.54 *francs* a metre
- Fifteen small buttons at 20 *centimes* a dozen
- Labour: 1.25 *francs*
- Total: 12.13 *francs*

Hungarian breeches:

- 1.50 m of green wool cloth, third quality, costing 18.76 *francs* a metre
- 0.45 m of ecru linen, costing 1.54 *francs* a metre
- 5.34 m of aurore wool flat braid, costing 20 *centimes* a metre
- Labour: 1.75 *francs*
- Total: 25.08 *francs*

Pantalons-à-cheval:

- 1.24 m of green wool cloth, third quality, costing 16.34 *francs*
- 0.14 m of scarlet wool cloth, costing 24 *francs* a metre
- 0.59 m of ecru linen at 1.54 *francs* a metre
- Forty-two large copper buttons at 48 *centimes* a dozen
- One leather hide, costing 8.50 *francs*
- Labour: 3 *francs*
- Total: 37.71 *francs*

Stable coat:

- 1.34 m of green wool cloth, fifth quality, costing 12.50 *francs* a metre
- 1.68 m of ecru linen costing 1.54 *francs* a metre
- Twenty large buttons at 48 *centimes* a dozen
- Labour: 1.330 *francs*
- Total: 21.44 *francs*

Bonnet de police:

- 0.37 m of green wool cloth, fifth quality, at 12.50 *francs* a metre
- 0.001 m of scarlet wool cloth at 24 *francs* a metre
- 0.20 m of ecru linen at 1.54 *francs* a metre
- 0.90 m of aurore wool lace, 34 mm wide, at 85 *centimes* a metre
- One embroidered hunting horn, costing 28 *centimes*
- 2.50 m of aurore round wool cord at 0.50 *centimes* a metre
- One aurore wool tassel, costing 25 *centimes*
- Labour: 50 *centimes*
- Total: 7.09 *francs*

Manteau:

- 4.05 m of green wool cloth, fifth quality, costing 12.50 *francs* a metre
- 1.30 m of green milled *serge*, costing 2.05 *francs* a metre
- 0.90 m of strong linen at 1 *franc* a metre
- Labour: 1.50 *francs*
- Total: 66.31 *francs*

Stable trousers:

- 0.39 m of ecru linen at 1.54 *francs* a metre
- 2.72 m of *treillis* at 1.98 *francs* a metre
- Thirty-six bone buttons
- Grey leather for foot straps, costing 20 *centimes*
- Labour: 1.20 *francs*
- Total: 7.64 *francs*

Porte-manteaux:

- 0.59 m of green wool cloth, fourth quality, at 16.34 *francs* a metre
- 0.03 m of scarlet wool cloth, costing 24 *francs* a metre
- 1.03 m of *treillis* at 1.98 *francs* a metre
- 0.89 m of aurore wool lace, 28 mm wide
- Labour: 2.50 *francs*
- Total: 15.66 *francs*

Schabraques:

- 1.80 m of green wool cloth, fourth quality, costing 16.34 *francs*
- 0.20 m of scarlet wool cloth at 24 *francs* a metre
- 3.02 m of *treillis* at 1.98 *francs* a metre
- 6.35 m of aurore wool lace, 45 mm wide, at 1.15 *francs* a metre
- Labour and leather panels: 6 *francs*
- Total: 58.48 *francs*

Above and opposite: The Musée de l'armée preserves this trooper's *habit*. It is cut in the *chasseur*-style, with pointed cuffs and narrow revers. The waistcoat is cut in the style of a *veste*, i.e. with two points on the bottom edge. This dates the garment to pre-1812. The tail facings of the *habit* are not sewn down, and simply hook together at the base, dating this garment to pre-1806, so it is either consular in date or very early empire. (Musée de l'armée)

Worth noting is that the *schabraque* eagles were supplied separately to the *schabraque*. It also seems to have had the leading edge piped in scarlet all the way around. The *porte-manteau* was also similarly piped. The *manteaux* clearly were unlined, bar the front opening and the shoulder cape, with the linen purchased providing the interlining to the collar. For example, in 1809, 358 eagles for *schabraques* embroidered in aurore wool costing 7.50 *francs* a pair were ordered along with 657 pompom cockades. The purchase account lists them as 'tricolour with an embroidered eagle', costing 1.25 *francs* each. It seems the pompom cockade on the colpack was the same item as used by the *grenadiers-à-cheval*, as well as the *grenadiers* and *chasseurs-à-pied* of the Guard.[44]

A second set of uniform specifications, also from 1813, are for the following garments:[45]

Pelisse:

- 1.25 m of scarlet wool cloth, first quality, costing 33.50 *francs* a metre
- 0.74 m of linen, blondine quality, at 1.64 *francs* a metre
- 0.29 m of ecru linen at 1.54 *francs* a metre
- 0.20 m of strong linen at 1 *franc* a metre
- 1.78 m of wool flannel at 3.75 *francs* a metre
- Twenty-eight large buttons at 30 *centimes* a dozen
- Seventy-two small buttons at 25 *centimes* a dozen
- One olive (toggle covered in a worsted crochet-type work) in yellow wool at 50 *centimes*
- 15.35 m of yellow square wool lace at 50 *centimes* a metre
- 1 m of cording at 32 *centimes*
- 8.91 m of yellow wool *soutache* at 8 *centimes* a metre
- 8.49 m of yellow wool flat braid at 20 *centimes* a metre
- One black sheepskin at 10 *francs*
- Labour: 4 *francs*
- Total: 72.33 *francs*

Of interest with the *pelisse* specification is that it is made from higher quality materials than the dolman. Also, the braiding and lace on the *pelisse* are clearly listed as yellow, whereas on the dolman they are aurore. Clearly, the colour of aurore used was a shade of yellow, as with the *grenadiers-à-cheval*, as both regiments class aurore as yellow, whereas under the Bardin regulations aurore was officially a deep orange, close to a modern scarlet. Clearly, the colour used by the Imperial Guard was yellow.

A *redingote* for sub-officers required the following materials:[46]

- 2.70 m of green wool cloth, second quality, costing 26.50 *francs* a metre
- 1.88 m of linen, blondine quality, at 1.64 *francs* a metre

- 0.59 m of gold lace, 22 mm wide, at 8.40 *francs* a metre
- 0.15 m of strong linen at 1 *franc* a metre
- Twenty large buttons at 30 *centimes* a dozen
- Six small buttons at 25 *centimes* a dozen
- Labour: 3.10 *francs*
- Total: 85.325 *francs*

The garment was double-breasted with four large buttons on the back and two rows of eight buttons on the front. The cuffs were cut point in the *chasseur*-style and closed with two small buttons each. Two buttons were at the shoulder to attach the epaulettes. The same tariff indicates the *redingote* of the trumpet-major was to be *bleu de ciel* second quality. The sergeant-major required 1.18 m of gold 22 mm lace, the trumpet-major 5.55 m of 22 mm gold lace and an additional 2.40 m of 12 mm gold lace, the corporal-trumpeter 3.50 m of 22 mm and 2.10 m of 12 mm, trumpeters 1.50 m of 22 mm and 1.4 0 m of 12 mm, the master farrier 0.45 m of 22 mm gold lace and corporals 1.18 m of aurore lace 20 mm wide.

A *habit* required the following materials:[47]

- 1.80 m of green wool cloth, first quality, at 26.50 *francs* a metre
- 0.20 m of scarlet wool cloth at 33.50 *francs* a metre
- 0.59 m of white milled *serge* at 1.50 *francs* a metre
- 1.18 m of linen, blondine quality, at 1.64 *francs* a metre
- 0.30 m of ecru linen at 1.54 *francs* a metre
- 0.24 m of wool lace, 10 mm wide, at 25 *centimes* a metre
- 0.20 m of strong linen at 1 *franc* a metre
- Twelve large buttons at 30 *centimes* each
- Six small buttons at 20 *centimes* each
- Four embroidered hunting horns at 1.10 *francs* for the four
- Labour: 3 *francs*
- Total: 62.76 *francs*

As with the *pelisse,* the *habits* were made from best quality cloth, whereas the dolman was made from the same grade cloth as the stable coat. Perhaps this was an economy drive to make clothing cheaper. Indeed, we note in the second clothing tariff of 1813 that the dolman cost 37.44 *francs* compared to the first tariff, which gives a price of 51.09 *francs*. By using cheaper materials, nearly 14 *francs* could be saved from the clothing budget. The same is true for the *manteaux*, the cost of which in the first tariff using fourth grade cloth was 85.22 *francs* dropped to 66.31 *francs*, a saving of nearly 20 *francs*.[48] Clearly, economy was a watch word in the re-clothing of the regiment in 1813.

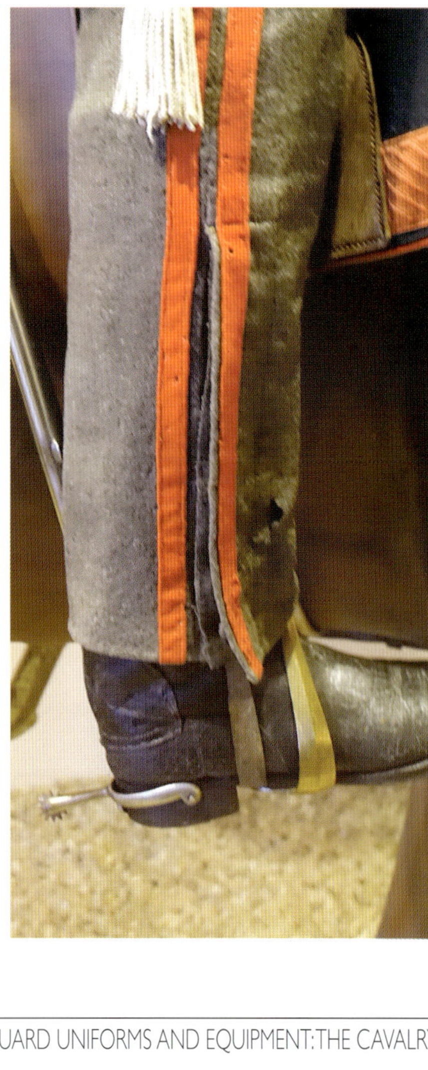

Above and opposite: The Musée d'Emperi preserves a *chasseur*-style *habit* for the regiment. It is accompanied by a scarlet braided waistcoat, cut flat at the bottom in the *gilet*-style, dating the garment to 1812 or later. The *habit* is cut in the style used from 1809 through to the end of the empire. The trooper wears *gris de Marengo pantalons*, introduced in the last years of the empire. We also see the trooper's buff belting, comprising *giberne* and *porte giberne*, *porte carabine* and carbine, waist belt with slings and sabre. (Musée de l'Empéri, Collections du Musée de l'armée, Anciennes collections Jean et Raoul Brunon)

Kettledrummer

The artist Nicolas Hoffmann presents the uniform of a kettledrummer of the *chasseurs-à-cheval* dressed like a *mameluke*. During September1803, the regiment began to contemplate the idea of adding a kettledrummer to the head of column of the regiment. Trumpet-Major Krettly had written to Colonel Beauharnais on 7 September 1803, asking that the order of the kettledrums be dealt with more speedily, so he could arrange the production of the undress uniform and also the squadron's standard.[49] The contract for the standards, trumpet banners and aprons for the kettledrums was passed on 12 August 1803 to Madame Chaillot:[50]

- Two standards on red silk
- Sixteen parade trumpet banners and trumpet cords on green silk
- Seventeen undress trumpet banners and trumpet cords on green silk
- Two *tabliers* for kettledrums on green silk

Krettly had organised the production of two squadron *guidons* from Madame Chaillot, of Paris, for 4,000 *francs*, trumpet banners costing 6,400 *francs* and the ornamented aprons for the kettledrums at the cost of 5,400 *francs*. However, the minister of war asked why the parade trumpet banners cost 500 *francs* each compared to the 700 *francs* of the items ordered by Krettly. The minister concluded that if the items had already been made, then they were to be paid for, failing that the order was to be cancelled.[51] The issue of authorisation to purchase these items, and the inflated prices charged by Madame Chaillot, rumbled on throughout autumn and winter 1803, generating numerous missives from the minister of war, the administrative council and Madame Chaillot. The order of parade trumpet banners and cords was duly suppressed, as on 5 March 1804 the items were finally delivered, comprising two *guidons*, sixteen undress trumpet banners and two kettledrum aprons.[52]

Detail of a troopers *sabretache*. The copper eagle was held in place by copper wire loops passing through the front face of the *sabretache*. (Musée de l'armée)

The contract for the kettledrum aprons states they were to be made on to green silk. Hoffmann, in his image of the trumpeter in the book of plates preserved in the Archives Nationales, shows the aprons and *schabraque* of the kettledrummer as crimson. In a second version of the plate housed in the A.S.K. Brown Library, USA, the *schabraque* and aprons are correctly shown as green. However, in the trumpeter in this series of images, the trumpet banner is shown as crimson/scarlet. No new kettledrum aprons/banners were obtained after March 1804, so we assume they were always green, likewise the trumpet banners up to 1806 were green, replaced in 1806 with crimson banners. This then appears to date this illustration to 1806 or later. The reliability of the Hoffmann image is, however, questioned as the trumpeter's parade *schabraque* was always crimson. Hoffmann shows *bleu de ciel* cloth ground with gold lace. The undress *schabraque* was indeed *bleu de ciel*, but the lace was always aurore. The kettledrummer ranking as corporal-trumpeter should, in theory, have had a *bleu de ciel schabraque* for undress and crimson for full dress. Hoffmann shows green and crimson. Crimson, we assume, was a standard trumpeter's *schabraque*. Was the green example an officer's model? We do not know, as no kettledrummer's *schabraques* were made. There are many details about this uniform that we simply do not know due to lack of period documentation and conflicting contemporary iconographic sources.

Trooper's *sabretache* preserved in the Musée de l'armée, Paris. On campaign, the front of the *sabretache* was protected by a leather cover to prevent the fragile embroidery becoming damaged or dirtied. (Musée de l'armée).

Returning to our narrative on the slow process of equipping the kettledrummer, the cost of kettledrums was raised at the meeting of the regiment's administrative council and also with the minister for war. Four quotes had been obtained ranging from 400 *francs* to 250 *francs* and to be the same quality and cost as those of the *grenadiers-à-cheval*.[53] Permission to buy a pair of kettledrums was passed on 25 September 1803.[54] The minister for war replied to the administrative council on 29 September 1803, stating the new drums were to be the same as those of the *grenadiers-à-cheval*, one drum nineteen inches in diameter, the other twenty-one inches, the bodies to be in copper. The minister further added that the officer placed in command of the regiment's music, along with the trumpet-major, were to oversee the purchase of the new drums. On 5 October 1803, a pair of kettledrums was ordered from M. Raoux, musical instrument manufacturer, of 8 rue Serpente, Paris, for the cost of 300 *francs*.[55] The kettledrummer was[56] MAT No. 904 Antoine Jean Bruneau Lemoin, son of Antoine Marcel Bruneau and (illegible) Amelot. Born on 23 December 1788 in Paris, he stood 1.34 m tall and had black hair and brown eyes. He had enlisted in the *grenadiers-à-cheval* on 3 January 1800 as corporal-trumpeter-kettledrummer, and had joined the *chasseurs* on 2 February 1803. He was killed at Madrid on 2 May 1808.

Above: Print by Vernet showing an officer of the regiment in parade dress.

Left: Trooper's *sabretache* preserved in the Musée l'Empéri. (Musée de l'Empéri, Collections du Musée de l'armée, Anciennes collections Jean et Raoul Brunon)

The position of kettledrummer does not seem to have been filled after the death of Lemoine, as no other kettledrummers were appointed. No specific kettledrummer's clothing was obtained, and given Hoffmann shows *mameluke* dress, it is likely that this was standard *mameluke* clothing. According to Boucquoy, the *sabretache* that belonged to Bruno Lemoine is housed in the Musée de l'Armée. This item is, however, very likely to be for the *grenadiers-à-cheval* rather than the *chasseurs-à-cheval*. This *sabretache* is mentioned in 1800 and is shown in the images by Hoffmann for the regiment, and is noticeably absent from Hoffmann's images of the kettledrummer of the *chasseurs*. The exact location of this item was not known in 2018.

CHAPTER 4

THE *MAMELUKES*

The word '*mameluke*' comes from the Arabic verb 'malaka', which means 'possess'. The *mamelukes* became the elite of the Ayyubid Army from the eleventh century. In the thirteenth century, the *mamelukes* of Egypt overthrew the Ayyubid dynasty, thus marking the beginning of several *mameluke* dynasties. In 1517, Selim I put an end to the independence of Egypt, making it an Ottoman province, itself divided up into twenty-four sub-provinces, each administered by a *mameluke* Bey. In 1767, Ali Bey, spokesman for the twenty-four Beys, seized power and proclaimed himself the 'great sultan of Egypt'.

At the moment Napoleon arrived in Egypt, this province was administered principally by Mourad Bey (army) and Ibrahim Bey (administration), both

Above left: *Mameluk* shown by the artist Nicolas Hoffmann, some time between 1805 and 1808.

Above right: *Mameluke* by Nicolas Hoffmann. This image shows the use of the shoulder-mounted holster, which carried two pistols as well as for the use of pommel holsters. We also see details of the *giberne*, which is seemingly a standard light cavalry type, with an eagle plate. The suggestion of lace to the flap of the *giberne* may indicate that this figure is of a *sous-officier*.

appointed by Constantinople. There were about 8,000–9,000 *mamelukes*, not one of whom was an indigenous Egyptian. On 21 July 1798, the French Army was victorious at the encounter known as the Battle of the Pyramids against 60,000 men, of which about 6,000 were *mamelukes*. Shortly after the disaster of Aboukir, Bonaparte decided to make up for losses by enrolling *mamelukes* (21 *Fructidor*, Year VI/7 September 1798). On 14 December 1799, Kleber created a company of mounted *mameluke* auxiliaries. General Menou re-organised this on 18 *Messidor*, Year VIII (7 July 1800) creating a regiment of *Mamelukes de la République*.

When the French capitulated at Alexandria on 8 *Messidor*, Year IX (27 June 1801), several hundred *mamelukes* and their families embarked with the French Army for France. On 21 *Vendémiaire*, Year X (13 October 1801), a measure passed by the first consul created the 1st Squadron of *Mamelukes* under the orders of Colonel Barthélémy, and later Brigadier General Rapp. The *Corps des Mamelukes* appeared for the first time on parade on 25 *Messidor*, Year X (14 July 1802). They distinguished themselves notably at Austerlitz and in the Peninsular War (2 May 1808). During the empire period, Frenchmen were allowed to enter the corps.

The *mamelukes* were disbanded in July 1814 by the new royalist government, and according to the historian Henry Lachouque, a decree of 24 April 1815 re-raised the *mamelukes*, and they were once more attached to the *chasseurs-à-cheval* of the Imperial Guard. It seems 120 or so *mamelukes* may have served with the *Armee du Nord*. What we do know for certain is that, during the battles that raged outside Paris on 30 June to 2 July, a composite formation of Guard cavalry, which included the 2nd Regiment of *Chasseurs à Cheval* of the Imperial Guard, also mustered lancers and *mamelukes*. Indeed, Major Schmidt, of the *chasseurs-à-cheval*, noted an *ad-hoc* squadron of lancers, *mamelukes* and *chasseurs* was posted at Saint-Cloud on 30 June. At Waterloo, *mamelukes* served in many regiments of the Imperial Guard. Pierre Phitily was an officer in the *grenadiers-à-cheval*, while others served in the Red Lancers (men such as Seraphin who was a first-lieutenant, Petros Roudjieri, Salloum and Daniel Mirza), the *chasseurs-à-cheval* (Jean Renno) as well as the equipment train of the Imperial Guard. So, the *mamelukes* were present at the last battles of the First Empire, if not at Waterloo as a squadron, but they served Napoleon in 1815 during the campaign.

Clothing and equipment

1803

The first detailed document for the clothing of the squadron is from 23 September 1803:[1]

- 71.40 *aunes* of scarlet wool cloth
- 71 *aunes* of crimson wool cloth
- 71 *aunes* of Saxony green wool cloth

- 65 *aunes* of yellow cassimere
- 65 *aunes* of crimson cassimere
- 65 *aunes* of nankeen from Rouen
- 150 *aunes* of linen
- Ninety *manteaux*
- Twenty-four *tarbouches*
- 296 shakos *des tarbouches*
- Thirty-six *etuis*

The clothing in 1803 was therefore mostly yellow, crimson and scarlet. The only clothing in the depot were the *manteaux* and two forms of headdress.

1804

The next document for the clothing of the squadron is from 23 September 1804:[2]

MATERIALS		*QUANTITIES* (AUNES)	*PRICE PER AUNE* (FRANCS)
Wool cloth	Crimson	64.43	21.00
	Scarlet	2.49	23.57
	Saxony green	146.64	21.88
	Bleu barbeau	121.58	21.88
	Bleu nationales, second quality	13.08	23.77
	Bleu nationales, fifth quality	4.28	8.84
Cassimere	Yellow	65.45	18.52
	Crimson	65.45	18.52
Treillis		28.51	1.75
Milled *serge*		90.49	1.75
Nankeen		105.34	2.07
Linen	Blondine quality	43.86	1.56
Flat braid	Gold and wool thread	109.35	0.32
Silver cord		1.37	1
Flat braid	woollen	1,687.67	0.21
Soutache		1,386.69	0.08
Square braid		777.54	0.17
Sixteen dozen *massif* buttons			
5.66 dozen large buttons			
Eight dozen small buttons			
Blue fringe for waist sash		97.10	2.10

Above: The waistcoat cut from scarlet wool cloth is decorated with cut glass imitation diamonds and gold applique embroidery. The shirt font is also embroidered. (Musée de l'Empéri, Collections du Musée de l'armée, Anciennes collections Jean et Raoul Brunon)

Left: Preserved ensemble for a *mameluke*. We see the highly ornate shoulder carried double pistol holster, as well as the highly ornate embroidery of the waistcoat. (Musée de l'Empéri, Collections du Musée de l'armée, Anciennes collections Jean et Raoul Brunon)

Clothing and equipment in the depot comprised:[3]

- Forty-three *charouls*
- Twenty-one Greek-style *vestes* with sleeves
- Ten Greek-style *vestes* with no sleeves
- Thirty *manteaux*
- Twenty-three *tarbouches*
- 200 shakos *de tarbouches*
- Eighty-four shakos *de cahouk*
- Fifty-six *yalek* in nankeen
- Fourteen sabre cords
- One *aiguillette* for sub-officer
- 100 handkerchiefs

1805

On 23 September 1805 the depot held the following items:[4]

MATERIALS		*QUANTITIES* (METRES)	*PRICE PER METRE* (FRANCS)
Wool cloth	Scarlet	151.65	23.57
	Diverse colours	246.46	23.57
	Bleu de roi	65	23.57
	Bleu nationales, fourth quality	480	9.89
	Grey *melange* for *capote*	660	15.15
Cassimere	Yellow	65.45	18.52
	Crimson	65.45	18.52
Treillis		211.88	1.75
Milled *serge*		90.49	1.75
Nankeen		51.88	2.07
Linen	Blondine quality	72.71	1.56
Flat braid	Gold and wool thread	81.01	0.32
Silver cord		24.35	1
Flat braid	Woollen	89.10	0.21
Soutache		108.92	0.08
Square braid	Gold and wool thread	89.10	0.17
Tresse	Wool	1507.48	0.21
Braid	Wool	2174.6	0.07
Soutache	Wool	186.46	0.07
Blue fringe for waist sash		97.10	2.10

Above left: *Mameluk* c.1804 by the print maker Chataignier and Poisson. He carries a short carbine over his left shoulder, and the cord over the right shoulder is for the suspension of his sabre.

Above right: *Mameluke* as observed by the artist Otto. He carries over his right shoulder a blunderbuss, a pair of pistols tucked into his waist-sash, along with a dagger, and his sabre. Otto nicely captures the look of this most exotic and unique regimental dress.

Clothing in the depot comprised:[5]

- Five *beniche* for sub-officers
- Twenty-five *beniche* for *mamelukes*
- Twenty-seven *charouls* for *mamelukes*
- Five Greek-style *vestes* with sleeves for sub-officers
- Forty-six Greek-style *vestes* with sleeves for *mamelukes*
- Fifty *fermelets* for *mamelukes*
- Forty-two *yaleks* in nankeen
- Eighteen *manteaux*
- Seven stable coats
- Twenty-nine *cahouks*
- Thirty shako *de cahouk*
- Twenty-three *tarbouches*
- 200 shakos *de tarbouches*
- Forty-two *porte-manteaux*
- Six *aiguillettes* for sub-officers
- Fifty-one sabre cords

Worthy of comment is the use of grey cloth for the *manteaux* of the squadron. The squadron seems to have had no two men dressed the same, given the wide array of different cloth colours in use. The inspection returns of 1 January 1807[6] and 1 January 1808[7] do not differ greatly from this return.

1809

The next document in sequence of returns is the 1809 stores inventory prepared on 1 January. The items of clothing and equipment in the depot at the time comprised:[8]

- 7.10 m of wool cloth of diverse colours
- 13.43 m of imperial blue wool cloth, first quality
- 10.72 m of imperial blue wool cloth, fourth quality, dyed by the piece
- 9.31 m of grey wool cloth for the *manteau*
- 130.90 m of casimir of diverse colours
- 90.17 m of milled *serge* (*blicourt*) for lining
- White *serge* (*cadis*)
- 50 m of ecru *tricot*
- 31.40 m of fringing in blue wool
- 153.41 m of mixed gold and wool flat braid
- 217.63 m of square braiding in gold and wool
- 254.07 m of *soutache* in gold and wool
- 97.25 m of wool flat braid
- 1,268.89 m of square wool braid
- 1,695.71 m of *soutache* in wool
- Eighteen small buttons for *surtouts*
- Twenty-one *grelots*, i.e. three-quarter round ball buttons
- 158.87 m of crimson and white lace 34 mm wide
- 67.41 m of green and white lace 28 mm wide
- 253.91 m of fringing in crimson and white

Without further archive sources, we have no idea at all as to the use of the different braids and laces that the unit held in its stores. The stores did, however, hold:[9]

- Sixty-seven *beniches*
- Fifty-three *charouls*
- Ninety-one Greek-style sleeved *vestes*
- One *fermelet* for sub-officer
- Seventy-seven *fermelet* for *mamelukes*
- Forty-six *jaluhl* in nankeen
- One *manteau*
- Eleven *bonnets de police*
- Thirty-one stable coats
- Five *cahouks*

A *fermelet* was a sleeveless waistcoat, *charouls* are the large baggy trousers worn by *mamelukes*, and the Greek-style waistcoats are also listed as *yaleks* in other documents. The *beniche* is the baggy shirt worn by *mamelukes*.

During 1808, the squadron had been on campaign in Spain. It returned to France in 1809 and headed off to Germany to fight the famous Austria campaign of 1809. While the regiment marched from one theatre of war to the other, the regiment's depot had been busy ordering new clothing, listed below:[10]

- Two *manteaux* for sub-officers, total cost 198.19 *francs*
- Eighteen *manteaux*, total cost 922.95 *francs*
- Two *fermelets* for sub-officers, total cost 128.38 *francs*
- Eighteen *fermelets*, total cost 441.36 *francs*
- Diverse items, total cost 15,345 *francs*

On the reverse of the same document is a list for the following items:[11]

- Fifty-seven stable coats, total cost 1,282.47 *francs*
- Forty *manteaux*, total cost 2,347.66 *francs*

1813

A large gap exists in the paper archive of almost five years. We cannot imagine any great changes were undertaken to the uniform during this time, but we cannot be certain. To clothe the *mamelukes* at the close of 1813, the following cloth was ordered on 3 November:[12]

- 94.80 m of wool cloth in diverse colours, costing 26.50 *francs* a metre
- 120 m of wool cloth in diverse colours, third quality, costing 18.76 *francs* a metre
- 423 m of wool cloth in diverse colours, fourth quality, costing 16.34 *francs* a metre
- Total: 11,689.92 *francs*

The same day a second batch of cloth was ordered:[13]

- 167.65 m of wool cloth in diverse colours, costing 26.50 *francs* a metre
- 109.20 m of wool cloth in diverse colours, third quality, costing 18.76 *francs* a metre
- 20 m of grey wool cloth, fourth quality, costing 16.34 *francs* a metre
- Total: 6,818.11 *francs*

From this it seems that the *manteau* was grey from 1804 until winter 1813. Some modern artists show the squadron with green *manteaux*, which is clearly an error.

1814

When the regiment was wound up in summer 1814, it prepared a list of all items of clothing, equipment, material, etc, that had been purchased by the regiment between January 1812 and August 1814. This remarkable resource of information is presented below. It means we can exactly reconstruct the dress of the regiment in these years using extant items in museum collections and this incredible document. Clothing made and issued 1812 to 1814 was as follows:[14]

Items for sub-officers and trumpeters

YEAR	*YALEKS*		*FERMELETS*		CHAROULS		*REDINGOTES*		*BONNETS DE POLICE*		*PANTALONS*		*CAHOUKS*		*PELISSE FOR SUB-OFFICERS*		*HABITS*	
	MADE	*ISSUED*	*MADE*	*ISSUED*	*MADE*	*ISSUED*	*MADE*	*ISSUED*	*MADE*	*ISSUED*	*MADE*	*ISSUED*	*MADE*	*ISSUED*	*MADE*	*ISSUED*	*MADE*	*ISSUED*	*MADE*	*ISSUED*
In magazine	0	0	5	0	0	0	0	0	7	0	7	0	1	0	1	0	2	0
1812	9	3	5	3	8	4	1	1	0	4	0	6	0	1	1	1	4	4
1813	21	14	13	14	12	14	13	10	14	10	14	10	8	8		1	3	5
1814	5	11	0	6	6	6	0	1	0	7	0	5	5	5	0	0	0	0
Total	35	28	23	23	26	24	14	12	21	21	21	21	14	14	2	2	9	9
In depot 1814	0	7	0	0	0	2	0	2	0	0	0	0	0	0	0	0	0	0

In addition, nineteen double-breasted waistcoats for trumpeters and sub-officers were made, eight being issued in 1812 and eleven in 1813. Furthermore, seven pairs of Hungarian breeches were made, three issued in 1812 and forty-seven in 1813. Fifty-six stable trousers were issued 1812-4, clearly to only a few other ranks. Sub-officers wore, it seems, both the *mameluke* uniform and a French-style uniform consisting of breeches, waistcoat, *habit*, *chapeaux* (of which four were issued in 1812 and three in 1813), as well as having *aiguillettes* and trefoils for the *habit*, four sets being made and issued in 1812 and the same number in 1813. A single *pelisse* was issued.[15]

As with the *chasseurs*, the sub-officers and trumpeters had their own pattern *giberne*, three being issued in 1812, twelve in 1813 and three in 1814.[16]

Items for other ranks were as follows:[17]

YEAR	*YALEKS*		*FERMELETS*		*CHAROULS*		*STABLE COATS*		*BONNETS DE POLICE*		*CAPOTE MANTEAUX*		*CAHOUKS*	
	MADE	*ISSUED*	*MADE*	*ISSUED*	*MADE*	*ISSUED*	*MADE*	*ISSUED*	*MADE*	*ISSUED*	*MADE*	*ISSUED*	*MADE*	*ISSUED*
In magazine	82	0	48	0	13	0	65	0	42	0	6	0	55	0
1812	1	28	32	25	72	23	27	31	46	26	25	26	0	14
1813	264	237	222	245	222	155	258	257	209	253	279	253	221	257
1814	59	100	150	111	61	84	41	103	75	93	75	93	76	75
Total	406	365	452	381	368	262	391	391	372	372	385	372	352	346
In depot 1814	0	0	0	0	0	0	0	0	0	0	0	0	0	6

Above left: Martinet presents us in a plate of 1809 yet another vision of a *mameluke*. The regiment's archive tells us that the clothing was made from 'diverse colours', so we must imagine each man could have been uniquely dressed. He carried the unique double pistol holster and a dagger tucked into his waist-sash as well as it seems a *giberne* carried from the leather belt passing over his right shoulder.

Above right: The *schabraque* used by the regiment was green-laced amaranth, as shown here by Martinet. The *portmanteau* was also green-laced amaranth, again correctly shown by Martinet. The baggy trousers are also seemingly amaranth.

In terms of equipment, 340 *gibernes* were issued between 1812 and 1814, along with 356 *giberne* belts and 337 carbine belts. Sub-officers, trumpeters and other ranks seem to have all used the same pattern *porte-manteaux*, with twenty-seven issued in 1812, 286 in 1813 and 106 in 1814. A mix of knee-length hussar-style boots and shorter ankle boots were used. Thirty of the former were presumably issued to trumpeters and sub-officers and 640 of the latter to other ranks.[18]

We learn something about the colour of the clothing from a clothing tariff or purchase account from 1814, which states the following:[19]

- *Yaleck*: *Soldat*: Facing cloth second quality, diverse colours, linen, half-domed buttons, flat wool lace, braided wool lace, square wool lace. Non-commissioned officer and trumpeter: Facing cloth first quality, diverse colours, gilded half-domed buttons, wool and gold flat lace, braided lace, square gold and wool lace, 1.38 m of 22 mm gold lace for sergeant-major, 0.65 m of 22 mm gold lace for sergeant, 0.48 m of 22 mm gold lace for farriers and 1.38 m of 22 mm wool lace for corporals.
- *Fermelet*: Scarlet facing cloth first quality, lined in *blicourt* (a fine woollen twill used almost exclusively as a lining material) in diverse colours, square flat wool lace for *soldat*, gold and wool for non-commissioned officers and trumpeters, 22.52 m of flat gold lace for non-commissioned officers and trumpeters.
- *Charoul*: Amaranth facing cloth of second quality, fine cow leather, 0.54 m of wool lace (gold and wool for non-commissioned officers and trumpeters).
- *Bonnet de police*: Imperial blue facing cloth third quality (second quality for non-commissioned officers), *bleu de ciel* third quality for trumpeters, 0.34 m of 30 mm wool lace for *soldat* (22 mm gold lace for non-commissioned officers and trumpeters), crescent (gilded for sub-officers), round wool lace, tassel in wool (gold and wool for non-commissioned officers).
- Stable trousers: Fourth quality grey wool facing cloth, linen for lining, black cow leather for reinforcement of inner seat of trousers, thirty-six bone buttons to close outside leg seam.
- Stable coat: Third quality imperial blue wool (*bleu de ciel* for trumpeters) linen for lining, fourteen buttons.
- Cloak: Fourth quality grey wool, wool lace 34 mm wide for brandenburgs, *treillis d'Alençon* (strong linen) for lining and collar interlining.
- Canvas trousers: Canvas, linen, nine bone buttons, leather for foot straps.

Disbandment

When the squadron was dissolved in July 1814, the depot contained, on 30 March 1814, the following items:[20]

- 2.14 m of wool cloth of diverse colours, first quality, total value 63.13 *francs*
- 17.13 m of wool cloth of diverse colours, second quality, total value 386.48 *francs*

- 0.23 m of wool cloth of diverse colours, third quality, total value 4.31 *francs*
- 508.16 m of *blicourt* for lining, total value 1,651.52 *francs*
- 42.88 m of ecru *tricot*, total value 111.48 *francs*
- 21.50 m of blue wool fringing, total value 45.15 *francs*
- 55.56 m of crimson wool fringing, total value 77.78 *francs*
- 1,001.77 m of grey ribbon, total value 100.17 *francs*
- 7.46 m of crimson wool lace, 34 mm wide, total value 8.58 *francs*
- 2.44 m of green wool lace, 28 mm wide, total value 2.20 *francs*
- 56.15 m of square braid in gold and wool, total value 85.92 *francs*
- 4,730.06 m of square wool braid, total value 993.31 *francs*
- 6,117 m of gold and wool *soutache*, total value 4,527.14 *francs*
- 4.29 m of amaranth braid for *charoul*, total value 11.95 *francs*
- 53.84 m of flat braid in wool and gold, total value 131.90 *francs*
- 2,223.08 m of flat braid in wool, total value 533.54 *francs*
- Twenty-four dozen small buttons *a grelot*, total value 7.30 *francs*
- Eighteen crescents embroidered in gold in, total value 15.75 *francs*
- Forty-six crescents embroidered in wool, total value 49.37 *francs*
- 396 pairs of brandenburgs, total value 456.60 *francs*
- Twenty-one black basane hides, total value 78.75 *francs*
- Six *yaleks* for sub-officers, total value 387.18 *francs*
- Fifteen *fermelets* for *mamelukes*, total value 330.30 *francs*
- Two *charouls* for sub-officers, total value 183.60 *francs*
- One *redingote* for sub-officer, total value 85.33 *francs*
- Five pairs of blue *pantalons* for sub-officers, total value 225.30 *francs*
- Eighteen stable coats, total value 457.20 *francs*
- Three *bonnets de police* for sub-officers, total value 75.75 *francs*
- Two *bonnets de police* for *mamelukes*, total value 16.28 *francs*
- Three *capotes manteaux*, total value 276.24 *francs*
- Six *cahouks* for *mamelukes*, total value 162 *francs*
- Thirty-five *schals de cahouk*, total value 140 *francs*
- Three covers for *cahouks*, total value 11.25 *francs*
- Sixty-two plumes and covers, total value 93 *francs*
- Thirty-three *porte-manteaux*, total value 725.12 *francs*
- One pair of boots, total value 18 *francs*

CHAPTER 5

EMPRESS DRAGOONS

Napoleon inherited twenty dragoon regiments in 1799 upon becoming first consul, their number rising to thirty by 1808, and reducing to twenty-four in 1811. In Napoleonic France, dragoons were formed for both service on foot and horseback and were the ideal troops for service in the Peninsular War, alongside light cavalry.

The Regiment of the Dragoons of the Guard, created on 15 April 1806, was initially composed of four squadrons and one of *velites*. Made up to five squadrons by the discontinuance of the latter on 1 April 1811, it numbered six squadrons in 1813 and 1814, four of which were Old Guard. A decree, dated from the Palace of Saint-Cloud on 15 April 1806, thus subjected the Imperial Guard to the following new organisation, namely:

> Cavalry:
> Art. 10. The regiments of *grenadiers*, *chasseurs* and dragoons are composed of:
>
> Four squadrons of two companies each. One squadron of *velites*.
>
> Art. 11. The staff of a regiment of *grenadiers*, *chasseurs* or dragoons will be composed of:

One commanding colonel	One sub-instructor (rank of *maréchal-des-logis-chef*)
Two majors	One quartermaster (*vaugmestre*) (rank of *maréchal-des-logis*)
Five squadron heads, of which one is for the *velites*	Two artist veterinarians, of which one is for the *velites*
One squadron head instructor	Four veterinarian *aides*
One quartermaster treasurer	One trumpet-major
One captain-instructor	Three corporal-trumpeters (brigadiers), of which one is for the *velites*
Two adjutant-majors, of which one is for the *velites*	One timpanist
Five sub adjutant-majors, of which one is for the *velites*	One master tailor
Four standard bearers	One master breech-maker
One adjutant-lieutenant for food	One master boot-maker

One adjutant-lieutenant for fodder	One master gunsmith (*armurier*)
One adjutant-lieutenant for clothing	One master saddle-maker
Five medical officers, of which two are first-class and three are second or third-class	One master spur-maker
	Two master sergeant-blacksmiths

Art. 12. Each company will be made up of:

One captain	One quartermaster (*fourrier*)
Two first-lieutenants	Ten corporals (brigadiers)
Two second-lieutenants	Ninety-six *grenadiers*, *chasseurs* or dragoons
One sergeant-major (*maréchal-des-logis-chef*)	Three trumpeters
Six sergeants (*maréchaux-des-logis*)	Two sergeant-blacksmiths

Art. 13. There will be a company of *mamelukes* attached to the Regiment of Horse *Chasseurs* of the Guard.

The *mameluke* refugees who are in Melun will be sent to Marseilles, where they will enjoy the same advantages and will be paid in same manner as in the past.

This company of *mamelukes* will be made up of:

One squadron head commandant	Two captains
One captain instructor French.	Two first-lieutenants
One adjutant-second-lieutenant French	Four second-lieutenants.
One standard-bearer, second-lieutenant French	One master sergeant (*maréchal-des-logis-chef*) French
One surgeon-major French	Eight sergeants, of which two French
One artist veterinarian French	One quartermaster French
One master saddle-maker French	Four *queues* bearers
One master gunsmith French	Twelve corporals, of which two French
One master boot-maker French	109 *mamelukes*
One master tailor French	Four trumpeters French
One corporal trumpeter French	Two sergeant blacksmiths French

Art. 14. There will be, for the regiment of cavalry of the Guard, a squadron of *velites*.

Each squadron of *velites* will be composed of two companies of 125 men, not including the officers and non-commissioned officers.

The officers, the non-commissioned officers and the sergeants will be provided by the regiments of horse *grenadiers* and *chasseurs*.

Art. 15. When a squadron of the Guard marches, for some type of service that it is, and this squadron will have sleep away for several days continuously, it will be changed to 250 men by the incorporation of fifty *velites* by squadron, so that, if the four squadrons went, they would form a total of 1,000 men, including 800 old soldiers and 200 *velites*.

The depot of each regiment, in Paris, will remain made up of forty-eight old soldiers and fifty *velites*, in all ninety-eight men.

Art. 16. On campaign, each regiment of *grenadiers*, *chasseurs* or dragoons will form two regiments.

Each regiment will be composed of two squadrons, and each squadron divided into two companies known as *manoeuvres*.

Each regiment will be commanded by a major under the orders of the two colonel commanders.

There will be only one administration per distinct body of cavalry.

The *grenadiers*, the *chasseurs* and the dragoons will have the same organisation.

Dragoons:

Art. 17. A regiment of dragoons of the Guard is created.

This regiment will be organised like the *grenadiers* and the *chasseurs*.

Art. 18. To this end, each regiment of dragoons of the line will provide, this year, for the formation of the dragoons of the Guard, twelve men having at least ten years of service. The emperor will name the officers: the regiments of *grenadiers* and *chasseurs* will provide the non-commissioned officers and sergeants.

The officers of the regiment of dragoons will be provided per third; the first two-thirds by the regiments of *grenadiers* and *chasseurs* of the Guard; the other third, by the thirty regiments of dragoons of the line.

The regiments of dragoons will appoint a lieutenant by squadron to be proposed as a candidate.

Art. 19. Two squadrons of dragoons will not be organised this year; next year a new call will be made for ten men to form the two other squadrons.

Art. 20. The final organisation of the regiment of dragoons of the Guard will take place only from the 1st of next July, except the squadron of *velites* and the staff, which will be trained immediately.

Art. 21. The regiment of dragoons will be mounted on black horses.

Art. 22. All the regiments of cavalry of the Guard will have to be supplemented, as old soldiers, from the 1st of next July.

Art. 23. The non-commissioned officers and sergeants, attached at this moment to the two squadrons of *velites* of the *chasseurs* and to the two squadrons of *velites* of *grenadiers*, will be divided, in equal portions, in each attached squadron of *velites*, by the present organisation, with each regiment of cavalry of the Guard; excess will be reincorporated in the regiment of dragoons, as well as the senior officers of the two regiments of *grenadiers* and *chasseurs* who would not be included in the present organisation.

It was Napoleon's intention that the regiment would comprise 1,000 men, 800 veterans and 200 *velites*, with fifty *velites* incorporated into each squadron.[1] By 13 December 1806, a squadron mustering 200 men were in Berlin and had marched by the way of Meudon. The formation of the first two squadrons was not as easy as the regiment's colonel had hoped. The Empress Dragoons had been ordered to march to Berlin at the start of November 1806, as Napoleon was in need of reinforcements following the defeat of the Prussians of Jena and the subsequent pursuit of their army. The dragoons left on 14 November 1806. These men were mounted by General Bourcier on captured Prussian mounts at the cavalry depot at Berlin.[2]

Six months later, Napoleon issued another decree regarding the formation of the dragoons. Article one of the decree of 8 July 1807 noted that the Guard cavalry needed 745 men to be brought up to full strength, 145 for the *chasseurs*, 200 for the *grenadiers* and 400 for the dragoons. To provide these men, article two stipulated that each of the twelve hussar regiments were to send ten men, as were the *chasseurs*. The *cuirassier* and *carabinier* regiments were to send ten men each and each Dragoon regiment eleven men. The men were to be veterans of Austerlitz and Jena, have good conduct, and have at least ten years' service before they could be considered for admission to the Guard, outlined under article three of the decree. Corporals and sergeants, however, only needed four years' service.[3]

Article four of the decree placed further constraints on the men that could be sent to the Guard. Each of the regiments of hussars, *chasseurs*, *cuirassiers* and *carabiniers* had to send five men between five feet 6.5 inches and five feet seven inches tall for the dragoons, three men five feet seven inches tall for the *grenadiers-à-cheval*, and two men five feet six inches tall for the *chasseurs-à-cheval*. The dragoons had to provide six men five feet 6.5 inches tall, three men five feet seven

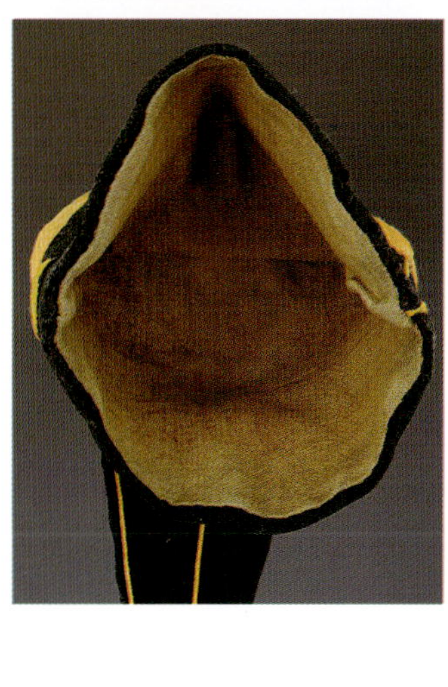

Incredibly well-preserved *bonnet de police* for the regiment. Of interest is the row of piping on the centre back seam rather than a single length of lace, which was more usual. (Photograph and collection of Bertrand Malvaux).

inches tall and two men five feet six inches tall. General Clarke was charged with the administration of the decree.[4]

On 13 December 1806, the regimental strength was 793 other ranks and sixty officers. The two squadrons of dragoons had 476 men, the *velites* 296 plus twenty-one non-commissioned officers, who were part of the headquarters staff. The officers were as follows:

Staff

Arrighi, colonel-general
Fiteau, colonel-major
Letort, major

Jolivet
Rossignol
Vacant
Vacant
Vacant
} Squadron heads

Delassus
Duvernoy
Vacant
Vacant
} Capt.-adj.-majors

Colommier
Alexandre
Vacant
Vacant
} First-lieut sub-adj.-majors
Vacant

Danglot, adj.-lieut for clothing

Vacant
Vacant
Vacant
Vacant
} Second-lieut standard bearers

Reiffer
Vacant
} Medical officers first-class

Poirson, medical officer second-class
Blondy, medical officer third-class

SDN.	COMP.	CAPTAINS	LIEUTENANTS			
			FIRST		SECOND	
1st	1st	Bureau de Pussy	Ligier	Chassin	Chamorin	Vacant
	3rd	Picard	Meunier	Paturel	Vacant	Vacant
2nd	2nd	Messier	Bernel	Belot-la-Digne	Vacant	Vacant
	4th	Desirad	Raquet	Meyronnet	Vacant	Vacant

Velites-dragoons, forming the 5th squadron:

COMP.	CAPTAINS	LIEUTENANTS			
		FIRST		SECOND	
1st	Mace	Villemetz	Vacant	Vacant	Vacant
2nd	Thierry	Garret	Vacant	Vacant	Vacant

Above left: Front view of a trooper's helmet. Trooper's helmets for the regiment are comparatively rare. This is an excellent example of the helmet worn by the other ranks from 1806 to 1815. (Collection de l'Office du Tourisme de Pontarlier. Dépôt au Musée municipal de Pontarlier – France)

Above right: This example seemingly dates from 1814/1815, as according to work by Bertrand Malavux, the flower bosses for the chinscales date from the 1814 restoration. (Collection de l'Office du Tourisme de Pontarlier. Dépôt au Musée municipal de Pontarlier – France)

The commanders, who were both Corsican officers, were the 28-year-old Colonel Jean-Toussaint Arrighi di Casanova and 22-year-old Philippe-Antoine d'Ornano, both of whom were related to the emperor. Arrighi had married the daughter of Napoleon's chamberlain, Montesquieu.

1806 – Formation of the regiment

On the formation of the regiment in 1806, the administrative council speedily started providing for the new unit's needs. Two inventories of the regimental stores and a document relating to items of equipment and dress for the dragoons and *velites* describe to us their first uniform. A purchase agreement made on 13 September 1806 by Colonel-Major Fiteau and counter-signed by Revue Inspector Chadelas for the tariff for the production of items of harnesses and saddlery was created on 13 September 1806 and was repeated on 21 May 1809 and 10 August 1811. Clearly, these items remained the same in the regiment prior to the Russian campaign. The tariff is as follows:[5]

Habits of sub-officers and dragoons:

- 1.41 m of green wool cloth
- 0.20 m of white wool cloth for *revers*
- 0.10 m of scarlet wool cloth for cuffs and piping
- 1.93 m of scarlet *blicourt* for lining
- 1.63 m of linen for lining, sleeve linings and pockets
- Epaulette *passants* for sub-officers
- Epaulette *passants* for dragoons
- Pair of contre-epaulettes and *aiguillettes* for dragoons
- Pair of contre-epaulettes and *aiguillettes* for sub-officers or trumpeters
- 0.40 m of scarlet wool cloth for lining contre-epaulettes
- 0.70 m of aurore wool lace for corporal's rank stripes
- Gold lace for rank stripes of sub-officers
- Gold grenades for sub-officers
- Dark yellow wool grenades for dragoons
- Eleven large eagle buttons
- Twenty-two small eagle buttons

Habits of trumpeters:

- 1.41 m of *bleu de ciel* wool cloth
- 0.20 m of white wool cloth for *revers*
- 6.20 m of gold garnitures
- *Surtouts* of sub-officers and dragoons
- 1.41 m of green wool cloth
- 1.93 m of scarlet *blicourt* for lining
- 1.63 m of linen for lining, sleeve linings and pockets
- Epaulette *passants* for sub-officers
- Epaulette *passants* for dragoons
- 0.70 metres of dark yellow wool lace for corporal's rank stripes
- Gold lace for rank stripes of sub-officers
- Gold grenades for sub-officers
- Dark yellow wool grenades for dragoons
- Eleven large eagle buttons
- Twenty-two small eagle buttons
- *Surtouts* for trumpeters
- 1.41 m of *bleu de ciel* wool cloth
- 1.40 m of gold lace for garnitures

Vestes:

- 0.59 m of white wool cloth
- 0.90 m of white *blicourt* for lining
- Ten small buttons
- Linen for *droit fils* (interlining)

Gilets d'ecurie:

- 1.12 m of green wool cloth
- 1.58 m of linen for lining
- Seventeen small buttons
- 0.70 metres of dark yellow wool lace for corporal's rank stripes

Pantalons d'ecurie:

- 2.38 m of *treillis*
- Thirty-six bone buttons

Bonnets de police:

- 0.30 m of green wool cloth
- 0.15 m of linen for lining
- 0.90 m of dark yellow wool lace, 25 mm wide
- 2.38 m of aurore cording
- One grenade
- One dark yellow wool tassel

Manteaux:

- 5.95 m of white wool cloth
- 1.48 m of scarlet *blicourt* for lining
- 1.04 m of linen for lining collar
- 0.40 m of green wool cloth for collar

The brass buttons bore a crowned eagle. Twenty-two small buttons and eleven large were used for the coat. For the full dress, the green coat with matching collar had white *revers*, scarlet cuffs with white, three-pointed flaps, long simulated vertical pockets bordered with red and red turnbacks decorated with grenades embroidered from dark yellow-coloured wool and mounted on white cloth.[6]

A *marche* account of 13 September 1806 lists *surclottes* in white canvas, stable trousers in white linen and breeches in sheepskin and doeskin. The same document notes that the first issue cloak was made from white wool cloth, piped in *serge* of unknown colour. The collar was green and lined with linen, as was the cloak.[7] The same document lists sixty helmets for sub-officers, 724 for dragoons, 793 plumes, eighty-seven sub-officer's *chapeaux*, 706 *chapeaux* for dragoons, eighty-seven sub-officer's sword knots and 793 dragoon's sword knots.[8]

1807

At the end of 1807, the regiment's staff drew up the following list of items in stores as of 1 January 1808:[11]

MATERIALS		*QUANTITIES (METRES)*	*PRICE PER METRE* (FRANCS)	*TOTAL VALUE* (FRANCS)
Green wool cloth	For *habits*	13.84	25.20	348.77
	For stable coats	0		
White		0		
Scarlet	First quality	0		
	Second quality	0		
Bleudeciel	First quality	7.52	30.30	227.86
	Second quality	0		
Blanc picque de bleu		7.52	9.66	216.38
Tricot	*Bleu de ciel*	0		
	White	0		
Milled *serge*	Scarlet	5.39	2.52	13.58
Linen	White	0		
White *coutil*		6.52	2.80	16.43
Treillis	d'Alençon	0		

Clothing and equipment in the magazine comprised:[12]

- 243 dragoon's *habits*
- Fifty-two dragoon's *surtouts*
- 243 white *vestes*
- 243 *bonnets de police*
- 243 *manteaux*
- 465 pairs of *surclottes*
- 344 stable coats
- 344 pairs of stable trousers
- 243 *pantalons du daim* (doe hide *pantalons*)
- Sixteen *capotes*
- 243 pairs of gauntlets
- 243 dragoon's sword knots
- 243 dragoon's *chapeaux*
- 243 dragoon's helmets
- 243 dragoon's *porte-manteaux*
- Fifty-two pairs of *bottes forte* (rigid knee boots)
- Eighteen trumpet cords
- Fifty-two pairs of spurs with straps

Above left: Dismounted trooper of the regiment by Hoffmann.

Above right: Trumpeter in parade dress by Hoffmann. The white-faced *bleu de ciel habit* has traditionally been ascribed to 1810 and later. Here we see it in use in 1806/1807, which is supported by archive documents, which in September 1815 clearly state twenty-four trumpeters dating from the creation of the regiment were in the regiment's magazine. Hoffmann is also correct in showing the lace as gold.

During 1807, the regiment had thirty-seven new officers join, 379 troopers from other regiments of line cavalry and thirty-four new entrants from the Guard. In that year, eleven men had been killed, eleven struck-off the muster role, fifteen were sent back to their original regiments due to bad conduct, one man had passed to the veterans, one had been sent to the military school at Fontainebleau and ten had been promoted as officers in the line.[13]

1811

We have a gap in the archive paperwork of five years. It is unlikely that any great changes to the dress of the regiment occurred during this time.

In August 1811, 700 m of *toile blondine* to line *habits* and 630 m of bleached white *coutil* for *surclottes* was ordered.[14] The same day wool cloth was obtained from Marianne et Sage, clothier, of 14 rue des Bourdonnais, Paris:[15]

- 400 m of green wool cloth, *de berry* quality, dyed in the piece
- 100 m of *bleu de ciel* wool cloth, *de berry* quality, dyed in the piece
- 800 m of white wool cloth for *vestes* and *revers* of *habits*
- 550 m of scarlet wool cloth for cuffs and piping of *habits*
- 500 m of scarlet *blicourt* for lining of *habits* and *manteaux*
- 900 m of white *blicourt* for the lining of *vestes*
- 2,740 m of *blanc de picque bleu* wool cloth for *manteaux*
- 150 m of grey wool cloth

Furthermore, forty-three pairs of *culottes de peau* were ordered in September 1811, costing 40 *francs* a pair.[16]

1812

As the army geared up for the invasion of Russia, on 28 May 1812 a *marche* was passed for the following amounts of cloth:[17]

- 1,000 m of green wool cloth, dyed in the wool, for *habits*, 142 cm wide
- 500 m of white wool cloth for *vestes*, 148 cm wide
- 64 m of scarlet wool cloth for cuffs, 148 cm wide
- 60 m of *bleu de ciel* wool cloth, dyed in the thread, for trumpeter's *surtouts*, 142 cm wide
- 500 m of green cloth, *de berry* quality, dyed in the piece, for *gilet d'ecurie*
- 60 m of *bleu de ciel* wool cloth, de berry quality, dyed in the piece, for *gilet d'ecurie*, *housses* and *chaperons* of trumpeters
- 1,788 m of *blanc de picque bleu* wool cloth for *manteaux*
- 300 m of scarlet *serge* (*blicourt*), 50 cm wide, for lining
- 1,100 m of white *tricot* for *vestes*

The same day a *marche* was passed for the purchase of linens:[18]

- 2,400 m of *toile laval dit blondine*
- 1,016 m of ecru Flanders linen
- 1,800 m of *treillis* d'Alençon
- 400 m of white *coutil*
- 370 m of strong linen from Abbeville

M. Mottet, master breeches-maker, of the 'place of the Palace Royale', Paris, was contracted to supply 400 pairs of gauntlets and 1,070 pairs of *culottes de peau*

Above left: Regimental headed notepaper enlivened with a naive sketch of a trooper of the regiment.

Above right: The Otto artist shows the regiment in campaign dress *c.*1807-1808. He wears the undress green surtout, which was replaced in 1809 for troopers and corporals, with a second undress *habit*. *Sous-officiers* always wore the surtout on campaign, as did trumpeters.

on 28 March 1812.[19] In addition, 900 pairs of boots and 900 pairs of spurs with straps were ordered from M. Dubois, chief boot-maker of the regiment.[20] Also, 530 m of oil cloth were ordered from M. Larroumet, cloth merchant, of 18 rue St Margueritte, in the *arondisment* of St Antoine.[21]

1813

Following the Russian campaign, the regiment had to be rebuilt and re-dressed. Cloth was ordered from Messrs Lisarge and Marianne, clothiers, of Paris, on 10 February:[22]

- 3,000 m of green wool cloth, dyed in the thread, for *habits*, 142 cm wide
- 1,000 m of white wool cloth, 148 cm wide, for *vestes*
- 280 m of scarlet wool cloth, 148 cm wide, for cuffs and piping
- 80 m of *bleu de ciel* wool cloth, 142 cm wide, for trumpeter's *surtouts*
- 3,000 m of green wool cloth, *de berry* quality, 142 cm wide, for *gilet d'ecurie*, *housses*, *chaperons*, *porte-manteau* and collars of the *manteaux*

- 130 m of *bleu de ciel* wool cloth, *de berry* quality, 142 cm wide, for *gilet d'ecurie*, *housses* and *chaperons* of trumpeters
- 7,700 m of *blanc de picque bleu* wool cloth for *manteaux*, 119 cm wide
- 2,800 m of grey wool cloth for *pantalons*
- 3,000 m of scarlet *blicourt* (milled *serge*), 50 cm wide, for lining of *habits* and *manteaux*
- 1,800 m of white *blicourt* (milled *serge*), 50 cm wide, for lining of *vestes*
- 1,440 m of white *tricot* for back of *vestes*

The following *marche* for linen was passed on 13 February 1813:[23]

- *Toile blondine*, 89 cm wide; 5,365 m for use and 1,860 m for replacements in 1813
- *Toile de Flanders*, 104 cm; 223 m for use and 1,236 m for replacements in 1813
- *Treillis d'Alençon*, 89 cm wide; 3,157 m for use and 426 m for replacements in 1813
- *Toile d'Abeville*, 80 cm wide; 260 m for use and 340 m for replacements in 1813

Every year, the regiment received funding for new items it needed to replace worn-out items, as well as money for items due to be replaced in the same year. Often, accounts list these amounts separately, but not in this case. Further, 465 m of oil cloth was supplied by M. Larroumets, clothier and maker of oil cloth.[24]

M. Lesage et Muraine was contracted on 30 June 1813 to provide the following lengths of cloth:[25]

- 476.33 m of green wool cloth for *habits* at 27.35 *francs* a metre
- 1,459 m of green wool cloth for *gilet d'ecurie* at 18.50 *francs* a metre
- 72.75 m of scarlet wool cloth for cuffs at 27.78 *francs* a metre
- 62 m of white wool cloth for *vestes* and *revers* at 22 *francs* a metre
- 2,409.80 m of white wool cloth for *manteaux* at 12 *francs* a metre
- 1,023.60 m of scarlet *serge* (*blicourt*) at 3 *francs* a metre
- 316.80 m of white *serge* (*blicourt*) for *vestes* at 1.60 *francs* a metre
- 571.30 m of white *tricot* for *vestes* at 2.60 *francs* a metre

A document of 27 October 1813 lists the purchase of cloth for the regiment:[26]

- 564.54 m of green wool cloth for *habits* at 27.35 *francs* a metre
- 1,826.74 m of green wool cloth for *gilet d'ecurie* at 18.50 *francs* a metre
- 41.71 m of *bleu de ciel* wool cloth for trumpeter's *surtout* at 26.94 *francs* a metre

- 33.70 m of *bleu de ciel* wool cloth for trumpeter's *gilet d'ecurie* at 18.50 *francs* a metre
- 87.15 m of scarlet wool cloth for cuffs at 27.78 *francs* a metre
- 386.72 m of white wool cloth for *vestes* and *revers* at 22 *francs* a metre
- 5,496.55 m of *blanc picque de bleu* (white with blue fleck) wool cloth for *manteaux* at 12 *francs* a metre
- 200 m of grey wool cloth for *pantalons* at 15.90 *francs* a metre
- 2,962.88 m of scarlet *serge* (*blicourt*) at 3 *francs* a metre
- 520.92 m of white *serge* (*blicourt*) at 1.60 *francs* a metre
- 200 m of white *tricot* for *vestes* at 2.60 *francs* a metre

Of interest, in 1813 it is clear that the trumpeters only wore the *surtout*,; a fact confirmed by the clothing returns for the regiment at the time of disbandment in 1814.

On 10 February 1813, 800 pairs of *culottes de daim* and 1,300 pairs of gauntlets were purchased.[27]

Equipment

On 10 February 1812, the following items of equipment were ordered from M. Kling, chief saddler of the regiment:[28]

- 1,000 waist belts, with plates and slings
- 1,000 *gibernes* complete with plates and *bonnet de police* slings
- 1,000 *banderoles de giberne*, complete with buckle, slide and tip
- 1,000 *grenadieres*
- 1,200 sword knots in buff leather
- 300 replacement long sword slings
- 1,000 lock covers

With regards the *grenadieres*, this is a term is used to describe the central band on the Year XI dragoon pattern musket, to which the musket sling attaches. A document dated 1 December 1812 states that the administrative council decided to have foul weather lock covers for the muskets of all other ranks. An order for 1,000 foul weather lock covers made from black leather, garnished with two straps and a buckle, was placed with M. Kling, master saddler, each cover to be furnished with two straps joined together at the end with a metal loop.[29]

On 23 February 1813, the dragoons of the Guard of Paris were disbanded into the Red Lancers. The following items surplus to requirements were passed to the Empress Dragoons on 28 June 1813:[30]

- 212 helmets
- 128 *bradoon* bridles

- 128 *musketoon* slings
- Forty-nine curb bridles
- Forty-three *bradoon* bridles in leather
- Thirty-nine *bradoon* bridles in white webbing
- Forty-nine *housses* and pairs of *chaperons*
- Forty-nine curb bits
- 219 sabres
- Ten pairs of pistols
- 154 muskets
- 139 bayonets

Passamenteries

A *marche* passed on 4 June 1812 for the lace and embroidery of the regiment with M. Beaurian, of 1 rue de la Monnaie, Paris, gives the turnback grenades for non-commissioned officers as being gold with nine flames, and in wool with nine flames for dragoons.[31] The complete *marche* comprises:[32]

- 11,108 large eagle buttons
- 60,000 small eagle buttons
- 3,017 large gilded eagle buttons for sub-officers
- 1,076 small gilded eagle buttons for sub-officers
- 103 grenades for sub-officers, embroidered in gold on white cloth with nine flames
- Twenty-five grenades for trumpeters, embroidered in gold on crimson cloth with nine flames
- 785 grenades for dragoons, embroidered in yellow wool on white cloth with nine flames
- 495 grenades, embroidered in wool for *bonnets de police*
- 131 m of gold lace 9 mm wide
- 140 m of gold lace 28 mm wide
- 180 m of dark yellow wool lace 16 mm wide
- 3,000 m of dark yellow wool lace 23 mm wide
- 1,021 m of dark yellow wool lace 41 mm wide
- 3,800 m of dark yellow wool lace 55 mm wide
- Seventy-eight *aiguillettes* and epaulettes for sub-officers in red wool and gold
- Thirty-five *aiguillettes* and epaulettes for trumpeters in crimson wool and gold
- 600 *aiguillettes* and epaulettes for dragoons in dark yellow wool
- 120 pairs of crowns embroidered in wool for the *housse*
- 2,116 m of dark yellow cord for *bonnets de police*
- 1,236 dark yellow wool tassels
- Twenty-four sets of trumpet cords in wool

From this list, it is very clear that sub-officers and trumpeters did not have gold lace, and either red and gold or crimson and gold cord to the *flamme* of the *bonnet de police*. Clearly, for dragoons, sub-officers and trumpeters, the cording, lace and tassel were always dark yellow.

Harness

The tariff for the production of items of harnesses and saddlery was created on 13 September 1806 and repeated on 21 May 1809 and 10 August 1811. Clearly, these items remained the same in the regiment prior to the Russian campaign. The tariff is as follows:[33]

Housses:

- 0.76 m of green wool cloth
- 1.50 m of *treillis* for lining
- 4.80 m of dark yellow wool lace 50 mm wide
- 4 m of dark yellow wool lace 22 mm wide
- One pair of crowns
- 1.19 m of oil cloth for interlining

Chaperons:

- 0.40 m of green wool cloth
- 0.63 m of *treillis* for lining
- 4.70 m of dark yellow wool lace 50 mm wide
- 3.60 m of dark yellow wool lace 22 mm wide
- 0.53 m of oil cloth for interlining

Porte-manteaux:

- 0.75 m of green wool cloth
- 0.75 m of *bleu de ciel* wool cloth for trumpeters
- 1.30 m of linen for lining
- 1.05 m of 22 mm dark yellow wool lace
- 1.35 m of 16 mm dark yellow wool lace

On 10 February 1812, the following items of harnesses and saddlery were ordered from M. Ling, chief saddler of the regiment:[34]

- 900 curb bits
- 110 saddles, complete with pistol holders, crupper, stirrup leathers and irons, breastplate, girth, *musketoon* bucket and sling
- 200 *bradoon* bridles in black leather
- 200 parade head collars with lead rope
- 900 stable head collars
- 900 watering bridles
- 100 *musketoon* slings

SABRES D'OFFICIER ET DE SOUS-
OFFICIER DES CHASSEURS À CHEVAL
DE LA GARDE IMPÉRIALE.

Above, opoosite and previous spread: General Philippe Antoine Ornano was the regiment's colonel. A cousin of Napoleon Bonaparte, Philippe-Antoine Ornano first became an officer at the young age of 15 as a *sous-lieutenant* of the 9th Dragoons in 1799. Over the next few years he served in Italy before traveling on the expedition to Saint-Domingue as an *aide-de-camp* to Napoleon's brother-in-law, General Leclerc. After Leclerc's death, in 1803 Ornano was promoted to lieutenant and attached to the general staff. A few months later he was promoted to captain and thereafter soon returned to France. Once back in France, Ornano served in the Army of the Coasts and became an *aide-de-camp* to Berthier. In March of 1805, as the Grande Armée prepared for war, he was appointed a *chef de bataillon* of the 3rd Battalion of Corsican *Tirailleurs*, serving in Legrand's division. Campaigning with the army, Ornano served with distinction at Austerlitz, Jena and Lubeck. In early 1807, he received a promotion to colonel and he took command of the dragoons in Beker's division.

Rewarded in 1808 by being made a Count of the Empire, Colonel Ornano would spend the next few years in Spain and Portugal. Serving in the 5th Division of Dragoons in 1809, he served at the crossing of the Navia and at Alba de Tormès. The next year he fought at Ciudad-Rodrigo and then served under Trelliard, and in 1811 he fought at Fuentes de Onoro, where he was promoted to *général de brigade* on the battlefield.

In 1812, Ornano returned to France to take command of the 16th Brigade of Light Cavalry for the Russian campaign. In Russia, he served at Mohilew, and then at the Battle of Borodino he charged the enemy at the head of the cavalry of IV Corps. In recognition of his performance, he was promoted to *général de division* the following day, and then a week later he received command of a division of cavalry of Prince Eugene's IV Corps. During the retreat, he fought at Maloyaroslavetz and then at Krasnoe, where he was wounded and left for dead on the battlefield.

After making it out of Russia, Ornano became a major colonel of dragoons in the Imperial Guard in early 1813, serving in Saxony. After the death of Marshal Bessières, General Ornano took command of all the cavalry of the guard for a time. He would go on to fight at Dresden, Kulm, Leipzig and Hanau before returning to France. Back in France, he took command of all the Imperial Guard troops defending Paris. It is comparatively rare to be able to link preserved items of clothing with historical men. (Musée de l'Empéri, Collections du Musée de l'armée, Anciennes collections Jean et Raoul Brunon)

Disbandment

The decree of 1 September 1814 laid out which men were to be retained by the regiment to implement the decree of 8 June. The titles of 'Regiment' and 'Guard' were abolished, at least for the former Imperial Guard, and replaced with the title of Royal Corps of France. This was not to be a royal guard.

The Empress Dragoons passed to the Royal Corps of Dragoons of France the following items:[35]

ITEM	*GOOD REPAIR*	*NEED REPAIRING*	*NEED REPLACING*
Habits	474	75	43
Vestes	557	7	48
Non-commissioned officer's and farrier's *surtouts*	81	6	21
Trumpeter's *surtouts*	16	4	2
Bonnets de police	479	13	87
Trumpeter's *bonnets de police*	17	0	4
Greatcoats	501	123	18
Porte-manteau	445	75	85
Trumpeter's *porte-manteau*	16	2	4
Stable coats	396	26	110
Trumpeter's stable coats	16	2	4
Canvas trousers	0	0	0
Grey overalls	0	0	0
Deerskin breeches	592	10	30
Gauntlets	362	1	18
Sword knots	640	2	0
Non-commissioned officer's sword knots	5	0	0
Chapeaux	0	0	5
Helmets	575	67	0
Plumes and covers	578	5	47
Boots	434	157	50
Spurs	615	21	0
Non-commissioned officer's and trumpeter's *aiguillettes*	89	0	18
Aiguillettes	460	7	59
Sabre belts	634	8	0
Sabre belt plates	637	5	0

ITEM	*GOOD REPAIR*	*NEED REPAIRING*	*NEED REPLACING*
Gibernes and plates	590	8	0
Giberne belts	598	0	0
Sabre slings	552	0	90
Saddles	392	301	10
Curb bridles	604	80	19
Bridoon head pieces	668	37	22
Stable head collars	0	0	0
Head collars and lead ropes	0	0	0
Parade head collars	488	130	60
Schabraques	502	97	98
Saddle blankets	0	0	0
Porte-manteaux	0	0	0
Sabres	493	149	0
Pistols	774	14	0
Epees for the five chief workmen	5	0	0
Drap vert dragon for *habits*	17.40 m	0	0
Drap vert for *veste d'ecurie*	65.80 m	0	0
Drap *bleu de ciel* for *habit d'trompette*	1.84 m	0	0
Drap blanc for *manteaux*	12.55 m	0	0
Drap ecarlette	9.83 m	0	0
Drap gris	28.45 m	0	0
Blicourt ecarlette	69.33 m	0	0
Blicourt blanc	71.26 m	0	0
Toile blondine	74.22 m	0	0
Toile des Flandres	49.67 m	0	0
Gold lace, 9 mm	0.68 m	0	0
Gold lace, 13 mm	4.20 m	0	0
Gold lace, 22 mm	4.30 m	0	0
Wool lace, 9 mm	39.86 m	0	0
Wool lace, 4 mm	73.14 m	0	0
Wool lace, 55 mm	50.42 m	0	0
Grenades for trumpeters	22	0	0
Grenades for *bonnets de police*	104	0	0
Pairs of crowns for *housses*	16	0	0

Above: Officer in full dress in a print by Aaron Martinet, published in Paris in 1810.

Left: A dragoon in campaign dress by the German artist Henschel. His print is worth comparing to that of Otto, as they both show virtually identical uniforms, which strongly implies that this is how the regiment appeared in the campaign of 1807.

the other rank's green stable coat, *bonnet de police*, *housses* and *chaperons*. The *habit* is listed as having a green collar, but we are ignorant of all other details of the garment.[39]

The first dress *habit* we have with firm details of what was produced was in September 1806. The twenty-three uniforms were made for trumpeters on 13 September 1806. They were cut in the same style as for the troopers, but the body was made from *bleu de ciel* wool cloth. All other details were the same as the others ranks, i.e. with white *revers*, cuffs, cuff patches, and scarlet turnbacks and piping. The coats were decorated with 6.20 m of 23 mm wide gold lace used to decorate the collar, *revers*, cuffs, pockets, the buttons at the waist in the rear of the coat, the buttonhole loops on the *revers*, plus three false buttonholes beneath each *revers*. The turnbacks had gold embroidered grenades. The epaulette bridles (loops) were made from 9 mm wide gold lace. The *aiguillette* was made from one-third gold thread and two-thirds *bleu de ciel* woollen thread.[40]

The trumpet-major wore sergeant-major rank stripes above each cuff. The collar and cuffs had a second, narrower 12 mm wide row of lace set below the 23 mm wide lace. His *aiguillettes* were two-thirds gold thread and one-third *bleu de ciel* wool. The three corporal trumpeters, one attached to the *velites*, and the corporal kettledrummer wore the trumpeter's uniform, plus the rank distinction of a sergeant, i.e. a single gold chevron above each cuff.[41]

In 1810, according to Rousselot, based on no archive documents but upon a Martinet print published in 1810, a new dress coat was produced for the trumpeters. It was white with *bleu de ciel* collar, *revers*, cuffs, pocket edging, lining and turnbacks. A gold braid 34 mm (15 *lignes*) wide, bordered the collar, the *revers*, the cuffs and the pockets. The braid formed a triangular shape at the buttons on the waist and formed three buttonholes below the lapels, seven on the lapels, and one on each pocket button. Each buttonhole had a gold fringe. The grenades on the turnbacks and the epaulette loops were also gold.[42]

Again, according to Rousselot, the *bleu de ciel* contre-epaulettes were bordered with gold, and *aiguillettes* made from *bleu de ciel* wool mixed with two-thirds gold braid were worn on the dress coat.[43] There is no archive evidence at all to

Above left: Trooper in full dress, as shown by Aaron Martinet in print of 1810.

Above right: Dismounted trooper in town or walking-out dress. His helmet is replaced by the more comfortable *chapeau*, and his stiff cavalry boots by softer Suvorov-style knee boots,

support this notion. Hoffmann, however, shows this coat in use in 1806/1807. Therefore, the Hoffmann plate coupled with archive evidence tells us that these twenty-four trumpeter's coats were made new in 1806, and Martinet was showing what was in use rather than newly made. These items were used rarely and for the most part of the empire were held in stores, and used perhaps two or three times a year. Certainly, no archive paperwork exists for the production of the coats, but they did indeed exist according to stores inventories and iconography.

No new trumpeter's *habits* were made from 1812, only *surtouts*. The old dress coats from 1806 were placed in store and seldom used, where they remained until 1815. Rousselot states the facings were changed to crimson in 1810 and retained until the end of the empire. However, no crimson cloth was purchased between 1806 and 1813, so again Rousselot has taken this detail from the Martinet print.[44]

Archive material shows that the *surtout* was cut in the same style as that of troopers, but was made from *bleu de ciel* wool cloth with scarlet piping and lining to the tails. The collar and cuffs were laced with gold and the turnback grenades and epaulette bridles were also gold.[45]

The trumpeter's helmet had a tuft and mane of white horsehair, and for the dress uniform a *bleu de ciel* plume was also added.

The cloak, which had the same style and dimensions as that of the dragoons, was *bleu de ciel* with scarlet lining. In 1813, the *manteaux-capote* was issued. It was distinguished from the other ranks by its *bleu de ciel* collar in lieu of green. Rousselot is again at error when he says the lining was crimson.[46]

The *bonnet de police* was again *bleu de ciel* with aurore wool lace, piping, tassel and embroidered grenade.

Trumpeter in parade dress in a print by Martinet published in 1810. The uniform *habit* is virtually identical to that shown by Hoffmann, so we can be sure that the *habit* shown did indeed appear as in this illustrations. The dismounted trumpeter wears the campaign dress *surtout*, cut from *bleu de ciel* wool cloth with crimson facings laced with gold.

CHAPTER 6

POLISH LANCERS[1]

Following the Battle of Jena, the Grand Armee moved east to Poland. In anticipation of Emperor Napoleon's arrival in Poznan, on 6 November 1806 General Dąbrowski met with civil dignitaries and agreed to form an honour guard of 100 riders from the youth of the city who were to greet the emperor on his arrival into the city. Command of this unit was given to Umiński, an old friend of Dąbrowski, who knew him from their time served in the Insurrection of Kościuszko. Upon receiving notification that the emperor was approaching Poznan, the honour guard marched immediately to beyond Miedzyrzecz, where it was to await him and welcome him onto Polish soil. However, at Bytyniem, where the honour guard bivouacked at night, the emperor arrived unexpectedly and immediately ordered the honour guard to escort his carriage by a mounted guard in front and behind it The *chasseurs-à-cheval* of the Guard, whose picket of an officer and twenty-five men had escorted the emperor up to this point, were ordered to march behind the Poles. While in Poznan, the honour guard were on duty around the emperor.

By the imperial decree of 6 April 1807, signed by the emperor at the Palace of Finckenstein, the honour guard was incorporated into the newly formed Polish Light Horse Regiment of the Guard, under Colonel Wincenty Kraśinski. Tyszkiewicz was transferred with the rank of colonel to the army of the Duchy of Warsaw on 11 May 1807.

The new regiment was organised exactly as the *chasseurs-à-cheval* of the Guard. It comprised a commanding officer and a regimental staff of fourteen officers, twenty-one sub-officers and four squadrons of two companies each. The companies in turn consisted of five officers, twenty sub-officers, three trumpeters and ninety privates. In its entirety, the regiment was made up of fifty-five officers and 981 sub-officers and men. The two 'gross majors' were Frenchmen assigned from the Imperial Guard, as were two senior *aides* and a captain instructor. Some of the trumpeters were also Frenchmen and came from the Guard cavalry trumpeters' school.

Contrary to French tradition, where the colour-bearer was an officer, the Poles created a special rank of 'cadet standard-bearer'.

The regiment took up residence at the Mirłowski Barracks near Ul. Chłodnej. Candidates for the regiment after first being interviewed at the Polish ministry of war were examined by the medical commission at Małachowski Palace, which was in turn followed by a more rigorous selection at the barracks. Here it was decided if the candidate would be accepted into the regiment or sent home.

The youth of Poland flocked to the regiment, but not all could aspire to the high ideals expected of the Guard. Those who passed were accepted and listed in the regimental manifest and equipped with basic kit. This was then followed by the issue of the uniform, which was fitted in the presence of the company commandant, and any necessary alterations were made by the master tailor at this time. The officers in 1807 were as follows:

Regiments of the light horse lancers, known as Polish lancers:

Staff:

Count Krasinksi (O. ✻), colonel	
Delaître (O. ✻) Dautancourt (O. ✻)	Majors
Cte. Lubeinsky (O.✻) Cte. Kozietuloki ✻ Stokiwski ✻ Depare ✻	Squadron heads
Duvivier ✻ Moreau ✻	Capt.-adjutant-majors
Raulet, first-lieutenant, quartermaster	
Pfeisser, first-lieutenant, adj. for clothing	

Deshayes Coulon Vianney	Sub-adjutant-majors
Zelaskowsky	
Cte. Jordain, eagle bearer, second-lieutenant.	
Ladroite, instructor, second-lieutenant	
Desplaces Girardot	Surgeon first-class
Gadowsky Courtiade	Surgeon second-class

SQN.	COMP.	CAPTAINS	LIEUTENANTS			
			FIRST		SECOND	
1st	1st	Lubienski	Jankowski	Olszewski	Sliwoski	Hoffmann
	5th	Szehtiski	Zaluski	Heyman	Korycki	Mierzeiewski
2nd	2nd	Jermanowski	Giedrové	Wibicki	Dubilcki	Malinowski
	6th	Radziminski	Prasmowski	Luszezewski	Vandernot	Balinski
3rd	3rd	Rostworouwski	Jaukowski	Niecolewski	Tedwen	Roman
	7th	Krazinski	Mikulouwski	Zelunki	Jaraczewski	Gutarlowski
4th	4th	Fredro	Zayoncher	Skrzynski	Jasinski	Hempel
	8th	Trezinski	Jordan	Broski	Kruszewski	Gnalowski

1809

The oldest extant document for the clothing of the regiment is a document of 2 February 1809, and gives the breakdown of the components and their cost for making a *czapka*:[2]

- Linen for headband, 75 *centimes*
- Leather for the headband, 40 *centimes*
- *Pavilion* in cardboard, 75 *centimes*
- Braid, 40 *centimes*
- Velvet, 60 *centimes*
- Peak with silvered metal edging (*jonc*), 1.25 *francs*
- Silvered lion head bosses, rosettes, hooks and pins, 2 *francs*
- Chinstrap in silvered chain, 40 *centimes*
- Wool cloth for lining chinstrap, 50 *centimes*
- Labour to make, 1 *franc*

The tariff implies the *pavilion* was made from cardboard covered with velvet. The order accompanying the tariff was for sub-officer's *czapka* at 58 *francs*, trumpeter's *czapka* at 58 *francs* and other rank's *czapka* at 35 *francs*, including the hooks and cords according to the model adopted by the administrative council of the regiment. Is it possible sub-officers and trumpeters had velvet covering to the *pavilion* and other ranks wool cloth? Perhaps, but more documentation is needed on this point. Extant items are covered in wool cloth. Of course, it could be velvet that has lost its raised knap.

The *kurtka* was blue with crimson collar, lapels, cuffs, turnbacks and crimson piping on the back seams of the tunic, sleeves, pockets and belt retention strap.

The *revers* were fastened by fourteen 17 mm tin buttons: fourteen on the lapels, two more appeared at the small of the back, six on the pockets, two on the bottom of the tails and two on the shoulders. A 15 mm button secured the belt strap and four small ones of 13 mm were found on the cuffs. Compared to the first model, the two buttons at the front of the tunic below the lapels disappeared and the pockets were aligned to fall parallel to the rear edge of the turn backs. Epaulette loops were white and the lapels were edged with 1.71 m of silver 15 mm braid. In the field and on the march the lapels of the *kurtka* were folded across towards the epaulette, with the blue lining edged in thin crimson piping showing.[3]

Very few items from the regiment can be found in museums outside of Poland. This *czapka* can be found in Les Invalides in Paris. (Musée de l'armée)

Under the *kurtka* was worn a plain blue waistcoat fastened down the front with twelve small buttons. Troopers also wore a white cotton epaulette lined with crimson cloth on the left shoulder and an *aiguillette* worn on the right shoulder. In 1809, with the introduction of the lance, the epaulette and *aiguillette* were changed to opposite shoulders to allow for comfort and practicality. When in the field, dark blue marching overalls were worn by the men. They were rather fuller than the trousers and were fitted with thin black leather on the inside leg and flap. They fastened at the sides on thirty-six tin buttons, eighteen on each leg, with the buttonholes cut into a crimson leather band, which ran the full outside length of each leg.[4]

Headdress

Czapki were supplied by M. Chardon, hatter, of Paris. M. Odier oversaw the order:[5]

- Thirty-five *czapki* for sub-officers, costing 41 *francs* each
- Fifteen *czapki* for trumpeters, costing 41 *francs* each
- 449 *czapki* for other ranks, costing 34 *francs* each

Clothing and equipment

Archive documents tell us a great deal about the amount, type and quality of materials used in the production of uniforms. The documents date primarily from 1811 and winter 1813.

M. Destrot was contracted to supply large quantities of cloth, overseen by M. Odier:[6]

- 104 m of linen, Abbeville quality
- 1,784.94 m of linen, blondine quality
- 1,317.63 m of ecru linen
- 2,666.79 m of white *treillis* for stable trousers
- 110 m of *treillis*, Alençon quality

In addition, for new items to be made in 1811 for 200 new entrants to the regiment:[7]

- 29.60 m of linen, Abbeville quality
- 475.20 m of linen, blondine quality
- 594 m of ecru *treillis*
- 953.40 m of *treillis*, Alençon quality, for lining the *schabraques*
- 535.33 m of white *treillis* for stable trousers

Wool cloth was obtained from M. Barbaud, clothier, of rue des petits-champs, Paris. The contract was overseen by Commissioner for War Odier:[8]

- 20 m of blue wool cloth, first quality 5/4, costing 24 *francs* a metre
- 2,012.10 m of blue wool cloth, first quality 5/4, costing 29 *francs* a metre
- 272.66 m of blue wool cloth, second quality 5/4, at 26 *francs* a metre
- 1,149.40 m of blue wool cloth, third quality 5/4, at 20 *francs* a metre
- 765.07 m of blue wool cloth, fourth quality 4/4, at 13 *francs* a metre
- 46.29 m of *bleu de ciel* wool cloth at 24 *francs* a metre
- 899.34 m of white wool cloth, second quality 4/4, costing 11 *francs* a metre
- 350.65 m of crimson wool cloth, first quality 5/4, at 31 *francs* a metre
- 259 m of crimson wool cloth, second quality 5/4, at 20 *francs* a metre
- 43.98 m of grey wool cloth, 4/4, at 14 *francs* a metre
- 505.78 m of white milled *serge* at 1.16 *francs* a metre
- 300 m of blue *tricot* at 3 *francs* a metre

For 200 new entrants to the regiment in 1811, the following cloth was ordered, again from M. Barbaud:[9]

- 521.62 m of blue wool cloth, first quality 5/4
- 409.20 m of blue wool cloth, second quality 5/4
- 368.28 m of blue wool cloth, third quality 5/4
- 287.70 m of blue wool cloth, fourth quality 4/4
- 101.57 m of crimson wool cloth, first quality 5/4
- 272.59 m of crimson wool cloth, second quality 5/4
- 1,254.80 m of white wool cloth, second quality 4/4
- 207.60 m of blue milled *serge*
- 118.80 m of blue *tricot*

The various grades of blue wool cloth were clearly destined for the production of garments for the various grades of sub-officer. The white wool cloth was intended for the production of the *manteaux*. The use of the blue milled *serge* is unknown, but likely used in the production of *vestes*, based on the archive of other regiments of the Imperial Guard who used milled *serge* in the back and lining of *vestes*. The *tricot* was, again, based on the quantity of purchases, likely to be used in the production of the *veste*. A document of 27 February 1809 lists the cloth for the *schabraque* being 3rd quality, Berry standard, and the fourth quality being used for the *gilet d'ecurie*. The first quality crimson was used for the *revers* of the *kurtka*, and the second quality for the *porte-manteau*. The white was meant for *manteaux*.[10] The use of the grey cloth is not known.

M. Raoul, of Saint-Denis, Paris, was contracted to supply 388 leather hides for the *pantalons-à-cheval* and for rubbing plates on the *schabraque*.[11] Also, 1,001 white plumes were supplied by M. Dufrenel, plume-maker, of 10 rue de Saint-Denis, Paris, at the cost of 3 *francs*. The contract stated the plumes were to be 50 cm long.[12] Furthermore, 166 saddle blankets were purchased from M. Barot, blanket-maker, of Paris.[13] Buttons were supplied by M. Sauer, button manufacturer, of Saint-Denis:[14]

- 2,415 dozen large silvered dome buttons for *pantalons-à-cheval*
- 1,550 dozen large silvered dome buttons for *kurtkas*
- 765 dozen medium silvered dome buttons for *kurtkas*
- 829 dozen small silvered dome buttons for *kurtkas*, *vestes* and *gilets*

Petty equipment

Czapka covers, plume covers, lance pennants and covers were supplied by M. Dupouvillon. The purchase was overseen by M. Odier:[15]

- 1,001 *czapka* covers
- 1,001 plume covers
- 377 lance pennants in taffeta
- 377 lance pennants in milled *serge*
- 754 lance pennant covers

The order was amended to also include:[16]

- 200 *czapka* covers
- 200 plume covers
- 200 lance pennants in taffeta
- 200 lance pennants in milled *serge*
- 200 lance pennant covers
- 200 black neck cloths (cravats)
- 200 white neck cloths (cravats)
- 400 shirts

Lance pennants measured 73 cm in length and 48.70 cm wide, with a central seam of 40.50 cm. They had two points and were crimson on top and white below, constructed from *serge* cloth for everyday use and taffeta for parades. In the field the *pennon* could be covered with a waxed linen case to protect it from the elements.

A contract for gloves and gauntlets was awarded to M. Gerel for 332 pairs of gauntlets and 1,001 pairs of wrist gloves. The order was supervised by Commissioner for War Odier.[17]

Passamenteries:

Passamenteries were supplied in 1811 by M. Hebert et Compagnie, of 14 rue St Fauvure, Paris, the order being overseen by Commission for War Odier:[18]

- 59.40 m of silver lace 34 mm wide
- 214.38 m of silver lace 22 mm wide
- 1,324.91 m of silver lace 14 mm wide

- 24.35 m of crimson and silver lace
- 32.07 m of Russian braid *dit soutache*
- 734.18 m of white wool lace 34 mm wide
- 120 m of white wool lace 14 mm wide
- 1,291.59 m of crimson wool lace 54 mm wide for *schabraques*
- 1,468.36 m of white wool lace for *bonnets de police*
- 618 white wool tassels for *bonnets de police*
- Fifty silver and crimson wool tassels for sub-officer's *bonnets de police*
- 59.40 m of crimson and silver cord for *bonnets de police* of sub-officers
- 1,786.40 m of crimson cord for *pantalons*
- Eight *aiguillettes* and epaulettes for sergeant-majors
- Fifty-seven *aiguillettes* and epaulettes for sergeants
- Fifty-three *aiguillettes* and epaulettes for corporals
- 545 *aiguillettes* and epaulettes for other ranks
- Sixty-five *czapka* cords for sub-officers
- 598 *czapka* cords for other ranks

As well as the items ordered for replacements in 1811, an order was placed again with Hebert et Compagnie for new items for the year 1811:[19]

- 342 m of silver lace 14 mm wide
- 237.60 m of white wool lace 34 mm wide
- 178.80 m of white lace 28 mm wide for *bonnets de police*
- 40 m of white wool lace 14 mm wide
- 1,247.40 m of crimson wool lace 45 mm wide
- 475.60 m of white wool cord for other rank's *bonnets de police*
- 200 white wool tassels for other rank's *bonnets de police*
- 440 m of crimson cord for *pantalons*
- 200 pairs of eagles embroidered in white wool for the *schabraques*
- 200 pairs of crowned 'N's for *schabraques*, embroidered in white wool
- 200 *czapka* cords for other ranks
- 200 *aiguillettes* for other ranks
- 200 epaulettes for other ranks

The cording for *pantalons* was used to provide a central narrow stripe down the outside leg seam of the parade *pantalons*. The outside leg of the *pantalons* was decorated with two rows of crimson cloth 30 mm wide. The seam itself was sewn with the crimson round cord.

The *marche* also poses other questions. What were the differences between sergeant-major, sergeant and corporal's items? Presumably, the sergeant-major had a ratio of two silver to one crimson, sergeant two crimson to one silver. The ratio for corporals is not known. Clearly, they were of sufficient difference to the other ranks as to be ordered separately.

1812

As the regiment prepared to go to war in Russia, new stocks of clothing were ordered for new entrants and to replace clothing that had expired its service life. A huge quantity of buttons was ordered in spring 1812:[20]

- 2,712 dozen large silvered dome buttons for *pantalons-à-cheval*
- 18,206 dozen large silvered buttons for *kurtkas*
- 1,266 medium silvered buttons for *kurtkas*
- 695 dozen small silvered dome buttons for *kurtkas*

For new entrants to the regiment, the following buttons were procured:[21]

- 1,050 dozen large silvered dome buttons for *pantalons-à-cheval*
- 354 dozen large silvered dome buttons for *kurtkas*
- 454 dozen medium silvered dome buttons for *kurtkas*
- 462 dozen small silvered dome buttons for *kurtkas*

A huge quantity of wool cloth was purchased from M. Barbaud, clothier, of Paris, the order being overseen by Imperial Guard War Commissioner Odier:[22]

- 2,300.20 m of blue wool cloth, first quality, costing 28 *francs* a metre
- 594 m of blue wool cloth, second quality, costing 25 *francs* a metre
- 1,405.40 m of blue wool cloth, third quality, costing 18 *francs* a metre
- 1,068.80 m of blue wool cloth, fourth quality, costing 13 *francs* a metre
- 407.60 m of crimson wool cloth, first quality, costing 30 *francs* a metre
- 285.30 m of crimson wool cloth, second quality, costing 25 *francs* a metre
- 30.40 m of white wool cloth, first quality, costing 24 *francs* a metre
- 1,247.40 m of white wool cloth, second quality
- 60 m of *bleu de ciel* wool cloth
- 356.40 m of white (illegible), second quality, costing 3 *francs* a metre
- 600 m of white milled *serge*, costing 1.60 *francs* a metre

The use of the first quality white cloth is of interest. Was it destined for *manteaux* of sub-officers? Or was it destined to make the white parade *kurtkas* of the trumpeters? The white *kurtka* was introduced in 1810, so it is possible that this was for the *kurtkas*. The *bleu de ciel* cloth was used to make the trumpeter's undress *kurtka* and *pantalons*, whereas the white was destined solely for the *kurtka*, hence the lower amount of cloth purchased. The parade dress for the trumpeters included crimson *pantalons* with two white side stripes. The *schabraque* was now crimson as well. In a second document, also from the first quarter of 1812, a further 18.40 m of *bleu de ciel* wool cloth was purchased for trumpeters, but no more first quality white. No first quality white was obtained in 1811, and only a small amount in 1813/1814. We know the trumpeters received new clothing in

Above: This painting made after the conversion of the regiment to lancers in 1809 captures very well the dress of the regiment, with the blue *kurtka* faced crimson.

Right: This portrait of an officer shows the elaborate dress of a field officer. He wears crimson *pantalons* laced with silver, elaborate embroidery to the revers of the *kurtka* and a panther skin seat to his *schabraque*.

Above: Officer's *kurtka* preserved in the Army Museum in Warsaw. The elaborate embroidery to the collar and cuffs can be clearly seen. (George Lubomski)

Left: Preserved uniform of a sergeant of the regiment in the Warsaw Army Museum. The *czapka* belonged to the 3rd Scouts attached to the 1st Regiment and has been added to complete the figure. (George Lubomski)

1812, as eleven trumpeter's *czapki* were purchased as replacements and six were purchased for new entrant trumpeters,[23] so clearly seventeen sets of trumpeter's clothes were made in the first quarter of 1812.

A fragmentary document, presumably drawn up in the first half of 1812, listed the items of clothing and equipment in use and when its service life would expire, dictating that new items were to be authorised for production. This is a unique document but, presumably, hundreds of these documents existed in the era so regiments could easily keep track of month-by-month expiry of clothing and equipment:[24]

DATE	1812 11 November	1812 18 December	1813 19 February	1813 1 April	1813 8 April	1813 10 April	1813 13 April	1813 14 April	1813 illegible	Total
KURTKAS	400	0	400	206	82	0	0	0	120	1,208
TRUMPETER'S *KURTKAS*	0	0	0	0	0	0	0	0	0	0
PANTALONS	400	0	400	290	158	0	0	0	0	1,248
TRUMPETER'S *PANTALONS*	0	0	0	0	0	0	0	0	0	0
PANTALONS-À-CHEVAL	400	0	600	173	51	0	0	0	0	1,224
VESTES	400	0	500	350	0	0	0	0	0	1,250
GILET D'ECURIE	400	0	510	128	10	0	0	0	0	1,048
SUB-OFFICER'S *BONNETS DE POLICE*	20	0	0	20	0	0	0	0	0	40
OTHER RANK'S *BONNETS DE POLICE*	300	0	600	140	95	0	0	0	0	1,135
CAPOTES	20	0	0	20	0	0	0	0	0	40
MANTEAUX	0	300	0	300	0	50	50	50	150	900
CZAPKI	300	0	100	324	0	0	36	36	0	796
TRUMPETER'S *CZAPKI*	0	0	0	0	0	0	0	0	0	0
CZAPKA COVERS	300	0	100	0	400	0	0	0	0	800
PLUMES	0	300	100	0	400	0	200	0	0	1,000
PLUME COVERS	300	0	100	0	340	0	0	0	0	740
SUB-OFFICER'S *CZAPKI CORDS*	0	0	0	15	0	0	0	0	0	15
OTHER RANK'S *CZAPKI CORDS*	0	300	0	300	0	0	360	0	0	960
SUB-OFFICER'S *AIGUILLETTES*	0	0	0	19	0	0	0	0	0	19
CORPORAL'S *AIGUILLETTES*	0	0	0	40	0	0	0	0	0	40
OTHER RANK'S *AIGUILLETTES*	300	0	300	330	0	0	0	0	0	930

Above left: Martinet shows a trooper in the process of mounting. However, he shows bastion loops to the buttonholes on the *revers*, also shown by Hoffmann, which implies these loops of lace were indeed a feature of the very early uniform for the regiment in French service.

Above right: Officer in a print by Aaron Martinet published in 1810. Martinet endeavours to capture the elaborate embroidery to the *revers* and collar.

Of interest from the table is the lack of renewal for any items of clothing or equipment for trumpeters. Furthermore, it seems both the sleeved cloak and the old-style *manteaux* were used side-by-side in the regiment, unless the term *capote* actually means *redingote*. The table, however, due to the events of 1812 would have become theoretical, given the large losses of the regiment in the Russian campaign.

Winter 1813

Headdress

Czapki were obtained from M. Chardon, hatter, of Paris, who supplied:[25]

- Twenty *czapki* for sub-officers at 41 *francs*
- Six *czapki* for trumpeters at 41 *francs*
- 220 *czapki* for other ranks at 34 *francs*
- Four *chapeaux* for sub-officers, costing 24 *francs*

A second order, again placed with M. Chardon, was for the following items:[26]

- Ten *czapki* for sub-officers at 41 *francs*
- Six *czapki* for trumpeters at 41 *francs*
- Fifty *czapki* for other ranks at 34 *francs*

Clothing and equipment

Over winter 1813, the regiment had to be re-formed and re-dressed. All purchases were authorised and overseen by M. Pellechet, a commissioner for war of the Imperial Guard. To re-dress the regiment, the administrative council ordered large stocks of material. Linen and canvas was supplied by M. Destrot, of Paris:[27]

- 31 m of linen, Abbeville quality, at 90 *centimes* a metre
- 621 m of linen, blondine quality, at 1.66 *francs* a metre
- 600 m of ecru linen at 1.56 *francs* a metre
- 360 m of *treillis* (herringbone-weave hemp canvas) at 1.95 *francs* a metre
- Total: 2,697.64 *francs*

A second order was made in the new year of 1814, also with M. Destrot:[28]

- 62.22 m of linen, Abbeville quality, at 80 *centimes* a metre
- 1,189.83 m of linen, blondine quality, at 1.66 *francs* a metre
- 1,196 m of ecru linen at 1.56 *francs* a metre
- 1,107.75 m of *treillis*, Alençon quality, at 1.95 *francs* a metre
- Total: 6,050.77 *francs*

Wool cloth was purchased from M. Barbaud, clothier, of Paris:[29]

- 889.58 m of blue wool cloth, dyed in the thread, first quality, costing 28.50 *francs* a metre
- 265.50 m of blue wool cloth, dyed in the thread, second quality, costing 25.50 *francs* a metre
- 826.74 m of blue wool cloth, dyed in the piece, third quality, costing 19.50 *francs*
- 327.60 m of blue wool cloth, dyed in the piece, fourth quality, costing 13 *francs* a metre
- 26.63 m of *bleu de ciel* wool cloth, costing 24 *francs* a metre
- 257.69 m of crimson wool cloth, first quality, costing 30.50 *francs*
- 403.30 m of crimson wool cloth, second quality, costing 25.50 *francs*
- 7.68 m of white wool cloth, first quality, costing 24 *francs* a metre
- 921.31 m of white wool cloth, second quality, costing 11.50 *francs* a metre
- 35.56 m of Saxony green wool cloth, costing 26 *francs* a metre
- 228 m of white milled *serge* at 1.60 *francs* a metre
- 151.25 m of white *tricot* at 3 *francs* a metre

The white wool of the first quality was, we suppose, for the *manteau* of a sub-officer. The use of the Saxony green wool cloth is not known. Could it be for grooms? Sub-officers did not undertake stable duties and were allowed grooms. Did the grooms get issued uniforms? Were they separate to the rank and file? We simply do not know the use of the green cloth. The white *tricot* and milled *serge* were undoubtedly used in the production of *vestes*.

Leather hides for the *pantalons-à-cheval* were obtained from M. Hugues, authorised by M. Pellechet, commissioner of war of the Imperial Guard. A total of 1,369 hides were obtained in 1813[30] and a further 607 in 1814.[31] M. Gerel, manufacturer of gloves and leather *calceons*, was contracted to supply 1,149 pairs of gauntlets, 1,500 pairs of white leather wrist gloves, and 974 *calceons* made from leather costing 8 *francs* a pair.[32]

Clothing was made by Master Tailor M. Koltz, the number of items, and cost to make per item, of the uniform made and delivered by 1 April 1814 was as follows:[33]

- 400 undress *kurtkas,* costing 3 *francs* each
- Twelve trumpeter's undress *kurtkas,* costing 3 *francs* each
- 500 *pantalons,* costing 1.95 *francs* a pair
- Twelve *pantalons* for trumpeters, costing 1.95 *francs* a pair
- 600 *pantalons-à-cheval,* costing 2.25 *francs* a pair
- 340 single-breasted waistcoats, costing 1.40 *francs* each
- 350 stable coats, costing 1.20 *francs* each
- Thirty *bonnets de police* for sub-officers, costing 50 *centimes* each
- 520 *bonnets de police* for other ranks, costing 50 *centimes* each
- Thirty *redingotes* for sub-officers, costing 3.10 *francs* each
- 150 *manteaux,* costing 2.60 *francs* each
- 150 hooks and eyes, costing 10 *centimes* each
- 512 leather foot straps for *pantalons,* costing 1 *centime* each
- 512 *voites,* costing 12 *centimes* each

The undress *kurtka* is a bit of an enigma. Clearly, it was different to the parade *kurtka*, but how was it different? Did it just have blue *revers* piped in crimson in the place of crimson, or did it have no silver lace?

Equipment

In spring 1814, 285 carbine lock covers, 130 bayonet scabbards and 450 lance straps were ordered.[34] Furthermore, ten trumpets costing 39 *francs* each were obtained from M. Reidlocker.[35] For footwear, M. Krewskie, master boot maker of the regiment, was employed to make 600 pairs of ankle boots, to be delivered by 1 April 1814 for the total cost of 11,400 *francs*.[36] A further 500 pairs were ordered from M. Fouchat for the total cost of 5,700 *francs*, again to be delivered by 1 April 1814.[37] For the boots, 450 pairs of spurs with straps were ordered from M. Courrier for the sum of 1,125 *francs*, along with 1,450 curb bits costing 8 *francs* each.[38] A further 200 curb bits were obtained from M. Hermivier.[39]

Above left: Trooper in full dress in a print by Martinet published in 1810, once the regiment had adopted the lance in 1809.

Above right: Martinet captures very well indeed the kettledrummer of the regiment. The *schabraque*, drums and banners, matching almost exactly to as shown by Martinet, can be found today in the Warsaw Army Museum, so we can be confident that the dress of the drummer was indeed as shown in the print.

Very little archive paperwork describes the leather equipment used. One of the few documents is from 1814, which tells us 840 *francs* was spent on 14 January 1814 for leather-work for the 1st Regiment, and 810 *francs* on leather-work for the 3rd *Èclaireurs*.[40]

Passamenteries

Passamenteries were supplied in 1814 by M. Hebert et Compagnie, of 14 rue St Fauvure, Paris, the order being overseen by Commissioner for War Odier:[41]

- 26.77 m of silver lace 34 mm wide
- 108.27 m of silver lace 22 mm wide
- 820.58 m of silver lace 14 mm wide
- 706.83 m of white wool lace 34 mm wide
- 193.78 m of white wool lace 14 mm wide

- 1,674.50 m of crimson wool lace 54 mm wide for *schabraques*
- 64.64 m of *ganse* in silver
- 1,227.80 m of white wool lace for *bonnets de police*
- 1,046.30 m of crimson wool lace
- Twenty-one silver and crimson wool tassels for sub-officer's *bonnets de police*
- 459 white wool tassels for other rank's *bonnets de police*
- 157 pairs of eagles
- 157 pairs of crowned 'N's
- 663.20 m of *soutache*

The white *soutache* was presumably used in the manufacture of either *bonnets de police* or the *czapka*. The document does not give a use for this material. As in 1811, it is clear sub-officers had crimson and silver tassels and silver lace on the *bonnet de police*, and other ranks had white lace, braid and tassels. The crimson lace was evidently for the *schabraque*. The trumpeter's *schabraque* used on parades had white lace, but none was purchased in 1813. Presumably, they were made once, and once only, we assume in 1810 as no trace of them being made in 1811 or 1812 can be found in the regiment's archive. Crucially, paperwork for 1810 is missing. M. Popard provided the regiment with *aiguillettes* and epaulettes:[42]

- Ten *aiguillettes* and epaulettes for sub-officers, costing 50 *francs* a set
- Fifteen *aiguillettes* and epaulettes for corporals, costing 13.50 *francs*
- 200 *aiguillettes* and epaulettes for corporals, costing 10 *francs*
- Thirty-five *czapka* cords for sub-officers, at 18 *francs* each
- 300 *czapka* cords for other ranks, at 1.90 *francs* each
- Fifteen *czapka* cords for trumpeters, at 7 *francs* each

As in 1811, we are at a loss in identifying the appearance for the corporal's *aiguillette* and epaulette. Was it white and silver in imitation of the sub-officers? Corporals are said to have had silver rank stripes, so silver and white would make sense for these distinctions, but no archive evidence exists to support this claim.

Petty equipment

Huge quantities of shirts were needed in winter 1813. M. Dupouvillon, of 13 rue Quincampoix, was contracted to supply:[43]

- 1,500 *czapka* covers in oil cloth
- 1,500 plume covers in oil cloth
- 715 lance pennant covers
- 715 lance pennants in taffeta
- 715 lance pennants in milled *serge*
- 1,948 shirts

Above left: Officer in full dress wearing blue *pantalons* in *lieu* of the crimson parade examples. The image nicely captures the elegance of this uniform.

Above right: Nicolas Hoffmann prepared this image in the autumn and winter of 1807, which was when the regiment first arrived in Paris. He captures very well the look of the uniform, even down to the use of wrist gloves and not gauntlets for parade dress, the crowned N and eagle on the *schabraque*. He also shows bastion loops on the *revers*, as does Martinet, along with the absence of collar lace. So it seems when first raised in French service, these bastion loops were worn on the *kurtka*, but replaced by c.1809 when the regiment converted to lancers from light horse.

A further 250 lance pennants in taffeta for parade use were obtained, also from M Dupouvillon, costing 4.20 *francs* each.[44] Some 500 *czapka* covers and 500 plume covers were ordered in spring 1814, again from M. Dupouvillon.[45] In winter 1813, 240 white plumes were ordered and a further 240 white plumes were ordered from M. Dufrenel, costing 3.50 *francs* each in spring 1814, with a further 600 being ordered to be delivered by 1 April 1814.[46] Buttons were ordered from M. Sauer, of Paris, comprising 21,576 large buttons for *pantalons-à-cheval*, 10,800 large buttons for the *kurtkas* and 3,612 medium buttons for the *kurtkas*.[47]

M. Gerel supplied 900 pairs of gloves costing 3.75 *francs* a pair in spring 1814.[48]

Harness

The regiment rode on light cavalry equipment. It comprised a Hungarian bridle, the same as used by the *chasseurs-à-cheval* of the Guard, but with tinned iron fittings. The saddle used was the wood arch Hungarian or hussar saddle. By the end of the empire the regiment also rode upon the French designed lancer saddle, adopted in 1811 for the use of the line lancers.

Under the saddle went a wool blanket to act as a *numnah*, of which 750 blankets were supplied in 1813 to measure Seven foot by six feet two inches, and to weigh 3 kg.[49] Saddles were ordered in 1814:[50]

- 112 French saddles, costing 67.50 *francs* each
- 213 wooden Hungarian saddles, costing 44.50 *francs* each
- 345 curb bridles, costing 10.60 *francs* each
- 326 black leather *bradoon* head pieces, costing 3.90 *francs* each
- 337 black leather head collars, costing 4.50 *francs* each
- 360 *surcingles* in black leather, costing 6 *francs* each
- 955 *schabraques,* costing 6.50 *francs* to make each
- Eleven *schabraques* for trumpeters, costing 6.50 *francs* to make each
- 225 carbine slings, buckets and straps, costing 3 *francs* each

Trumpeters[51]

According to the regimental orders of Dautancourt and the memoirs of Załuski, the *czapka* was crimson with mixed silver/white piping. All metal elements were as for troopers. *Czapka* cords were mixed silver/white. The *kurtka* and trousers were of crimson cloth with collar, lapels, cuffs, turnbacks, piping and trouser stripes in white cloth. The collar, cuffs and lapels were edged in silver braid *galon.* A white epaulette was worn on the left shoulder and an *aiguillette* on the right shoulder. These were constructed of blocked cord silver/white.

The trumpeter's *schabraque* was crimson edged in white braid with embroideries as for troopers in white thread. All belting was as for troopers. Trumpets were silvered with silver/white cords and tassels.

In the field and for everyday wear, the *czapka* was worn without a plume and cords and was encased in a black waxed cloth cover. The *kurtka* was the same as for *grande tenue,* but with the lapels crossed over to cover the white facing cloth. The crimson trousers were replaced with the blue service trousers fastened at the sides with metal buttons and lined in black leather.

In 1810, a white *czapka* was issued, edged in crimson cord with all fittings as for troopers. Around the body of the *czapka* was sewn a 35 mm *galon* braid in silver. All *czapka* cords and tassels were mixed silver/crimson. With the *czapka* was worn a crimson plume topped with a white tuft. The crimson *kurtka* was replaced by a white *kurtka* with all facings in crimson and edged in silver braid. This was also added to run around the buttonholes on the lapels of the *kurtka*.

A silver crimson mixed epaulette was worn on the right shoulder and a silver/crimson blocked *aiguillette* was worn on the left.

Crimson trousers with two white stripes on the outside of each leg were worn and for parade belts were white (some sources state silver with two crimson stripes). *Schabraques* were as used in the earlier period.

Kettledrummer[52]

In 1810 there was relative peace in Europe and in honour of the emperor's marriage to Marie Louise of Austria numerous fetes and parades were held in Paris.

It was at this time that in line with the tradition of the musicians of the Guard cavalry a kettledrummer or *timbalier* was added to the Polish Guard Lancers. His name was Louis Robiquet, a Frenchman, born in Lille on 25 February 1787. He joined the regiment on 1 February 1808 as a trumpeter and was selected to be the kettledrummer by Major Dautancourt on 1 July 1810, promoting him to the *petit etat-major*. He served in Spain in 1808 and Germany in 1809. He entered Russia in 1812, but was lost in the course of the retreat at Borissov. It is not certain if he was replaced by another kettledrummer following the retreat from Russia.

The regimental kettledrummer was dressed in Polish national costume. On his head he wore a Polish hat *konfederatka,* which had a crimson cloth top edged and piped in gold thread and a body of black lamb's wool. To the *konfederatka* were attached gold cords, tassels and white and crimson feathers. The Polish traditional tunic from the late fifteenth century known as the *zupan* was crimson with the cuffs, front fastening and collar in gold thread. Over the *zupan* was worn a white coat known as a *kontusz,* also edged in gold braid. The *kontusz* was fastened with a long sash that was of crimson silk with gold thread embroidery.

Light blue baggy Turkish trousers were worn. These had a strip of gold braid on each outside leg. The trousers tucked into tan brown boots. To complement his outfit the kettledrummer carried a Turkish *mameluke* sabre in a black scabbard with gold fittings.

The kettledrummer's horse and harness were just as elaborate. It is preserved in the Warsaw Museum. The saddlecloth or *dywdyk* was in crimson velvet and highly embroidered with classical vases and flowers in gold thread with a heavy gold fringe around its edge. It measured 1.50 m in length at its shortest side, 1.30 m at its centre and 1.60 m at its rear points. The saddle was of Turkish design, covered in crimson velvet with silver embroidery.

The horse wore a seventeenth-century Turkish headstall with gilded metal scales and a headband being turquoise with a jade centre and that was tassels at the sides and front with crimson fringes. The horses bit, also gilded, had *bossettes* (outer discs) with a central motif of an uncrowned imperial eagle surrounded by stars.

On his head the horse wore white and crimson feathers surrounding a central white plume.

The horse's breast-strap was also covered in gilded scales and large tassels in gold with crimson fringes. At both sides of the saddle were attached kettledrums made by the firm Riedlocker, in Paris. They were constructed from beaten brass sheet and were fitted with a metal band at the top for tightening the drum skins.

The first drum had a circumference of 50 cm and a depth of 40 cm, the second a circumference of 57 cm and a depth of 37 cm. On the inner base was a small hole to assist with the resonance of the drum.

On the outer base of each drum were engraved the make's details: *fait par riedlocker rue foin no. 4- Paris.*

There was also an inscription in Polish below the metal hoop that read *koty regimentu szwolezerow gwardii fracusko – polshiej* (regimental kettledrums of the Polish-French Guard Lancers). The kettledrums were covered in crimson velvet cloth that was heavily embroidered, measuring 1.19 m in length and 57 m wide. In the centre was a laurel leaf wreath within which was a gold eagle on a thunderbolt. Above the wreath was a white banner with the following inscription in black thread: *chevau legers polonais.*

Surrounding the wreath was a field of eighty-eight embroidered silver stars. The cover was edged in heavy gold thread embroidery comprising swirls and leaves with a large embroidered gold crown in each corner set at 45 degrees. At the edge of the cover was a wide gold braid border terminating in gold tassels.

Disbandment

With the first abdication, the Allies allowed Napoleon a bodyguard of 500 infantry, 120 cavalry and 120 artillerymen. The cavalry was formed almost exclusively from the Polish lancers, and those men who were not able to follow Napoleon returned to Poland and entered the service of the future Congressional Kingdom of Poland. The Elba Squadron was commanded by Major Jan Paweł Jerzmanowski and comprised two companies, each mustering six officers, eleven sub-officers, eight corporals, two trumpeters, one farrier and eighty-one troopers. Only twenty troopers were mounted.

At the start and end of the empire, the *grenadiers-à-cheval* were armed with light cavalry musketoons, carried from a shoulder belt. Here we see a trooper of the Corps Royal des *grenadiers-à-cheval* de France in late 1814. The uniform shown is the classic uniform of the regiment. The grey breeches were adopted in February 1813 for campaign use, as well as for parade use and stable dress. One can only begin to imagine how smelly and dirty these must have become.

The *chasseurs-à-cheval* were dressed in flamboyant Hussar dolmans. On campaign the elaborate hungarian breeches were replaced with cloth and leather *charivari* or riding trousers. The costly embroidered *Sabretache* on campaign had a leather cover to protect the embroidery from wear and dirt.

From 1813, when the regiment was rebuilt following the Russian campaign, the dress of the regiment underwent some radical changes. Grey broadcloth breeches replaced the doe hide breeches for all ranks. For non-commissioned officers and trumpeters, the habit was abolished in favour of the much cheaper single-breasted surtout we see here.

An integral part of the Consular and Imperial Guard since 1800, the mamelukes wore the most distinctive and elaborate uniform of any regiment during the Napoleonic wars.

Raised in Poland in 1807 as a regiment of Light Horse i.e. *chasseurs-à-cheval*, the regiment became lancer-armed in 1809. Their uniform was one of the most easily recognised in the French Army.

Formed in 1810, the Red Lancers, after the *mamelukes*, had one of the most distinctive and famous uniforms of any regiment of the French Army in the Napoleonic wars. The scarlet *kurtka* with mid-blue facings, set off with scarlet hungarian breeches in parade dress, literally led to the term 'Red Lancers'. On campaign, the hungarian breeches were replaced with blue *charivari*. From 1813, this type of leg wear was worn universally, for parade, camapaigns and stable dress.

CHAPTER 7

DUTCH LANCERS

The 1st Regiment of Dutch Hussars, disbanded by a decree of the King of Holland dated 16 June 1810, would have been joined by the Regiment of the Horse Guards when the imperial decree of 13 September came to incorporate the Royal Dutch Guard into the Imperial Guard.

The Regiment of Hussars was to form the 2nd Regiment of Light Horse Lancers of the Imperial Guard, more often known as 'The Red Lancers'. The corps arrived at Versailles at the end of August 1810. Organised the following month into four squadrons, it was completed by means of bodyguards and elements of the 3rd Dutch Hussars.

This organisation continued in 1811 and, on 17 February 1812, the regiment left Versailles for Hanover and from there towards the Niemen. A decree of 11 March 1812, had augmented the regiment by a 5th Squadron, formed partly by Frenchmen and partly by a squadron of hussars of the former Dutch Guard who had returned from Spain. The nominal strength of the corps was to have been 1,212 men, but on 1 September 1812, its effective strength was 1,406 men, of whom 171 were *velites*.

Re-constituted and formed into eight squadrons by the decree of 10 January 1813, it was increased to ten by a decree of the following 6 March. The five premier squadrons were of the Old Guard and the others of the Young Guard. The royal ordinance of 12 May 1814 reduced the regiment to four squadrons and gave them the name of the Royal Corps of Light Horse Lancers of France. This formation was dissolved by a decree of 8 April 1815. It was immediately re-formed with four squadrons under the name the Regiment of Light Horse Lancers of the Imperial Guard.

The regiment was dressed in the same manner as the Polish Lancers of the Guard, save that the blue *kurtka* was now scarlet faced in blue, and the *pantalons* became scarlet with two blue side stripes and a blue round woollen cord sewn onto the seam, as with the Polish lancers, to provide a narrow side stripe between the two large pieces of cloth. Yellow lace, cords and embroideries were identical to those of the Poles. The *czapka* was the same as the second model used by the Poles, 22 cm tall, and was covered in scarlet cloth with yellow lace. The dress of the new regiment, copied from that of the Polish light horse, had been issued at the end of July 1811 and worn for the first time at the review of 15 August 1811.

1811

When first created the regiment was clothed in the manner of *chasseurs-à-cheval*, only becoming dressed in the manner of the Polish lancers under the decree of

10 February 1811. The decree stated that new *kurtkas* were to be scarlet, like the *habit*, but to be faced in *bleu de ciel*. The decree clearly came at a time when the regiment was completing its *chasseur*-style uniform, as the decree made it clear that items in use were to be conserved until worn-out. So, we must imagine in 1811 that part of the regiment was dressed as lancers and another part as *chasseurs*. Despite the decree of February 1811, new items for the *chasseur* uniform were still ordered. The master workmen of the new lancers had all served since the regiment's formation on 21 September 1810:[1]

Nicholas Borsu was born at Waremme on 29 October 1772. He enlisted in September 1810 and was discharged on 22 October 1815 as the master tailor.

Joseph Wilmotte was born on 2 May 1779 at Voroux-Lez-Liers. Admitted as saddler in 1810, in 1813 he was appointed as master saddler. He was discharged on 22 October 1815.

It was Borsu who oversaw the production of uniforms at Versailles under the direction of Squadron Commander de Watteville.

In May 1811, a large order for headdress was placed with Chardon et Compagnie, of Paris:[2]

- Ninety-five *czapki* for sub-officers, costing 40 *francs* each
- 874 *czapki* for other-ranks, costing 32 *francs* each
- Five *chapeaux* for master workmen, costing 25 *francs* each
- Six *chapeaux* for regimental waggon drivers, costing 12 *francs* each
- One colpack for trumpet-major, costing 514 *francs* each
- 107 shakos, costing 13 *francs* each
- 992 white plumes and also white and black for *velites*, both with covers, costing 4.25 *francs* each
- 874 sets of *czapka* cords for corporals and troopers, costing 2 *francs* each
- 138 *czapka* covers, costing 3.30 *francs* each
- 138 lance pennants in silk taffeta, costing 5.25 *francs* each

Passamenteries came from Hebert, of Paris:[3]

- Ninety-five *czapka* cords for sub-officers, costing 15 *francs*
- One colpack cord for trumpet-major, costing 20 *francs*
- 107 sets of shako cords, costing 3.90 *francs*
- Twenty-seven sets of trumpet cords in wool, costing 7 *francs*
- Thirty-one sets of *aiguillettes* and trefoils in wool, costing 7.50 *francs*
- Two *aiguillettes* and trefoils for trumpeters, costing 35 *francs*
- 104 *aiguillettes* and epaulettes for sub-officers and trumpeters, costing 16 *francs* each
- 874 epaulettes for other ranks, costing 5 *francs*

- 970 pairs of crowned eagles embroidered in yellow wool, costing 2.50 *francs* a pair
- 200 yellow wool tassels for *bonnets de police*, costing 25 *centimes* each
- Two sets of brandenburgs with fringes

We propose that the *aiguillettes* and trefoils were destined for the *chasseur* uniform. The gold lace brandenburgs could have been applied to either the *chasseur*-style or lancer-style coat of the trumpet-major. For the *chasseur*-style uniform, we assume a braided hussar-style waistcoat was worn, as 10.80 m of square gold braid, 9.60 m of gold *soutache*, 43.20 m of gold and wool *soutache* and 54 m of square gold and wool braid were purchased. The sub-officers seem to have had mixed red and gold braid to the waistcoat. For the troopers, 350 m of square yellow wool braid were purchased. Also purchased in 1811 were pairs of hussar boots. Again, these were worn when the regiment was dressed in *habits*.[4] In a second order placed on 5 July to equip all men in the regiment with new clothing, no *soutache* or square braid was purchased, nor were trefoils, which confirm these items were only for the *chasseur* uniform.[5]

When first raised, the regiment seems to have had much lighter blue facings than in later years. The facing colour, it seems, became lighter in 1811. On 24 May 1811, three different qualities of *bleu de roi* wool cloth was purchased: 840 m costing 29 *francs* a metre, 1,280 m costing 27 *francs* a metre and a further 1,180 m of the same colour costing 20 *francs* a metre.[6] Was this cloth destined for *habits* or for new *kurtkas*? It is likely the *bleu fonce* was the same as the *bleu de ciel* listed in the February 1811 decree.

On 5 July 1811, 64.23 m of *bleu fonce* wool cloth costing 27.50 *francs* was purchased, along with 157.73 m of the same colour costing 29.75 *francs*, the latter clearly being of a higher quality. This cloth was certainly destined for the manufacture of *kurtkas*. For the *gilet d'ecurie*, two qualities of *bleu celeste* were purchased: 720 m at 14 *francs* and 106 m at 21 *francs* a metre. The trumpeters from the point of creation of the regiment wore white *kurtkas* faced in scarlet.[7] In 1812, the facing colour reverted back to *bleu de roi*, which was retained through to 1813, when *bleu fonce* was re-adopted. The light blue was only used for a very short period.

The colour *bleu de roi* was the facing colour of the 9th and 13th Hussars, which based on extant garments was notably a lighter blue than imperial blue, but not as light in tone as the *bleu de ciel* stated in the February 1811 decree, based on cloth samples preserved in the Musée d'Emperi, France.

Of interest, three qualities of iron-grey cloth were purchased in May 1811: 24 m costing 21.50 *francs* a metre, 35 m costing 19 *francs* a metre and 14 m costing 14 *francs* a metre. Eleven metres of black wool cloth costing 23 *francs* was also purchased. The use of this cloth is hard to assess without further archive material suggesting its use.[8] Given that in May 1811 hats for waggon drivers were

Above and opposite: This officer's *czapka* was worn by Captain Soufflot, who served in the regiment during the Waterloo campaign. It is no doubt representative of officers' *czapka* for the regiment. The 'N' on the sunray plate is missing, no doubt removed after the fall of the emperor in 1815, or perhaps in 1814. (Photograph and collection of Bertrand Malvaux)

ordered, and the equipment train, like the artillery train, wore iron-grey, it is very likely that this cloth was used in the production of clothing for the six regimental waggon drivers. The appearance of the dress is not known, however.

1812

It was only in 1812 that the regiment was entirely dressed in the manner of lancers and the *chasseur* uniforms presumably replaced. To do so, large orders for all types of material and equipment were placed.

Headdress

In spring 1812, M. Chardon, hatter, of Paris, was contracted to supply:[9]

- Twenty-nine *czapki* for sub-officers, costing 40 *francs*
- Twelve *czapki* for trumpeters, costing 410 *francs*
- 411 *czapki* for other ranks, costing 32 *francs* each
- 450 *czapka* covers at 3.30 *francs* each
- 438 plumes and covers, costing 4.25 *francs*
- Twelve plumes and covers for trumpeters, costing 4.25 *francs*
- 450 lance pennants with covers, costing 5.25 *francs*
- 450 lance pennants in milled *serge* (*blicourt*) with covers costing 3 *francs* each
- 411 *czapka* cords for other ranks, costing 2 *francs* each

Clothing

A vast quantity of wool cloth was ordered from Messrs Muraine et Leface, clothiers, of 14 rue des Bourdonnais, Paris, on 21 March 1812 to provide:[10]

- 657 m of scarlet wool cloth at 31 *francs* a metre
- 720 m of scarlet wool cloth at 28.50 *francs* a metre
- 591 m of scarlet wool cloth at 23 *francs* a metre
- 445 m of *bleu de roi* wool cloth, dyed in the thread, at 29.75 *francs* a metre
- 993 m of *bleu de roi* wool cloth, dyed in the thread, at 27.50 *francs* a metre
- 3,160 m of *bleu celeste* wool cloth at 14 *francs* a metre
- 980 m of *bleu celeste* wool cloth, dyed by the piece, at 20 *francs* a metre
- 22 m of white wool cloth for trumpeters at 27 *francs* a metre
- 87 m of yellow wool cloth at 21 *francs* a metre.

For lining of newly made items of uniform, M. Destrot, clothier, of Paris, was contracted on 21 March 1812 to provide:[11]

- 1,606 m of linen, blondine quality, at 1.64 *francs* a metre
- 2,791 m of ecru linen at 1.54 *francs* a metre
- 215 m of strong linen at 1 *franc* a metre
- 3,291 m of *treillis*, Alençon quality, at 1.98 *francs* a metre

Buttons and brass work were purchased off M. Mionet, of 16 Rue de St Martin, Paris:[12]

- 959 dozen buttons, size one, at 30 *centimes* a dozen
- 783 dozen buttons, size two, at 25 *centimes* a dozen
- 170 dozen buttons, size three, at 20 *centimes* a dozen
- 1,500 dozen buttons, size four, at 48 *centimes* a dozen
- 1,350 dozen bone buttons at 5 *centimes* a dozen
- 450 sets of hooks for *manteaux* at 50 *centimes* a dozen
- 450 buckles at 25 *centimes* each

Presumably, the size one buttons were solid cast for the sides of the *pantalons-à-cheval*, the three other sizes corresponding with large, medium and small for the *kurtka*, *veste* and *gilet d'ecurie*.

M. Fossey, leather merchant, supplied 450 leather hides for the *pantalons-à-cheval* and *schabraques*.[13]

Passamenteries:
Lace and braid was obtained from M. Hebert, of Paris:[14]

- 33 m of gold lace 22 mm wide
- 130 m of gold lace 12 mm wide
- 27 m of round gold cording
- 2,807 m of wool lace 54 mm wide at 1.30 *francs* a metre
- 450 m of wool lace 32 mm wide, costing 90 *centimes* a metre
- 3,005 m of wool lace 22 mm wide at 55 *centimes* a metre
- 137 m of wool lace 12 mm wide at 30 *centimes* a metre
- 450 tassels in wool, costing 25 *centimes* each
- 600 m of round wool yellow cording at 5 *centimes* a metre
- 900 m of round wool blue cording at 5 *centimes* a metre
- 66 m of (illegible) lace for *schabraques*
- Twenty-seven sets of *czapka* cords for sub-officers at 15 *francs* a set
- Twelve sets of *czapka* cords for trumpeters at 15 *francs* a set
- Twenty-seven *aiguillettes* for sub-officers at 18 *francs* each
- Twelve *aiguillettes* for trumpeters at 18 *francs* each
- Twenty-seven epaulettes for sub-officers at 16 *francs*
- Twelve epaulettes for trumpeters at 16 *francs*
- 411 *aiguillettes* for other ranks, costing 7 *francs* each
- 411 epaulettes for other ranks, costing 2.25 *francs*
- Twelve waist, belts for trumpeters, costing 42 *francs* each
- Twelve trumpet cords, costing 36 *francs* each
- Twelve trumpet banners, costing 135 *francs* each
- Twelve trumpet cords in wool costing 7 *francs*

- 1,200 *gibernes* and *giberne* belts, line pattern, costing 14 *francs* each
- Sixty *gibernes* and belts for trumpeters costing 102 *francs* each
- 1,500 *bradoon* headpieces in yellow lace, costing 6 *francs* each
- 1,224 carbine belts with *surpicquer* stitching, costing 14 *francs* each
- 1,100 carbine belts, line pattern, costing 12.50 *francs* each
- Sixty trumpeter's waist belts or girdles, costing 12 *francs* each
- 2,500 sword knots, costing 1.10 *francs* each
- 1,250 black sheepskins garnished and lined, including sixty in white for trumpeters, costing 22 *francs* each
- 1,250 black sheepskins to be sewn to cloth *schabraques* as seat covers, costing 10.50 *francs*
- 2,200 lance straps, costing 1 *franc* each
- 2,500 sets of braces, costing 1.50 *francs* each
- 5,000 nose bags and straps, costing 1 *franc* each
- 2,500 forage ropes with iron rings, costing 1.10 *francs* each
- 2,500 body brushes, costing 2.80 *francs* each
- 2,500 curry combs, costing 1.40 franc each
- 1,900 shoe pouches, costing 2.90 *francs* each
- 2,250 carbine lock covers, costing 3.25 *francs* each
- 2,500 bayonet frogs, costing 3.50 *francs*
- 2,440 *schabraques* in cloth, costing 8.50 *francs* each to make
- Sixty *schabraques* for trumpeters with *galon a systeme*, costing 9 *francs* each to make
- 2,500 *porte-manteaux*, costing 2.50 *francs* each to make
- 2,500 sponges, costing 1.10 *francs* each
- 2,000 water bridles, bit and reins, costing 4.50 *francs* each
- 2,500 wooden combs, costing 35 *centimes* each
- 200 stable head collars and lead ropes in *cuir de hongre* (i.e. Alum-tanned buff), costing 4.50 *francs*
- 2,200 pistol lanyards

It is clear from the tariff that the cloth *schabraque* in some instances had a sheepskin cover sewn to the seat area. It also seems that the sheepskins that were lined and had a garnish no doubt around the edge just like the sheepskin *schabraque* of cuirassiers, dragoons, hussars and chasseurs were able to be used as *schabraques* in their own right. Were these reserved for the Young Guard squadrons who received the line pattern equipment? Perhaps so, as it is a logical conclusion to make. The painter, Gericault, shows the trumpeter with a scarlet cloth *schabraque* with white false seat, so clearly they could be used as a cover to the cloth *schabraque* and on their own as a sheepskin *schabraque* we assume. For the *schabraques*, sixty pairs of embroidered crowned eagles were purchased for use by the trumpeters, costing 29 *francs* each, and 2,440 eagles embroidered in yellow wool for sub-officers and other ranks for 5 *francs* a pair. Other rank's *schabraques* still had a double row of lace, one 22 mm wide, and the other 54 mm wide. Presumably, trumpeter's *schabraques* still had gold lace. Certainly, the *schabraque* never had in the front corner a crowned 'N' device like the Polish lancers.

Winter 1813-4

Following the arduous 1813 campaign, the regiment had to be re-built again from new entrants and totally re-equipped.

Headdress

Items of headdress purchased in 1814 were as follows:[23]

- Eighty *czapki* for sub-officers, costing 43.30 *francs* each
- 824 *czapki* for other ranks, costing 32 *francs* each
- 1,200 *czapka* covers, costing 3.30 *francs*
- 960 sets of other rank's *czapka* cords, costing 2 *francs* each
- 1,350 plumes and covers, costing 4.25 *francs*
- 476 lance pennants in silk taffeta with covers, costing 5.25 *francs* each
- 476 lance pennants in milled *serge* with covers, costing 3 *francs* each
- Four laced *chapeaux* for master workmen, costing 25 *francs* each

Clothing

Ordered on 3 November 1813 was the following amount of cloth for the manufacture of uniforms:[24]

- 10 m of scarlet at 31 *francs* a metre
- 58.35 m of scarlet wool cloth at 28.50 *francs* a metre
- 395.50 m of scarlet wool cloth at 23 *francs* a metre
- 10.50 m of *bleu fonce* wool cloth, costing 29.75 *francs* a metre
- 307.05 m of *bleu fonce* wool cloth, costing 27.50 *francs* a metre
- 734.18 m of *blue fonce* wool cloth, costing 20 *francs* a metre
- 1,921.78 m of *bleu celeste* wool cloth, costing 14 *francs* a metre
- 26.94 m of white wool cloth, costing 27.50 *francs*
- 33.95 m of ecru wool cloth, costing 13 *francs*

The white wool cloth would have been bleached white, whereas the ecru wool cloth was in essence fleece-coloured, i.e. an off-white. The bleached white was destined for trumpeter's *kurtkas*. Was this also the destination of the ecru wool cloth? A contract dated 1 May 1813 is for the production of a *capote-manteau* in white wool cloth for 95.58 *francs* and a single waist-belt, in *system d'or,* costing 42 *francs*.[25] Therefore, it seems highly plausible that the ecru cloth was used in the production of similar garments in 1814.

Above and opposite: This excellently preserved trooper's *czapka* is no doubt representative of the *czapka* used by the regiment. The lace to the body of the *czapka* masks the join between the cloth-covered cardboard pavilion and the leather headband. (Photograph and collection of Bertrand Malvaux)

The purchase of cloth was overseen by M. Boulles, commissioner for war of the Imperial Guard. The cloth was procured from M. Sage Muraine, clothier, of Paris:[26]

- 986 m of scarlet wool cloth, costing 28.50 *francs* a metre
- 774 m of scarlet wool cloth, costing 23 *francs* a metre
- 2,677 m of *bleu fonce* wool cloth, costing 27.50 *francs* a metre
- 6,090 m of *bleu celeste* wool cloth, dyed in the thread, costing 14 *francs* a metre
- 2,892 m of *bleu fonce* wool cloth, dyed by the piece, costing 20 *francs* a metre
- 30 m of white wool cloth, costing 27.59 *francs* a metre

In neither purchase account is there any yellow wool cloth destined for the piping on the *porte-manteaux*. Was this feature no longer used in 1814?

Buttons were supplied by M. Mionet, of 5 rue de Saint Martin, Paris:[27]

- 5,465 dozen buttons, size one, at 30 *centimes* a dozen
- 3,940 dozen buttons, size two, at 25 *centimes* a dozen
- 560 dozen buttons, size three, at 20 *centimes* a dozen
- 6,346 dozen buttons, size four, at 48 *centimes* a dozen
- 5,462 dozen bone buttons at 5 *centimes* a dozen.

Black leather hides for the rubbing panels on the cloth *schabraque* and for the *pantalons-à-cheval* were purchased from M. Fossey, leather dealer, of Paris, who provided 1,100 hides at a cost of 7.75 *francs* each.[28] Even in the hasty improvision of 1814, 1,000 handkerchiefs were obtained from M. Berard, as well as 1,000 shirts, 1,000 white stocks, 100 pairs of *calceons*, 1,200 *sac a distribution*, 1,000 forage ropes and 2,000 nose bags that doubled up as grooming kit-holders from M. Destrot, of Paris.[29]

Equipment

M. Gerel, of 8 rue de Echelle, Paris, glover and breeches-maker, supplied 1,175 pairs of gauntlets.[30] In addition, 736 pairs of boots were supplied by M. Gaignaison, master boot-maker, for 18 *francs* a pair.[31]

Harness and saddlery

Master Saddler Wilmotte was contracted to provide:[32]

- 1,500 saddles complete for 91.56 *francs* each
- 1,500 bridles, costing 13.10 *francs* each
- 1,130 head collars and lead ropes, costing 5.50 *francs*
- 1,500 curb bits and *bradoons,* costing 6 *francs* for the two
- 500 *surcingles* and girths, costing 1.60 *francs*

- 1,050 waist-belts, costing 10.40 *francs*
- 1,015 *gibernes* and belts for 12.50 *francs* per set
- 1,064 carbine belts, costing 12.50 *francs* complete with hook and straps
- Thirty trumpeter's waist-belts, costing 12 *francs*
- 626 other rank's sword knots, costing 1.10 *francs*
- 1,500 black sheepskins for false saddle seats, costing 10.50 *francs* each
- 653 sets of sword slings, costing 1.50 *francs* each
- 1,000 shoe pouches, costing 2.90 *francs* each
- 1,500 *schabraques,* costing 8.50 *francs* to make
- 1,100 *porte-manteaux,* costing 2.50 *francs* to make

Disbandment

The Royal Corps of Light Horse Lancers of France needs to be seen as a new formation as opposed to a continuation of the former 2nd Regiment of Light Horse Lancers of the Imperial Guard. It was the most thoroughly purged regiment of the former Guard, and the new corps had little to do with its predecessor. The corps' new organisation was set as follows on 4 August 1814:[33]

One colonel with three horses, one major with three horses, two squadron commanders each with two horses, two adjutant-majors each with two horses, one lieutenant-quartermaster with one horse, one standard-bearer with one horse, one surgeon major with one horse, one assistant surgeon with one horse, two adjutant-sub-officers each with one horse, one master veterinarian with one horse, one second-class veterinarian with one horse, one corporal-trumpeter, one tailor, one saddler, one boot-maker and one armourer.

Each of the eight companies was to comprise:[34] one captain, one first-lieutenant, two second-lieutenants, one sergeant-major, four sergeants, one quartermaster-corporal, eight corporals, two trumpeters, forty mounted troopers, sixteen dismounted troopers and two farriers.

The following officers were discharged from the regiment, or returned to the Netherlands:[35]

Surgeon-major: Mergell, Steenis

Captain instructor: van Balveren

Squadron commander: Post

Captain: Bocher, Royen

First-lieutenants: Baumann, Brietenbach, de Bellefroid, de Groot, Eschweiler, Gisser, Leutner, Omphal, Spiers, Stutterheim, Ziegler

Second-lieutenants: Bazin, Barth, Bidault-Corness, Breedenabch, Chomel, de Jongh, Hoevenaar, Jouet, Lasage, Leutner, Mareilhac, Retterich, Spies, Le Sueur, Van de Linden, Veldhuys, Verhaegen, Vermaesen, Werner, Willich, Ziegler.

Placed on half-pay were:[36]

Squadron commander: de Briqueville, de Tiecken

Surgeon-major: Hennige

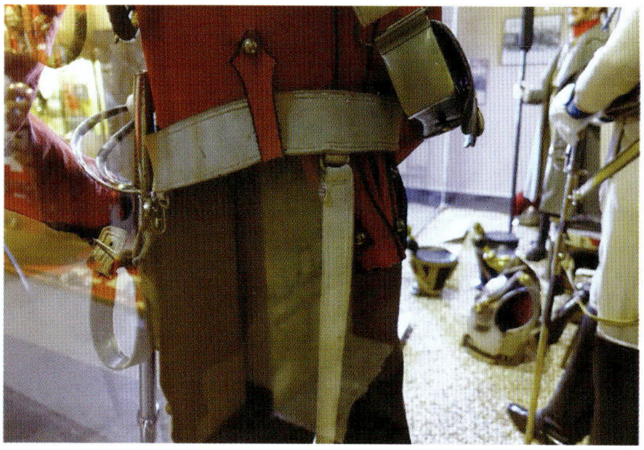

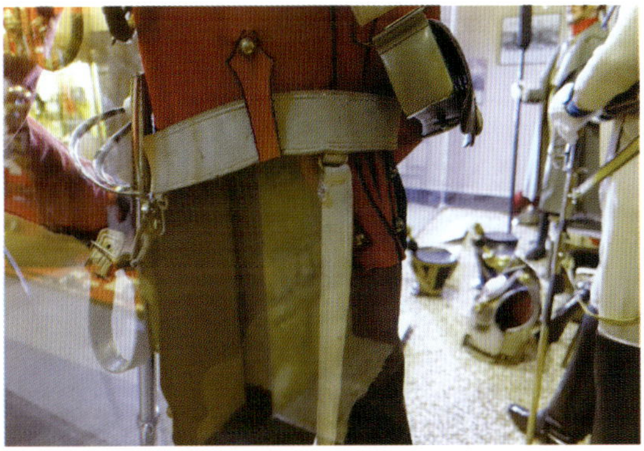

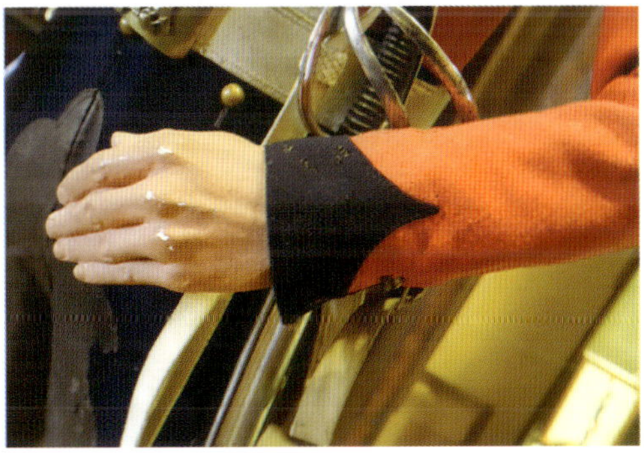
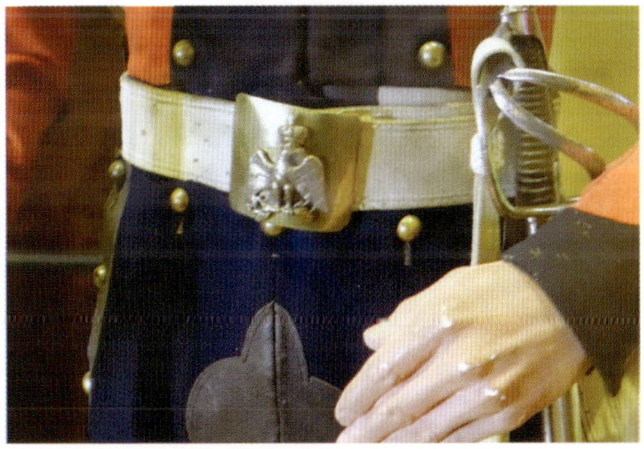

Above and opposite: This well preserved *kurtka* matches in nearly all respects the other preserved *kurtka* for the regiment. The *kurtka* dates to before 1813, when two small additional buttons appeared at the base of the tail facings. *Kurtkas* were not worn in the campaign of 1812, in their place, the stable coat was worn on the campaign. We also see details of the under-arm loop and button to support the waistbelt. The *giberne* has brass flanks with grenade plate, which may indicate that this item is actually from the *grenadiers-à-cheval*, or even line *carabiniers* rather than belonging to the Red Lancers, who seem to have used eagle plates on the *giberne* like the 1st regiment. Archive documents do not actually tell us what the plate was, so it is not impossible a grenade was used. The *porte-giberne* is as one would assume for a guard light cavalry regiment. Brass flanked *gibernes* were traditionally used by trumpeters and *sous-officiers*. No doubt it has been added to the figure to give a complete impression of the uniform. (Musée de l'Empéri, Collections du Musée de l'armée, Anciennes collections Jean et Raoul Brunon)

Above and opposite: This *kurtka* is housed in Les Invalides. It is an excellent example of the *kurtka* used by the regiment. It dates to the period 1813 to 1815 as the bottom of each tail carries a small button, which we know from archive sources was added in March 1813. (Musée de l'armée)

Captain: Salvetat
Lieutenant: Collins de Ham
Second-lieutenant: Dejean, Delaizement, Lannoy.

Without the men of the Young Guard, the Royal Corps of Light Horse Lancers of France would cease to exist. With the reduction in size of the cavalry regiments of the former Imperial Guard, it allowed a number of officers and sub-officers to be retained and passed to the Royal Corps of Lancers of France. The Young Guard squadrons were distributed to the light horse lancer regiments of the line.

To the 3rd Regiment of Light Horse Lancers, renamed the Light Horse Lancers of the Dauphin, were transferred five officers along with eighty-two sub-officers and men. Also transferred were their horses, noted as being very mediocre. The clothing and harness was, however, noted to be in good condition.[37]

To the 4th Regiment of Light Horse Lancers, two squadrons of the former Young Guard lancers who were based at Angers were transferred. This comprised twelve officers with twenty horses and 180 sub-officers and troopers. Of the troopers, thirty-nine deserted and ten were sent home before they joined their new regiment.[38] The regiment required 282 men to bring it up to full strength. General Pully noted on 11 August 1814 that the regiment needed one veterinarian, three sergeants, one corporal-quartermaster, thirty-one corporals and 246 troopers. Also required were four sub-lieutenants as temporary appointments until serving officers were returned as prisoners-of-war. One hundred and twenty seven horses were also needed.[39] Of the two squadrons sent to join the regiment from the Young Guard Regiment of Light Horse Lancers, the destination regiment had no items of clothing for them and they arrived at the regiment with their clothing in terrible condition. It was a matter of urgency General Pully noted to clothe and feed them. The spirit of the officers and men was good, and in time they would become fond of the regiment they had been taken into.[40]

Other elements of the former Young Guard were passed to the 5th Regiment of Light Horse Lancers, notably the former 15th and 20th Companies.[41] One such officer of the 8th Squadron was Adolphe Herval. He was born on 29 January 1794 at Voust. Admitted to the military school at Saint-Germain on 18 February 1812, he graduated as a second-lieutenant into the 2nd Regiment of Light Horse Lancers of the Imperial Guard on 18 March 1813. Admitted to the 5th Regiment of Line Lancers on 6 June 1814, he was admitted into the Regiment of Light Horse Lancers of the Imperial Guard on 14 April 1815.

The men remaining in the original five squadrons formed the nucleus for the new Royal Corps. On 24 April 1814, these five squadrons mustered thirty-two officers, 352 sub-officers and men with 418 horses. By 2 August 1814, the Royal Corps mustered thirty-two officers and 482 sub-officers and other ranks, the increase being due the detachment at Douai of fifty men and 113 horses. Of the needed fifty officers, the Royal Corps lacked twenty-two, namely four captains, eight first-lieutenants and ten second-lieutenants. Of the required 617 sub-officers and men, 482 were present. There was a shortfall of one sergeant-major, 162 troopers and sixteen cadet trumpeters. The regiment had one officer and forty-four men surplus, namely one major, one sergeant-veterinarian, ten sergeants, five corporal-quartermasters and twenty-eight corporals. Of these, one officer and seventeen men were removed. A further seven officers were with the regiment awaiting re-assignment. This shortfall of men was to be made up with a draft of deserving men from the line. Of the 597 horses, 104 were declared unfit and were sold or put down.[42] However, after the removal of the non-French officers, the regiment had barely any left.

The remaining officers with the regiment were as follows:[43]

Staff:

Major: Dubois
Major supernumerary: Brousse
Squadron commanders: Coti, de Tiecken, de Briqueville, Trentinian
First-lieutenant-adjutant-major: Delafargue, de Steurs, Chappat
Second-lieutenant-adjutant-major: Bisaux
Adjutant-sub-officers: Gouat, Gondre
Quartermaster: Dufour, Seran.

Company officers:[44]

Captains: de Brack, de Duranti, Gauthier, de Potier
First-lieutenants: Doyen

Above left: Officer of the Red Lancers in parade dress by Aaron Martnet. The close similarity in the uniform, bar colours, to the Polish lancers is very evident.

Above right: Trooper of the Red Lancers in parade dress in a print published in Paris in 1812.

Second-lieutenants: Arnaud, Boudgout, Dejean, Gourel, Hayot, Lethuillier, Reckinger, Vincent.

In order to make up the shortfall of officers, many now redundant officers of the former Imperial Guard were sent to the regiment. In total, twenty-five officers from the Guard and one from the line were transferred to the corps. Article four of the ordinance of 21 June 1814 stated that no officer who had been appointed after 19 March 1813 or the Young Guard were not to be retained in the new Royal Corps. However, it seems that the officers sent from the *grenadiers* and *chasseurs-à-cheval*, as well as the majority of retained officers from the 2nd Regiment of Light Horse Lancers, had all been appointed after 19 March 1813 or served in the Young Guard. Clearly, this article of the decree was flouted in order to retain deserving officers within the Royal Corps. It also seems that the edict to remove non-French offices was also overlooked in the case of Italian officers and those from the *mamelukes*.[45]

Of the regiment's fifty-two officers, seventeen came from the former 2nd Regiment of Light Horse Lancers, fifteen from the former *chasseurs-à-cheval* of the Imperial Guard, twelve from the former *grenadiers-à-cheval*, three from the *mamelukes*, two from the 1st Regiment of Scouts of the Imperial Guard, one from the line and one from the Guards of Honour, thus thirty-eight percent of the officers had been with the 2nd Regiment of Light Horse Lancers of the Imperial Guard.[46]

The regiment lacked men, horses, clothing and equipment. Marshal Ney, on 2 August 1814, noted that the regiment had thirty-two officers and 482 men. The report stated that:[47]

> Uniforms and equipment, etc.
> Uniforms: shabby and irregular. Clothing needs much repair. Moreover, it is very incomplete and lacks all uniformity since the regiment has received soldiers from various units – the Guards of Honour etc – who have not been issued with full lancer uniforms,
>
> Equipment: that of the troops also needs repairing and its amount is insufficient. The minor equipment is complete. That for the horses is, like the men's major equipment, insufficient.
>
> Armament: the unit is short one hundred carbines, 269 pistols and twelve lances. The arms are in good condition.
>
> Stores: there are no uniforms, nor materials for their manufacture, with the exception of some shakos. There is very little equipment, and the quantity of harness is very low.
>
> Horses: the standard of the horses is very poor; their numbers exceed that of the lancers.

The new Royal Corps of Light Horse Lancers of France had the following items of uniform and equipment upon formation. It was to retain the uniform of its proceeding formation:[48]

ITEM	*ITEMS IN SERVICE*	*IN NEED OF REPAIR*	*IN NEED OF IMMEDIATE REPLACEMENT*	*IN NEED OF REPLACEMENT IN ONE YEAR*	*ITEMS MISSING*
Czapki	245	89	27	45	150
Czapka covers	200	13	85	49	269
Czapka cords	297	3	8	13	182
Plumes and covers	186	4	36	14	292
Chapeaux for adjutants	3	0	0	0	0

ITEM	*ITEMS IN SERVICE*	*IN NEED OF REPAIR*	*IN NEED OF IMMEDIATE REPLACEMENT*	*IN NEED OF REPLACEMENT IN ONE YEAR*	*ITEMS MISSING*
Kurtkas	133	60	181	30	289
Surtouts for adjutants	3	0	0	0	0
Aiguillettes and epaulettes	176	10	125	7	296
Redingotes (stable coat used in their place) for sub-officers and trumpeters	11	7	14	12	52
Sleeved overcoats	215	71	11	36	196
Hungarian breeches	3	2	11	0	477
Riding trousers	129	55	144	51	298
Stable caps	277	22	83	11	183
Stable coats	181	26	94	16	192
Stable trousers	159	9	40	6	257
Underwear	320	0	0	0	162

Sadly, we are ignorant of any items made for the corps during the First Restoration or any items produced during the Hundred Days campaign, as the paperwork has not survived that the author has been able to locate in the French Army Archives in Paris.

CHAPTER 8

LITHUANIAN LANCERS AND TATARS

On 23 June 1812, the Grande Armée crossed the River Niemen, which separated Poland from Lithuania, heading towards Vilna (now Vilnius), the capital of the Grand Duchy of Lithuania. Filled with hope for the restoration of a fully independent Poland, the Polish Diet in Warsaw jumped the gun and proclaimed unilaterally the restoration of the Kingdom of Poland, uniting the Grand Duchy of Warsaw with the Grand Duchy of Lithuania. The confederation of Poland named Prince Adam Czartoryski as president. This had not been done with Napoleon's blessing for fear of alienating the tsar with whom he wished to conclude a peace. Napoleon had promised the Poles that he would create an independent state, the Duchy of Warsaw being an interim measure. This action guaranteed an army of loyal Poles, but enraged Alexander and his nobles, who demanded that Napoleon abandon the duchy. Poland was important to Napoleon, as it created a buffer between the empire and Russia. However, this act had an even worse effect on Lithuanian landowners, who were uneasy about an association with Poland and Napoleon's threat to free the serfs, and whose support he needed for the invasion of Russia. Napoleon himself kept the issues cloudy, neither recognising the Kingdom of Poland beyond its status as a grand duchy, nor squelching Polish or Lithuanian national aspirations.[1]

Indeed, Napoleon actively encouraged them. On 1 July Napoleon created a temporary government for the Grand Duchy of Lithuania as well as raising a national guard of two battalions and a police force of gendarmerie at Vilna, Grodno, Minsk and Byalistock. Both organisations were to be uniformed like the Poles. Napoleon also authorised the creation of another regiment of lancers, recruited from wealthy Lithuanian landowners, and honoured them by admitting the regiment to his Imperial Guard as the 3rd Regiment of Light Horse Lancers. Napoleon explained that 'by paying the light horse the same as my Guard, I intend to procure educated and experienced horsemen, and no peasants who need polishing, which would be a lengthy operation'. At the same time a regiment of Tatars was also raised. With the formation of two Lithuanian regiments attached to his Guard, Napoleon was attempting to establish political support among the conquered western provinces of Russia. Such political support would minimise the threat to his lines of communication across this conquered territory, as well as encourage the recruitment of new troops for his cause. On 5 July, Napoleon signed a decree to form a regiment for the French Imperial Guard from Lithuanian volunteers. This regiment became the 3eme Regiment des Chevau-legers-Lancier (light horse lancers). The regiment was to consist of five squadrons of two companies each for a total of 1,280 men (sixty-two officers and 1,218 enlisted men). However, only four squadrons were formed.[2]

Very few items of clothing and equipment exist from this most enigmatic regiment. This headdress is one of the few that which does. The body of the headdress was original covered in amaranth cloth with a green bag laced in gold. (George Lubomski)

Other ranks' headdress preserved in a private collection. (Private Collection Switzerland)

Major General Konopka, of the 1ere Regiment des Chevau-Legers-Lancier de la Garde Impériale, was named colonel of the newly formed regiment.[3] On 19 October, the regiment was suddenly attacked in Slonim by Russian General Chaplitz and was completely destroyed. General Konopka, thirteen officers and 253 men were captured. The only survivors came from its depot. The paperwork for the regiment was fire damaged in 1944 and is heavily water-stained. What paperwork that exists is mostly illegible. On 22 March 1813, the regiment was disbanded into the 1st Polish Lancers of the Guard. The new regiment was to comprise six squadrons each of two companies.[4]

Lithuanian Tatars

The squadron was formed on 24 August 1812 from Muslim nobles. The idea for the unit was proposed in July of that year to one of the emperor's *aides-de-camp*, General Count Van Hogendorp, then governor-general of the grand duchy.[5] By 30 August 1812, a squadron of thirty Tatars, commanded by Captain Samuel Murza Utan, were at the headquarters in Potsdam.[6] On 22 March 1813, Marshal Bessières incorporated the squadron of the Lithuanian tartars, now reduced to fifty men and three officers, into the debris of the 3rd Regiment of Lancers of the Guard. At the same time the 3rd Guard Light Horse was disbanded and the remnants became the 7th Squadron of the 1st Polish Lancers. The tartars became the 15th Company. On 16 April 1813, the squadron still only mustered thirty men.[7] The strength of the tartar squadron was recorded at twenty-four men on 22 June 1813, and at twenty-six tartars on 11 July, of which six still wore the old uniforms. Fifty men and three officers were recorded present at the Battle of Dresden on

27 August 1813. As a consequence of the re-organisation of 9 December 1813, the last eight companies of the 1st Lancers became the 3rd *Éclaireurs*. This regiment was placed under the overall command of its colonel, General Count Kraśinski. The squadron commander of the 3rd *Éclaireurs* was Major Jean Kozietulski. It was as scout lancers that the Lithuanian tartars fought the campaign of France. As well as incorporating the Tatars, fifteen officers and eighty-two other ranks of the Polish battalion were transferred to the 3rd *Éclaireurs*.[8]

One of the very few documents to exist concerning the squadron is a from 1814 authorising the production of sixty-five *schabraques* costing 55 *francs* each and sixty-five *surcingles* costing 6 *francs* each.[9] Furthermore, M. Chardon, hatter, of Paris, provided seventy *tatares* hats at 27 *francs* each according to a document from spring 1814.[10] The following items of clothing were produced by M. Kotz, master tailor, of the 1st Polish Lancers, for the agreed sums listed below:[11]

- Seventy *vestes manche dit spencer* at 3 *francs*
- Seventy *vestes sans manche dit keibik,* costing 3.50 *francs*
- Seventy *pantalons de tatares,* costing 9 *francs*
- Seventy *pantalons de route,* costing 2.55 *francs*

It is very likely that the 35.56 m of Saxony green wool cloth, costing 26 *francs* a metre, purchased from M. Barbaud, clothier, of Paris, in January 1814 was destined for the unit.[12]

CHAPTER 9

ÉCLAIREURS

The *éclaireurs* of the Guard was a corps of cavalry *éclaireurs* of the French Imperial Guard, which included three cavalry regiments created by Napoleon when he re-organised the Imperial Guard following the disaster of the 1812 campaign in Russia. The corps was created in Article one of the decree of 4 December 1813. The 1st Regiment was divided into the Old Guard and Young Guard squadrons, with the first two wearing a uniform of the hussars and the others wearing a *habit-kinski* similar to the *chasseurs-à-cheval* of the line. All three regiments were organised into four squadrons with 250 sabres in two companies each. Due to insufficient recruits, an appeal was made for volunteers from the cavalry of the line, and 1,005 troopers were eventually added to the regimental rolls. Although half of the *éclaireurs* were armed with 2.75 m long lances issued in 1812 to the line regiments, and the rest with carbines, the regiments were rarely employed as lancers in battle. The decree of 9 December read:[1]

> Title one
> Organisation of the cavalry.
>
> Article 1.
> There is to be created in the cavalry of the Guard three regiments of *éclaireurs-à-cheval*, the first to be attached to the *grenadiers-à-cheval*, to be under the orders of the colonel of the *grenadiers-à-cheval* and their administrative council will administer the regiment.
>
> The 2nd Regiment is to be attached to the dragoons, it will be under the orders of the colonel of the dragoons and will be administered by the administrative council of the dragoons.
>
> The 3rd Regiment will be attached to the 1st Regiment of Lancers, commanded and administered by that regiment.
>
> Article 3.
> The regiments of *grenadiers-à-cheval*, dragoons, *chasseurs* and the 2nd Lancers will retain their current organisation, the 1st Regiment of Lancers will be organised in according to the table attached to this decree.
>
> Title 2
> Recruitment
>
> Article 4.
> There will be chosen from among each of the regiments of guards of honour 200 men to complete the regiments of cavalry of the Guard.

Thirty men will be destined to complete the regiment of *grenadiers-à-cheval*, they must be over five foot 5.5 inches.

Thirty men will be sent to the dragoons, to measure five foot four inches.

One hundred and forty men to the 2nd Regiment of lancers to measure five foot 1.5 inches.

The chosen 200 men from each of the regiments of guards of honour will be sent to Paris, where they will be clothed and mounted in their new regiments.

Article 5.
Furthermore, each of the four regiments of guards of honour will supply 250 men to enter the 1st Regiment of *Éclaireurs*, they will be sent dismounted to Paris carrying their arms and uniforms.

The 2nd Regiment of *Éclaireurs* will be formed from the '*postillions* of the empire'. The minister of finances will create a report to be sent to the mayors of those men to be sent to Paris.

The 3rd Regiment of *Éclaireurs* to be created by the taking the surplus dismounted men of the 1st Regiment of Lancers not placed in the new organisation, and from the 800 Polish solders at the depot at Sedan, the men to be '*bonne volonte*' and have long experience in the French service.

These 800 men will be sent to Givet where they will be clothed and mounted.

Title 3
Remounts

Article 6.
The colonels of the regiments of Guard cavalry are to purchase the following number of horses:

For the *grenadiers-à-cheval*	300 horses
For the dragoons	450 horses
For the *chasseurs*	700 horses
For the 1st Lancers	200 horses
For the 2nd Lancers	1,000 horses
Total	2650 horses.

Clothing of the regiments was dealt with under 'Title four, Article eight, Clothing'. The 1st Regiment was to be dressed as guards of honour, the 2nd as *chasseurs* of the line, and the 3rd as Polish lancers of the line. Article nine noted that the officers, sub-officers and men of the 1st Regiment of *Éclaireurs* would receive the pay and status as the 1st Regiment of *Chasseurs-à-Cheval* of the Guard. The officers of the staff of the 2nd and 3rd Regiments would be paid as for the Guard, with the sub-officers and men being paid the same as the men of the line, as with

Above and opposite: The *Éclaireurs* of the Guard were the corps of cavalry scouts of the Imperial Guard created by Napoleon when he reorganised the Imperial Guard following the 1812 campaign in Russia. The corps was created in Article one of the decree of 4 December 1813. Claude Testot-Ferry was named colonel of the first regiment. In 1803, he left for Russia as a young lieutenant with his friend Colonel Auguste François-Marie de Colbert-Chabanais on a diplomatic mission. On Colbert-Chabanais's recommendation, he became a captain and *aide-de-camp* of General Marmont. Testot-Ferry and Marmont became great friends and were buried in the same cemetery, the *cimetière* Saint-Vorles in Châtillon-sur-Seine. In 1805, Testot-Ferry distinguished himself at the Battle of Reifling (Austria), where he captured a whole Austrian battalion (450 soldiers and nineteen officers). In 1807, he fought at the Battle of Castel Nuovo (Albania).

On 3 March 1808, having strongly impressed Napoleon on their first meeting, Napoleon personally named Claude Testot-Ferry *chef d'escadron*, and he set out to join the 13th *Cuirassiers* for the Peninsular War. In that campaign he recovered General Auguste François-Marie de Colbert-Chabanais' body shortly after his death and distinguished himself at the *Siege* of Saragossa.

In 1811, Napoleon summoned him to join the regiment of dragoons in the Imperial Guard, known as the 'Empress's Dragoons', at the rank of major. In 1813, he was put in command of the 3rd squadron of the Old Guard at the Battle of Leipzig, then the 2nd squadron at the Battle of Hanau. At Hanau he received twenty-two sabre and lance cuts before safely reaching the rear to have his wounds treated. On this campaign he was promoted to colonel, then colonel-major in 1813, and took command of the *1er Régiment des Eclaireurs de la Garde Impériale*, with whom he served throughout the campaign in France in 1814. The images show his full dress dolman. (Musée de l'Empéri, Collections du Musée de l'armée, Anciennes collections Jean et Raoul Brunon)

the 2nd Regiment of *Chasseurs-à-Cheval* of the Guard. Men sent from the Old Guard to the 2nd and 3rd Regiments, however, would retain their status and pay as Old Guard, the same as with the men from the guards of honour.[2]

1st Regiment

The 1st Regiment was attached to the *grenadiers-à-cheval*, who provided the cadre of the regiment.

Officers sent to the 1st *Éclaireurs* from the *grenadiers-à-cheval* were as follows:

Francois Gaudinot was born on 3 July 1778. He was admitted to the 16th Cavalry Regiment in 1798 and admitted to the *grenadiers-à-cheval* in 1801. Promoted to quartermaster-corporal in 1803 and to sergeant and sergeant-major in 1805, he was awarded the Legion of Honour on 14 March 1806 and was promoted to second-lieutenant on 16 February 1807. Promoted again to first-lieutenant with the rank of captain on 6 December 1811, he was transferred as captain of the 1st Regiment of *Èclaireurs* of the Imperial Guard on 21 December 1813. Upon the return of the Bourbon monarchy and disbandment of the *èclaireurs* on 1 September 1814, he was placed on half-pay. Appointed as squadron commander in the 6th *Cuirassiers* on 23 April 1815, he was passed to the 3rd *Cuirassiers* on 29 May 1815 and placed on half-pay again on 1 August 1815, being discharged on 1 September 1815.

Marcel Marthurin Grival was born at Toulon on 24 January 1770 to an aristocratic family. He enlisted as a cadet in the school of marine engineers on 21 March 1789 and he left the school on 31 December 1790 when it was closed. Under the *levee en mass,* he was conscripted into the 3rd Hussars on 30 May 1792, promoted to quartermaster-corporal on 6 March 1799, and a month later to sergeant on 22 April 1799. Following the Battle of Jena in October 1806, he was promoted to sergeant-major on 22 November 1806 and was awarded the Legion of Honour on 14 April 1814. Promoted to adjutant on 24 August 1808 and to third-lieutenant on 19 December 1808, he passed as a second-lieutenant in the *grenadiers-à-cheval* on 9 February 1813 and served in 4th Company, which was part of 4th Squadron. He was made first-lieutenant on 20 December 1813, served with the 1st Regiment of *Èclaireurs* of the Imperial Guard, and then passed as an *aide-de-camp* on 27 July 1814. He remained at Saumur during the Hundred Days campaign and retired on 30 September 1816.

Jean Baptiste Richard was born on 6 November 1766 at Vesoul. In 1801 he was serving as a third-lieutenant. He passed to the *grenadiers-à-cheval* in December 1805 as a second-lieutenant and served in 7th Company, which was part of 3rd Squadron. In 1809, he was promoted to first-lieutenant and remained in 7th Company. During the 1812 campaign, he served in 8th Company, which was part of 4th Squadron. He returned from Russia and passed to 7th Company of 1st Squadron. On 27 December 1813, he passed to the 1st Regiment of *Èclaireurs* of the Imperial Guard as a captain.

Medard Lepot was born on 5 April 1778, the son of Martin Lepot, a farm labourer, and Marguerite Baudet. He enlisted with the 4th Hussars in 1799 and passed in 1802 to the *grenadiers-à-cheval* of the Guard of the Consuls. Promoted to quartermaster-corporal in 1804 and to sergeant-major in 1805 following the Battle of Austerlitz, he was appointed as second-lieutenant-adjutant of the *velite* squadron in January 1806, a post he held until promoted to first-lieutenant on 5 April 1809. He served on the staff as lieutenant-adjutant-major. Following his return from the Russian campaign, he was promoted to captain-adjutant-major on 9 March 1813. Appointed as squadron commander of the 1st Regiment of *Èclaireurs* of the Imperial Guard on 21 December 1813, with the disbandment of the Young Guard in July 1814 he was placed on half-pay. He was then admitted as major supernumerary in the 5th Dragoons on 16 November 1814. With the return of Napoleon, he was made major of the 6th *Chasseurs-à-Cheval.* He was placed on the non-active list on 1 August 1815. He had been made a knight of the Legion of Honour on 14 March 1806 and an officer of the Legion of Honour on 14 September 1813.

Antoine Jean Gabriel Verne was born in Paris on 15 October 1784. He was serving in the 9th Hussars as a third-lieutenant in April 1809 and was promoted to first-lieutenant in February 1811. He was admitted to the *grenadiers-à-cheval* as a second-lieutenant in February 1813 and served in 12th Squadron, which was part of 6th Company, which was in turn the 2nd Regiment of *Grenadiers-à-Cheval* of the Young Guard. He passed on to the 1st Regiment of *Èclaireurs* of the Imperial Guard on 27 December 1813.

Cesar Waldner de Freundstein was born in Strasbourg on 8 September 1792. Admitted to the 11th *Chasseurs* in 1807 as a third-lieutenant, in September 1813 he entered the *grenadiers-à-cheval* as a second-lieutenant. He passed to the 1st Regiment of *Èclaireurs* of the Imperial Guard on 27 December 1813 as first-lieutenant. His service under the First Restoration is not clear.

The decree stated 250 men were to come from the guards of honour, and by consulting the regiment's two muster lists we can trace the origins of the men who made up the regiment:[3]

• 1st, 3rd and 4th Guards of Honour	337 men
• *Grenadiers-à-cheval*	forty-five men
• *Chasseurs-à-cheval* of the Guard	three men
• *Grenadiers-à-pied*	one man
• 5th *Voltigeurs* of the Guard	one man
• 2nd, 3rd and 11th *Cuirassiers*	seven men
• Line dragoons	twenty-five men
• 3rd and 4th Line Lancers	seven men
• 2nd and 14th *Chasseurs-à-Cheval*	four men
• 6th Horse Artillery	one man
• *Chevau-Leger* of the Guard of Spain	twenty-five men
• *Pupilles* of the Guard	twenty-five men
• Other regiments	thirty-seven men

Five hundred and one men listed in the first register were classed as Old Guard, the 608 in the second register ranked as line. From the 1st Regiment of *Grenadiers*, thirty-nine men were transferred and from the 2nd Regiment six men. Those sent from the 1st Regiment included:[4]

Jean Joseph Sabathie was born on 3 June 1770. Admitted as a farrier to the artillery equipment train on 7 September 1791, he was admitted to the *grenadiers-à-cheval* as farrier in January 1800. Promoted to sergeant-farrier on 1 August 1806, he was admitted to the 1st Regiment of *Èclaireurs* of the Imperial Guard as farrier in December 1813 and admitted as sergeant-farrier to the Royal Corps of *Cuirassiers* of France on 23 July 1814. He served on the staff in 1815 and was discharged on 1 October 1815.

Jean Baptiste Florent Brailly was born at Amiens on 15 August 1782. He was admitted to the 1st *Chasseurs-à-Cheval* in 1800 and then passed to the *grenadiers-à-cheval* in 1803. Promoted to corporal in the 1st Regiment of *Èclaireurs* of the Imperial Guard on 1 January 1814, he was appointed as a corporal in the Royal Corps of *Cuirassiers* of France on 23 July 1814. He served in 5th Company, which was part of 1st Squadron, in 1815 and passed on 22 May 1815 to the regiment of light horse lancers of the Imperial Guard. However, he was discharged from

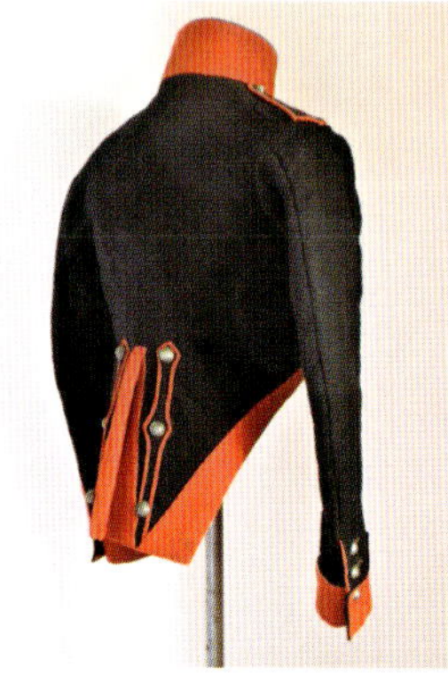

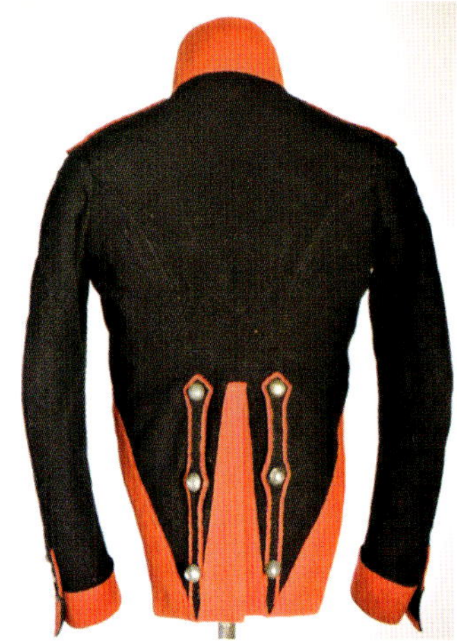

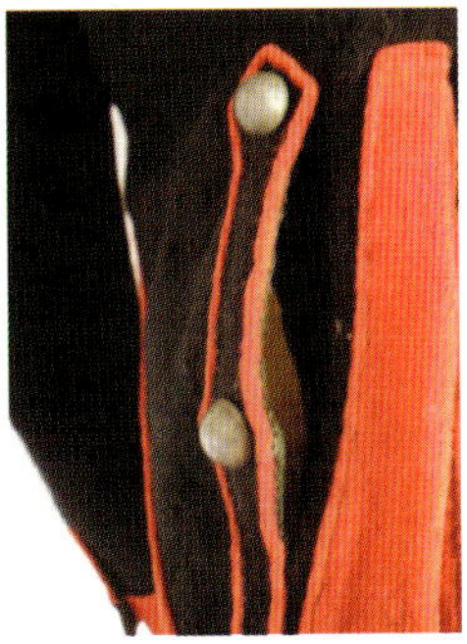

Above and opposite: A single trooper's *habit* exists for the 1st regiment. It is cut as a single-breasted *kinski*. This is a remarkable item and belonged to the Young Guard squadrons of the 1st regiment, which were clothed and equipped like *chasseurs-à-cheval* of the line. (Private collection Switzerland)

the *grenadiers-à-cheval* on 24 October 1815, so it seems he did not take up this appointment.

Jean Baptiste Delbart, born on 23 April 1793, stood 1.77 m tall. He was the son of Joseph Delbart and Jeanne Clement. He entered the 58th Regiment of Line Infantry on 1 January 1791, and passed to the 1st Regiment of Foot Artillery of the Line on 13 January 1793. Admitted thence to the 5th Hussars in 1800, he passed to the *grenadiers-à-cheval* on 23 June 1806. Promotion followed quickly to corporal on 14 July 1806 and he was awarded the Legion of Honour on 28 November 1813. Passed as a sergeant into the 1st Regiment of *Èclaireurs* of the Imperial Guard, from 1 July to 21 October 1814 he was in hospital in Danzig. Being discharged from the 1st Regiment of *Èclaireurs* on 15 July 1814, he was accepted to the Royal Corps of *Cuirassiers* of France on 24 August 1814 and promoted to sergeant-major on 21 September 1814. He passed to 10th Company on 1 April 1815 and was discharged from the regiment on 28 November 1815.

Edme Lazard Cresnard was born on 12 March 1780 at Villepart. Admitted to the stood 1.75 m tall. Admitted to the 25th Dragoons in 1803, he was promoted to corporal on 1 July 1806, to sergeant on 20 September 1813 and passed as sergeant to the 1st *Éclaireurs* on 22 January 1814. He then passed to the regiment on 20 July 1814 and was discharged on 25 November 1815.

Sebastian Narcisse Hachette was born on 20 January 1787 at Verlus in the Marne. He was conscripted into the 25th Dragoons on 8 November 1805, promoted to quartermaster-corporal in November 1810, to sergeant on 1 July 1812 and was admitted into the 1st Regiment of *Grenadiers-à-Cheval* of the Imperial Guard on 23 January 1813. At the close of the 1813 campaign, he was transferred to the 1st Regiment of *Èclaireurs* of the Imperial Guard, which was attached to the *grenadiers-à-cheval*, with the rank of sergeant on 1 January 1814. With the fall of Napoleon and disbandment of the junior elements of the Guard cavalry, he was admitted to the Royal Corps of *Cuirassiers* of France on 23 July 1814. With the return of Napoleon, he was admitted back to the *grenadiers* on 1 April 1815. He was placed on half-pay from 11 July 1815 and awarded the Legion of Honour on 27 February 1814.

Guillaume Victor Lecoq was born at Caen on 7 October 1783. He entered the 1st Regiment of Guards of Honour on 13 July 1813. He transferred to the 1st Regiment of *Èclaireurs* of the Imperial Guard on 15 December 1813 and arrived at the depot on 6 January 1814. He deserted the army on 30 May 1814, but was allowed back into the Guard as a trooper in 3rd Company of the *grenadiers-à-cheval* on 8 May 1815. His matricule entry notes he stood 1.70 m tall.

Louis Sevrette was born at La Harve in 1795. He was conscripted to the Imperial Guard depot on 22 September 1813 and admitted to the 1st Regiment of *Èclaireurs* of the Imperial Guard on 2 January 1814. In April 1814, he appears to have been discharged from the army. He re-enlisted in the *grenadiers-à-cheval* in May 1815. Following Waterloo, he passed to the 7th *Cuirassiers* in November 1815, and thence to the 2nd Regiment of *Grenadiers-à-Cheval* of the Royal Guard in January 1816. He was then transferred to the *Garde du Corps de Monsieur* in 1817 and left the army on 8 October 1819.

Jean Baptiste Paymal was born on 12 July 1788 in Paris. He was admitted to the 10th Hussars on 1 November 1805. Promoted to corporal on 1 January 1812, he was admitted to the *grenadiers-à-cheval* on 26 December 1812. Following his return from the Russian campaign he was promoted to corporal on 28 January 1813. He was promoted to sergeant on 1 January 1814 with the 1st *Éclaireurs*. He passed to the Royal Corps of *Cuirassiers* of France on 23 July 1814 with the rank of sergeant and was appointed to sergeant in the re-formed *grenadiers-à-cheval* on 8 April 1815. Following service at Waterloo, he was admitted as sergeant to the 2nd Regiment of *Grenadiers-à-Cheval* of the Royal Guard on 1 November 1815. He was still serving in 1816. He had been wounded on 12 February 1807 with a sabre cut and a gunshot wound and was awarded the Legion of Honour on 27 February 1814.

Antoine Nicholas Guyot, born on 4 July 1783, was admitted to the *grenadiers-à-cheval* on 28 January 1812, passing to the 1st *Éclaireurs* on 27 December 1813. He was admitted to the *Cuirassiers* de France on 23 July 1814 and served with the *grenadiers-à-cheval* at Waterloo, where he was captured.

Jean Baptiste Arma Auguste Hoguet, born on 13 March 1794, was admitted to the regiment on 10 March 1812 as a cadet trumpeter. He passed to the 1st *Éclaireurs* as a trumpeter on 27 December 1813 and was admitted to the 12th *Chasseurs-à-Cheval* on 23 June 1814.

Otto Neuhausen, born on 10 April 1787, was admitted to the regiment on 11 January 1809 and was promoted to corporal on 24 February 1813. He passed to the 1st *Éclaireurs* as sergeant on 1 January 1814, then to the 4th *Chasseurs-à-Cheval* on 6 June 1814.

Francois Valette, born on 24 May 1788, was admitted to the 15th Dragoons in 1800 and promoted to corporal on 16 May 1811, to *fourrier* on 1 November 1811 and was admitted to the regiment on 6 April 1813. Admitted to the 1st *Éclaireurs* on 1 January 1814, he was wounded on 7 March 1814 with a sabre cut. He passed to the 4th *Chasseurs-à-Cheval* on 6 June 1814.

Martin Desmedt was born on 1 January 1787 and was admitted to the regiment on 9 May 1811. He passed with the rank of corporal to the 1st *Éclaireurs* on 1 January 1814 and to the 4th *Chasseurs-à-Cheval* on 6 June 1814.

Nicolas Lambert Lenars was born on 6 December 1786. He was admitted to the regiment on 24 July 1811 and passed with the rank of corporal to the 1st *Éclaireurs* on 1 January 1814. He deserted on 30 May 1814.

Jean Philippe Kaisermann (born on 16 December 1790) was admitted to the 24th Dragoons on 6 June 1809 and admitted to the regiment on 21 January 1813. Passed with the rank of corporal to 1st *Éclaireurs* on 1 January 1814, he then passed to the 4th *Chasseurs-à-Cheval* on 6 June 1814.

Pierre Nicolas Thiebault (born on 8 November 1777) was admitted to the regiment on 15 October 1808 and promoted to corporal on 27 November 1811.

He passed with the rank of sergeant to the 1st *Éclaireurs* on 1 January 1814, then to the 12th *Chasseurs-à-Cheval* on 6 June 1814.

Jean Pierre Pequrier was born on 3 March 1780 and was admitted to the regiment on 23 July 1812. He was promoted to corporal on 21 January 1813, then passed with the rank of sergeant to the 1st *Éclaireurs* on 1 January 1814 and to the 12th *Chasseurs-à-Cheval* on 6 June 1814.

Francois Joseph Precelle, born on 31 December 1782, was admitted to the regiment on 1 October 1812 and promoted to corporal on 22 January 1813. He passed with the rank of sergeant to the 1st *Éclaireurs* on 1 January 1814 and to the 12th *Chasseurs-à-Cheval* on 6 June 1814.

Pierre Joseph Hebrin was born on 10 January 1782. He was admitted to the regiment on 16 December 1812, having served with the 10th Hussars since 13 February 1804. Promoted to corporal on 28 January 1813, he passed with the rank of sergeant to the 1st *Éclaireurs* on 1 January 1814, passing back to the *grenadiers-à-cheval* on 8 May 1814.

Jean Baptiste Ramage (born on 7 April 1784) was admitted to the regiment on 15 October 1808, promoted to corporal on 12 February 1813 and passed with the rank of sergeant to the 1st *Éclaireurs* on 1 January 1814. He passed back to the *grenadiers-à-cheval* on 8 May 1814.

Hyacinthe Renaud, born on 1 March 1779, was admitted to the regiment on 3 April 1806, promoted to corporal on 21 February 1813 and passed with the rank of sergeant to the 1st *Éclaireurs* on 1 January 1814. He was killed on 7 March 1814.

Jean Joseph Jacques Watrin (born on 9 March 1785) was admitted to the regiment on 17 October 1811 and promoted to corporal on 21 February 1813. He passed with the rank of sergeant to the 1st *Éclaireurs* on 1 January 1814. Wounded at Brienne with a sabre cut, he passed back to the *grenadiers-à-cheval* on 8 May 1814.

Charles Barthelemy Dusand was born on 12 October 1782. Admitted to the regiment in 1804, he was awarded the Legion of Honour on 14 April 1807, promoted to corporal on 1 March 1813 and passed with the rank of sergeant to the 1st *Éclaireurs* on 1 January 1814. He passed back to the 12th *Chasseurs-à-Cheval* on 6 June 1814.

Jean Amant Marcel (born on 17 January 1778) was admitted to the regiment in 1803 and promoted to corporal on 1 March 1813. He passed with the rank of sergeant to the 1st *Éclaireurs* on 1 January 1814, then back to the *grenadiers-à-cheval* on 8 May 1814.

Jean Germain Comment, born on 25 September 1785, was admitted to the regiment on 23 January 1813 and promoted to corporal on 1 March 1813. Passed with the rank of sergeant to the 1st *Éclaireurs* on 1 January 1814, he passed back to the 12th *Chasseurs-à-Cheval* on 6 June 1814.

Jean Cesar Paquien, born on 25 February 1785, was admitted to the regiment on 1 May 1807, having served with the 9th *Chasseurs-à-Cheval* since 1800.

Passed with the rank of corporal to the 1st *Éclaireurs* on 1 January 1814, he went to the 12th *Chasseurs-à-Cheval* on 6 June 1814.

Joseph Prasso (born on 14 October 1775) was admitted to the regiment on 9 July 1807, having served with the 1st Regiment of Piedmontese Dragoons since 23 January 1794. Passed with the rank of corporal to the 1st *Éclaireurs* on 1 January 1814, he was placed on half-pay from 23 July 1814, passing to the Royal Corps of *Cuirassiers* of France on 27 January 1815.

Philippe Joseph Rembert, born on 28 July 1780, was admitted to the regiment on 23 September 1808, having served with the 11th *Chasseurs-à-Cheval* since 1803. He passed with the rank of corporal to the 1st *Éclaireurs* on 1 January 1814, then to the *grenadiers-à-cheval* of the *Maison du Roi* on 23 August 1814.

Jean Louis Sabron (born on 3 October 1787) was admitted to the regiment on 23 October 1809 from the 8th *Cuirassiers*, which he had joined on 6 April 1804. He passed with the rank of corporal to the 1st *Éclaireurs* on 1 January 1814 and was wounded on 7 March 1814, dying on 15 May 1814 from his wounds.

Andre Maucorps was born on 13 July 1780. He was admitted into the 2nd Regiment of *Carabiniers* on 6 September 1802. Entering the *grenadiers-à-cheval* on 28 October 1809, he was one of the 127 members of the regiment who returned from Russia and served in the 1813 campaign. On 1 January 1814, he was appointed corporal with the 1st *Éclaireurs*. Passed back to the *grenadiers-à-cheval* on 6 June 1814, following the disbandment of the regiment he was admitted as corporal in the 2nd Regiment of *Grenadiers-à-Cheval* of the Royal Guard on 13 December 1815. At Waterloo he took a gunshot wound to his left leg and had his horse killed under him. He failed to recover his *porte-manteau*, which contained the brevet of his Legion of Honour, which had been awarded on 28 November 1813.

Jean Manceaux, born on 2 February 1781, was admitted to the regiment on 24 November 1810 from the 4th *Cuirassiers*, which he had joined in 1803. He passed with the rank of corporal to the 1st *Éclaireurs* on 1 January 1814, then to the 12th *Chasseurs-à-Cheval* on 6 June 1814.

Jean Baptiste Gerard (born on 19 April 1785) was admitted to the regiment on 27 April 1811 from the 8th *Cuirassiers*, which he had served with since 1805. Passed with the rank of corporal to the 1st *Éclaireurs* on 1 January 1814, he passed to the 12th *Chasseurs-à-Cheval* on 6 June 1814.

Pierre Pierret, born on 19 May 1785, was admitted to the regiment on 1 May 1811 from the 2nd *Carabiniers*, which he had joined on 12 December 1805. Passed with the rank of corporal to the 1st *Éclaireurs* on 1 January 1814, he deserted on 23 May 1814.

Frederic Frison, born on 24 April 1781, was admitted to the regiment on 11 May 1811 from the 7th *Cuirassiers*, with whom he had served since 25 January 1804. Passed with the rank of corporal to the 1st *Éclaireurs* on 1 January 1814, he passed to the 4th *Chasseurs-à-Cheval* on 6 June 1814.

Francois Nicolas Bremont (born on 18 April 1784) was admitted to the regiment on 1 September 1812 from the 22nd Dragoons, with whom he had

CHAPTER 10

ELITE *GENDARMES*

The consular decree of 12 *Thermidor*, Year XI (3 July 1801), reorganised the national *gendarmerie* into twenty-seven legions, one of which was elite. This last, made up of 260 unmounted and 312 mounted men with a staff of twenty-seven officers, was formed by means of brigadiers (corporals) and *gendarmes* drawn from the other legions, but who nevertheless remained on the nominal roles of those legions. It was charged with maintaining public safety and policing those places where the government resided.

The decree of 28 *Ventôse*, Year X (19 March 1802) completed the organisation of the elite legion. It was to comprise of a staff, four mounted companies forming two squadrons, and a demi-battalion of two foot companies.

The legion of elite *gendarmerie* was incorporated into the Consular Guard by the decree of 14 *Prairial*, Year XI (3 June 1803). Ranked with the *grenadiers-à-cheval*, it enjoyed the same privileges in terms of pay, clothing and barrack allowance.[1] The decree of 29 July 1804 gave the regiment the following organisation:[2]

The regimental staff to comprise:
One colonel
One major
Three squadron commanders, of which one was to be instructor
One quartermaster
One adjutant-major
Two sub-adjutant-majors, one for the infantry, one for the cavalry
Two surgeons
Two standard-bearers
One flag-bearer
One veterinarian
Twelve musicians, of which one was the band-master
One master tailor gaiter-maker
One master saddler
One master leather breeches-maker
One master boot-maker
One master armourer and spur-maker

Each mounted company to comprise:
One captain
Two first-lieutenants
One sergeant-major

Three sergeants
One *fourrier*
Six corporals
Seventy-two *gendarmes*
Two trumpeters, plus a corporal trumpeter to command all the trumpeters
One farrier

Each foot company to comprise:
One captain
Two lieutenants
One sergeant-major
Five sergeants
One *fourrier*
Ten corporals
100 *gendarmes*
Two drummers, plus a drum-corporal to command all the trumpeters

No archive paperwork exists to confirm the existence of the twelve musicians in the regimental band.

The decree of 15 April 1806, which re-organised the Imperial Guard, kept the elite *gendarmerie* at four mounted companies with a strength of 456 horsemen. The foot companies were disbanded and almost all the *gendarmes* transferred to the mounted companies. The decree stated:[3] 'Art. 24. The four companies of the elite *gendarmerie* will have the same organisation and will have the same strength as a company of a regiment of the cavalry of the Guard.'

The decree in Article ten set out the organisation of the Guard cavalry as follows:[4]

Art. 10. The regiments of *grenadiers*, *chasseurs* and dragoons are composed of:

Four squadrons of two companies each. One squadron of velites.

Art. 11. The staff of a regiment of *grenadiers*, *chasseurs* or dragoons will be composed of:

One commanding colonel. One sub-instructor (rank of *maréchal-des-logis-chef*).

Two majors
One quartermaster (*vaugmestre*) (rank of *maréchal-des-logis*)
Five squadron heads, of which one is for the *velites*
Two artist veterinarians, of which one is for the *velites*
One squadron head instructor
Four veterinarian aides
One quartermaster treasurer
One trumpet-major

One captain instructor
Three corporal trumpeters (brigadiers)
Two adjutant-majors, of which one is for the *velites*
Five sub adjutant-majors, of which one is for the *velites*
One timpanist
One master tailor
Four standard-bearers
One master breeches-maker
One adjutant-lieutenant for food
One master boot-maker
One adjutant-lieutenant for fodder
One master gunsmith (*armurier*)
One adjutant-lieutenant for clothing
One master saddle-maker
Five medical officers, of which two are first-class and three are second or third-class
One master spur-maker
Two master sergeant blacksmiths

Art. 12. Each company will be made up of:

One captain. One quartermaster (*fourrier*).

Two first-lieutenants
Ten corporals (brigadiers)
Two second-lieutenants
Ninety-six *grenadiers*, *chasseurs* or dragoons
One sergeant-major (*maréchal-des-logis-chef*)
Three trumpeters
Six sergeants (*maréchaux-des-logis*)
Two sergeant blacksmiths

Presumably, however, the *gendarmes* never had *velites*. The decree officially allowed for a kettledrummer. Can the Hoffmann print of the kettledrummer really date from 1806? Possibly, given in the same series Hoffmann shows the trumpeters and troopers of the Empress Dragoons, as well as the Polish Lancers created in 1807.

One has to wait until the decree of 1 March 1813 before a change was made to the organisation of this corps. This decree fixed its strength at 1,174 men, including officers, and to achieve this 640 further *gendarmes bis* (additional) were added, taken from among the conscripts.

The decree of 12 December reduced the number of *gendarmes bis* to 540. The decree of 16 January 1814 reduced them to 300, to which were to be added twenty Old Guard *gendarmes* and 160 pupil *gendarmes*.

It is not certain that events allowed this project to be realised and on 23 April 1814 the elite *gendarmerie* was disbanded. Part of its strength was used to form the *gendarmerie* company known as *des voyages et chasses du Roi* (journeys and hunts of the king), created in July 1814.

Portrait of Baron J.P. Henry, commanding officer of the Elite *Gendarmes*. (private collection)

Clothing and equipment

Very little paperwork exists for the clothing of the regiment – just three documents. There is, therefore, very little we can say about the dress of the regiment. We know the dress of the kettledrummer and trumpeter from the works of Hoffmann, but we are not able to confirm or deny what this source depicts. We must treat with utmost caution the work of Rousselot, Jouineaux and other twentieth-and twenty-first-century illustrators, as their work is based on guesswork and not hard fact. The master workmen of the regiment were:[5]

MAT. No. 468 Xavier Fert, born on 2 February 1765 and admitted to the regiment on 8 April 1802 as master boot-maker.

MAT No. 476 Pierre Louis Grosselin, born on 19 August 1758 and admitted to the regiment on 8 April 1802 as master armourer; discharged on 23 March 1806.

MAT No. 518 Nicolas Dieudonne, born on 15 October 1748, admitted to the regiment on 8 April 1802 as master saddler and died on 20 April 1804.

MAT No. 519 Joseph Francois Bonnaud, born on 11 July 1760 and admitted to the regiment on 8 April 1802 as master tailor.

MAT No. 672 Honore Bondonnauxm, born on 20 May 1767 and admitted to the regiment on 23 January 1803 as *gendarme-à-cheval*. Named as master saddler on 21 April 1804, he was dismissed from the regiment on 20 April 1805.

MAT No. 967 Pierre Deroch, born on 17 February 1754 and admitted to the regiment as master saddler on 20 April 1805.

MAT No. 1039 Joseph Pery was admitted to the regiment on 23 March 1806 as a master armourer.

The regiment, confusingly, has two additional muster lists for the period 1802 to March 1807. In this supplementary book we find:[6]

> MAT No. 336 *bis* Nicolas Hany, born on 4 October 1766 in Paris and admitted to the regiment on 7 October 1804 as master breeches-maker; discharged on 1 February 1809.
>
> MAT No. 360 *bis* Pierre Deroche.

In the additional book from 1802 to 1814 we again find:[7]

> MAT. No. 468 Xavier Fert
>
> MAT No. 476 Pierre Louis Grosselin
>
> MAT No. 518 Nicolas Dieudonne
>
> MAT No. 519 Joseph Francois Bonnaud
>
> MAT No. 672 Honore Bondonnauxm
>
> MAT No. 967 Pierre Deroch

These men have double entries. Clearly, at some stage the paperwork for the regiment at the time became hopelessly confused, resulting in three muster lists, one being a duplicate.

1802

A document of 19 March 1802 lists the following items as the clothing for the mounted companies:[8]

- *Habit* to last two years, costing 49.50 *francs*
- *Surtout* to last one year, costing 48.50 *francs*
- *Veste* to last two years, costing 10 *francs*
- *Culottes de daim* to last two years, costing 36 *francs*
- *Culottes de mouton* to last two years, costing 12 *francs*
- Stable coat to last two years, costing 12 *francs*
- *Bonnet de police* to last two years, costing 8.80 *francs*
- Stable trousers to last one year, costing 5.36 *francs*
- *Manteau* to last six years, costing 143.10 *francs*
- Full dress *chapeau* to last two years, costing 46.25 *francs*
- Undress *chapeau* to last one year costing 20.50 *francs*
- *Aiguillette* and trefoil to last three years, costing 10 *francs*
- Shirt to last one year six months, costing 6 *francs*
- Cotton socks to last six months, costing 4 *francs*

- Wool socks to last six months, costing 4 *francs*
- Linen socks to last six months, costing 4 *francs*
- Black gaiters to last one year, costing 6.30 *francs*
- Black neck stock to last six months, costing 2.50 *francs*
- Pair of gauntlets to last one year, costing 8 *francs*
- A pair of braces to last one year, costing 75 *centimes*
- Plume to last two years, costing 4.30 *francs*
- Knee guards (*manchette du botte*) to last six months, costing 1 *franc*
- Shoe buckles to last six years, costing 1.25 franc
- Waist belt to last ten years, costing 17.90 *francs*
- *Giberne* to last ten years, costing 6.50 *francs*
- *Giberne* belt to last ten years, costing 14 *francs*
- *Porte-mousqueton* to last ten years, costing 19 *francs*
- *Musketoon* sling to last ten years, costing 3.70 *francs*
- Pair of boots to last one year, costing 26 *francs*

The same document goes on to comment that for the *housse* and *chaperons*, they were to last eight years, but the lace on the *housse* and *chaperons* was to be replaced every two years and the grenades on the *housse* every four years. A *housse* cost 43 *francs* and the *chaperons* 36 *francs*, a considerable investment. The *porte-manteau* cost 26 *francs* and was to last six years. Oddly, the regiment is also listed as receiving *schabraques*, to last four years and cost 6.50 *francs*. It cost 322.93 *francs* to equip a mounted *gendarme*, and 253.64 *francs* for a member of the foot company.[9] The equipment and clothing of the foot company was as follows:[10]

> *Habit* to last two years, *veste* to last two years, cloth *culottes* to last six months, *surtout* to last one year six months, *capote* to last four years, *chapeau* to last two years, *bonnet de police* to last two years six months, red fringed epaulettes to last one year.

Equipment-wise, the foot company had standard infantry equipment, the belts being left as natural buff, edged with 5 mm white worsted lace. The white lace to the natural buff belting was a unique feature of the *gendarme's* clothing for the foot and mounted companies, as well as shared with the *carabiniers-à-cheval* of the line. The foot company, from the list of items, had red epaulettes instead of white *aiguillettes* and trefoils of the mounted companies. On 19 March 1802, the foot companies mustered 211 men, short of twenty-nine men, and the mounted 339 men, and were two men short of regulation strength.

1803

On 22 March 1803, a report issued to the minister of war records that, as a matter of economy, the blue wool cloth used to produce the *manteaux* of the mounted

Above left: Mounted officers in parade dress by Nicolas Hoffmann c. 1807-1808. The resemblance to the uniform of the *grenadiers-à-cheval* is most notable in this image.

Above right: Due to a lack of archive documents, for the dress of the trumpeters we have to rely upon period iconography to inform us of how the uniform may have appeared. Hoffman shows a *habit* in reverse colours laced silver, which is a perfectly acceptable understanding of how the trumpeters were dressed.

company was henceforth to cost 16.75 *francs* a metre, a saving of 100 *francs* in the production of forty-nine new *manteaux*. At the same time, for the matter of economy, the *chamois* coloured cloth to make 292 *vestes* and 142 *culottes* for the foot company was to cost between 7.29 *francs* and 7.50 *francs* a metre. The report further adds that the cloth purchased in 1802 was as follows:[11]

- Blue wool cloth at 25 *francs* a metre
- Scarlet wool cloth at 24 *francs* a metre
- Scarlet *blicourt* (milled *serge*) at 2.75 *francs* a metre
- Linen for lining at 2.85 *francs* a metre

- Linen for pockets at 1.40 *francs* a metre
- *Chamois* wool cloth for *culottes* and *vestes* at 21 *francs* a metre

By purchasing lodeve cloth of lower qualities a major saving could be made. A mounted *gendarme's* clothing and equipment would cost, under the new scheme, 700 *francs* rather than 852.50 *francs*. A further saving was made by changing the supplier of the *culottes du daim*, the price going from 40 *francs* a pair to 36 *francs*, for which the inspecting officer noted in the purchase of 257 pairs was a considerable saving of 1,028 *francs*. Overall, the inspecting officer reported that a saving of 300 *francs* per mounted *gendarme* and 200 per foot *gendarme* could be made a year, to bring the cost of equipping the regiment into line with the same cost as a *grenadier-à-pied* and a *grenadier-à-cheval*, as the regiment at that time was the costliest in the Guard.[12]

The report added that the following items were in the magazine:[13]

- 17 m of blue wool cloth for *habits* at 25 *francs* a metre
- 43 m of blue wool cloth for *manteaux* at 22.50 *francs* a metre
- 13 m of scarlet wool cloth at 24 *francs* a metre
- 2 m of white wool cloth for piping at 36 *francs* a metre
- 20 m of *chamois* wool cloth at 21 *francs* a metre
- 112 m of scarlet milled *serge* at 2.64 *francs* a metre
- 69 m of blue *tricot* at 7 *francs* a metre
- 89 m of cotton at 2.85 *francs*
- 194 m of linen, Abbeville quality, at 1.95 *francs* a metre
- Thirty-eight hooks for *manteaux* at 7 *centimes* each
- 9 m of silver lace 22 mm wide at 8 *francs* a metre
- 11 m of silver lace 18 mm wide at 4 *francs* a metre
- 24 m of silver lace 8 mm wide at 2 *francs* a metre
- Thirteen *bands de chapeaux* at 25 *francs* each
- Sixteen cockade straps for *chapeaux* at 1.25 *francs* each
- 40 m of white worsted lace 28 mm wide at 60 *centimes* a metre
- 54 m of white worsted lace 13 mm wide at 30 *centimes* a metre
- Eighty *garnitures de brandenburg* at 3 *francs* each
- Seventy *garnitures* for *bonnets de police* at 50 *centimes*
- Nine *chapeaux* at 10.89 *francs*
- Ten sets of trefoils for musicians at 12 *francs* a pair
- Thirty-two *aiguillettes* for *gendarmes* at 9.25 *francs* each
- Sixteen trefoils for *gendarmes* at 1 *franc* a pair
- 150 dozen large uniform buttons at 1 *franc* a dozen
- Sixty-three dozen small uniform buttons at 50 *centimes* a dozen
- Thirty-four dozen bone buttons at 5 *centimes* a dozen
- Eleven leather hides at 1.50 *francs* each

Uniform items in the magazine were:[14]

- Eleven full dress *habits* at 49.50 *francs* each
- Two *surtouts* at 48.50 *francs* each
- Ten *chamois vestes* at 10 *francs* each
- Ten *culottes* in *chamois* wool cloth at 15.44 *francs* each
- Thirty-six stable coats costing 12 *francs* each
- 210 sets of stable trousers costing 5.36 *francs* each
- Eight *surtouts* at 8 *francs* each
- Nine *manteaux* costing 143.10 *francs* each
- Five *capotes* costing 63.32 *francs* each
- Six full dress *chapeaux* costing 46 *francs* each
- One undress *chapeau*, costing 15 *francs*

Other items in the magazine were:[15]

- Four *baudriers* costing 11 *francs* each
- One infantry *giberne* costing 5.50 *francs*
- Eighteen cavalry *gibernes* costing 6.50 *francs*
- Three infantry *giberne* belts costing 9.75 *francs*
- Nineteen cavalry *giberne* belts costing 14 *francs* each
- Ten *porte-carabines* costing 19 *francs* each
- Twenty-one musket slings costing 3.60 *francs* each
- One carbine sling costing 3.70 *francs*
- Six pairs of boots costing 24 *francs* a pair
- Two pistol ram rods costing two *francs* each
- 234 double-headed brass studs at 2.50 *francs*
- One haversack costing 7.50 *francs*

The brass studs were undoubtedly used to fasten the musket and carbine slings and also used on the sword slings of the mounted companies. The slings had a buckle at one end and a stud at the other. The studs were easily lost, hence a ready supply in the regiment's magazine for these small items. The reference for the cavalry *giberne* is likely a reference to the 1786 or 1801 pattern *gibernes* issued to the cavalry regiment, i.e. the regiments that were to become *cuirassiers*. The *giberne*, unlike the *giberne* of the dragoons and light cavalry, was in essence a smaller version of the infantry *giberne*, in as much it was carried off a simple shoulder belt with no buckle, slide and tip, and the *giberne* itself was the same as the infantry type, just smaller. However, re-enactors and twentieth-century and more modern illustrators show the regiment with curved *gibernes* in the manner of the light cavalry, with light cavalry-style shoulder belts that cannot be supported by archive material, which clearly shows the use of the heavy cavalry-style equipment. Given the *gibernes* issued in 1802 had a lifespan of ten years, it is very likely that all

Above left: Kettledrummer of the regiment by Hoffmann. No kettledrummer existed in the regiment till autumn 1807, so clearly this image must date from then. The kettledrummer wears presumably a trumpeter's *habit*. This is the main source of information about the dress of the kettledrummer due to a lack of period archive documentation.

Above right: *Gendarme* in full dress by Hoffmann. The print is notable for one or two points of comment. Firstly, the sabre belt is worn over the shoulder in the manner of the carabiniers, and the sabre itself is of an unusual pattern, and not the expected sabre as used by the *grenadier-à-cheval* or dragoons. Secondly, the *giberne* and *porte-giberne*, rather than being the expected light cavalry style, is in fact the 1801 heavy cavalry type. This *giberne* was a smaller version of the standard infantry *giberne*, carried from a single-piece *banderole*, just as in the infantry. The *giberne* clearly sits on the *portmanteau*. The *portmanteau* is shown with a cross on the ends – which is arguably an artist's error, but one he shows also for the *grenadiers-à-cheval*. Overall, however, the print is very believable for the regiment's appearance in the period 1806-1808 after the adoption of the bearskin.

subsequent issues would be of the same pattern, thus the heavy cavalry-style leather-work could have remained in use through to 1815. Nicolas Hoffmann shows this heavy cavalry *giberne* and belt in use in his paintings of 1805/1806. We can date the image to 1805 and later, as both the foot and mounted *gendarmes* wear the bearskin, adopted in that year. Here we seem to have iconographic sources corroborating with archive textual sources.

A stores inventory of 23 September 1803 lists the following materials:[16]

MATERIALS		*QUANTITIES* (AUNES)	*PRICE PER AUNE* (FRANCS)
Blue wool cloth	For *habits*	228 5/6	25
	For *manteaux*	21 7/8	21
Scarlet	First quality	29 1/3	30
Chamois	First quality	16.25	21
Milled *serge*	Scarlet	52.25	2
Tricot	Blue	9 7/8	5

The *chamois* coloured cloth is clearly for the production of *vestes* for the mounted and foot companies, and for the knee breeches of the foot companies.

The stores also list fourteen *gibernes de cavalerie*, i.e. 1801 regulation heavy cavalry *gibernes*, with fifteen *porte-gibernes de cavalerie* and six *porte-carabines*.[17] The magazine held the following items:[18]

- Fifty-nine full dress *chapeaux*
- Sixty-two undress *chapeaux*
- Two sub-officer's *aiguillettes*
- Eight sub-officer's trefoils
- Two trumpeter's *aiguillettes* and trefoils
- Fifty-eight *gendarme's aiguillettes* and trefoils
- Thirty-one *gendarme's* trefoils
- Thirty-five pairs of scarlet epaulettes
- Two grenades embroidered in silver
- 127 large buttons
- 194 small buttons
- Fourteen *habits*
- Five *surtouts*
- Sixteen *vestes*
- Four pairs of knee breeches in wool cloth
- 112 *stable coats*
- Thirty-five *bonnets de police*
- 202 pairs of stable trousers
- Twenty pairs of *surclottes*
- Two *manteaux*
- Two *capotes*

A year later the stores held the same cloth types and a similar cross section of clothing. The *gibernes* for the mounted companies were still listed as of the cavalry type. In addition, thirty-four pairs of *culottes de daim* and thirty-three pairs of *culottes de mouton* were in the depot. It is clear the mounted companies never had *chamois* woollen cloth breeches.[19]

1805

Adopted in 1805 was a black bearskin. The date of adoption is known only from the work of the artist Nicolas Hoffmann. The bearskin had a black leather peak with white metal edging, white metal chin scales, white cords and the scarlet back patch bore a white embroidered grenade. On 28 August 1809, 350 bearskins were ordered, costing 31.20 *francs* each.[20] Eighty-five were purchased in 1812, costing 34 *francs* each.[21]

On 23 September 1805, the depot held the following materials:[22]

MATERIALS		*QUANTITIES* (AUNES)	*PRICE PER AUNE* (FRANCS)
Blue wool cloth	For *habits*	102 41/144	28.50
	For *manteaux*	27 1/8	25.50
	For stable coats	84 2/3	11.50
Chamois		103 23/120	24
Scarlet	First quality	33	30
Crimson	First quality	1	28
Bleu de ciel	First quality	4.25	26
Milled *serge*	Scarlet	396.50	2.90
	Crimson	5	3

The *bleu de ciel* and crimson must be destined for the trumpeters. The presence of crimson milled *serge*, which was used as lining material, suggests the *habit* was *bleu de ciel* faced in crimson. The silver lace in the depot was destined to lace the *habits* and came in widths of 28 mm, 14 mm and 10 mm. This document is the first evidence of the trumpeters wearing *habits* in *bleu de ciel*, as for the Guard cavalry as a whole. We have to imagine that presumably the trumpeters of the elite *gendarmes* appeared like those of the *grenadiers-à-cheval*, but with silver lace as opposed to gold.[23] Of interest, Nicolas Hoffmann shows the trumpeter wearing a bearskin, so the image dates to the second half of 1805, but it also shows a scarlet *habit*. Was the scarlet *habit* kept as undress? Or had the regiment not yet fully received the new *bleu de ciel* trumpeter's clothing? Were these *habits* a one-off manufacture? More than likely, as over the next few years only very small purchases of *bleu de ciel* cloth were made.

The year when 1805 was the bearskin was adopted, with the depot holding ninety-four of these, valued at 26 *francs* each. The depot also held 185 *habits*, nineteen *surtouts*, six pairs of breeches in *chamois* wool cloth, thirty pairs of knee breeches in doe hide, seventy stable coats, fifteen *bonnets de police*, fifteen pairs of stable trousers, one pair of *pantalons* in *coutil*, three pairs of *surclottes*, eight greatcoats and one *giberne de cavalerie* with two *porte-gibernes de cavalerie*, showing that the *cuirassier*-style *giberne* remained in use beyond 1805.

1807

We have a regrettable gap in the records for the unit. The next document is a list of what the depot held in terms of raw materials on 1 January 1807:[24]

MATERIALS		*QUANTITIES* (AUNES)	*PRICE PER* AUNE (FRANCS)
Blue wool cloth	For *habits*	231 5/6	25.50
	For *manteaux*	143 13/24	23
Scarlet	First quality	0	
Crimson	First quality	0	
Bleu de ciel	First quality	6 5/8	28
Milled *serge*	Scarlet	383	2.90
	Crimson	0	3

In terms of clothing, sixty-two *surtouts* were in the depot, along with forty-seven *vestes*, twenty-eight pairs of knee breeches in doe hide, sixty stable coats, 108 *bonnets de police*, 189 pairs of stable trousers, 160 pairs of *surclottes*, twenty-eight *manteaux*, 120 full dress *chapeaux*, 126 undress *chapeaux*, nine *aiguillettes* for sub-officers, fifty-five trefoils for sub-officers, five sets of *aiguillettes* and trefoils for trumpeters, thirty-eight gendarme's *aiguillettes* and trefoils and four *porte-carabines*. Trumpeters used the same *housse* and *chaperons* as the *gendarmes*, as no specific *housse* or *chaperons* for the trumpeters are in the depot. The depot also contained linen *manteaux* covers. Seemingly these were the same principle as *etui d'habit* used by the infantry of the Guard to protect clothing on campaign. Forty-six cloak covers, costing 2.70 *francs*, were in the depot. No bearskins or bearskin cords were in the depot.[25] New trumpet banners had been purchased in 1806.[26]

The *bonnet de police* was blue, decorated with red cording on the seams of the *flamme*, with a woollen red tassel at its end, and a white cloth grenade on the front of the turban, which also had two white stripes: one 27 mm wide placed at the outer edge and one 13 mm wide inside that. The tariff for the *bonnet de police* was established on 3 July 1807:[27]

- 0.29 m of blue wool cloth at 18.52 *francs* a metre, total 5.50 *francs*
- 0.14 m of *toile blondine* at 1.68 *francs* a metre, total 25 *centimes*
- 0.89 m of white wool lace, 27 mm, at 40 *centimes*
- 0.89 m of white wool lace, 13 mm wide, at 20 *centimes*

- 2.37 m of white wool cording at 50 *centimes*
- One white wool tassel at 50 *centimes*
- One grenade at 48 *centimes*
- Labour: 50 *centimes*
- Total: 8.33 *francs*

The clothing records of the elite *gendarmes* are very incomplete. Only two documents exist that give details of the regiment's clothing. The *habit* coat of the *gendarmes* was that determined by the law of 28 *Germinal*, Year VI (17 April 1798). It was of national blue with collar, lapels and cuffs of scarlet edged in white, lining and turnbacks of madder-red, blue grenades on the turnbacks, horizontal

Above left: Trumpeter in full dress c.1804 by Chataignier and Poisson. We see here the rear of the trumpeter's *habit*. It is in reversed colours. Indeed, the uniform shown here is worth comparing to that shown by Hoffmann, the main point of divergence being the absence of swallows' nests on the print by Hoffmann.

Above right: The foot company of the regiment existed from 1801 to April 1806. This is one of the very few period images of this short-lived formation. He is dressed like a mounted *gendarme*, save for the scarlet fringed epaulettes at the shoulder, the use of black gaiters in *lieu* of boos, and presumably the sabre was exchanged for a *sabre-briquet*.

pockets simulated by red piping, shoulder strap on the right and cuff-patches of blue edged in scarlet, *aiguillette* on the left, tricoloured or white. The waistcoat was of *chamois* coloured cloth. The breeches were in sheep or doe hide. They were covered on campaign either by canvas or grey wool *surclottes*. The consular decree of 21 *Pluvoise*, Year X (10 February 1802) authorised that collars became blue without coloured piping, and the white edgings of the lapels, collar and cuffs were done away with. In undress a *surtout* was worn, which was blue with scarlet tail facings and piping.

The tariff for the *surtout* was established on 3 July 1807:[28]

- 1.48 m of blue wool cloth at 23.57 *francs* a metre, total 35 *francs*
- 0.14 m of scarlet wool cloth at 23.57 *francs* a metre, total 3.49 *francs*
- 2.36 m of scarlet *serge* at 2.53 *francs* a metre, total 6.01 *francs*
- 0.59 m of linen for pockets at 1.52 *francs* a metre, total 90 *centimes*
- 1.03 m of *toile blondine* at 1.68 *francs* a metre, total 1.75 *francs*
- Buttons at 63 *centimes*
- Labour: 2.50 *francs*
- Total: 50.28 *francs*

The sleeveless *veste* was made from *chamois* coloured wool cloth and was worn under the *surtout* and *habit*. The tariff for the *veste* was established on 3 July 1807:[29]

- 0.39 m of *chamois* wool cloth at 19.36 *francs* a metre, total 7.66 *francs*
- 0.89 m of cotton for lining at 2.53 *francs* a metre, total 2.25 *francs*
- 0.19 m of linen for pockets at 1.52 *francs*, total 30 *centimes*
- Twelve small buttons at 38 *centimes*
- Labour: 1.20 *francs*
- Total: 11.79 *francs*

The tariff for the *gilet d'ecurie* was established on 3 July 1807:[30]

- 1.36 m of Lodeve wool cloth at 8.84 *francs* a metre, total 11.81 *francs*
- 1.78 m of *treillis* for lining at 1.52 *francs* a metre, total 2.70 *francs*
- Labour: 1.30 *francs*
- Total: 15.81 *francs*

The tariff for other items of clothing was established on 3 July 1807:[31]

- Doe hide breeches: 35 *francs*
- Boots: 26 *francs*
- Pairs of spurs with straps: 1.25 *francs*

1808

A year later the following materials were in the depot.[32]

MATERIALS		*QUANTITIES* (AUNES)	*PRICE PER* AUNE (FRANCS)
Blue wool cloth	For *habits*	1	25
	For *manteaux*	0	
	Lodeve quality for stable coats	299 21/24	6.75
Chamois		18.75	22
Scarlet	First quality	21 7/24	26.50
Crimson	First quality	0	
Bleu de ciel	First quality	6 5/8	28
Milled *serge*	Scarlet	125.50	2.90
	Crimson	0	

No crimson cloth was purchased to line the trumpeters' clothing, so it seems the *bleu de ciel* was used for either repairs or other items of clothing. The same amount was in the depot since 1 January 1807, so none had been used in the year up to 1 January 1808. The old pattern *chapeaux* were still in use, as the depot, compared to the previous year, held just seventeen parade dress items and fifty-five undress *chapeaux*. Trumpeters do not seem to have had their own pattern *bonnet de police*, as only 175 *bonnets de police*, worth 8.45 *francs*, were in the depot. In addition were twelve sets of trumpeter's bearskin cords at 27 *francs* each and six trumpeter's *aiguillettes* at 54 *francs* each. Sixteen sub-officer's bearskin cords, costing 27 *francs*, were in the depot, along with 126 for *gendarmes*, costing 3 *francs* each.[33]

After 1808, the paperwork for the regiment becomes piecemeal.

1811

A purchase dated 3 December 1811 was for the following amounts of cloth:[34]

- 297 m of Lodeve quality wool cloth, dyed blue for stable coats, at 8 *francs* a metre
- 205.60 m of blue wool cloth, de Berry standard, dyed in the thread, for *habits*
- 202.60 m of grey wool cloth for *surclottes*

From this tariff found among the paperwork for the 3rd Regiment of *Grenadiers-à-Pied*, we see that by 1811 the canvas *surclottes* had been replaced with ones made from grey wool cloth, presumably closed down the outer leg by cloth-covered buttons. This type of *surclotte* became standardised for all heavy cavalry of the line,

Above left: Drummer of the short-lived foot company. Based on this image, it seems the drummers and trumpeters wore exactly the same *habit* in reversed colours laced silver.

Above right: Kettledrummer in a print by Chataignier and Poisson. This print shows the uniform of the kettledrummer soon after the addition the kettledrummer to the regiment's organisation in autumn 1807. The uniform shown here is virtually identical to that shown by Hoffmann.

as well as dragoons and some hussar regiments under the Bardin regulations of 1812. The other heavy cavalry regiments of the Guard only adopted grey *pantalons* in 1813 and entered the Russian campaign with *surclottes* made from white *coutil*.

1812

A *marche* from the third quarter of 1812 provides a list of cloth used by the regiment:[35]

- 363.75 m of blue wool cloth for *habits* at 27.90 *francs* a metre
- 975.85 m of blue wool cloth for *manteaux* costing 24.85 *francs* a metre
- 18 m of scarlet wool cloth at 25.50 *francs* a metre
- 52.86 m of *chamois* wool cloth costing 18.52 *francs* a metre
- 59.22 m of grey wool cloth at 15 *francs* a metre
- 1,079.17 m of scarlet milled *serge* at 2.89 *francs* a metre
- 428.22 m of powder blue wool cloth for *gilet d'ecurie* at 8 *francs* a metre
- 148.06 m of cotton at 3 *francs* a metre

- 794.08 m of linen for pockets at 1.60 *francs* a metre
- 493.65 m of *toile laval* at 2 *francs* a metre
- 19.40 m of *coutil* at 2.60 *francs* a metre
- 26.87 m of *treillis* at 14.55 *francs* a metre

It seems, therefore, that the stable coat changed from imperial blue to a much lighter shade in 1812. The *gilet d'ecurie* was a lighter shade of blue, which is rather unexpected as this has never been commented upon before. Furthermore, the madder-red (*garance*) facings had been changed to scarlet by 1812. From this cloth the following items were made in the last quarter of 1812 to re-clothe the regiment before the 1813 campaign began:[36]

- 112 *habits* costing 60.72 *francs* each
- Seventy-four *vestes* at 11.85 *francs* each
- Eight *culottes de daim* (doe hide breeches) at 45 *francs* a pair
- Ten *culottes de mouton* (sheep hide breeches) at 12.50 *francs* a pair
- 471 *pantalons de treillis* at 5.50 *francs* a pair
- Forty-three *surclottes* in *coutil* costing 7.50 *francs* each
- Five *manteaux* costing 149 *francs* each

Lace and *passamenteries* purchased were as follows:[37]

- 9.36 m of silver lace, 27 mm wide
- 7.78 m of silver lace, 14 mm wide
- 2.69 m of silver lace, 10 mm wide
- 1,599.69 m of white wool lace, 50 mm wide
- 2,576.20 m of white wool lace, 27 mm wide
- 2,155 m of white wool lace, 14 mm wide
- 10.34 m of white wool cording for *bonnets de police*
- Eleven grenades at 4 *francs* a set
- 172 metal buttons at 40 *centimes* a dozen
- 199 large uniform buttons
- 630 small uniform buttons
- 552 bone buttons at 5 *centimes* a dozen
- Nine trumpeter's *aiguillettes* at 63 *francs*
- 168 *gendarme's aiguillettes* in white thread at 7 *francs* each
- Six bearskin cords for sub-officers at 27 *francs* each
- Nine bearskin cords for trumpeters at 27 *francs* each
- 142 bearskin cords at 2.82 *francs* each

1813

Between 1802 and 1813, no documentation exists to confirm the items of equipment in use. Given the list of items in 1813 is the same as 1802, we assume

Horse equipment purchased in 1813 was as follows:[43]

- Forty-three complete saddles costing 88 *francs* each
- 194 *bradoon* bridles for parades at 3.75 *francs* each
- Thirty watering bridles at 6 *francs* each
- Ten girths at 3.50 *francs* each
- Two *surcingles* at 2 *francs* each
- 165 *housses* at 27 *francs* each
- 204 pairs of *chaperons* at 22 *francs* each
- Forty-five rosettes for the bridles
- Fifty-one ribbons for the cruppers
- Four *porte-manteaux*
- Four *manteau* covers
- 427 pairs of white embroidered crowns for the *housse* at 5.50 *francs* a set

We don't know when the crowns for the *housse* were adopted. Hoffmann shows grenades. Martinet, in a print of *c.*1810, shows crowns. No archive paperwork exists to give a precise date of adoption.

Petty equipment

The earliest list of items of petty equipment is from March 1803:[44]

- 216 plumes
- 114 *trousse* (housewifes, i.e. a sewing and cleaning kit)
- Three pairs of black gaiters
- Forty-eight black neck stocks
- Seventy-three brushes for cleaning the *gibernes*
- Fifty-five pairs of gloves
- Twenty-four rosettes in leather stamped with grenades
- Fifty-nine pompoms
- Fifty-one full dress *chapeaux ganses*
- 108 undress *chapeaux ganses*
- 116 cockades
- Fifty-three sword knots for *gendarmes*
- Seven pairs of shoe buckles
- Thirty-eight brushes for cleaning the *habit*
- 108 shoe cleaning brushes
- Thirty-four powder bags
- Sixty-nine combs
- 107 *combes retapeur*
- Thirty-four pairs of spurs with straps
- Seventy-nine grease boxes
- Fifty-five pairs of (illegible)

- Fifty body brushes
- Ninety-eight curry combs
- Fourteen main *combes*
- Thirty-five sponges
- 178 nose-bags
- Fifty-five oat bags
- Seventy-three forage ropes

The use of the leather rosettes stamped with grenades is not known, nor can a use be speculated by the author. These items are unique to the regiment with no comparable items in use in the Imperial or Consular Guards. We know nothing more for a decade about the petty equipment used. Petty equipment purchased at the close of 1813 comprised:[45]

- One pair of rigid boots (*bottes forte*) at 30 *francs*
- 169 pairs of semi-soft boots at 30 *francs* each
- Two plumes at 4.50 *francs*
- Nineteen pompoms at 90 *centimes* each
- One sword knot for *gendarme* at 6.10 *francs*
- Sixty-six cockades
- Two sub-officer's sword knots at 5.50 *francs* each

Trumpeters, drummers and kettledrummers

We have to rely on contemporary iconography to give us an impression of the dress of the trumpeters and drummers. The plates by Chataignier and Poisson show both trumpeter and drummer in reverse colours, i.e. a scarlet *habit* faced in imperial blue. The trumpeters appear to have retained the scarlet *habits* until the end of the empire. For the trumpeter, the plates give imperial blue swallows' nests laced in silver with silver and blue trefoils worn over it with a silver and crimson *aiguillette*. The paper archive makes no mention of this item. The silver lace in the depot was presumably destined for these men, as well as the sub-officers. Chataignier and Poisson show silver lace to the pockets on the back of the *habit*, to the collar and at the small of the back. The plates of the regiment from this series consistently show the cuff of the *habit* having no flap, which correlates exactly with a preserved *habit* thought to be of the regiment in the Musée de l'Emperi, which carries royalist buttons of the First Restoration. The drummer in the series, like the trumpeter, sports a silver-laced *chapeau* and has blue and silver trefoils worn over blue swallows' nests laced in silver. Silver lace appears at the collar and also the *revers*. It is highly likely that the trumpeters and drummers wore the same *habit*, which Chataignier and Poisson show the back of in the print of the trumpeter, and the front in the print of the drummer, which allows us to potentially accurately reconstruct the dress of these men, at least in the Consular period. The trumpet-corporal was MAT No. 150 *bis* Antoine Stulz

Above left: *Gendarme* wearing campaign uniform c.1806-1807 by the German artist Henschel. As with the other regiments of the Guard, on campaign a *surtout* was worn to save the *habit* for parades. By this date, it seems the regiment had adopted the *porte-carabine* to support the light cavalry carbine.

Above right: Officer in full dress in a print by Aaron Martinet published in 1809. Oddly, the colourist of the plate gives the officer white waistcoat and breeches in *lieu* of the *chamois*-coloured items.

was born on 7 April 1781 and admitted to the regiment on 20 May 1802. He was named as trumpet-corporal on 3 February 1805 and as trumpet-major on 1 October 1807.[46]

By the time that Nicolas Hoffmann is working, the swallows' nests had been discontinued and the bearskin had replaced the *chapeau*. Hoffmann shows a *habit* in all respects the same as Chataignier and Poisson, although Hoffmann has added cuff flaps. However, in 1805 *bleu de ciel habits* faced in crimson were made for the regiment – perhaps a one-off event. Boessweilwald shows the *bleu de ciel habit* faced in crimson, but for the band of the regiment. This is of course entirely possible, as the regiment was authorised a band in July 1804. So, perhaps this is the only archive evidence of the band, as no other traces of the band ever existing can be found in archive documents.

Hoffmann also shows a kettledrummer, dressed in the same manner as the trumpeter. The image exists in two forms. In one the figure sports a *chapeau*, in the other a bearskin. Chataignier and Poisson also show a trumpeter wearing a *chapeau*. Both images by Hoffmann and Chataignier and Poisson of the kettledrummer in a *chapeau* are remarkably similar. The image by Hoffmann dates from 1805 to as late as summer 1807, as the series that included the kettledrummer also includes Polish lancers, created in 1807, as well as Empress Dragoons created in April 1806. The regiment was officially allowed a kettledrummer from 15 April 1806.

Consulting the regiment's meagre archive for references to the kettledrummer provides no documents. However, upon consulting the regiment's muster list of 22 November 1801 to 2 January 1808, we do find mention of a kettledrummer:[47]

> MAT No. 1134 Nicolas Lemaigre, son of Theodore Lemaigre and Elisabeth Oudot, was born on 30 August 1790 in Paris and stood 1.66 m tall. He was admitted to the regiment on 1 October 1807 as *timbalier*.

More details can be found in a duplicate copy of the book made during the empire:[48] 'Passed to the lancers of the Guard 21 July 1811'.

Clearly, Lemaigre held the post of kettledrummer from 1807 to 1811. His replacement was:[49]

> MAT No. (illegible) Joseph Othon Vandenbrock, son of Dieudonne Joseph Othon Vandenbrock and Louise Borde. Born at Toul on 19 September 1797, he was admitted to the regiment on 19 October 1811 and passed to the 'Garde du Corps du Roi' on 4 September 1814.

Seemingly, the regiment only ever had two kettledrummers, and perhaps just one set of uniform. Given that kettledrummers are clearly listed in the regimental muster lists, the absence of any such person before 1807 is proof that no kettledrummers were in the regiment before October 1807.

Therefore, does the Hoffmann image actually date from the end of 1807? The only chance Hoffmann had of witnessing the Polish lancers, raised in early 1807, would have been their entrance to Paris in November 1807. Therefore, this is the earliest time from which Hoffmann's image can date, assuming he actually observed a Polish Lancer rather than working from a published print. Therefore, is the Hoffmann image of the kettledrummer also from winter 1807? Given no mention is made at all, at any point, between 1801 and 1807 of another kettledrummer, it is likely that such an appointment was only made on 1 October 1807 in enacting the decree of 15 April 1806. Until more archive material can be found for the regiment's kettledrummer, it seems that the post was created in 1807. What do we make, therefore, of the image by Chataignier and Poisson? The image, purporting to be from 1802/1803, does imply the existence of a kettledrummer at this date.

A second state of the print by Martinet is correctly coloured giving chamois waistcoat and breeches. Like with the plate by Vernet published in 1810, the officers *habit* has horizontal pockets on the back. It seems, therefore, that officers retained this distinction in *lieu* of adopting the long pockets used by other regiments of the Guard.

No archive paperwork exists to confirm the existence of a kettledrummer in the regiment pre-1807. It is an unanswerable question if one existed before 1807, or indeed what the uniform actually was. Certainly, no kettledrummer existed between 1801 and 1803, as the very comprehensive inspection returns make no mention at all of a kettledrummer's clothing or the kettledrums themselves.

A band was authorised for the regiment, the only musician the regiment seems to have had was:[50]

> Mat No. 319 *bis* Pierre Klingberg was born in 1771 and admitted to the regiment as a trumpeter on 21 April 1804, then passed to the staff as a musician on 31 December 1805. He left the regiment on 6 November 1808.

A single musician on the staff could imply that the bandmaster was a member of the regiment and the other band members being hired in *gagistes*. The dress of a band, if indeed it existed (as the only proof of its existence is the decree and the presence of a bandmaster), is not known. It could have been similar to that of the trumpeters.

CHAPTER 11

HORSE ARTILLERY

The Light Artillery of the Guides of Bonaparte was formed on 30 May 1797 and consisted of thirty mounted gunners. On 6 July 1798, the artillery became the Artillery of the Guides of the Army of the Orient, and consisted of sixty gunners commanded by a lieutenant and captain, serving three 4-pounders. The decree dated 7 *Frimaire*, Year VIII (8 November 1799) enlarged the half-company to a full-strength company manning eight guns. In 1804, the company was expanded to two squadrons manning four batteries of guns.

The decree of 12 April 1808 created a regiment of foot artillery within the Guard, reducing the mounted regiment to two squadrons each of two companies. At this point, each company was to have six 6-pounders and two Howitzers, listed in a report of 1 July 1809 and 7 February 1811. On 13 March 1813, the mounted regiment was re-established once again to three squadrons and, at the end of 1813, a mounted company of Young Guard was created. This Young Guard company was in fact not a new formation, but had been transferred into French service from the former Spanish Royal Guard of King Joseph. Kit and equipment, in theory, was as under Spanish administration. These seven companies were disbanded in July 1814.

Clothing and equipment

The oldest document relating to the dress of the regiment was compiled on 17 September 1800 and lists the following items:[1]

Passamenteries:

- 3,314.67 m of *soutache* in red wool at 30 *centimes* a metre
- 1,983.17 m of red flat wool braid, 12 mm wide, at 75 *centimes* a metre
- 6,828.94 m of red square wool braid at 60 *centimes* a metre
- 3,985.78 m of red and gold square braid
- 1,838.12 m of square wool braid in red and gold for sub-officers
- 500 red *aiguillettes* at 7.75 *francs* each
- 330 red hat cords at 6 *francs* each
- 1,600 grenades in red wool for *bonnets de police* at 60 *centimes* each
- 1,040 red tassels for boots at 65 *centimes* each
- 590 pairs of tassels for *schabraques* at 2 *francs* a pair
- Twenty trumpet cords in red and gold at 96 *francs* each
- Fifty-three sets of shako cords in red and gold at 18 *francs* each
- 159 *sabretache* at 18.25 *francs* each
- Twelve *sabretache* for trumpeters at 50.50 *francs* each

Equipment:

- Fifteen trumpets at 160 *francs* each

Headdress and sundries:

- 150 plumes at 6 *francs* each

Leather-work:

- 100 *gibernes* at 6.50 *francs* each
- 100 *gibernes* belts at 7 *francs* each
- Fifty waist belts at 9.50 *francs* each

Harness:

- 352 saddles at 80 *francs* each

The document is frustratingly vague on several issues. The headdress is not listed, nor are *schabraques*, boots or uniform items. Clearly, the hussar uniform was in use by this date, as the braid and lace for dolmans and *pelisse* of gunners and sub-officers was purchased.

Above left: Painting by Nicholas Hoffmann of an officer of Guard Horse Artillery c.1805, wearing the elaborate and costly parade dress uniform.

Above right: Gunner in hussar-style full dress of the Guard Horse Artillery by Hoffmann c.1805.

What we do know from the work of Hoffmann and from later archive documentation is that the regiment had two uniforms: a more sombre and practical *chasseur* dress and an elaborate hussar dress. The *chasseur* dress comprised a blue *habit* with scarlet facings and piping, which was worn over the simple blue double-breasted *gilet* or a hussar-style *gilet* with scarlet braiding. The dolman was imperial blue with scarlet braid and lace. Sub-officers had mixed red and gold braid and lace. In full dress with both uniforms, tight fitting decorated Hungarian breeches were worn, tucked into hussar boots. On campaign, with both orders of dress, *pantalons-à-cheval* made from imperial blue wool cloth were worn. The outside leg seams were closed by a row of eighteen large brass buttons. The button stand was reinforced with a stripe of scarlet cloth. Sub-officers seem to have worn *pantalons*, also reinforced with leather, but lacking the side opening. The *pelisse* was, as we shall see from later documentation, rarely worn. However, we cannot be sure when the hussar-style dress was adopted. Archive documentation, as we see later, makes no mention at all of any items of the uniform, so we are left to postulate that the uniform was adopted in 1806.

1805

On 23 September 1805, the depot held the following lengths of cloth:[2]

MATERIALS		*QUANTITIES (METRES)*	*PRICE PER METRE* (FRANCS)	*TOTAL VALUE* (FRANCS)
Blue wool cloth	First quality	86.68	24.40	2,090.59
	Second quality	104.78	23.90	2,304.24
	Third quality	41.40	20.43	845.80
	Fourth quality	108.59	14.50	1,552.83
	Fifth quality	1,128.88	9.68	10,927.55
Scarlet	First quality	55.44	23.56	1,306.16
	Second quality	29.34	20.19	592.37
Crimson	First quality	19	23.56	156.67
Bleu-celeste	First quality	7.43	19.35	143.77
For *capotes*		16.19	16.83	272.47
Tricot	White	212.93	2.10	447.13
Milled *serge*	Scarlet	485.98	2.73	1,326.62
	White	429.04	1.47	630.68
Linen	Blondine	696.58	1.53	1,065.76
Treillis	d'Alençon	283.43	1	8,535.52

In addition, the depot held the following items of clothing:[3]

- Fourteen pairs of gunner's Hungarian breeches
- Seven pairs of Hungarian breeches for trumpeters
- Three pairs of breeches for trumpeters with no lace
- Two pairs of Hungarian breeches for sub-officers
- One braided *gilet* for sub-officer
- Sixteen gunner's *gilets*
- Five trumpeter's *habits*
- Eighty-six gunner's *habits*
- Seven pairs of *pantalons-à-cheval* lace for trumpeters
- Eighty-seven pairs of *pantalons-à-cheval* for gunners
- Eight *gilets* for trumpeters
- Eighty-four *gilets* for gunners
- Three *redingotes* for sub-officers
- Sixty *caracots* for gunners, i.e. stable coats
- Two sub-officer's *chapeaux*
- Two gunner's *chapeaux*
- 106 stable coats
- 129 pairs of stable trousers
- 122 *gilet d'ecurie*
- Fifteen *aiguillettes* for sub-officers
- Six *aiguillettes* for trumpeters
- 101 *aiguillettes* for gunners
- Thirteen *sabretache* for gunners
- Two colpacks for sub-officers
- 396 shirts
- 137 black stocks
- Fifteen pairs of *calceons*
- Thirty-eight plumes for colpacks
- Sixteen plumes for *chapeaux*
- Eight plume covers
- Six *manteaux*
- Fifty *porte-manteaux*
- Ten *bonnets de police*
- Forty-seven *capotes*
- Twelve sets of sub-officer's colpack cords
- Three sets of gunner's colpack cords
- Six sets of trumpet cords
- Five workmen's *habits*

Worthy of comment is the total absence of *pelisse*, dolman and barrel sash. Were none in use, or more prosaically were none in the depot. Also of comment is

Above left: Gunner of Guard Horse Artillery wearing the more sombre, and more practical, *chasseur*-style uniform, in painting by Nicholas Hoffmann, *c.*1805.

Above right: Trumpeter pf Guard Horse Artillery in full dress uniform. This uniform was styled after the *Chasseurs-à-Cheval* of the Guard. From 1811, the same uniform, the one shown here, was worn by the trumpeters of both the Guard Horse Artillery and the Artillery Train.

the absence of a white colpack for trumpeters. Hoffmann shows the use of such a colpack, but it cannot be verified through archive documents. The previous inspection of the regiment is from 23 September 1804 and also makes no mention of a trumpeter's colpack or the hussar dress for the regiment.[4] The stores list of 1803 lists a single white trumpeter's colpack, which cost 87 *francs*, but again no hussar clothing is mentioned.[5] We are left, therefore, with a quandary – when did the regiment gain the hussar-style uniform?

Equipment in stores in the summer of 1805 comprised:[6]

- Four gunner's *gibernes*, costing 2.50 *francs* each
- Six *giberne banderoles*, costing 12 *francs* each
- Five hussar-pattern waist-belts, costing 11 *francs* each
- 198 *giberne* plates, costing 1.30 *francs*

Horse equipment included:[7]

- One undress *schabraque* for trumpeter, costing 54.74 *francs*
- 159 *schabraques* for gunners, costing 56.35 *francs*
- Twenty-five sheepskin hussar *schabraques,* costing 26.91 *francs*
- Fifty hussar bridles, costing 6.30 *francs*

Of interest is the presence of the sheepskin *schabraque*. Its use is confirmed, it seems, by the painting by Nicolas Hoffmann showing a gunner in undress wearing the *chasseur* clothing

1809

The archive documents leave us with a gap of four years, a period that is key to understanding the evolution of the uniform, as in these missing years it is likely the hussar dress was adopted. The next document concerning the dress of the regiment is dated 5 March 1809. The regimental depot held the following items:[8]

- Seven Hungarian breeches for sub-officers of artillery
- Thirteen Hungarian breeches for trumpeters
- 156 Hungarian breeches with braid for other ranks
- Twenty-nine Hungarian breeches
- Five braided *gilets* for sub-officers
- Five braided *gilets* for trumpeters
- Thirteen braided *gilets* for other ranks
- 106 double-breasted *gilets* for other ranks
- Twelve double-breasted *gilets* for trumpeters
- Three sub-officer's *habits*
- 100 other rank's *habits*
- Twelve trumpeter's *habits*
- Seven *redingotes* for sub-officers
- 200 *pantalons-à-cheval* for other ranks
- Twelve *pantalons-à-cheval* for trumpeters
- Six *vestes d'ecurie*
- Five *caracots*
- Six *gilets d'ecurie*
- Six *pantalons d'ecurie* in blue wool cloth
- Sixty-one *bonnets de police*
- Five *capotes-manteaux*
- Eleven pairs of *calceons*
- Six *porte-manteaux*
- Five trumpeter's *porte-manteaux*
- Five trumpeter's *schabraques*
- Five colpacks for sub-officers

Officer of Guard Horse Artillery wearing full dress. (Musée de l'Empéri, Collections du Musée de l'armée, Anciennes collections Jean et Raoul Brunon)

- Five sets of colpack cords for sub-officers
- 931 pairs of gloves
- Fifty sets of colpack cords
- 106 gunner's *aiguillettes*
- Twelve *aiguillettes* for trumpeters
- Six sword knots for trumpeters
- 320 sword knots for gunners
- Fifty-five colpack cockades
- 200 pairs of trefoils
- Eleven shirts
- Eleven cravats
- 300 pairs of shoes
- Six *chapeau* plumes for gunners
- Fifty-five colpack plumes with covers
- Eleven sabres for gunners
- Five *gibernes* and *porte-gibernes* for sub-officers
- Eleven gunner's sabre belts
- 400 pairs of spurs

Yet again, no hussar uniform items are listed in the depot. Why is this? Did no spare hussar items, like the *pelisse*, dolman and barrel sash, exist to be in stores? Perhaps so.

1811

A gap of almost three years exists in the paper archive of the regiment and the next documents date from July 1811.

Clothing made and issued 1811 to 1814 was as follows for the sub-officer:[9]

YEAR	PELISSE		*DOLMAN*		*HUNGARIAN BREECHES*		GILET TRESSE		HABITS		REDINGOTES		*COLPACK CORDS*		AIGUILLETTE		SABRETACHE	
	MADE	*ISSUED*	*MADE*	*ISSUED*	*MADE*	*ISSUED*	*MADE*	*ISSUED*	*MADE*	*ISSUED*	*MADE*	*ISSUED*	*MADE*	*ISSUED*	*MADE*	*ISSUED*	*MADE*	*ISSUED*
In magazine 1 July 1811	2	0	3	0	1	0	19	0	0	0	3	0	30	0	11	0	7	0
Third quarter of 1811	0	0	1	0	30	0	1	0	3	1	4	2	0	0	1	3	6	0
Fourth quarter of 18141	0	1	0	1	2	12	0	1	1	1	2	2	1	0	0	1	0	0
Total	2	1	4	1	33	12	20	1	4	2	9	4	31	0	12	4	13	0
In depot 1 January 1812	0	1	0	3	0	21	0	19	0	2	0	5	0	31	0	8	0	13

Items for other rank's clothing were as follows:[10]

Gunner of the Guard Horse Artillery during the consular period in full dress, in a print by Chataignier and Poison.

YEAR	PELISSE		*DOLMANS*		*HUNGARIAN BREECHES*		GILET TRESSE		GILETS		HABITS		BONNETS DE POLICE		PANTALONS-À-CHEVAL		CAPOTE-MANTEAUX	
	MADE	*ISSUED*	*MADE*	*ISSUED*	*MADE*	*ISSUED*	*MADE*	*ISSUED*	*MADE*	*ISSUED*	*MADE*	*ISSUED*	*MADE*	*ISSUED*	*MADE*	*ISSUED*	*MADE*	*ISSUED*
In magazine 1 July 1811	3	0	97	0	127	0	123	0	209	0	203	0	429	0	171	0	131	0
Third quarter of 1811	6	3	3	4	190	7	15	10	7	29	0	7	403	559	155	10	25	18
Fourth quarter of 18141	0	0	0	9	0	140	1	15	4	35	59	28	49	131	7	155	70	74
Total	9	3	100	13	317	147	139	25	220	64	261	35	881	690	333	165	226	92
In depot 1 January 1812	0	6	0	87	0	170	0	114	0	156	0	226	0	191	0	168	0	134

The *caracot* listed for stable dress was double-breasted. Exactly the same item was used by the marines of the Guard in undress, although that of the Guard horse artillery may not have had scarlet braid replicating the aurore of the marines' example. These items were in the depot in 1811 and are first mentioned in 1809, along with *gilet d'ecurie* and *veste d'ecurie*. These items needed the following cloth amounts:[13]

Veste d'ecurie:

- 1.36 m of blue wool cloth, fifth quality, at 9.68 *francs* a metre
- 1.19 m of linen at 1.51 *francs* a metre
- Fourteen bone buttons, total 3 *centimes*
- Labour: 1.20 *francs*
- Total: 16.18 *francs*

Caracots:

- 1.36 m of blue wool cloth, fifth quality, at 9.68 *francs* a metre
- 1.64 m of linen at 1.51 *francs* a metre
- Fourteen large buttons at 29 *centimes*
- Four small buttons at 6 *centimes*
- Labour: 1.40 *francs*
- Total: 17.38 *francs*

Gilet d'ecurie:

- 0.40 m of blue wool cloth, fifth quality, at 9.68 *francs* a metre
- 0.59 m of white *tricot* at 2.10 *francs* a metre
- 0.14 m of white milled *serge* at 1.47 *francs* a metre
- 0.30 m of linen for lining at 1.51 *francs* a metre
- Twelve bone buttons at 3 *centimes*
- Labour: 75*centimes*
- Total: 8.09 *francs*

Clearly, the *caracot* were sleeved garments, the *vestes* were also sleeved, whereas the *gilet* was without sleeves. These garments for the sub-officers were worn with stable trousers made from blue wool cloth, with the outside leg seam closed by bone buttons.

As in 1811, the *pelisse* was, it seems, not worn, with only two examples issued between 1812 and 1814. The *manteaux-capote* must have fulfilled the function of this item of dress.

Equipment issued in the same period was as follows:[14]

YEAR	SABRETACHE		ETUIS DE *SABRETACHE*		*EAGLE AND CROSSED CANNON FOR ETUIS*		*WAIST BELTS*		*SWORD KNOTS*		GIBERNES		PORTE-GIBERNES		*EAGLES FOR* GIBERNES		*BOOTS*	
	MADE	*ISSUED*	*MADE*	*ISSUED*	*MADE*	*ISSUED*	*MADE*	*ISSUED*	*MADE*	*ISSUED*	*MADE*	*ISSUED*	*MADE*	*ISSUED*	*MADE*	*ISSUED*	*MADE*	*ISSUED*
In magazine	71	0	10	0	0	0	64	0	0	0	46	0	59	0	69	0	252	0
First quarter of 1812	0	30	89	33	250	171	0	30	400	173	27	36	28	26	184	38	110	246
Second quarter of 1812	0	40		41	0	40	0	34	0	40	0	38	0	38	0	38	0	42
Third quarter of 1812	0	0	0	0	0	0	20	3	0	2	0	0	0	0	0	0	150	5
Fourth quarter of 1812	18	17	0	21	0	21	0	17	0	174	10	18	0	18	0	28	150	358
First quarter of 1813	483	60	708	70	636	70	407	68	610	109	350	116	300	116	350	120	452	118
Second quarter of 1813	0	121	0	166	0	166	100	129	0	298	301	234	301	234	301	242	430	285
Third quarter of 1813	0	1	0	3	0	3	0	1	0	7	0	3	0	3	0	10	200	16
Fourth quarter of 1813	213	292	60	272	38	272	101	208	0	207	0	257	0	257	0	257	2	376
Total	785	561	867	606	924	743	692	490	1,010	1,010	734	702	688	692	904	733	1,746	1,446
In depot 1 January 1814	0	217	0	217	0	181	0	202	0	22	0	42	0	54	0	169	0	300

Above left: Gunner wearing the more sombre *chasseur*-style uniform, worn on campaign. Henschel captures very well the soldierly appearance of this uniform.

Above right: Officer in parade dress in a print by Aaron Martinet.

Left: Gunner wearing the hussar-style dress. Martinet shows the gunner not carrying a *pelisse*. This observation is corroborated by the regiment's paper archive, which shows that from 1811 very few *pelisses* were made and issued.

Of interest, the *sabretache* cover made from black leather was decorated with a brass device eagle over crossed cannon – the same device as worn on the shako of the Young Guard foot artillery and the *gibernes* of the Guard foot artillery. Also of interest is the fact that the sub-officers, and presumably trumpeters, had their own pattern *giberne,* with forty-two made from 1812 to 1814, along with forty-two *porte-gibernes*. Sub-officers and gunners had the same pattern cloth *schabraque* decorated with 50 mm wide scarlet lace. Trumpeters' examples were *bleu de ciel* with gold lace and gold grenades in the back corners, with 1,158 gunners' and twenty-three trumpeters' being made from 1812 to 1814. Trumpeters had their own *porte-manteaux*, again *bleu de ciel*, of which twenty-six were made.

In terms of arms, trumpeters and sub-officers had hussar-pattern sabres, and gunners for Year XI light cavalry pattern sabre. All ranks, it seems, had a pair of pistols.

Trumpeters

Our first document for the dress of the trumpeters dates from 1811:[15]

YEAR	PELISSE		*DOLMANS*		*HUNGARIAN BREECHES*		GILETTRESSE		GILETS		HABITS		PANTALONS-À-CHEVAL		CAPOTE-MANTEAUX		REDINGOTE TROMPETTE MAJOR	
	MADE	*ISSUED*	*MADE*	*ISSUED*	*MADE*	*ISSUED*	*MADE*	*ISSUED*	*MADE*	*ISSUED*	*MADE*	*ISSUED*	*MADE*	*ISSUED*	*MADE*	*ISSUED*	*MADE*	*ISSUED*
In magazine 1 July 1811	0	0	1	0	6	0	2	0	0	0	2	0	2	0	0	0	1	0
Third quarter of 1811	2	1	1	2	6	0	0	0	7	2	1	2	6	0	5	2	0	0
Fourth quarter of 18141	0	0	0	0	0	4	0	0	8	9	0	0	7	11	1	1	0	1
Total	2	1	2	2	12	4	2	0	15	11	3	2	15	11	6	3	1	1
In depot 1 January 1812	0	1	0	0	0	8	0	2	0	4	0	1	0	4	0	3	0	1

Trumpeters also had their own pattern colpack, but it seems used the same pattern colpack cords, *aiguillettes* and *sabretache* as the sub-officers. Parade and undress cords were in use, two parade sets being in the depot on 1 January 1812,

Senior officer's off-duty cap, a *bonnet de police*. The heavy bullion tassel at the front tells us it belonged to a squadron commander or above. (Musée de l'armée)

Officer's parade *sabretache*. These costly and expensive items were replaced on campaign with a *sabretache* made from black leather. This parade example is highly ornate. (Musée de l'armée).

fourteen undress sets, accompanied by six trumpet banners, were in the depot in January 1811 to January 1812. Clearly, these items were used for parades in Paris only. The trumpeter's *habit* was made from *bleu de ciel* cloth, with crimson facings. The dolman was also *bleu de ciel*, and the *pelisse* was crimson. Rousselot states that pink (rose) was used in place of crimson, but is wrong on this matter, as the regiment only purchased, between 1811 and 1814, crimson wool cloth for trumpeters, along with *bleu de ciel*.[16] Between 1812 and 1814, a single *pelisse* was made for a trumpeter but never issued. Forty-five dolmans were made, as well as thirty-one *habits* with thirty-eight double-breasted waistcoats, thirty-one braided Hungarian breeches, thirty-one braided hussar waistcoats, fifty-seven pairs of *pantalons-à-cheval*, thirty-one *capote-manteaux* and two *redingotes* for the trumpet-major. The trumpeter's *habit* was made from the following materials:[17]

- 1.80 m of *bleu celeste* wool cloth at 19.35 *francs* a metre
- 0.20 m of imperial blue wool cloth for *revers* at 23.90 *francs* a metre
- 0.08 m of crimson wool cloth at 23.56 *francs* a metre
- 1.19 m of linen for lining at 1.61 *francs* a metre
- 3.57 m of gold lace, 22 mm wide, total 32.68 *francs*
- Four grenades embroidered in gold, total 3.50 *francs*
- Twenty large buttons at 41 *centimes* a dozen

Gunners carried an elaborately embroidered *sabretache* only when wearing the hussar uniform, although *sabretache* covers were issued for use on campaign to stop the fragile embroidery becoming dirty and damaged. (Musée de l'armée)

Officers of Guard Horse Artillery also wore the more sombre *chasseur*-style uniform, as shown here in a painting by the German artist Otto, executed between 1806 and 1808.

- Four small buttons at 6 *centimes* a dozen
- Labour: 3 *francs*
- Total: 83.68 *francs*

The *schabraque* required:

- 1.50 m of *bleu celeste* wool cloth at 19.35 *francs* a metre
- 0.15 m of scarlet wool cloth, second quality, at 20.19 *francs* a metre
- 2.97 m of herringbone weave linen at 1.89 *francs* a metre
- 5.94 m of wool lace, 50 mm wide, at 1.70 *francs* a metre
- Two embroidered eagles, total 8 *francs*
- Labour: 5 *francs*
- Total: 60.74 *francs*

CHAPTER 12

ARTILLERY TRAIN

The artillery train of the Consular Guard was created under article nine of the decree of 21 *Fructidor*, Year VIII (8 September 1800) and was to comprise of one company commanded by a captain and a lieutenant, with one sergeant-major, three sergeants, one *fourrier* (company clerk), eight corporals, eighty drivers, two trumpeters and a master smith and a master saddle-maker.[1] The single company was increased to four companies with the decree of 11 *Brumaire*, Year XII (3 November 1803).[2] Article nineteen of the decree of 29 July 1804 organised the regiment as follows:[3] one lieutenant or sub-lieutenant, one sergeant-major, four sergeants, one *fourrier*, six corporals, two trumpeters, two farriers, twenty-six soldiers first-class and seventy-two soldiers second-class.

On 15 April 1806, the train was formed into one battalion and counted six companies. The staff comprised:[4] one captain commandant (Devarennes), one lieutenant-adjutant-major (Deroy), one sub-lieutenant-quartermaster (Monnin), one adjutant-sub-officer, one veterinarian, one master saddler-maker, one master boot maker, one master harness-maker, one master tailor and one master rope-maker.

Each company had:[5] one lieutenant, one sub-lieutenant, one sergeant-major, four sergeants, one *fourrier*, five corporals, sixty-eight drivers, two smiths, two harness-makers and two trumpeters. So, with the eight men on the staff the regiment had 510 men in six companies, with 220 horses in times of peace and 1,000 horses in times of war.

This eagle plate was likely to have been carried on the *giberne* of the regiment, which we know from archive sources carried a tin eagle over crossed cannon. (Photograph and collection of Bertrand Malvaux).

On 24 October 1807, the corps had two battalions, one active or principal battalion and one double battalion or *bataillon bis*, each having six companies. The *bataillon bis* became, on 22 August 1808, the 13th Line Battalion, the Guards depot company becoming the new *bataillon bis*.[6] The *bataillon bis* was formed like their line counterparts and had sixteen officers and 463 non-commissioned officers and drivers.[7]

In April 1809, the two battalions had twelve companies, to which three new companies were added in October to draw the regimental guns attached to

Above left: Officer of Artillery Train by Nicolas Hoffmann. Uniquely, or not as no other images exist of an officer, the officer is shown in an entirely imperial blue *habit* rather than the iron-grey we know to have been worn by *sous-officiers*, adjutants and drivers.

Above right: Driver of artillery train by Hoffmann. The figure dates to pre-1809, as in that year the *chapeau* was replaced by the shako, and the tail facings seemingly became dark blue.

the corps of fusiliers, *tirailleurs* and conscripts. Entry into the Guard was set at 1.678 m in height.[8]

Napoleon, like Frederick the Great, placed a greater emphasis on massing his guns at a single point to smash a hole in the enemy line for the cavalry, supported by horse artillery, to exploit, followed up infantry assault. Napoleon also believed that the well-trained and battle-hardened veterans, as well as the conscript, needed close artillery support.[9] Just at the time when Prussia (in 1807) and Austria (in 1808) had abandoned their battalion artillery and Russia its regimental artillery (in 1808), Napoleon was busy re-introducing battalion guns. It is overly simplistic to consider the return of battalion guns to the French Army in 1809, after being abolished at the end of the Revolutionary Wars, as being due to a tactical decline of the French. First (Davout) Corps and the Imperial Guard were the cutting edge of the Grande Armee of 1812. It received the highest allocation of battalion artillery.

This portrait shows a trumpeter of the regiment. The coat is seemingly dark blue, with crimson collar, and a mixed silver and light blue *aiguillette*. In 1811, this ensemble was replaced by the same uniform as worn by the Horse Artillery of the Imperial Guard. We are not sure when this image was made, but it is likely to be 1800-1806. (Musée de l'Empéri, Collections du Musée de l'armée, Anciennes collections Jean et Raoul Brunon)

This resulted in the French infantry having its own dedicated artillery support, in addition to that at divisional level, which in effect freed up guns from infantry support to be used in larger, and higher-level, artillery formations. To support the newly formed Young Guard, Napoleon raised three companies of *artillerie-conscrits* for service with the Guard in Spain on 9 June.[10]

Uniform and equipment

From the formation of the artillery train of the Consular Guard in September 1800, the company kept, if not the clothing, more or less the same colours of the old artillery carters, that is to say an iron-grey *habit-veste* with dark blue facings. The 'statement or the cost for each soldier of the train', established in September 1800, mentions the different articles destined for them: *habit-veste*, waistcoat, trousers, sheepskin breeches, hat, forage cap and boots.[11]

In addition, clothing included an iron-grey waistcoat, leather breeches and the canvas knee guards (*manchettes du botte*), iron-grey *pantalons-à-cheval*, semi-soft long knee-length boots as worn by dragoons, with detachable spurs, the iron-grey cape-overcoat, the forage cap and the waist-belt. Beside this, each soldier had an iron-grey *porte-manteau*.[12]

1803

The next document to mention clothing and equipment is an inspection made in 1803. A stores inventory of 23 September 1803 lists the following materials, items of clothing and equipment:[13]

- 135.50 *aunes* of iron-grey wool cloth
- 794 *massif* (i.e. Solid cast) tin domed buttons
- 174 large tin domed hussar buttons

- 4,804 medium tin domed hussar buttons
- 288 small tin domed hussar buttons
- 123 head collars
- One *chapeau* for sub-officer
- Two *aiguillettes* for sub-officers
- Three sets of colpack cords for sub-officers
- Three sub-officer's sword knots
- Five pairs of boots
- One driver's *chapeau*

Clearly, the sub-officers had *aiguillettes* as early as 1803 and it also seems wore colpacks, which heretofore has not been commented upon.

1804

The next document for the clothing of the regiment is from for 23 September 1804:[14]

- 326 *aunes* of iron-grey wool cloth, first quality, at 21 *francs* a metre
- 339 *aunes* of iron-grey wool cloth, second quality, at 14 *francs* a metre
- Thirty-five *aunes* of *drap blanc picque de bleu* for *manteaux* at 12 *francs* a metre
- Twenty-four large buttons
- 140 medium buttons
- 240 small hussar buttons in tin
- 645 *massif* buttons
- Ten sub-officer's sword knots
- Sixty-nine plumes for *chapeaux*
- Twenty-eight *porte-manteaux*
- Fifty-nine sabres
- Two sub-officer's *surtouts*
- Two pairs of *pantalons-à-cheval* for sub-officers
- Two pairs of hung rein breeches with crimson and silver braid for sub-officers
- Two red *gilets* with crimson and silver braiding for sub-officers
- Ninety iron-grey *gilets*
- Eighty-four *habit-vestes*
- 124 *culottes de mouton*
- Thirty-five *chapeaux*
- Two waist-belts with plates
- Twenty heavy cavalry saddles
- Twenty-seven heavy cavalry bridles
- Two bridles for sub-officers
- 497 plumes for *chapeaux*
- Two *redingotes* for sub-officers
- 127 pairs of *manchettes du botte*

Of interest, the *manteaux* were not iron-grey, which is something of a surprise. In the year up to September 1804, two officers had joined the regiment and 301 drivers. Of the men in the regiment, eighty-nine were discharged, four sent to other regiments, twenty-one had died, nineteen had deserted and five had been made officers.

1805

On 23 September 1805, the depot held the following items:[15]

- 20.68 m of white wool cloth, first quality, at 16.83 *francs* a metre
- 109.64 m of iron-grey wool cloth, first quality, at 18.51 *francs* a metre
- 2,288.25 m of iron-grey wool cloth, second quality, at 11.78 *francs* a metre
- 594 silvered large buttons at 9 *francs* a dozen
- 4,888 medium buttons in tin at 2.40 *francs* a dozen
- 159 silvered buttons at 4.50 *francs* a dozen
- 686 *boutons massif* at 3.30 *francs* a dozen
- Four grenades in silver embroidery for *habits* of sub-officers at 3 *francs* each
- Three sub-officer's *aiguillettes*
- Twenty-five sword knots for sub-officers
- Forty-four *porte-manteaux* costing 16.67 *francs* each
- 106 *bonnets de police* costing 9.90 *francs* each
- Thirty-one sabres for drivers
- 216 pairs of boots costing 23 *francs* a pair
- 187 pairs of spurs costing 3 *francs* a pair
- Eleven white waistcoats costing 12.17 *francs* each
- 131 iron-grey waistcoats costing 9.90 *francs* each
- Two full dress *habit-vestes* costing 32.88 *francs* each
- 109 undress *habit-vestes* costing 26.57 *francs* each
- Ninety-eight pairs of iron-grey wool knee breeches costing 10.52 *francs* each
- 126 pairs of *culottes de peau* costing 9 *francs* each
- Sixty-eight driver's *chapeaux* costing 8.50 *francs* each
- 383 sabre waist-belts in cow hide costing two *francs* each
- 394 waist-belt plates costing 2.55 *francs* each
- Five waist-belts in buff costing 8 *francs* each
- 337 plumes at 3 *francs* each
- 142 *surclottes* in *treillis* at 3.88 *francs* each
- Four *schabraques* in wool cloth, dragoon-style, costing 24.91 *francs* each
- Sixty-two pairs of *manchette du botte* costing 76 *centimes* a pair
- 451 trefoils in wool costing 80 *centimes* a pair

Worthy of comment is the use of, presumably whitened, cow hides for the driver's waist-belts and good quality buff for the waist-belts of the sub-officers. The price difference is notable, with the cow hide belt costing less than the buckle to fasten the belt.

Preserved in the Musée de l'armée is the only item of clothing for the regiment, this *habit*-veste. It dates from 1813, when this garment was adopted, and was only used during the campaigns of 1813 and 1814, as from 1811 a *habit-kinski* was worn, and was re-adopted in 1815. However, it is also possible that this garment dates from 1816-1830. The artillery train of the Royal Guard wore identical *habits* to this example. The buttons are not original and are not the regimental issue of tin, half-domed, with an eagle over crossed cannon. Given that the garments of 1813 and 1816 were identical, bar buttons, we cannot be sure that this item is actually 1st Empire. (Musée de l'armée)

wool cloth. The *marche* further comments that the method of covering the *fonts* (pistol holsters) had not yet been agreed upon, and that in one holster a pistol was carried, in the other a small hatchet.[22]

A few days later, on 11 April 1809, 600 pairs of shoes were ordered. At the same time 600 shirts were ordered, to measure 0.96 m from collar to tail and 0.68 m wide. The same document also gives us the details of the nose-bag (*musette*) which was to be made from canvas and measure 0.50 m by 0.45 m wide, with leather strap and buckle. The *sac a distribution* was to measure 1.30 m long by 0.65 m wide. Linen of blondine quality was purchased for the lining of *habits*, *vestes*, *gilets* and *redingotes* of the sub-officers and trumpeters, and Hungarian breeches. Linen *bisomme* was ordered for lining the *capotes*, stable coats, stable trousers and for making the pockets of the *habit*. Herringbone weave canvas of Alençon quality was obtained to line the *schabraque* and *porte-manteaux*, as well as for the production of the *musette* and *sac a distribution*. Buttons were also ordered: large silvered buttons mounted on wood, large solid cast silvered, small and medium-sized silvered solid cast buttons and horn buttons for gaiters.[23]

Wool cloth purchased comprised:[24]

- Iron-grey wool cloth, costing 14 *francs* a metre
- *Bleu de roi* wool cloth for *revers*, cuff facings and tail facings of driver's and sub-officer's *habit-vestes*, for the trumpeter's stable coat, and for the cloth stripe on the side of the *pantalons-à-cheval*, costing 30 *francs* a metre
- *Bleu de ciel* wool cloth for the clothing of the trumpeters of both battalions, costing 25 *francs* a metre
- Scarlet wool cloth for piping and grenades for both battalions, costing 25 *francs* a metre

The cloth was used to make 662 pairs of Hungarian breeches of the 1st Battalion and 1,650 pairs for the men of the 2nd Battalion. Some 1,650 black calf skins were purchased for the *pantalons-à-cheval*.

Footwear was ordered on 2 June 1809:[25]

- Sixty-two pairs of boots for sub-officers
- 600 pairs of shoes with hob nails
- Sixty-two pairs of spurs with straps

Master Saddler Waemar was engaged to supply the following items of leatherwork on 7 August:[26]

- Sixty-two *gibernes* with belts of the same pattern used by the Guard horse artillery. Each *giberne* to be supplied with a plate in red copper. The *porte-giberne* to be 65 mm wide, with *surpicquer* stitching, with buckle, slide, tip and double-headed buttons in red copper.

- The *gibernes* for sub-officers to have the flanks in copper.
- The price for the sub-officer's *giberne* to be 18 *francs*
- The price of the *giberne* with belt for drivers: 13.25 *francs*

Later the same month, 300 belt plates were issued for the *baudrier*, along with 1,600 *gibernes* and belts for the drivers.[27] This means that, contrary to Rousselot in his plate No. 80, which states that the *baudrier* was adopted in 1810, despite no archive paperwork existing from 1810, it was adopted in 1809. This is also the first mention of *gibernes*. They are absent in the images by Hahlo and Hoffmann, so we assume they were newly adopted in 1809.

On 5 March 1809 the depot held:[28]

- Seventeen Hungarian breeches for sub-officers
- Thirteen braided *gilets* for sub-officers
- 200 iron-grey *gilets*
- Four *habits* for sub-officers
- Three *redingotes* for sub-officers
- Twelve *pantalons-à-cheval* for sub-officers
- 200 undress *habit-vestes* for other ranks
- Fifty *bonnets de police*
- 600 pairs of *surclottes* in iron-grey wool cloth
- Five sword knots for sub-officers
- Three *chapeau* plumes
- 300 pairs of spurs

The tariff for the *habit* was as follows:[29]

- 1.40 m of iron-grey wool cloth, second quality, at 11.75 *francs* a metre
- 0.20 m of blue wool cloth at 14.30 *francs* a metre
- 0.09 m of scarlet cloth for piping at 23.56 *francs* a metre
- 1.78 m of linen for lining at 1.51 *francs* a metre
- Twenty-four medium buttons at two *francs* a dozen
- Labour: 2.50 *francs*
- Total: 27.05 *francs*

This item seems to have been the same as the *habit-veste* proper, but made from cheaper materials. Presumably fourteen buttons were on the *revers*, two at the shoulder, four on each cuff and four on the back. In both cases, the tail facing and lining was blue piped in scarlet.

Hungarian breeches for sub-officers required the following materials:[30]

- 1.06 m of iron-grey wool cloth, second quality, at 23.90 *francs* a metre
- 0.40 m of linen for lining at 1.61 *francs* a metre

- 6.53 m of flat scarlet wool and silver braid, total 10.50 *francs*
- Labour: 1.70 *francs*
- Total: 32.46 *francs*

The braided *gilets* for sub-officers needed:[31]

- 0.30 m of iron-grey wool cloth, first quality, at 18.51 *francs* a metre
- 0.59 m of *tricot* at 2.10 *francs* a metre
- 1.19 m of white milled *serge* at 1.47 *francs* a metre
- 0.45 m of linen for lining at 1.31 *francs* a metre
- 3.57 m of scarlet wool and silver flat braid, total 5 *francs*
- 9.51 m of silver and scarlet *soutache*, total 2.29 *francs*
- Labour: 1.50 *francs*
- Total: 22.98 *francs*

The sub-officer's *habits* were made from the following materials:[32]

- 1.80 m of iron-grey wool cloth, first quality, at 18.54 *francs* a metre
- 0.20 m of imperial blue wool cloth, second quality, at 23.90 *francs* a metre
- 0.08 m of scarlet wool cloth, first quality, at 23.56 *francs* a metre
- 1.45 m of linen for lining at 1.61 *francs* a metre
- 0.59 m of silver lace, total 3 *francs*
- Four grenades embroidered in silver, total 3 *francs*
- Four silvered large buttons, total 25 *centimes*
- Twenty silvered medium buttons, total 60 *centimes*
- Labour: 2.50 *francs*
- Total: 52.60 *francs*

As with the driver's *habit*, the tails were, we are told by Rousselot, faced and lined in blue piped in scarlet. However, comparison of the amount of blue cloth issued correlates with the same amount of white cloth issued to make the *revers* and cuff flaps of *habits* for the *grenadiers-à-cheval* and Empress Dragoons. Therefore, we can be sure that the tail facings were indeed iron-grey not dark blue.

1811

The earliest document from 1811 is dated 5 April and is an order for 200 dragoon bridles and saddles.[33] A further 600 bridles with curb bits were ordered on 7 May 1811.[34] Cloth was purchased later the same month:[35]

- 368 m of iron-grey wool cloth for the *capotes*, *schabraques* and *porte-manteaux* of sub-officers
- 368 m of iron-grey wool cloth for the *pantalons-à-cheval*, stable coats, *capotes* and *porte-manteaux* of the men of the 2nd Battalion

- 58 m of *bleu de celeste* wool cloth for the *capotes-manteaux*, *porte-manteaux* and *schabraques* of trumpeters
- 60 m of *bleu de celeste* wool cloth for Hungarian breeches, *gilets* and *habits* of trumpeters
- 30 m of crimson wool cloth for lining and piping of trumpeter's *habits*
- White milled *serge* for lining of trumpeter's dolman

Hussar-style copper buttons were purchased for the trumpeter's dolman, along with medium and small solid cast buttons for the trumpeter's *pantalons-à-cheval*. Tin buttons were purchased for the driver's *habit*, and solid cast tin buttons for the driver's *pantalons-à-cheval*.[36] The lace and braid ordered in May 1811 was as follows:[37]

- Silver lace 32 mm wide for shakos of sub-officers
- Gold lace 22 mm wide for trumpeter's *habits*
- Silver braid for trumpeters
- Wool braid 12 mm wide for lacing of trumpeter's Hungarian breeches, *gilet*, dolman and *pelisse*
- Scarlet wool braid 12 mm wide for lacing driver's Hungarian breeches and *gilet*
- Scarlet wool lace 12 mm
- Scarlet wool lace 32 mm wide for driver's shako and *bonnet de police*
- Scarlet wool lace 50 mm wide for driver's *schabraques*
- Scarlet wool *soutache* for lacing driver's *gilet*
- White wool lace 22 mm wide
- White wool lace 50 mm wide
- Silver and red braid for sub-officers
- Silver braid for sub-officers
- Square braid in silver and red for sub-officers
- Round scarlet wool cord for driver's *bonnet de police*
- Ten sets of four gold embroidered grenades for the trumpeter's *habits*
- Twenty-six sets of four grenades, embroidered in silver on red cloth patch, for sub-officers
- 356 grenades embroidered in red wool on iron-grey cloth for *bonnets de police*
- 369 scarlet wool tassels for *bonnets de police*
- Twenty-five olives in gold and red for trumpeter's *pelisse*
- Twenty-five pairs of grenades embroidered in red wool for trumpeter's *schabraques*
- Twenty-nine pairs of eagles embroidered in red wool for sub-officer's *schabraques*
- Two pairs of epaulettes and *aiguillettes* for adjutants
- 1,153 pairs of scarlet fringed epaulettes

- Twenty-five trumpeter's sword knots
- Sixteen trumpeter's *aiguillettes* with 27 mm in gold thread and 52 mm in crimson wool thread
- Sixteen trumpeter's trefoils
- Two sets of shako cords for adjutants
- Four sets of shako cords for sub-officers
- Twenty-five colpack cords for trumpeters

Based on this order the drivers in 1811 wore scarlet fringed epaulettes at the shoulder. Artists, like Rousselot and others, show the regiment with trefoils, which clearly is not the case. Trumpeter's headdress was the colpack. The trumpeters had two uniforms: a parade dress dolman and an undress *habit*.

Leather-work ordered was as follows:[38]

- Twenty-six hussar waist-belts with the hook and rings in copper of the same model as used by the Guard horse artillery, for use of the trumpeters
- Twenty *gibernes* and *porte-gibernes* for drivers, each costing 13 *francs*
- Twenty-six hussar saddles complete with breastplate, crupper, stirrup leathers and irons, girth and *surcingle* and pistol holsters conforming to the model used by the horse artillery of the Guard
- 336 plates with the eagle in copper
- Four pairs of hussar boots for adjutants edged in silver lace with silver and red tassel
- Ninety-four pairs of hussar boots for sub-officers with red and silver lace and red and silver tassel
- Twenty-five pairs of hussar boots for trumpeters with red and gold lace and tassels
- 1,784 pairs of hussar boots, complete with hobnails and scarlet lace and tassels
- 2,000 pairs of hussar spurs
- 336 leather hides for *pantalons-à-cheval*
- 436 shakos made from leather covered in black cloth, complete with eagle plate and chin scales in copper and oil cloth cover

Later, on 29 July, 350 sets of shako cords in wool were ordered, along with 300 scarlet plumes 30 cm tall with covers.[39] At the close of the year, eighteen saddles were purchased for trumpeters costing 36 *francs*, along with twenty-five dragoon saddles for sub-officers costing 84 *francs* each, 1,392 pairs of leather breeches costing 15 *francs* each, 1,392 pairs of braces costing 1.25 *francs,* and twenty-five colpacks for trumpeters costing 42 *francs*.[40]

In summer 1811, a store's inventory was made showing what was in stock on 1 January 1811 and had been made in the first quarter of the year:[41]

Sub-officers

	Pantalons-à-cheval		*Gilet tresse*		*Habits*		*Redingotes*		*Capotes*		*Shakos*		*Aiguillettes*	
	Made	Issued	Made	Issued	Made	Issued	Made	Issued	Made	Issued	Made	Issued	Made	Issued
In magazine	45	0	47	0	40		31	0	15		4	0	54	0
First quarter	0	0	0	0	0	0	0	0		0	9	0	0	0
Second quarter	0	13	0	13	1	17	0	15	0	10	4	14	0	19
Total	43	13	47	13	41	17	31	15	15	10	17	14	54	19
In depot 1 July 1811	0	30	0	34	0	24	0	16	0	5	0	3	0	35

Above left: Driver of the artillery train wearing the pre-1809 uniform but sporting the 1809 shako. No doubt it took time for the new clothing to be introduced across the entire regiment, which witnessed the leather breeches and white waistcoat replaced by hussar-style Hungarian breeches and braided waistcoat.

Above right: Martinet's depiction of the 1809 to 1811 uniform, comprising *habit*, braided waistcoat, and braided Hungarian breeches. The presence of shoulder straps in *lieu* of scarlet fringed epaulettes tells us this figure is actually of the 2nd Young Guard regiment who never adopted epaulettes.

Drivers

		In magazine	First quarter	Second quarter	Total	In depot 1 July 1811
PANTALONS-À-CHEVAL	*MADE*	400	450	229	1,079	0
	ISSUED	0	429	69	498	584
GILET TRESSE	*MADE*	355	0	8	363	0
	ISSUED	0	26	25	51	312
GILETS	*MADE*	617	1	251	869	0
	ISSUED	0	0	0	0	0
HABITS, *OLD MODEL*	*MADE*	0	0	196	196	0
	ISSUED	0	0	0	0	196
HABITS, *NEW MODEL*	*MADE*	690	6	0	696	0
	ISSUED	9	15	24	48	0
HUNGARIAN BREECHES	*MADE*	675	256	0	931	0
	ISSUED	0	81	32	113	818
STABLE COATS	*MADE*	1,276	3	313	1,592	0
	ISSUED	0	41	716	757	935
BONNETS DE POLICE	*MADE*	793	0	0	793	0
	ISSUED	0	28	96	124	669
CAPOTE-MANTEAUX	*MADE*	15	25	74	114	0
	ISSUED	0	18	19	37	84

Furthermore, drivers had 358 pairs of scarlet fringed epaulettes, 369 pairs of stable trousers, 226 sword knots, 618 *porte-manteaux* and 719 pairs of shoes for stable duties. Seemingly, both an iron-grey waistcoat braided in scarlet and a simple white waistcoat were in use side-by-side.

Trumpeters

	PANTALONS-À-CHEVAL		GILET TRESSE		GILETS		HABITS, *FULL DRESS*		HABITS, *UNDRESS*		*HUNGARIAN BREECHES*		AIGUILLETTES, *FULL DRESS*		AIGUILLETTES, *UNDRESS*		*SWORD KNOTS*	
	MADE	*ISSUED*	*MADE*	*ISSUED*	*MADE*	*ISSUED*	*MADE*	*ISSUED*	*MADE*	*ISSUED*	*MADE*	*ISSUED*	*MADE*	*ISSUED*	*MADE*	*ISSUED*	*MADE*	*ISSUED*
In magazine	4	0	5	0	33	0	5	0	2	0	3	2	21	0	25	0	14	0
First quarter	0	0	0	0	0	0	0	0	0	0	17	4	0	0	0	0	0	0
Second quarter	1	2	0	2	0	2	0	2	0	0	2	6	0	2	0	0	0	4
Total	5	2	5	2	33	2	5	2	2	0	22	12	21	2	25	0	14	4
In depot 1 July 1811	0	3	0	3	0	31	0	3	0	2	0	0	0	19	0	25	0	10

In addition, trumpeters had twenty-three *porte-manteaux* made, of which three were issued, ten trumpet banners, of which two were issued, fourteen sets of parade trumpet cords and twenty-six sets of undress trumpet cords.

Equipment

	BAUDRIERS		GIBERNES, *SUB-OFFICERS*		GIBERNES DE TROUPE		PLAQUE *DU* BAUDRIER		CEINTURON D'ADJUTANT		CEINTURON D'TROMPETTE		*HUSSAR SPURS*		BOTTES *OF SUB-OFFICERS*		BOTTES DE SOLDAT	
	MADE	*ISSUED*	*MADE*	*ISSUED*	*MADE*	*ISSUED*	*MADE*	*ISSUED*	*MADE*	*ISSUED*	*MADE*	*ISSUED*	*MADE*	*ISSUED*	*MADE*	*ISSUED*	*MADE*	*ISSUED*
In magazine	169	0	16	0	261	0	133	0	0	0	1	0	1,489	0	48	0	1,427	0
First quarter	0	8	0	0	0	9	0	8	0	0	0	0	0	1,248	16	64	25	1,184

	BAUDRIERS		GIBERNES, *SUB-OFFICERS*		GIBERNES DE TROUPE		PLAQUE *DU* BAUDRIER		CEINTURON D'ADJUTANT		CEINTURON D'TROMPETTE		*HUSSAR SPURS*		BOTTES *OF SUB-OFFICERS*		BOTTES DE SOLDAT	
	MADE	*ISSUED*	*MADE*	*ISSUED*	*MADE*	*ISSUED*	*MADE*	*ISSUED*	*MADE*	*ISSUED*	*MADE*	*ISSUED*	*MADE*	*ISSUED*	*MADE*	*ISSUED*	*MADE*	*ISSUED*
Second quarter	69	26	0	15	70	17	433	26	2	0	0	0	259	52	13	10	671	42
Total	238	34	16	15	331	26	566	34	2	0	1	0	1,748	1,300	77	74	2,123	1,226
In depot 1 July 1811	0	204	0	1	0	305	0	532	0	2	0	1	0	848	0	5	0	897

Equipment included thirty-one sub-officer's *porte-manteaux* and 618 driver's *porte-manteaux*, 226 driver's sword knots, 506 shakos with 298 scarlet cords and 274 plumes. Senior sub-officers and trumpeters were issued hussar-pattern sabres, and drivers carried standard infantry sabre *briquets* of the model used by the Guard infantry. Trumpeters rode on twenty-one hussar saddles, and drivers had 180 dragoon-pattern saddles. The sub-officers had fifty-six *schabraques*, and the trumpeters ten.

1812

In spring 1812, huge quantities of materials were purchased:[42]

- 46 m of gold lace *a la batons*, 22 mm wide, for trumpeter's *habits*
- 124 m of red and gold thread braid for lacing Hungarian breeches and *gilets* of trumpeters
- 160 m of *soutache* in red and gold for lacing *gilets* of trumpeters
- 1,000 m of scarlet wool lace, 22 mm wide, for rank stripes and *porte-manteaux*
- 1,394 m of scarlet wool lace, 32 mm wide, for *bonnets de police*
- 518 m of scarlet wool lace, 50 mm wide, for *schabraques*, *housses* and *chaperons*
- Sixteen pairs of grenades in silver or possibly gold For trumpeter's *habits*
- Seventy-five sets of four grenades embroidered in silver on red cloth for sub-officers
- 923 grenades embroidered in scarlet wool on iron-grey cloth for *bonnets de police*
- 1,212 scarlet wool tassels for *bonnets de police*
- 564 pairs of epaulettes in scarlet wool
- 189 pairs of trefoils in scarlet wool

- Twenty-six sword knots for trumpeters of the new model in buff leather with tassel in red wool and gold, the same model as used by the Guard horse artillery
- Thirty-one *aiguillettes* for sub-officers, of one-part silver to two-parts scarlet
- Twelve *aiguillettes* for trumpeters, of one-part gold to two-parts crimson
- Twenty-six trumpeter's cords, the same as used by the Guard horse artillery
- Twenty-six *sabretache* for trumpeters, the same as used by the Guard horse artillery

It is likely that the epaulettes were worn by the 1st, or Old Guard, Battalion from 1809 onwards, and the trefoils by the 2nd, or Young Guard, Battalion. The two battalions were seemingly dressed identically, bar the shoulder decoration. It must have been a Young Guard driver that Martinet shows in his print and was copied by Rousselot in his plate No. 80 as being Old Guard.

Leather-work and equipment ordered comprised:[43]

- Twenty-six waist-belts for trumpeters, the same as used by the Guard horse artillery
- *Gibernes* and *porte-gibernes* complete with buckle, slide, tip and double-headed buttons in red copper
- *Baudriers*, 65 mm wide, with *surpicquer* stitching with sword frog in the manner of an *epee* shoulder-belt, along with bayonet frog
- Hussar-style waist-belts
- Sixty whips
- Four pairs of boots for trumpeters, bordered with gold and crimson braid and gold and crimson tassels
- Twenty-four pairs of hussar boots for cadet trumpeters, with scarlet wool lace and tassel
- 957 sets of heavy cavalry spurs and straps
- 957 pairs of Russian boots, i.e. rigid knee-length boots as worn by the *grenadiers-à-cheval*, for the conscript battalion
- 1,300 pairs of shoes with nails

Buttons purchased were large and small copper buttons for trumpeter's *habits*, medium-sized copper buttons for the trumpeter's *gilet* and small copper buttons for the braided waistcoat of the trumpeters. Other items ordered from M. Mason were:[44]

- Large solid cast copper buttons for *pantalons-à-cheval* of the trumpeters
- Medium-sized tin buttons for *habit-vestes*
- 164 sets of shako brasses comprising a crowned eagle over crossed cannon plate, three crowns in copper, one garnished with a hook, and chin scales in copper
- 169 shakos
- Twenty-four trumpets in copper

On 27 May the following tariffs for clothing was established:[50]

Habit-veste:

- 1.28 m of iron-grey wool cloth
- 0.62 m of *bleu impériale* wool cloth
- 1.58 m of linen *bisomme*
- 0.10 m of scarlet wool cloth for piping
- Eight large buttons in tin
- Twenty-three small buttons in tin
- Labour: 3 *francs*
- Total: 61.24 *francs*

We note the increase in blue wool cloth for a *habit*. The increase is likely to correlate with the tail facing and lining changing from iron-grey to imperial blue. Under the Bardin regulations, a *habit-veste* required 1.36 m of imperial blue wool cloth for the body, 0.24 m of white wool cloth for the *revers* and 1 m of white milled *serge* for tail facings and linings.[51] Clearly, the *habit-veste* adopted in 1813 was not a standard Bardin *habit-veste*. Of interest, the 1809 specification allows for 1.40 m of iron-grey wool cloth, which included the facings, is a difference of 0.12 m. The blue cloth has increased by 0.42 m. The amount of scarlet cloth for piping increased fractionally. The *habit-kinski* adopted in 1815 required 1.40 m of iron-grey wool cloth and 0.40 metres of blue.[52] These single-breasted garments had blue collars, blue round cuffs and blue tail facing and lining. The 0.22 m difference between the 1813 tariff and 1815 for the amount of blue cloth can be accounted for by the addition of *revers* and pointed cuffs. In 1815, the garment needed 1.40 m of iron-grey wool for the body. The difference in cloth amount could be simply representing that the *habit-veste* of 1813 was as in previous years – cut away rather than being closed to the waist – and, therefore, it seems likely that the 1813 *habit-veste* was the same type as in previous years, but with the addition of blue tail facings. The lack of any waistcoats to be worn under the garment precludes a cut-away coat, however. When compared to the stable coat tariff, the *habit* needed just 0.80 m more of iron-grey wool cloth, which seems totally insufficient to make full-length tails, which we know existed, as eight large buttons were purchased: two at the small of the back and three on each long pocket. We know the garment had *revers*, as buttons were issued to fasten them back to the *habit* body. So, we are left with a conundrum about the appearance of the regiment's *habit* in 1813 – was it a Bardin-style garment or the older style? It is easy to be distracted by the *habit-veste*, said to be for the regiment, in the Musee de l'Armée. However, given the artillery train of the Royal Guard wore *habit-vestes* from 1816 to 1830, and the garment on display retains no original buttons, it is likely to be 1815 and later, as far more of these items were made and existed than were made in 1813 for the Imperial Guard. Without detailed examination of the garment to locate issue numbers and inspection stamps, we cannot verify this suggestion.

The tariff for the other items of cloth was as follows:[53]

Stable coat:

- 1.20 m of iron-grey wool cloth
- 0.10 m of blue wool cloth
- 1.58 m of Flanders linen
- Labour: 2.25 *francs*
- Total: 27.64 *francs*

Pantalons-à-cheval:

- 1.78 m of iron-grey wool cloth
- 1.20 m of Flanders linen
- Labour: 2.25 *francs*
- Total: 27.54 *francs*

Capote-manteaux:

- 4 m of iron-grey wool cloth
- Flanders linen
- Twelve large tin buttons
- Seven small tin buttons
- Labour: 2 *francs*
- Total: 61.24 *francs*

Bonnet de police:

- 0.35 m of iron-grey wool cloth
- 1.20 m of scarlet wool lace 32 mm wide
- 2.38 m of round scarlet wool cording
- 0.28 m of Flanders linen
- One grenade embroidered in scarlet wool on iron-grey cloth
- One tassel in scarlet wool
- Labour: 50 *centimes*
- Total: 7.28 *francs*

Porte-manteau:

- 0.90 m of iron-grey wool cloth
- 1.40 m of Flanders linen
- 1.19 m of scarlet wool lace 22 mm wide
- *Hongroise de peau* (doe hide Hungarian breeches): 15 *francs*
- Pair of scarlet epaulettes: 5 *francs*
- Plume and cover: 3.65 *francs*
- Shako: 11.25 *francs*

- Shako plate and chin scales: 4.70 *francs*
- Shako cover: 2.50 *francs*
- Scarlet wool shako cords: 2.70 *francs*
- *Baudrier* with *surpicquer* stitching: 8.50 *francs*
- *Baudrier* plate in copper: 2.70 *francs*
- *Giberne* and *porte-giberne*: 13 *francs*
- Boots: 30 *francs*
- Spurs and straps: 2.25 *francs*
- Sword knot in buff: 1.10 *francs*
- Gloves in doe hide: 3.75 *francs*

From this we see that the *pantalons-à-cheval* no longer opened laterally down the outside seam, and neither where they reinforced with black leather, but rather by a second layer of iron-grey wool cloth. Given no *gilets* are issued, we suppose the *habit-veste* was the 1812 style. Clearly, the regiment wore fringed epaulettes much as it had done since 1809, with trefoils being reserved for the 2nd, or Young Guard, Regiment as in previous years. The Young Guard Regiment also seems to have had standard infantry *capotes* in *gris-beige* cloth rather than the cavalry-style in iron-grey. The only cloth ordered for the 2nd Regiment was beige and iron-grey wool cloth and *tricot*. Does this mean that the regiment's *habits* were entirely iron-grey? Perhaps so, as no blue is listed. It seems the facings of the 1st Regiment changed in 1813 from the much lighter *bleu de roi* (the same facing colour as the Red Lancers, 12th Hussars, 13th Hussars and 5th Lancers) to the darker imperial blue.

For the 2nd Regiment, the following *marche* was passed on 13 April:[54]

- 2,000 shakos
- 2,000 pairs of chin scales in copper with star *bossettes* and fifteen scalloped scales
- 2,000 cockades in varnished leather for shakos
- 2,200 *houpettes* for shakos
- 1,730 pairs of rigid heavy cavalry boots, complete with spurs
- *Gris-beige* wool cloth for *capote*
- Silver lace, 22 mm wide, for sub-officer's rank stripes
- White wool lace, 22 mm wide, for trumpeter's *habit*
- 1,000 *culottes de peau de mouton*
- 1,700 *baudriers*

The Dresden manuscript shows two drivers from the Guard artillery train. The first is a front view showing a covered shako, the short-tailed *chasseur*-style coat, as adopted in 1809, with imperial blue facings piped in scarlet. He also wears an iron-grey waistcoat and leather-reinforced *surclottes*. The other view shows the rear view of a driver. He wears the same uniform as the first figure, and the tails of the jacket are embellished with scarlet grenades. He carries a cavalry-style ammunition belt with an infantry ammunition box. Both figures have an infantry-style sabre *baudrier* and sabre *briquet*. The preserved 1812 style *habit* in the Musée de l'Armée seems likely to have been the dress coat adopted by the corps in 1813, or even the coat adopted in September 1815, which was certainly a *habit-veste*. Archive sources only list the making of *habit-vestes* in 1812-3 and we cannot be sure of their style, but the absence of sleeveless *gilets* makes us suppose the cut was the 1812-style as noted earlier. However, the Dresden manuscript implies that the old-style coats were re-adopted as opposed to the 1812-style coat.

Trumpeters

The dress of the trumpeters can be readily reconstructed from the various *marches* passed between 1809 and 1813. The trumpeters seem to have had two orders of dress:

1. *Chasseur*-style *habit-longe* cut from either *bleu de ciel* or the much brighter *bleu de celeste* with crimson facings, domed copper hussar buttons, 22 mm gold lace to collar and cuffs, gold turnback grenades.
2. Hussar-style dolman, with gold and crimson flat braid, gold and crimson *soutache*, lined in white milled *serge* introduced in 1811.

Both orders of dress were complemented from 1809 to 1811 by a shako covered with crimson cloth, and from 1811 a colpack, hussar-style waist-belt and boots, and the same *sabretache* as carried by trumpeters of the Guard horse artillery.

The *chasseur habit*, with gold lace and copper buttons, was undoubtedly the same as used by the Guard horse artillery. In both the horse artillery and artillery train the *schabraque* was the cloth light cavalry-style with scarlet grenades in the back corners and 50 mm scarlet lace edging. The body of the *schabraque* was *bleu de ciel* or the brighter *bleu de celeste*. We assume the plume was scarlet, as no plumes specifically for the trumpeters were purchased.

The colour of the dolman is open to debate. The archive paperwork lists no specific cloth for this garment bar the white milled *serge* lining. Rousselot, in his plate No. 80, states it was crimson based on no archive documentation. We know very little about this garment, but it is likely to have been crimson faced in *bleu de celeste*, as this was adopted by the trumpeters of the Guard horse artillery in summer 1806. This seems a likely scenario, as the trumpeter's *sabretache*, colpack, *giberne* and belt, waist-belt and boots were the same pattern as used by the Guard horse artillery. The trumpeters of the 2nd Regiment had white lace for the *habit-veste* in 1813, and the white lace purchased in 1811 is again, we suppose, likely to have been used in the construction of the *habit-vestes* for the trumpeters. Rousselot and Jouineau attribute this lace to the *porte-manteaux* and *housse* of corporals with no support for this attribution.

CHAPTER 13

EQUIPMENT TRAIN

The decree dated 24 August 1811 created the equipment train of the Guard. This new formation replaced the regimental level equipment drivers sanctioned by the decree of 15 April 1806.

The 1811 decree stipulated that the 1st Company was to be charged with the transportation of the Guards' paperwork, and to do so was to have thirty wagons – nine for the Corps of *Grenadiers-à-Pied*, nine for the Corps of *Chasseurs-à-Pied* and twelve for the cavalry. Furthermore, the company was to handle twelve field forges, making a total of forty-two vehicles and 180 draught

This enigmatic image by Nicolas Hoffmann may show a trumpeter of the equipment train as it was pre-1811, when the train was part of the Administration Battalion. The *habit* is chestnut brown-faced *bleu de ciel*. No documentation exists to prove that this uniform existed.

horses.[1] The 2nd Company was charged with transporting the Guard's thirty-two ambulances, as well as twenty-four four-wheeled carts and one wagon, making fifty-two vehicles moved by 180 horses. The Third Company was responsible for forty wagons, one cart and one forge, totalling forty-two vehicles drawn by 180 horses. Numbers 4, 5 and 6 Companies each were to have forty wagons of the new model, one cart and one forge, making forty-two vehicles again drawn by 180 horses, of which twelve were lead. In total, the battalion had six companies, and totalled seventeen officers, 755 men, 117 saddle horses and 1,048 draught horses.[2]

The battalion's staff was to comprise:[3] One captain commandant, one adjutant-major, one sub-lieutenant-quartermaster, one sub-lieutenant pay master, one assistant surgeon, one sub-assistant surgeon, one veterinarian, one master smith, one trumpet-major, one master armourer, one master saddler, one master wagonwright, one master boot-maker and one master tailor.

Each company was to comprise:[4] One lieutenant, one sub-lieutenant, one sergeant-major, four sergeants, one fourrier, eight corporals, two trumpeters, seven workmen and 104 soldiers.

The battalion was complete by 21 December 1811 and had an effective strength of seventeen officers, 771 men and 1,179 horses. The battalion was in charge of thirty wagons and twelve forges for the various corps of the Guard, and twenty-eight ambulances, fifty-two ration wagons, 120 new model wagons, six old model wagons and four *prolonges*.[5]

Following the Russian campaign, the battalion was re-formed with the decree of 26 February 1813. Each company was to have forty caissons of the new model, driven by eighty soldiers. Six soldiers were to drive two field forges, a further two were to drive a single *prolonge* and twenty were dismounted to lead pack horses. With the defeat of Napoleon, the battalion was disbanded on 22 July 1814.[6]

Clothing and equipment

The paper archive for the regiment provides a great wealth of information for the dress of the regiment. A document of 30 October 1811 states:[7]

- 600 m of iron-grey wool cloth, Elbeuf quality, for *habits*
- 200 m of iron-grey wool cloth, Lodeve quality, for working jackets, *pantaloons* and *porte-manteaux*
- 54 m of chestnut brown wool cloth for *revers*, cuffs and collars.

This document confirms that the collars, cuffs and facings of the *habit* were in chestnut brown as per the equipment train of the line. Boucquoy shows an iron-grey *habit-veste* with imperial blue piping to the collar, *revers* and cuffs, and imperial blue tail facing and lining. This is clearly incorrect, as the regiment always had chestnut brown facings.

The total number of *habits*, *vestes* and other items of clothing made and issued was as follows:[8]

- 3,876 *habits*
- 3,959 *vestes-manche*
- Fifty-eight *veste sans manche*
- 3,912 *pantalons* in iron-grey wool cloth reinforced with leather
- 3,528 stable trousers
- 234 *surclottes* in iron-grey wool cloth
- 359 *surclottes* made in white *treillis*
- 4,130 *capotes*
- 3,871 *bonnets de police*

A document dated 24 December 1811 lists the purchase of 200 *habits*, 200 stable coats, 200 pairs of *pantalons* in cloth reinforced with leather, 400 *bonnets de police* and 200 *capotes*.[9] A second order for 100 *habits*, 100 stable coats and 100 pairs of *pantalons* was placed the same day.[10]

Boisselier states that the *pantalons* in iron-grey wool cloth with leather reinforcement were only issued in 1813. Again, we can see from original documents that they were worn from 1811. Oddly, the stable coats do not appear in the purchase accounts, unless one assumes that they were the *vestes-manche*. This then leaves us with a quandary. Only fifty-eight *vestes sans manche* were made to go with 936 *habits* in the period 1 October 1811 to 1 January 1813. Was the *habit* worn over a multi-purpose *veste-manche*? Or did the regiment always have the *habit-veste*?

Cloth purchased and used between 8 October 1812 and 14 July 1814 was as follows:[11]

- 19,334.31 m of iron-grey wool cloth
- 1,314.99 m of chestnut brown wool cloth
- 431.73 m of scarlet wool cloth
- 140,000 m of beige wool cloth for *capotes*
- 331.13 m of green wool cloth
- 23.73 m of black wool cloth
- 23.74 m of *bleu de ciel* wool cloth for trumpeters
- 2,418.48 m of iron-grey *tricot*
- 4,439.90 m of chestnut brown milled *serge*

From these purchase accounts, it appears that from these the regiment was dressed in an iron-grey *habit*, which had chestnut brown facings, with the tails of the *habits* lined in chestnut brown milled *serge*. The scarlet cloth appears to have been used in piping. The use of the green cloth is not known, unless it was used to dress the trumpeters in green *habits*. No green cloth was purchased after 1 April 1813, so its use was limited to the period 8 October 1812 to 1 April 1813. The *bleu de ciel* cloth delivered to the depot on 17 August 1813 was surely used in the production of trumpeter's *habits*. Enough cloth was purchased for twelve *habits*. We suppose they were faced in chestnut brown or iron-grey. The beige cloth purchased was destined for *capotes*. The black cloth, it seems, was used to make gaiters.

Lace purchased in the same period was as follows:[12]

- 18.02 m of silver lace 14 mm wide
- 34.96 m of silver lace 20 mm wide
- 183.89 m of silver lace 22 mm
- 10.33 m of scarlet and silver braid
- 267.87 m of scarlet wool lace 22 mm wide
- 6.40 m of scarlet wool lace 32 mm wide
- 4,491.20 m of white wool lace 22 mm wide
- 181.40 m of white wool lace 28 mm wide for *porte-manteaux*
- 813.60 m of white wool lace 50 mm wide for *housse*
- 12,113 m of round wool cord for *bonnets de police*
- 4,054 tassels for *bonnets de police*
- 134 sets of eagles embroidered in silver
- Thirty sets of cut out cloth eagles

The mixed silver and scarlet lace may have been used in the production of trumpeter's clothing. The regiment did not have any light cavalry affectations like the artillery train, which had braided waistcoats and Hungarian breeches, with sub-officers having mixed gold and scarlet braid. Thus, we have to assume that this braid was used on trumpeter's *habits*. Boisselier, however, shows white and red lace and iron-grey *habits*. Boucquoy shows a trumpeter wearing a chestnut-brown *habit*, faced in *bleu de ciel*, and dates this uniform to 1812. Clearly, Boucquoy is at error on this point, as no *bleu de ciel* cloth existed prior to August 1813, so if this uniform did indeed exist, it cannot have done so until after August 1813. He clearly copies a painting by Hoffmann, which dates to 1805-8. No equipment train of the Guard existed at this time, and the caption merely tells us the image of a trumpeter attached to the artillery of the guard. He does wear a brown *habit*, from which it is assumed Hoffmann shows the equipment train of the Guard. Given the regiment did not exist until 1811, we have to suppose the image is an invention by Hoffmann, as it is impossible to accurately ascribe the image to a specific regiment.

Headdress for the regiment was a shako, of which 4,131 examples were purchased, decorated with a pompom and white cords, which it seems were only issued to corporals or merely sub-officers, as 324 sets were purchased in October 1811 and never replaced.[13]

Equipment comprised the following items:[14]

- 3,671 *culottes de peau*
- 3,993 pairs of gauntlets
- 3,995 *porte-manteaux*
- 3,733 pairs of braces
- Twelve sets of spurs
- 3,658 *gibernes*
- 3,616 *porte-gibernes*
- 3,554 waist-belts
- Fifteen waist-belt plates
- Seventy-three trumpets
- Fifty-five trumpeter's *gibernes*
- 356 hussar-pattern sabres for trumpeters and sub-officers
- 2,783 sabre *briquettes* for drivers

It is interesting to see that the trumpeters had their own pattern *giberne*. No doubt this had brass flanks as for the *gibernes* of the trumpeters in the Guard horse artillery and artillery train. Footwear was always the semi-soft boots worn by the dragoons, along with shoes and gaiters for stable and dismounted duties. When mounted, it seems only trumpeters and sub-officers had *housses* and *chaperons*, with nine issued in 1811, ninety-nine in 1813 and three in 1814. Some 100 sets of pistol holsters were issued. Sub-officers, corporals and trumpeters rode on dragoon saddles, of which 365 were issued between 1811 and 1814. Some 1,937 sheepskin *schabraques* were issued to drivers in the same period. A number of twentieth- and twenty-first-century illustrators give the drivers *housses*. This is incorrect. Boucquoy gives the trumpeter a hussar saddle and *schabraque*. No such items were ever ordered, casting further doubt on the accuracy of the often cited and respected work of Boucquoy.

In summary, the regiment wore an iron-grey *habit* faced in chestnut brown with scarlet piping. Headdress was always a shako. In full dress, *culottes de peau* were worn. For sub-officers on campaign they were covered by *surclottes* in white *treillis*. Other ranks always seem to have worn iron-grey *pantalons* reinforced with black leather. Only sub-officers had *housses* and *chaperons*. Trumpeters appear to have had green *habits*, and later *bleu de ciel*.

CHAPTER 14

GENDARMES D'ORDONNANCE

In an effort to bind the old aristocracy of France to his regime, Napoleon decreed the formation of the *Gendarmes d'Ordonnance*. Very little archive paperwork exists concerning the organisation and dress of the regiment.

The uniform was regulated on 24 September 1806, a, copy being held in the Rijksarchiv Maastricht. It states that the uniform was to be a green *chasseur habit* without coloured piping, silvered domed buttons, a scarlet waistcoat with silver lacing with three rows of buttons and green Hungarian breeches with knots on the upper thigh and lace on the outer seam. Headdress was to be a shako, with silver lace and a plate bearing the imperial eagle. The sabre had a silver sword knot and the *schabraque* and horse harness were to be the same as for the *chasseurs-à-cheval* of the Guard. Pay was to be the same as the *chasseurs-à-cheval* of the line. A silver *aiguillette* was to be worn on the right shoulder and a trefoil on the left. A *chapeau* was worn in undress and the *bonnet de police* was to be in the Polish style of a *konfederatka*. The greatcoat was to be all green with large sleeves and collar. The equipment straps were to be blackened and varnished.[1] This was repeated with an order of 11 April 1807:[2]

> The uniform is to be the *chasseur* coat, all green, no coloured piping, waistcoat, scarlet, laced in silver, breeches in Hungarian style also laced: shako plate and domed buttons in white metal. The sabre of the *chasseur*, the horse, to be as tall and the equipment to be the same as the *chasseurs-à-cheval*. There will be furnished from the magazines at Mayance, carbines and the pistols.

The September decree did not specify certain aspects of the uniform, which appear to have been left to the section of war of the council of state to deal with. M. Lacuee, in a letter to the minister of the interior, noted that the lining of the *habit* was not yet determined, but he commented that it should be either scarlet or red garance. The riding trousers were to be all green. Henschel shows red cuffs, collar and turnbacks, and white piping to the *revers* and facing of the tail. Zimmerman shows white piping to the *revers* and long pockets on the tails, as well as to the collar. Weiland and Otto show the *habit* as entirely green. The portrait of Sergeant Nadillac shows an entirely green *habit*.[3]

A note of 7 September 1807 lists that the breastplate buckles and plate, the bridle buckles and strap ends as all silvered. The *schabraque* was green with silver

The unit existed for less than eighteen months, thus period iconography is very limited indeed. This image by Henschel shows the regiment's uniform. The paucity of original documents means that we have to rely on period iconography to gain an understanding how the regiment appeared. This means we have no idea at all as to the dress of the trumpeters, or if the uniform was actually as shown by Henschel.

eagles in the rear corners. It was bordered with garance cloth. The Otto manuscript shows silver lace to the *schabraque* and *porte-manteau*, but does not show any eagle devices on the *schabraque*. The presence of the eagles is confirmed by Lieutenant de Norvins who, in a letter dated 11 December 1806 written at Mayence, notes that his *giberne* cost 5 *louis*, the *schabraque* 9, the saddle, bridle, bits and eagles 6. He also lists the purchase of three horses, a second *habit*, and lace for his breeches, waistcoat and shako.[4] The head collar was in natural leather. The *porte-manteau* was green with silver lace to the outside edge. The *habit* was green, lined in scarlet casimir.[5]

The *aiguillette*, according to a circular of 20 October 1806, was to be worn on the right shoulder. However, the contemporary images by Zimmerman, Weiland, Hahlo, Otto and Hendschall show it on the left shoulder. A portrait of Sergeant Nadillac shows the *aiguillette* on the right shoulder, dated 30 January 1807, in accordance with the dress regulations. Is it possible that non-commissioned officers and officers wore their *aiguillette* on the right and the troopers on the left? No archive documents exist to tell us about the dress of the trumpeters or drummers in the foot company. Any reconstruction of the uniform without supporting documentation is guesswork.

Contemporary iconography also disagrees about the appearance of the shako. Hendschell and Weiland show the *raquettes* at the left of the headdress, though Hendschell shows both cords at the front. Zimmerman and Otto show the inverse of the *raquettes*, with Zimmerman adding silver lace to the top band

Above left: Stunning portrait of a *gendarme* wearing the full dress uniform.

Above right: Portrait presumably of an officer of the regiment. Troopers wore silver trefoils, and officers fringed epaulettes. (Photograph and collection of Bertrand Malvaux)

of the shako. Lieutenant de Norvins mentions silver lace for the shako in his letters.[6] The shako plate is shown as diamond by Hahlo, Zimmerman, Weiland and Hendschell, but as a silvered eagle by Otto. All sources agree with the regulations that white plumes were worn by troopers and non-commissioned officers.

CHAPTER 15

ATTACHED REGIMENTS

Berg Light Horse

A regiment of light horse of the Grand Duchy of Berg was raised by a decree of 21 May 1807 from a cadre of German-speaking and non-commissioned officers. These men were drawn from various French cavalry regiments in France and Italy as a bodyguard to Murat. Napoleon, in March of 1807, granted Murat permission to enlist one trooper from each French cavalry regiment in Italy and one from each regimental depot in France. The regiment was organised with one depot company and four war squadrons of two companies of eighty-seven men each. The 1st Squadron received the title *Garde du Corps*. However, as he was in Poland at the time, Murat improvised a short-term solution to this situation by making personal use of a troop of fifty Polish horsemen from the new levies raised after the French liberation of Warsaw. On 15 March 1807, the emperor ordered Murat to relinquish control of that particular unit, although he softened the blow by simultaneously authorising Murat to replace it with a special independent company of 100 Polish Honora Guards to serve as his personal escort. These were to become the Polish lancers. Poniatowski was placed in command and chose his recruits from the youth of some of the most aristocratic families in Poland, and by mid-April 1807, he had already assembled ninety guards and forty horses who were taken into the Guard.

When initially formed, the uniform of the regiment appears to have been a buff-coloured *habit-veste* with crimson facings. A crimson shako appears to have been used as headdress. This striking colour scheme is not surprising, given that Marshal Murat's *aides-de-camp* were adorned in buff and crimson uniforms.[1] The period terminology for the colour buff was *ventre de bitche*. However, it does seem that the buff uniform was not made in any great number, as a letter from 30 June 1807 testifies:[2]

> The grand duke was informed this morning that ten men of his escort were uniformed in yellow because not enough *chamois* cloth could be found. His imperial highness has charged me to tell you that not a single one of these men should be sent to Tilsit and instead they should be kept at Konigsberg with the others.
>
> You will suspend the uniforming process until further orders. In the meanwhile, you are to have four uniforms made as quickly as possible (using the best men as models) and send them by the first courier.

What these four different examples of uniforms looked like we cannot say for sure. The model uniforms referred to in the passage above were probably made from buff-coloured wool cloth. The total number of buff uniforms made beyond these four, and ones made earlier in the year, we can only guess at. In response to this letter, subsequent entries in the register of correspondence indicate that an immediate decision was made to consider alternate colour schemes for the dress of the light horse. In order to assess stocks of cloth available from which to make uniforms, a letter was sent on 6 July 1807 to the intendant general of the *Grande Armee* to enquire about the colour of and types of cloth held in the magazines at Danzig. The letter specifically requested the quantities of 'yellow, *ventre-de-bitche*, aurore, grey and white cloth' that could be found in the magazine.[3] Having received a report confirming that the magazine did hold cloth in the desired colours, a detachment of two sub-officers and seven men under the command of Lieutenant Luyarts were subsequently ordered to Danzig to collect the cloth and to transport it back to Berg. The detachment was furthermore authorised to collect *en route* to Berg additional items of clothing and equipment from the magazines at Thorn, Spandau and Berlin.[4] Despite collecting cloth and equipment, we know nothing about the uniform. There is a major gap in the records concerning the appearance of the uniform until it was disbanded in 1809 – almost a full two years since the issue of dressing the regiment was raised.

Berg Light Horse, as depicted by the artist Nicolas Hoffmann, who had confusingly called the figure a member of the Hanoverian Legion.

An inspection report dated 9 February 1809 for the 5th Depot Company lists eighty-eight *habits-vestes blancs*, eighty-eight *habits-vestes gris* and eighty-eight *bonnets polonaise,* which were no doubt *czapki*.[5] This report also refers to grey *pantalons d'ecurie*, sheepskin saddlecloths and armaments consisting of pistols, carbines and sabres. Unfortunately, the report neither specifies a facing colour, gives details of the style of the uniform nor refers to ornaments such as lacing, epaulettes, *aiguillettes*, plumes or shako cords. We get an idea of what the white uniform looked like from a plate by Martinet. Presumably the regiment wore white *habit-vestes* or *kurtkas* faced in crimson, with crimson *pantalons* and a crimson *czapka*.

Contemporary iconography helps to an extent in filling in the gaps in our knowledge of what the uniform looked like. In his famous series of coloured lithographic plates

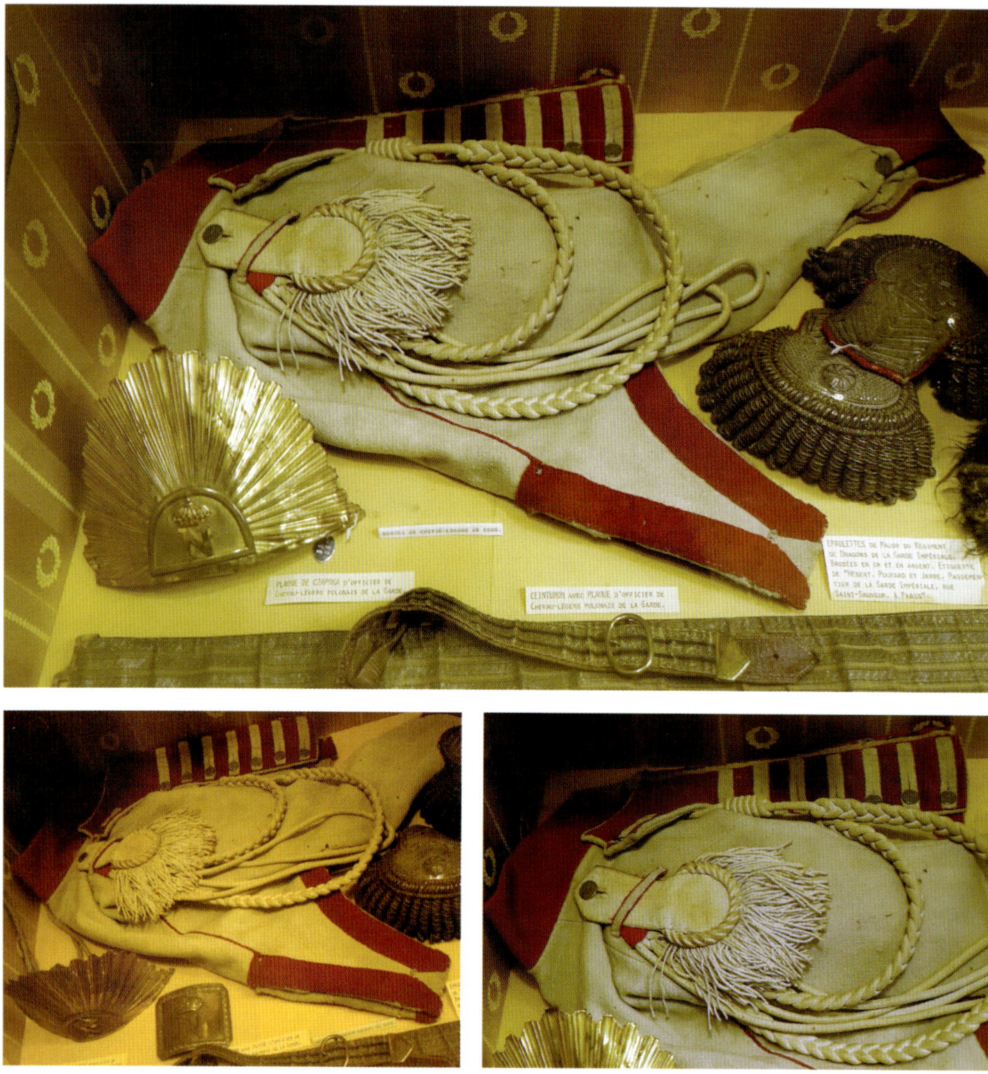

Preserved in the Musée d'Emperi is this white *kurtka* faced amaranth said to be Berg Light Horse, although it is possible for the *kurtka* to have also have belonged to Murat's Polish bodyguard. (Musée de l'Empéri, Collections du Musée de l'armée, Anciennes collections Jean et Raoul Brunon)

of soldiers of the First Empire, Aaron Martinet features a mounted trooper of the *Cavalerie Polonaise du Grand Duc de Berg* (Polish Cavalry of the Grand Duke of Berg). In the plate, the trooper is shown mounting his horse. In terms of the dress and equipment of the figure, the plate shows a white *kurtka* with crimson facings. The *revers* are laced in white with white brandenburgs. The *kurtka* tail facings are also crimson. A *kurtka* preserved in the Brunon collection is identical to that shown. Can we relate the two items as being from the same regiment? Potentially yes. Another undoubtedly contemporary image is by Nicolas Hoffmann in his series of prints. The plate shows a remarkably similar uniform to the extant garment and the Martinet image. The plate is entitled *Legion Hanoverienne*. The Hanoverian Legion wore scarlet jackets, so clearly this is not that unit. It is likely that the term Hanoverian is a cover-all term for German. The strong similarity between the figure shown by Hoffmann and by Martinet, as well as the extant habit, makes us believe that all three items show the same unit, i.e. the Berg regiment.

An image produced by Martin Engelbrecht in 1808 is the third depiction of this white *kurtka* faced in crimson, with white lace to the *revers*. The plate is entitled *Polish Officers with Mameluke*.

However, it seems that the three prints more likely depict the Polish Honour Guard raised for Murat by Poniatowski rather than the Berg Light Horse. The first issue is the title of the Martinet plate. It specifically identifies the figure as 'Polish Cavalry of the Grand Duke of Berg'. Thus, if the title is correct, it is a depiction of a soldier in Murat's Polish unit than of a soldier of the Berg Light Horse dressed in Polish-style uniform. Concerning the image made by Hoffman in Paris, for the Hoffmann artist to have observed the regiment, if he ever did, the regiment would have had to have been in France. The likelihood is, therefore, given the Light Horse of Berg (as far as can be ascertained) never entered Paris, we must be dealing also with a figure of the Polish Honour Guard, which did indeed enter Paris in November 1807, before the Polish Honour Guards were re-equipped as the Polish Light Horse. However, neither of the two hypotheses can be proved. We do know the Berg regiment wore white faced in crimson, just like the Polish Honour Guard, so ascribing the plate to a specific regiment is fraught with difficulty.

Martinet print of a Berg Light Horse regiment officer. The uniform shown by Martinet matches almost exactly that shown by Hoffmann and the possible original *kurtka*.

Only a single squadron acting as bodyguard to Murat was taken on campaign with him. It entered Spain on 5 April 1808, but only consisted of the bodyguard squadron (fully mounted) and 100 dismounted troopers of the 1st Company of the 2nd Squadron. The regiment organisation included an elite company that was designated by Murat as his *Garde du Corps*, or bodyguard.

Murat apparently hoped that this company would be recruited exclusively from the sons of the most prominent families of his realm, who would provide their own mounts, uniforms and equipment. To this end, he accordingly granted the company the same privileges of rank and pay enjoyed by the light cavalrymen of the French Imperial Guard. When Joachim Murat became King of Naples on 1 August 1808 and relinquished his title of Grand Duc de Berg, Napoleon attached the *Garde du Corps de Berg* to the Imperial Guard. On 17 November 1808, Napoleon instructed his minister of war to inform the new king of the two Sicily's that the bodyguard was being incorporated into the Imperial Guard. The squadron, in December 1808, had four officers and 105 other ranks. The bodyguard was attached for operational purposes to the mounted *chasseurs*, and so it was present when Lefèbvre-Desnoëttes rashly led the Guard light cavalry across the storm-swollen Esla River to attack the English rearguard at Benevante on 29 December. The French were routed, Captain Charinet, of the bodyguard, was wounded and the other ranks of the unit may have suffered casualties, according to Martinien.

The regiment was dissolved on 11 January 1809. The decree read:[6]

> Art. 1
> The squadron of light horse of the Grand Duchy of Berg to be dissolved.
>
> Art. 2
> The officers named in the attachment number one to be taken with their rank into the cavalry of the duchy.
>
> Art. 3
> The sub-officers and men named in attachment number two to be incorporated into the *chasseurs-à-cheval* of the Guard, and to retain their rank.
>
> Art. 4
> The sub-officers and men listed in attachment number three to be taken into the *grenadiers-à-cheval* of the Guard and to retain their rank.
>
> Art. 5
> The sub-officers and men listed in attachment number four to be sent to Düsseldorf where they will be taken into the cavalry of the Grand Duchy of Berg with the rank of sergeant.

By the terms of the decree, the officers were to return to Berg to serve in the cavalry force of the duchy, namely:[7]

> Squadron Commander Stanislas Lanougarde
> Frederick Schorder, surgeon-major

Captain Charles Reinach
Captain Benjamin Charinet
Marie Mousse, first-lieutenant
Nicolas Beckery, second-lieutenant
Melchoir Forti, second-lieutenant

Melchoir Fortin, who was born in 1785 and volunteered to the 20th *Chasseurs-à-Cheval* on 24 September 1803, was promoted to corporal-quartermaster on 31 March 1804 and to sergeant on 11 November 1804. He was promoted to sub-lieutenant on 8 February 1808 in the *Garde du Corps*, and then named as *aide-de-camp* to General Dommanmget on 6 December 1812, then *aide-de-camp* to General Montbrun from 28 January 1813. Admitted as a first-lieutenant in the *grenadiers-à-cheval* on 3 April 1814, he was placed on the non-active list of the *Corps Royale des Cuirassiers de France* on 22 July 1814 and appears to have served in 1815.[8]

Of the *Garde du Corps*, eighty-six men were sent to the *chasseurs-à-cheval* of the Guard and fourteen to the *grenadiers-à-cheval*, with thirty-eight sent back to Berg.[9]

On 7 February, the 1st Squadron mustered 160 men and ten officers, of which 143 men and seven officers were sent to Naples to form the cadre of the new Naples Royal Guard. The 2nd Squadron had 208 men and twenty-one officers, of which 2nd Company had 107 men and four officers. Of these men, seven officers and 139 men were sent back to the duchy, with six officers and ninety men taken into the Guard.[10] All of the officers and thirty-nine of the troopers (including almost all of those with Germanic surnames) were re-assigned to the regiment of *chasseurs*, which had been created in Berg in August 1808 from the cadre of the squadrons that remained in the regiment's depot.

The Guards of Honour[11]

Never part of the Imperial Guard, but associated with it, were four regiments of Honour Guards. The decree of 3 April 1813 ordered the creation of four regiments of *Gardes d'Honneur*, and were to be formed from French-born volunteers who were to wear an elegant hussar-style uniform. Their garrisons were to be at Versailles (1st Regiment), Metz (2nd Regiment), Tours (3rd Regiment) and Lyon (4th Regiment). Each regiment comprised a staff of sixty-five men and 156 horses, and no less than ten squadrons. Each squadron was to consist of two companies, each of 122 men with 127 horses. The establishment of each of the twenty companies was to be 2,440 men with 2,540 horses, the staff making a total of 2,505 men with 2,696 horses. The four regiments would provide the Guard with 10,000 well-equipped and trained men, who would in due course provide the leadership cadres for the *Grande Armee*. The regimental colonels were chosen from among the divisional generals. The majors were to be colonels in the line, though all officers would keep the same rank that they had held in the line.

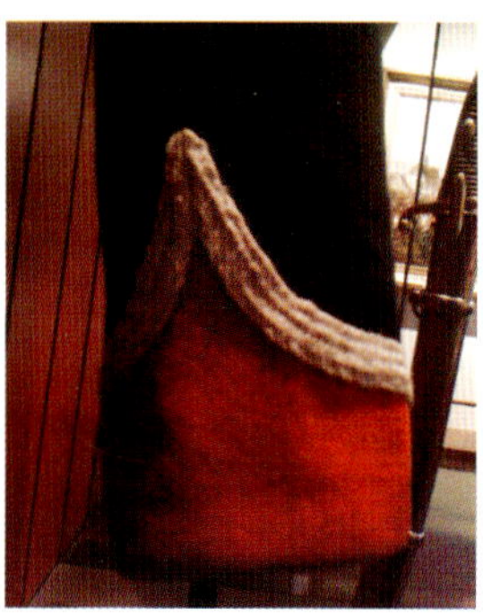

Housed in the Musée de l'armée is this dolman, in almost perfect condition. It is one of many dolmans to exist from the regiment, and all are very consistent in cut, colours, number of rows of buttons, lacing and braiding, so we can be sure that this garment is representative of the dolman used by the four regiments. (Musée de l'armée)

The new recruits were to be unmarried, aged between 19 and 30 years old, and not to have a profession. Unsurprisingly, former officers in one of the allied armies were allowed to join these new regiments, and for these valuable veterans the age limit was raised to 45. Each new recruit had to provide himself with his uniform, though there was some financial support available for those who could not afford to pay for their equipment. The *Gardes d'Honneur* received the same pay as the *chasseurs-à-cheval*, and after twelve months' service they would be promoted to sub-lieutenants.

By summer 1813, the 1st and 2nd Regiments were mostly up to strength and had a total of five squadrons in the field. The 5th Squadrons of the 1st and 2nd Regiments left Mainz on 1 October and marched toward Kassel, where they were united with the 5th Squadron of the 4th Regiment. The Guards of Honour had their first experience of battle at Dresden, even though the squadrons present were kept away from the fighting. The first fighting in which they were involved was at Leipzig and then Hanau. General Dautancourt, colonel-major of the Polish lancers, was made commander of the corps of Guards of Honour on 17 October, giving a total of forty-eight officers and 853 men coming from all the available squadrons of the four regiments.

During the campaign of France, the Guards fought with some distinction, charging at Montmirail, Château-Thierry, Rheims and other engagements. There followed almost daily skirmishes. On 1 April 1814, General DeFrance gathered his division near Saint-Germain. By this time the Guards of Honour could muster the combined strength of a weak squadron. The royal ordnance of 24 June 1814 dissolved the 1st Regiment at Versailles on 14 July, the following day the 4th was dissolved. The 3rd was dissolved at Tours on 17 July and the 2nd at Rambouillet on the 22nd. Nine hundred of the remaining Guards of Honour entered the companies of the *Garde du Corps*, and all were made sub-lieutenants.

With Napoleon's return in 1815, a single regiment was reformed.

Uniform

According to the decree and organisation of the corps, the ministry of the interior wrote to the prefects on 20 April 1813 specifying that:[12]

> The buttons are silver or silver plated, like those of the officers. The braid and lace are in white wool for the uniforms and in white cord for the shako. The shako will be as the model you receive; but the shako plate, the chin scales and other metal pieces on it will be silver-plated. The shako will have a green plume with the tip in a different colour for each regiment. This will be red for the 1st, imperial blue for the 2nd, yellow for the 3rd, and white for the 4th Regiment. The plume will have a pompom as base. This will be in a different colour for each company. The metal ornaments on the *sabretache* will be silver plated.

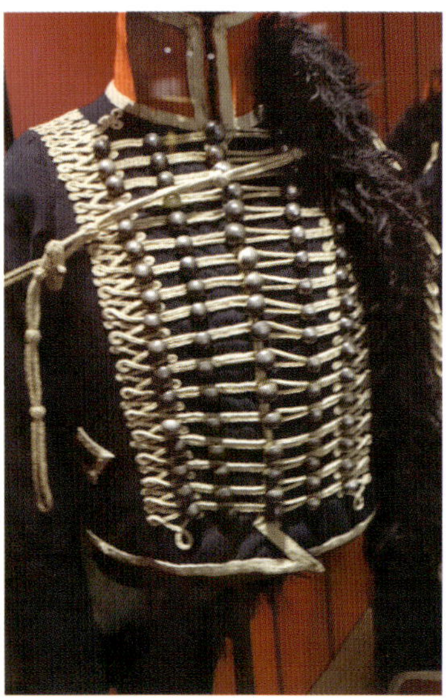

Above and opposite: This dolman, in the Musée de l'armée, is by the far the most ornate example for other ranks. The braiding to the outer most row of buttons that continues onto the shoulder and beyond the shoulder seam, is unique to this garment. Given that the regiment was formed in theory from the affluent middles classes, clearly the owner of this garment could afford to have more elaborate braiding applied to his dolman. (Musée de l'armée)

The *Journal Militaire* of 5 April 1813 listed the following items as being issued to the Guards:[13]

> *Pelisse*, dolman, sleeveless waistcoat, stable jacket, Hungarian breeches, underwear, riding trousers, sleeved overcoat, *porte-manteau*, *bonnet de police* and a pair of braces.

The *pelisse* was also in dark green, lined with white flannel and edged on the collar, cuffs and front edges with black fur. The specification was established on 12 April 1813:[14]

ITEM	*MATERIAL*	*COMMENT*	*SIZE 1*	*SIZE 2*
Pelisse	Green wool cloth 119/100	For the body of the dolman and lining the collar, as well as shoulder strap	1.23 m	0.99 m
	White flannel 79/100	For lining	2.36 m	2.12 m
	Linen 104/100	For lining, pockets and *droit fils*	0.15 m	0.15 m
	Square braid in white wool	For braiding	11.90 m	11.90 m
	White wool flat braid 10 mm wide	For edging the dolman, collar, false pockets and cuffs	9.40 m	9.20 m
	Black sheepskin	For cuffs, collar and extremity	5.27 m	5.27 m
	Cord	Square wool cording to secure *pelisse*	0.76 m	0.76 m
	Buttons	Large	27	27
		Medium	42	42
	Hooks and eyes	For cuffs	4	4

The *pelisse* had eighteen rows of white cording, but with five rows of eighteen buttons rather than three as on the dolman. The edge of the collar, the waist and pockets were piped in white. The dolman was in dark green cloth lined with white canvas. The collar and facings were scarlet. The front bore eighteen rows of white cord. The false pockets, collar and cuffs were laced in white. The buttons, like those of the officers, were semi-domed. The specification for the dolman, and other items of clothing, was published in the *Journal Militaire* for the first quarter of 1813, on 12 April 1813:[15]

ITEM	*MATERIAL*	*COMMENT*	*SIZE 1*	*SIZE 2*
Dolman	Green wool cloth 119/100	For the body of the dolman and lining the collar, as well as shoulder strap	1.23 m	0.96 m

ITEM	MATERIAL	COMMENT	SIZE 1	SIZE 2
Dolman	Scarlet wool cloth	0.38 m for collar, 0.42 m for cuffs	0.80 m	0.80 m
	Linen 104/100	For lining, pockets and *droit fils*	1.42 m	1.18 m
	Red Moroccan leather	For lining the bottom of the dolman, 25 mm tall	1.48 m	1.24 m
	Square braid in white wool	For braiding	11.90 m	11.90 m
	White wool flat braid 10 mm wide	For edging the dolman, collar, false pockets and cuffs	9.40 m	9.20 m
	Buttons	Large	19	19
		Small	42	42
	Hooks and eyes	For collar and cuffs	9	6

The specification for the *gilet* worn under the dolman was established on 12 April 1813:[16]

ITEM	MATERIAL	COMMENT	SIZE 1	SIZE 2
Gilet	Scarlet	For the body of the *gilet* and lining the collar	0.48 m	0.44 m
	Linen 104/100	For lining, pockets and *droit fils*	0.70 m	0.66 m
	Buttons	Small, round	10	10

The stable coat was to be made from the following materials, as specified on 12 April 1813:[17]

ITEM	MATERIAL	COMMENT	SIZE 1	SIZE 2
Veste d'ecurie	Green *tricot* 69/100	For the body of the *veste*, collar, sleeves and cuffs	1.88 m	1.74 m
	Linen 104/100	For lining, pockets and *droit fils*	1.34 m	1.26 m
	Buttons	Medium size, round	14	14

The specification for the Hungarian breeches was established on 12 April 1813:[18]

ITEM	MATERIAL	COMMENT	SIZE 1	SIZE 2
Culottes Hongroise	Scarlet 119/100	For the body of the *gilet* and lining the collar	1.15 m	1.05 m
	Linen 104/100	For lining, pockets and *droit fils*	0.42 m	0.38 m
	Lace	White wool lace 10 mm wide	2.95 m	2.95 m

This *pelisse* is one of two known original items. Both are cut from dark green cloth, braided and laced in white, with black fur edging. In full dress, the *pelisse* was worn slung over the left shoulder. In the winter it was worn over the waistcoat in place of the dolman. It was never worn over the dolman. (Musée de l'armée)

This *sabretache* is unique in that we know who owned the item, one Leopold Neuville-Kaisson, who enlisted in the 2nd regiment on 3 July 1813. Shown here is a photograph of the *sabretache* as well as his service papers. (Musée de l'armée)

Breeches of Hungarian-style were worn. These were scarlet with white lacing on the outer seams and decorated with pointed *pique*s on the front of the thighs. These were worn tucked into black light cavalry-style boots. Some had white lacing to the top edge, others had simple black leather tassels stitched to the front. For field dress, the red breeches were replaced by green riding overalls, fastening up the outside leg by the means of eighteen large buttons, stitched into a stripe of scarlet cloth. They had a 25 mm wide leather instep strap and buckskin reinforcement sewn into the crotch and inner legs. Towards the end of the empire, trousers made from grey cloth were worn.

A hussar-style barrel sash was worn, made up of forty-four crimson cords with twenty barrels. At 2.60 m long, the sash was wrapped three times around the body, over the waistcoat. The voluminous cavalry greatcoat was also green, with a straight collar, fastened by two tabs.

In undress, uniform similar to the undress uniform of the *chasseurs-à-cheval* of the Guard was worn. The *frac* was green with red collar and pointed cuffs, green Hungarian breeches laced in white, and a hussar-style waistcoat in scarlet laced in white. The cost of this uniform was 150 *francs*. However, a circular of 10 November 1813 notes that the uniform cost 59.35 *francs*. An *aiguillette* was allowed to be worn by the 2nd Regiment in undress. A second undress uniform was

Portrait of Honour Guard de Bieville who served in the 1st regiment. (Musée de l'Empéri, Collections du Musée de l'armée, Anciennes collections Jean et Raoul Brunon)

also worn and consisted of a *redingote* worn with *pantalons*. This normally comprised the uniform of the senior officers of the Guard in the mornings, though it was worn by a great number of officers on campaign.

The intention was that every guardsman had to pay for their own uniform, equipment and horse, and was to leave his department fully equipped and in uniform. In practice, however, the idea did not live up to expectations. The worst, according to General Nansouty, was the 4th Regiment. Some Italians in the regiment had not a single piece of uniform or equipment with them when they arrived at the depot, while eighty-six asked to be sent back to their homes so that they could have their uniforms made, promising to return once they had been kitted out. In some cases, shakos were made too large and pads had to be made to make them fit, as well as *pantalons* being made too short. With guardsmen coming to their regiments from across the empire, the quality and colours of materials used varied dramatically. On parade, one would have seen many shades of green and red in a single regiment. Although the officers and the more affluent troopers of the regiment could afford finely cut uniforms in the best materials, conforming to their social status, many of the guardsmen were badly or incompletely dressed. As an economy drive, any department that had purchased material and equipment for the Guards of Honour had often skimped on the quality either through carelessness or council officials lining their pockets with government money.

In theory, trumpeters wore imperial livery, like the light cavalry regiments of the line. The dark green dolman and *pelisse* bore seven chevrons on each arm in imperial lace. This was yellow with scarlet edging, divided into rectangles by transverse black lines. Alternate rectangles bore a green eagle and a green 'N'. A trumpeter of the 4th Regiment is depicted in a print held in the Bibliotheque Marmottan as wearing a red dolman and *pelisse* with green facings. The use of reverse colours for musicians in the French Army was more or less traditional. The *pelisse* appears to have been trimmed in white sheepskin. Boucquoy shows trumpeters with *bleu de ciel* dolmans faced in scarlet, but gives no sources for this reconstruction. The paper archive that exists does not resolve this issue.

Officers' uniforms were similar to the rank and file, but of finer quality material and silver replacing white in all respects. Some officers wore a black colpack with a scarlet bag piped in silver and with a silver tassel. All leather equipment was red with silver lacing and ornaments. Like the *chasseurs-à-cheval*, a service dress uniform was introduced, consisting of a green *chasseur*-style *habit* with scarlet collar, pointed cuffs and turnbacks, with the long pockets piped in scarlet. Silver trefoils were worn at the shoulder in place of epaulettes. This was worn in conjunction with green riding breeches and a scarlet waistcoat. In place of the shako or colpack, a *chapeau* was worn.

Portrait of a surgeon of one of the four regiments of Honour Guards. We know he is a surgeon as, under magnification, the collar and cuffs of the *habit* carry the distinctive embroidery ascribed to surgeons under the 1801 regulations. (Musée de l'Empéri, Collections du Musée de l'armée, Anciennes collections Jean et Raoul Brunon)

Some comments below are concerning the dress of the two regiments. Because clothing was a private purchase, in theory, little documentation exists regarding its purchase and production.

1st Regiment

An inspection report of 30 July 1813 states that in undress *surtouts* or *fracs* were allowed to be worn, to be made from Elbeuf cloth of the second quality:[19]

- 1.56 m of green wool cloth costing 23.03 *francs* a metre
- 0.15 m of scarlet wool cloth costing 27.60 *francs* a metre
- 1.10 m of linen for lining costing 1.35 *francs* a metre
- Fourteen silvered medium-sized dome buttons costing 2.80 *francs* a dozen
- Six small silvered buttons costing 1.35 *francs* a dozen
- Labour: 2 *francs*
- The epaulette and trefoil cost 7 *francs*[20]

At a revue of the 1st Regiment on 4 December 1813, the thirty-five officers and 500 non-commissioned officers and guards are reported to have been wearing *pantalons* made from *tricot* with leather reinforcements, as well as non-regulation grey wool *pantalons*. The report was also critical of the colour and quality of the

Opposite left: Print of an Honour Guard by Aaron Martinet and published in Paris in summer 1813.

Opposite right: This shako belonged to Colonel Randon de Pully. Born into a noble family, Charles-Joseph Randon de Malboissière de Pully first joined the French Army at age 16 in 1768. The following year he was admitted with the rank of lieutenant to the 1st Company of Musketeers of the King, and then in 1770, he was promoted to *capitaine* in the dragoons of La Rochefoucauld. Pully continued to serve in France, serving under Marshal de Broglie in 1776 and then Marshal de Vaux in 1783. In 1784, his commanding colonel d'Autichamp wrote in a report that Pully 'is a good officer but would never be but a poor senior officer'. Pully received a promotion to *chef d'escadrons* in 1788 and then another promotion to lieutenant-colonel in 1789.

Despite his noble birth, Pully rallied to the Revolution and, in 1792, was promoted to colonel and placed under General Kellermann in the Army of the Center. The day before the Battle of Valmy, Pully received a promotion to *maréchal de camp*. Next, he was assigned to the Army of the Moselle and, in December, he took command of the reserve of this army. In March of 1793, Pully was promoted to *général de division* and he took command of the Corps of Vosges in the Army of the Moselle. Six months later in September, he was suspended from the army and imprisoned as a suspected anti-revolutionary. Pully avoided the guillotine but remained in prison until he was released in November 1794.

Pully remained without a command in the army until June 1795 when he was sent to the Army of the North. In August, he was given command of a division, but only a month later was asked to give up the command. Pully remained without employment until May 1796, when he was named inspector general of cavalry in the Army of the Rhine and Moselle, but he did not take up the command. He finally took up a permanent position in April 1797, when he was named inspector general of cavalry in the Army of Italy.

In November 1799, Pully was given command of a division in the Army of Italy, and then in January 1800 was named commander of the 15th military division at Rouen. In this position, he helped Gardanne to disarm the Chouans in the 14th military division and afterwards was sent to the Army of the Rhine. Later that year, Pully was sent to the Army of Grisons, where he served at the crossing of the Splugen and then at Trente before he occupied part of the Tyrol. In September 1811, he was given command of a cavalry corps in the Cisalpine Republic.

General Pully remained in Italy throughout the years of peace that followed, and when war was declared in 1805, he took command of a division of *cuirassiers* under Marshal Masséna in the Army of Italy. That November he distinguished himself at the crossing of the Tagliamento. Pully continued to serve in Italy over the following years, for a time serving as inspector general. In 1809, he took command of a division of dragoons for the war against the Austrians. Serving in Prince Eugene's army, Pully fought at the Battle of the Piave and then at the Battle of the Raab. After the successful conclusion of the campaign, Pully was named a Count of the Empire and then ordered to form new cavalry regiments and inspect their depots. In 1812, he was appointed governor of the imperial palace at Meudon and then in 1813 was named colonel of the 1st Guard of Honour at Versailles.

After Napoleon's abdication in 1814, the restored Bourbons named Pully a Grand Officer of the Legion of Honour. When Napoleon returned from exile and resumed power in 1815 for the Hundred Days campaign; Pully did not leave the country and was therefore put at the disposition of the Ministry of War. In June he was ordered to inspect the depots and then help prepare the defence of Paris. After Napoleon's second abdication, Pully retired from the army in September of 1815. (Private collection Switzerland)

wool for the *pelisses* and dolmans. The guardsmen from the depot at Lys had uniforms made from very good wool cloth. Saddles also differed between civilian styles and the regulation issue as for the hussars.[21]

2nd Regiment

A document of 10 November lists the costs for sub-officer's clothing. They wore the same uniform as the men, but silver lace replaced white:[22]

- Silver cord for the *pelisse* and shako, 54 *francs* rather than 1.50 *francs*
- Silver lace for the shako, 8 *francs* rather than 0.75 *francs*
- Silver lace for the *porte-manteau*, 5 *francs* rather than 0.75 *francs*
- Silver barrel sash, 60 *francs* rather than 16 *francs*
- Waist-belt with lion heads at 32 *francs*
- Varnished *giberne*, with silvered buckles and ornaments at 30 *francs*
- *Pantalons-à-cheval* in cloth with silvered buttons with leather reinforcements

Thus, a non-commissioned officer's uniform cost 304.15 *francs* more than a trooper's.

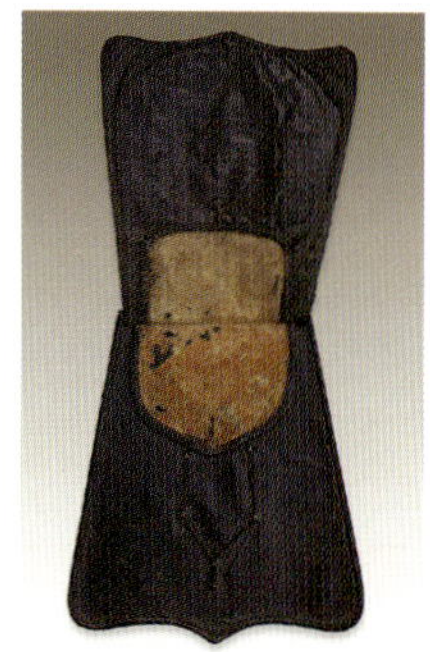

Sabretache of the 4th Honour Guards. Uniquely, this *sabretache* also has its campaign cover to protect the silvered eagle and numeral. (Photograph and collection of Bertrand Malvaux)

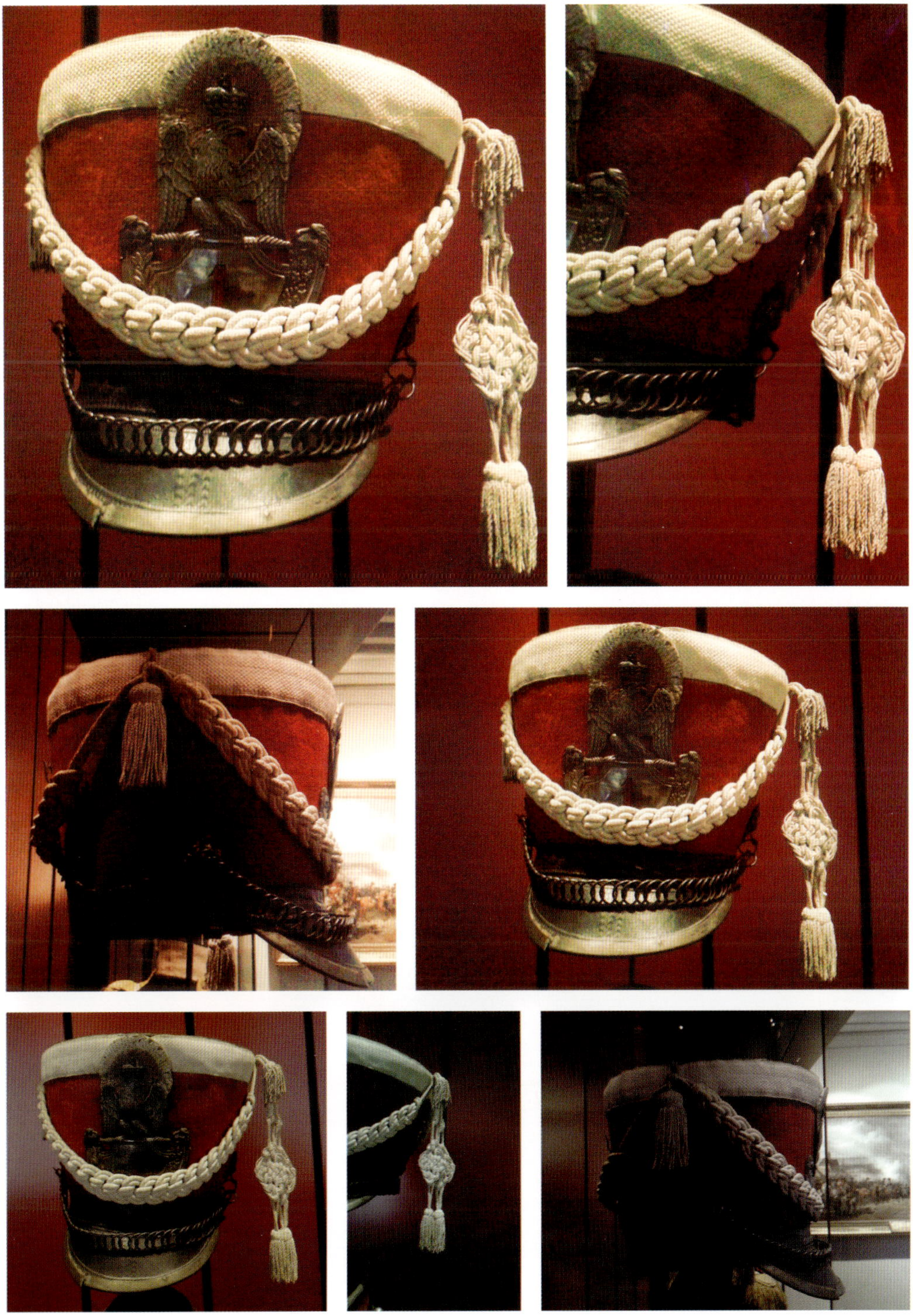

Shako belonging to the 1st Regiment of Honour Guards. It matches the uniform regulation, which was vague in the appearance of the chin strap, which in this case is a chain rather than chin-scales. (Musée de l'armée)

Above and opposite: The regulation shako of the Honour Guards was to have a scarlet body with lace and cords, and with metal fittings. A great deal of difference can be seen among the number of original shakos. This example has grenade bosses and cut-out chin scales, whereas others have chin chains with lion bosses. (Musée de l'armée)

Honour Guards, coming from an affluent background could afford to have their portraits painted. Here we have an unknown sergeant, his rank indicated by the silver stripe above the cuff. *Sous-officers* were allowed silver and crimson braid and lace, but this portrait shows white. An example in the Musée de l'Empéri, likewise for a sergeant, also has white lace and braid, so clearly not all *sous-officers* had such distinctions. (Musée de l'Empéri, Collections du Musée de l'armée, Anciennes collections Jean et Raoul Brunon)

In the 2nd Regiment, the colonel ordered, on 11 December 1813, that the company officers were to tell their men to wear the *bonnet de police* and stable jacket up to ten o'clock in the morning. When not on service, this order of dress was to be worn after ten o'clock in the morning. When on service, the *bonnet de police* or shako was to be worn with the *pelisse*, closed, without the dolman underneath.

The squadron commanders of the 3rd Regiment were ordered by the colonel, Le Comte d'Astorg, to wear a colpack with a red flame laced in silver, a white *aigrette* and to have a red Morocco leather cover for their *giberne* belt. Green *pantalons* were to be worn, laced in silver. The other ranks wore a double set of shako cords, having two at the front and two at the back. This appears to have been the case for the sub-officers of the 1st Regiment, as a portrait of Sergeant Antoine Dahlas shows his shako having two cords at the front (and back?), and the use of an officer's style *giberne* belt cover.

This mannequin presents the full dress uniform for a sous-officer of the 4th Regiment. The rank is shown by the silver chevron above the cuff. The flat lace to the dolman is mixed silver and crimson, as is the braid used on the frogging. The barrels on the barrel sash are also crimson and silver, as is the braid on the Hungarian breeches. The shako cords are likewise silver and crimson. The mannequin presents a very convincing vignette of how a sous-officer, no doubt with deeper pockets than others as he could afford the costly silver and crimson lace and braid, appeared in 1813. (Musée de l'Empéri, Collections du Musée de l'armée, Anciennes collections Jean et Raoul Brunon)

Above and opposite: Shako of the 2nd regiment of Guards of Honour. (Photograph and collection of Bertrand Malvaux)

CHAPTER 16

ROYAL CORPS OF CAVALRY

When the Bourbon monarchy was restored to power in 1814, they inherited a bankrupt and demoralised country, fatigued after almost twenty-five years of fighting. The army was ill-equipped and under-strength. Some regiments were little more than a battalion or squadron strong. The army was to be remade. The eleven-month history of the *Corps Royale des Grenadiers de France* is invariably overlooked (as is much during the Restoration of 1814) as a mere hiccough or mistake on the inexorable road to Waterloo. But it would be a mistake to overlook the history of the *Corps Royale* when trying to understand the history of the Imperial Guard.

Article three of the decree of 1 September 1814 further stipulated the regiment was to be organised in the same manner as the *cuirassiers* of the line under the decree of 8 June 1814 concerning the line cavalry. Under this earlier decree, the staff of the regiment was to comprise:[1] One colonel with three horses, one major with three horses, two squadron commanders each with two horses, two adjutant-majors each with two horses, one lieutenant-quartermaster with one horse, one standard-bearer with one horse, one surgeon-major with one horse, one assistant surgeon with one horse, two adjutant-sub-officers each with one horse, one master veterinarian with one horse, one second-class veterinarian with one horse, one corporal-trumpeter, one tailor, one saddler, one boot-maker, one breeches-maker and one armourer.

Each company was to comprise:[2] One captain, one first-lieutenant, two second-lieutenants, one sergeant-major, four sergeants, one quartermaster-corporal, eight corporals, two trumpeters and sixty troopers, of which forty-four were mounted and sixteen dismounted.

In total, the staff had ten officers with eighteen horses and ten sub-officers with five horses, and each company had four officers with five horses and seventy-four men with fifty-eight horses: a total of forty-two officers with fifty-eight horses and 602 men with 469 horses. This order was repeated on 13 March 1815 and 1 September 1815.

Article four of the royal order stipulated that:[3]

> All men belonging to the Old Guard, who have been seconded to perform the duties of sub-officers in the squadrons of the Young Guard may be recalled to join the regiment of *cuirassiers*, dragoons, *chasseurs* or light horse lancers, according to their arm, or shall be placed in the regiments of the line, who squadrons of the Young Guard will be part, and with the rank given to them by the decree of 19 March 1813. The minister of war may give some men another destination according to circumstances.

Article six stated about the cadet trumpeters that:[4]

> There will be two children of the company, chosen from the sub-officers and soldiers of the regiment, they will receive half-pay, and enjoy other benefits received by the regulations.

Article seven was concerned with returning prisoners-of-war, noting:[5]

> Sub-officers, corporals and trumpeters, the *grenadiers*, *chasseurs*, dragoons and lancers of the Old Guard who return from the prisons of the enemy after the organisation has been made, will be allowed into the new body of their arm, and will according to their seniority, occupy the vacant job of their rank.

Clearly, the army had a lack of good sub-officers to fill out the newly re-organised royal army.

Article eight dealt with the retirement of officers who had joined the regiment since 1 January 1812 or were too old or infirm due to injuries. Officers and sub-officers who had held their posts from 1 April 1813 to 1 April 1814 would retain their posts under section two of Article eight.[6]

Furthermore, Article nine stated that each royal corps was to retain for the depot a squadron commander, a major, two captains, two first-lieutenants, four second-lieutenants and a quartermaster. Officers who had returned from prison after the new organisation of the regiment had been made and had no post were allowed to return to their homes on half-pay according to their rank. The same was also true for sub-officers, trumpeters and troopers. Article eleven stated that until those officers and men returning to their homes had received the order for departure, they were to remain with the royal corps.[7]

Article sixteen of the order of 21 June 1814, repeated on 1 September 1814, noted that the uniforms of the royal corps of dragoons, lancers and *chasseurs* were to be retained, while the *cuirassiers* were to be equipped in the same manner as those of the line. The buttons of the eagle were to be replaced with those of the *fleur-de-lis*.[8]

Article seventeen of the order stated that recruitment to the four corps of royal cavalry would be by specific order. Each royal corps was to be inspected once a year by the regiment's colonels, who were to be lieutenant-generals. The commander-in-chief of the Guard cavalry was also to be the inspector-general.[9]

Even with these measures, Marshal Ney, who had been charged with organising the Royal Corps of Cavalry, was having difficulties in forming the four regiments. What remained of the Imperial Guard cavalry had been given a month's pay from the emperor's funds that had been retained in France. Officers for the four new regiments were not appointed until 19 November 1814, when the four regiments were finally organised.

GLOSSARY OF UNIFORMS

It is important to define the various items of headdress, clothing and equipment used in the Napoleonic era. This glossary is intended to provide a succinct description of items of clothing and equipment mentioned in the text.

Bonnet a poil

Colloquially known as the beehive, the most characteristic feature of the uniform of the *grenadiers* was their tall *bonnet a poil* (literally fur hat) for *soldats* and *bonnet d'ourson* (bearskin hat) for the officers – the same item of uniform made to the same patterns, but with a different fur covering.

The 1801 dress regulations stated that the *bonnet* was to be 352 mm tall and 231 mm wide, the back patch to be 162 mm in diameter, the cordon to be 921 mm long, the tassels to be 88 mm long and the *raquettes* to measure 115 mm deep by 74 mm wide.

Bonnet de police

The first *bonnet de police* or off-duty cap, was introduced in 1767. This was called a *pokalem* and copied then Polish-style clothing. The top was formed from a large disc of cloth, gathered into a headband. The headband had a cloth plaque at the front bearing the regimental number, and also had a second piece of cloth sewn to the headband, which could be lowered down to provide ear flaps and a neck guard. The ear flaps passed through two slots in the headband and were buttoned together. Despite being practical, on 1 April 1791 the *pokalem* was replaced by the more stylish *dragonne*-style *bonnet de police*. It comprised a triangular *flamme*, or wing, which was often laced in the regiment's facing colour and terminated with a tassel. The headband was decorated at the top edge with a row of lace. At the front appeared the regiment's number or a cut-out cloth device of a grenade or hunting horn. The *pokalem* was re-adopted under the Bardin regulations of 1812.

Shako

The Young Guard cavalry wore the 1812 pattern shako, described thus by the Bardin regulations:

Ordinance 12 September 1812: The body of the shako to be 217 mm tall, the cow hide cap to be 271 mm in diameter. The top band was to be 41 mm in depth, the bottom 27 mm, and was fastened at the back by a buckle 27 mm square. The peak was 54 mm deep and made a circle of 325 mm in diameter.

Czapka

Czapka is a Polish and Belorussian generic word for a cap. However, it is perhaps best known to English speakers as a word for the nineteenth-century Polish cavalry headgear, consisting of a high, four-pointed cap with regimental insignia on the front. This headdress developed initially as a square-topped variant of a shako. In bad weather the *czapka* was covered by a black oilskin cover.

Habit

The uniform *habit* of Napoleon's army had its origins in the 1660s, and over time its cut and form evolved into the garment we recognise today. The regulations of 1786 and 1791 were the starting point for *habits* used in the first half of the empire.

The *habit* used prior to 1809 had long tails. The *revers* (lapels) were either cut square (*grenadier*) or pointed (*chasseur*). The cuffs were either cut round with a three-button vertical flap (*grenadier*) or pointed with a two-button closure on the centre back of the sleeve (*chasseur*). The collar of the *habit* was cut to be closed in front. The tails of the *habit* were decorated with a three-pointed false pocket piped in scarlet. The tail linings were in scarlet milled *serge*. At the start of the empire, the tails had each bottom corner hooked together, which over time became stitched down, as the cut of the *habit* became tighter.

In 1809 a short-tailed *habit* was introduced, cut either *grenadier-* or *chasseur-*style. The bottom of the tails was to be 30 cm from the floor with the man on bended knee. The *habit-longe* was cut so that when the man was on bended knee, the bottom of the tail was just touching the back of the knee.

Yet another *habit* was adopted in 1812. This was the *habit-veste* or coatee. Rather than being closed only to the depth of the rib cage, the 1812 style was closed to the waist. This appears to have been worn by the 2nd Regiment of *Éclaireurs*.

Kurtka

The *kurtka* was in essence a precursor to the *habit-veste*. The cut of the *kurtka* was similar to the *habit-veste*: the *revers* closed to the waist, the collar was cut to be open. The sleeves were one-or two-part construction, with the back seam piped. The cuffs were pointed in the manner of the *chasseurs*. The back of the *kurtka* was a single piece of cloth, with the arm syce piped in the facing colour. On the tails of the *kurtka* were two vertical simulated pockets, which terminated the tail facings. Rather than following the shape of the tails, the facing's top edge was a horizontal line that went from centre front at the base of the *revers* to the small buttons at the centre back.

The *kurtka* required twenty-six 17 mm diameter buttons, of which fourteen were on the *revers*, four at the waist, six on the pockets and two on the shoulders. A solitary 15 mm button secured the belt strap on the left hip. In addition, each cuff was closed by a pair of 13 mm buttons.

Vestes and *gilets*

Under the uniform coat, the *habit*, the cavalryman wore a *veste* (waistcoat). This garment existed in four forms:

- *Veste* – sleeved waistcoat
- *Veste sans manche* – unsleeved waistcoat
- *Veste du travaille* – short jacket with sleeves
- *Veste d'ecurie* – short-sleeved jacket

The front was made from facing cloth, with the sleeves and back made from *tricot*, and was lined in either milled *serge* or *tricot*.

It was cut so it had a short 'skirt' at the front so that the top edge of the front pockets was on the natural waist, and the pocket flaps themselves and the front of the *veste* extended below the waistline and over the hips. The front tended to dip down towards the centre front, with a 'V' notch. Although worn under the *habit*, it could be worn as a fatigue coat. The *veste* had a low collar, the front being fastened by a row of small uniform buttons. The back panels were joined to the fronts by means of an underarm seam. The *veste manche* worn under the *habit* only had the sleeve cap of the arms sewn to the body of the *veste*. This allowed for a better fit under the *habit* and allowed greater freedom of movement in the shoulder.

Veste sans manche:
The *veste* could also be sleeveless. The front was cut as before, but it was also cut like a waistcoat, i.e. it had underarm seams joining the front to the back, rather than an army syce and centre back seam. At the centre back was a large triangular gusset that ran the full vertical length of the back of the garment. This allowed the *veste* to be adjusted to fit by the means of tapes.

Veste du travail/veste l'exercice:
The *veste manche* was also issued as a work jacket as a separate item. The *grenadiers-à-pied* and the foot artillery of the Guard were issued fatigue coats or work jackets. These were *veste manche*, but the sleeve was totally sewn to the *veste* body. The *veste* was cut like the *habit*. It was officially regulated in 1812.

Gilet-veste/gilet d'ecurie:
Introduced in 1812 were *gilets* (short jackets). The *gilet* was, in essence, a *veste du travail*, but without the skirts. The bottom edge of the *gilet* was to be extended to be at the natural waist. These garments were cut a lot higher than a *veste*. They, like the *veste*, had collars, shoulder straps and cuff facings. The cuff facings and collars were often in the facing colours of the regiment in the line. It is not certain if the Imperial Guard had the collar and cuffs in any other colour beyond white/ecru.

Dolman

The name 'dolman' was also given to the uniform coat worn by hussars. The close-fitting, short-cut coat was heavily braided. It had, a single-piece back and single-piece sleeves. It had a standing collar. The front was decorated wither either three or five rows of buttons, up to eighteen rows deep, down the front of the jacket. The seams on the back of the coat were covered with flat braid. The pointed cuffs, collar, false pockets, leading and bottom edge were also covered in flat braid either 10 mm or 12 mm wide. They were lined internally with linen. Around the bottom edge of the dolman, on the side, appeared a band of red basane or Moroccan leather. This reinforced the lining and stopped the sabre waist-belt rubbing through the lining. Over the duration of the empire, the cut of the dolman changed – the bottom, or leading edge, increasingly moved up the torso as the waistline of civilian garments increased up the torso. At the start of the empire, the bottom of the dolman was just below the natural waist and by 1815 the dolman often finished above the natural waist. It was complemented by a *pelisse*.

A *pelisse* was originally a short, fur-lined or fur-trimmed jacket that was usually worn hanging loose over the left shoulder of hussar light cavalry soldiers, ostensibly to prevent sword cuts. The name was also applied to a fashionable style of woman's coat worn in the early nineteenth century. The style of uniform incorporating the *pelisse* originated with the hussar mercenaries of Hungary in the seventeenth century. As this type of light cavalry unit became popular in Western Europe, so too did their dress. In the nineteenth century, *pelisses* were in use throughout most armies in Europe, and even some in North and South America.

In appearance the *pelisse* was characteristically a very short and extremely tight-fitting (when worn) jacket, the cuffs and collar of which were trimmed with fur. The jacket was further decorated with patterns sewn in bullion lace. The front of the jacket was distinctive and featured several rows of parallel frogging and loops, and either three or five lines of buttons. For officers of the British hussars this frogging, regimentally differentiated, was generally of gold or silver bullion lace to match either gold (gilt) or silver buttons. Other ranks had either yellow lace with brass buttons or white lace with white-metal buttons. Lacing varied from unit to unit and country to country. The *pelisse* was usually worn slung over the left shoulder in the manner of a short cloak. It was held in place by a shoulder cord. It was cut to be longer than the dolman. It was never worn over the dolman. In the winter it was worn over the *veste*, the dolman being placed into storage. In foul weather the *pelisse* or dolman would be covered by the *manteaux*.

Pantalons

As fashion changed during the early nineteenth century, the use of *culottes* began to be gradually abandoned. *Pantalons*, or trousers, became increasingly commonplace.

The use of *pantalons* became more prevalent in civilian fashion and military clothing as the era progressed, so much so that *culottes* were abandoned under the

1812 regulations in favour of *pantalons*. The heavy cavalry and train troops used *pantalons* made from leather, as well as from wool cloth.

Light cavalry used Hungarian breeches. These were in essence *pantalons* made from wool cloth and decorated on the side seams with lace, which also passed around the back of the *pantalons*. The front fall was decorated with lace, either in a complex Hungarian knot or in a simple *pique* (inverted arrow).

Cavalry also used two variations of *pantalons*. The first are called *pantalons-à-cheval*. These were *pantalons* made from wool cloth with the inside leg reinforced with leather and also at the bottom of each leg. The side seams were either sewn closed or fastened by a row of eighteen buttons down each leg.

In stable dress, *pantalons de treillis* were used. These were either simple *pantalons* or had the side seams closed by a row of eighteen bone buttons. Both forms are recorded as *pantalons d'ecurie*. A shorter version of the side-closing type, which closed at the knee, were called *surclottes*. These were made from *coutil* and worn to protect the expensive leather breeches in the heavy cavalry regiments. From 1812, these items were made from grey wool cloth for the line.

Gaiters

Some cavalry regiments of the Guard had gaiters issued. These were the same items as used by the infantry. Gaiters had been adopted in the French Army by 1714, and by 1786 were an integral part of the dress of the soldier. In normal full dress for the *grenadiers*, *chasseurs* and fusiliers, long, black, wool gaiters were closed with twenty to twenty-four small brass buttons, which were often replaced on campaign with short black or grey gaiters worn under the long trousers. The long black wool gaiters cost 4.20 *francs*, the short grey gaiters between 2.20 *francs* and 3.10 *francs*. The tradition of wearing white gaiters on parade was abandoned for the line with the circular of 20 December 1805, with the tradition maintained by the Old Guard alone.

The buttons were not sewn onto the gaiters. Rather, they were plugged on and held in place with a length of leather thong. The button stands and foot were lined in heavy, coarse linen. The regulations refer to knee buckles, i.e. the buckles that fastened the bottom of the legs were the same as those used on the gaiter straps. The half-gaiters were closed by sixteen to twenty horn buttons, later changed to copper buttons for the black gaiters by 1813. Gaiters were used by infantry and mounted regiments alike.

Calceon le toile

These would be full-length linen or wool flannel drawers, with a button-up fly and a cord around the waist or at the back to fit.

Boots

Various types of boots were used:

- Bottes *forte* – rigid knee-high boots with a knee cuff in front of the knee
- *Demie-forte* – made from a more supple leather

- *Écuyer* – made from soft leather, worn when dismounted
- *Bottines* – ankle boots very much like a modern Chelsea boot
- *Hussard* – a tight fitting riding boot, coming to below the knee, the top edge being decorated with braid

Sac a toile

This was the French soldier's bread bag. It was made from a coarse heavyweight canvas. It had several purposes, the main one for holding food and rations that were distributed to a squad.

This is confirmed in the *ordonnance sur l'habillement* of 1786, Article eleven, as well as *Service de Campagne 1791 section 1 Preparations*, which also confirmed it could be slept in.

It was slung over the shoulder *en sautoir*. On either shoulder it would have been an encumbrance with backpack, *giberne* and musket. It surely would have been dropped when in action, as it's a hindrance to either loading the musket or getting open the *giberne*. In 1801, it was regulated to be made from a double thickness of canvas and measure 157 cm long by 76 cm wide.

Stock

Not wearing something round your neck was not done in eighteenth- and nineteenth-century society. Every soldier would receive two *cols noirs* (black stocks) and one *col blanc* (white stock). The regulations issued by the Kingdom of Italy to harmonise Italian uniforms with French note that the stock was to be pleated in front with up to fourteen pleats. The document further notes that the stock was to be lower than the jacket collar, between 55 mm and 60 mm tall, and cost 2 *francs*.

Capote

The greatcoat was an item of clothing that was not issued to the soldier during the late eighteenth century and first years of the empire. The *capote* was issued to men on sentry duty in bad weather or at night. Thus, the *capote* was part of the equipment of the guardhouse and not of the solider as general issue. The Imperial Guard alone adopted the greatcoat in 1804.

The form of the *capote* was not officially regulation until 1812. Under these regulations it was to be made from beige cloth, to be double-breasted and closed with two rows of five buttons, with buttonholes on both sides so that it could be buttoned up right over left and *vice versa* to save wear on the buttonholes. They were adjusted to fit by means of a half-belt and button on the back. In theory, they were able to be worn over the cross belts. The equipment and artillery trains appear to have made use of these items rather than the cavalry *manteaux*.

Manteau

Rather than a *capote*, the cavalry used a large cloak. At first this was a cape with a standing collar, introduced in 1791. By 1801 the garment had developed a short shoulder cape. The front of the cape was closed by a row of six hooks and eyes. An innovation of the Bardin regulations was a sleeved cavalry cloak, called a *manteaux-capote*. It was of the same proportions as before, but now had sleeves, and the front was closed by a row of five cloth-covered buttons. It was no longer cut like a cloak, but like a *capote*, having the arm syce seam and centre back seam. Both types of *manteaux* and *manteaux-capote* were used side-by-side from 1812. The lining of the shoulder cape, the front opening of the body and the back vent were lined in the facing colour of the regiment. When folded and placed on the *porte-manteau*, the facing colour was visible.

Equipment

Cavalry *giberne*

This was ostensibly the same as the infantry type, but was far smaller. It came into basic types: heavy cavalry, which was a smaller version of the standard infantry *giberne*, and for other arms of the cavalry. This had a curved body. Inside both examples were wooden blocks to take musket cartridges, the oil bottle, etc. The belt for the heavy cavalry *giberne* was in essence the same as used by the infantry – a long leather strap with tabs at each end to buckle to the buckles on the *giberne*. The cavalry *giberne* belt came in two widths: 40 mm or 70 mm. They had large cast buckles, slides and tips. The same slides, buckles and tips were found also on the axe-case belt of the *sapeurs* of infantry.

Cavalry waist-belt

Cavalry waist-belts came in two basic types: heavy cavalry and light cavalry. The heavy cavalry type was 68 mm wide and had two rings from which the sabre slings were suspended. The belt for sub-officers had no bayonet frog.

Light cavalry belts were 40 mm wide and had three rings, two for the sabre slings and each ring also having the three slings for the *sabretache*. The bayonet frog was either held in place with a double-headed button, or was a piece of buff leather sewn to the belt.

Heavy cavalry saddles

The heavy cavalry rode on the French-style saddle, described variously as heavy cavalry or dragoon style. This was the final development of the medieval great saddle. The saddle consisted of a wooden tree reinforced with iron plates. The seat was made from birch and 360-400 mm long, the front points to be 290 mm long and the rear 260 mm long. The seat was made from two pieces of *serge* web that were nailed to the tree and crossed in the centre. Over these, two more webs, again from *serge*, were nailed running tangentially to the tree, all this in turn being covered in a double thickness of white *serge* or linen.

It had a high cantle and pommel. The pommel was reinforced with an iron plate on its underside and had points to prevent the saddle from rolling from side-to-side on the horse's withers. The pommel also sported a ridge board covered in leather and a cantle, covered in leather and stuffed with horse hair, which wrapped around the buttocks of the rider. The tree and seat were covered in a large panel of leather. Beneath it was placed the *panneau* or padding for the saddle, very similar to the panels of the modern hunting or English saddle. The *panneau* was made from a piece of fine cow leather 57 cm square, with a 160 mm gusset between the two stuff panels, each 20 cm by 57 cm. The heavy cavalry saddle presented in the French Army 1801 and 1812 regulations is little different from the seventeenth-century saddle preserved in the Scottish Army Museum in Edinburgh Castle. The form of saddle is preserved in the modern-day Spanish dressage saddle.

The stirrup leathers were attached to the pommel of the saddle, giving a leg forward, slightly bent knee seat, the same as the English hunting seat. The seat of the saddle was protected on campaign with a *serge* cover lined in thin leather.

Light cavalry saddle (Hungarian saddle)

The Hungarian saddle was almost entirely made out of wood. It comprised the following parts:

The front and rear arches were made of beech and reinforced with iron plates. The front arch formed the pommel and the rear arch the cantle. Both arches were secured to the side bars with a mortice and tenon joint.

The side bars were that portion of the saddle that rests on the horse's back, and to which the front and rear arches are secured, thus distributing the weight of the rider along the animal's back. The side bars were also made of wood and carved to fit the shape of the horse's back. The girth was attached to the side bars by means of rawhide thronging.

The seat is the portion of the saddle on which the rider sits. The seat, which was made of alum tanned buff leather, was 10 cm wide and nailed to the front and back arches and thronged to the side bars with rawhide. The saddle had a removable seat called a pilch, which was made from hemp canvas stuffed with horse hair. Over the saddle the *schabraque* was placed.

Lancer regiments used a variation of this saddle, whereby it was totally encased in leather.

Schabraque

Under the saddle a decorative saddle blanket was used, called a *schabraque*. These were made from thick wool cloth lined with wool blanketing and thick linen. They were cut either square or rectangular, the period term being *housse*. When used with a *housse*, the pistol holsters at the front of the saddle were covered with cloth covers. These were called *chaperons*.

For the light cavalry the *schabraque* totally concealed the saddle and was either made from wool or sheepskin. Both types were lined with a heavy linen canvas. The cloth type was often decorated with lace and embroidered emblems.

Blanket
Under the saddle another saddle blanket was used. The was made from heavyweight white wool, and measured four feet six inches by four feet.

Practical experimentation with a replica period blanket shows it could be folded several ways. The heavy cavalry blanket was smaller than that of the light cavalry. With a horse of normal shape and condition the following method, entitled the 'double fold', is recommended. Double the blanket lengthwise, then double it again crosswise. It should then be placed lengthwise across the horse's back with the selvedge edges on the near side and to the rear. The size when folded is two feet 8.50 inches by two feet four inches.

The light cavalry blanket was folded to have twelve thicknesses of cloth and to make it the same size as the heavy cavalry blanket when folded. The heavy cavalry type when folded had six thicknesses of cloth.

Porte-manteau
Behind the saddle for both light and heavy cavalry, a *porte-manteau* was carried. The *porte-manteau* was used to carry the trooper's personal belongings and to carry his cloak. The 1805 cavalry regulations list the contents of the *porte-manteau* as being two shirts placed along the bottom of the *porte-manteau*, with the breeches and stock placed over these, a bag of pistol powder and spare stocks on top of the breeches, along with the night cap, handkerchiefs, brushes for cleaning the *habit*, spare knee guards, then the *surtout* and stable bag. The ration bag was to envelop the watering bit and spread out at the top of the *porte-manteau*. Under the cover of the *porte-manteau* were to be placed the *bonnet de police*, a pair of shoes and the soldier's small equipment. Under the *porte-manteau* was to be the horse's nose-bag and rations, on top the rolled cloak. As well as carrying their own equipment, the *grenadier* had to also carry necessary items to look after his horse. A store return of September 1804 for the *grenadiers-à-cheval* lists the grooming kits then in store consisting of a metal curry comb (108 being in store each costing 1.40 *francs*), a stiff bristled brush (seventeen in store, costing 1 *franc* apiece), a comb (twenty-three in store costing 33.50 *centimes*) and a sponge (twelve in store costing one *franc* apiece). In addition, the cavalry regulation listed that a hoof-pick combination screwdriver was to be carried and a whisp was to be made from twisted straw and a stable rubber (piece of high grade linen). As well as this, each *grenadier* had to carry one or two hay nets and a ration bag/nose, bag to carry the horse's hard feed like oats or bran. This was often carried under the *porte-manteau*. Brietenbach shows this as being made from stripped ticking. The 1801 regulations describe the nose-bag as being made from natural linen, the bag being sixteen inches long and fourteen inches wide, on a strap three foot three inches long and an inch wide. The stores of the *grenadiers-à-cheval* holding twenty-seven of these in 1804, and costing 1 *franc* apiece. The stores list also includes a folding canvas bucket costing 90 *centimes*, twenty examples being in store for the *grenadiers-à-cheval*.

The trooper's *gamelles* and other eating equipment would also have needed to have been stowed as well.

Bridles (*tetiere*)
The first part consisted of a head-collar (*le licol*), nose-band, throat-lash and cheek-pieces. It fastened off at the side with a buckle, a *bridoon* bridle (*le filet*) consisting of cheek pieces, headpiece and brow-band and a second bridle (*le bride*) for the snaffle bit (*mors*), consisting of headpiece, brow-band, cheek-pieces and nose-band and throat-lash were used.

Watering bit (*bridon d'abrevoir*)
This was a head-collar made from natural leather or white canvas. It was designed to allow a bit to be fitted to the rings at the bottom of each cheek piece by a 'T' bar on a piece of chain at each end of the bit. This enabled the horse to be ridden bare-back to the place of watering, the bit to be removed, the horse allowed to drink, and then walked or ridden back to camp. This was often done in pairs.

Martingales
Most of the reliable contemporary prints that show the regiment depict the wearing of standing *martingales* as part of the harness. These are a non-military issue item, evidentially purchased at regimental expense, as fifty-three items, costing 2.50 *francs* each are listed in stores for 23 September 1804. The standing *martingale* is a length of leather attached at one end to the girth and would have passed through a loop on the breastplate (Nicholas Hoffmann, in his series of prints of the troops at the coronation of Napoleon in 1804, shows this loop decorated with a metal boss) and thence fasting to the nose-band of the bridle.

It is designed to prevent the horse throwing or putting their head up above the angle of control, a bad habit that can be dangerous, and the rider receiving a bang on the nose or worse, in the trumpeter's case. When the horse's head is carried in its normal position, the *martingale* should be long enough to be pushed up in the horse's gullet and follow the line of the neck.

BIBLIOGRAPHY

Archives Nationales, Paris:
AFIV 170
AFIV 1140
AFIV 1170 *Garde Impériale et Garde des Consuls*
AFIV 1171 *Garde Impériale*
AFIV 1172 *Garde Impériale*
AFIV 1173 *Garde Impériale 1813*
AFIV 1380
AFIV 1381 *Compatabilitie* Year X and Year XIII
AFIV 1382 *Compatabilitie* Year XIV and 1807
AFIV 1940 *Garde Impériale 1815*
LH/2676/11

Musée de l'Armee:
2747 B1/110
2747 B1/111
2747 B2/51
2747 B2/54
2747 B4 79
MV6354

Service Historique Armee du Terre, Paris:
C2
C15
GR 20 YB 74
GR 20 YB 87
GR 20 YC 4
GR 20 YC 133
GR 20 YC 135
GR 20 YC 136
GR 20 YC 137
GR 20 YC 139
GR 20 YC 140
GR 20 YC 141
GR 20 YC 142
GR 20 YC 145
GR 20 YC 165
IX 285

Xaa 3
Xab 3
Xab 4 *Garde Consulaire-à-Pied et-à-Cheval*
Xab 15
Xab 29
Xab 32 *Cavalerie Generalities*
Xab 33 *Grenadiers-à-Cheval*
Xab 34 *Grenaders-à-Cheval*
Xab 35
Xab 36
Xab 37
Xab 38
Xab 39 *Gendarmes d'Ordonnance*
Xab 40 *Gendarmes d'Ordonnance*
Xab 41 1e *Chevau-Legers*
Xab 42 2e *Chevau-Legers*
Xab 43 3e *Chevau-Legers et Corps Divers*
Xab 44
Xab 51
Xab 58
Xab 59
Xab 60
Xab 61
Xab 62
Xab 73
Xab 74
Xab 78-79 *Decrets Garde Imperiale*
Xac 3
Xac 4
Xc 190
Xc 264

Printed Sources:

Anon, *Ordonnance Provisioire sur l'exercise de la cavalerie An XIII troisieme*, Paris, Chez Magimel, 1815

G. Dempsey, *Napoleon's Soldiers. The Grande Armee of 1807 as depicted in the painting of the Otto Manuscript*. Arms and Armour Press, London, 1994

J.B. Gassendi, *Aide Memoire Chez Magimel*, Paris, 1809

Thomas Hemmann, *Die Bilderhandschrift des Samuel Hahlo aus den Jahren 1807-1808*, Noderstedt, Books on Demand, 2010

Les Gupil, *Administration du masses*, Paris, 1812

Perrot et Amoudru, *Histoire de la ex-Garde*, Deluany, Paris, 1821

Colonel J. Thomas, *Un Regiment Rhenan Sub Napoleon*, Liège, 1936

J.B. Du Vergier, *Collection Complet des Lois, Décrets, Ordonnances, Reglements et Avis du Conseil*, Paris, Guyot et Scribe, 1827

Periodicals:

Carnet de la Sabretache
Journal Militaire
La Giberne
Le Passepoil
Reglement Pour la Cavalerie
Soldats Napoleonienne

Websites:

Marco de Saint Hilaire, available at www.Napoleon-series.org
www.Napoleon-online.de/html/augsburgerbilderserie.html

ENDNOTES

Introduction

1. Perrot et Amoudru, *Histoire de la ex-Garde*, Deluany, Paris, 1821, p. 36.
2. *Reglement Pour la Cavalerie*, 1 January 1791, point 20.
3. *Reglement Pour la Cavalerie*, 1 January 1791, point 20.
4. Service Historique du Armee du Terre (SHDDT): Xab 3.
5. SHDDT: Xab 3 *Décret* 28 Floréal, Year XII.
6. '*Velite Grenadiers-à-Cheval de la Garde*' in *Carnet de La Sabretache*, 1900, p. 64.
7. Archives Nationales (AN): AFIV 1170 *Projet De Décret Portant création d'un corps de Velites à cheval*, 29 Fructidor, Year XIII.
8. AN: AFIV 1170 *Projet De Décret Portant création d'un corps de Velites à cheval*, 29 Fructidor, Year XIII, points 3 and 4.
9. AN: AFIV 1170 *Projet De Décret Portant création d'un corps de Velites à cheval*, 29 Fructidor, Year XIII, point 2.
10. AN: AFIV 1170 *Projet De Décret Portant création d'un corps de Velites à cheval*, 29 Fructidor, Year XIII, point 12.
11. Perrot et Amoudru, pp. 81-2.

Chapter 2

1. Perrot et Amoudru, p. 36.
2. AN: LH/2676/11.
3. SHDDT: 20 YC 137.
4. SHDDT: Xaa3 *Inspection de la Garde Constitutionnalle du Directoir-Executif faite par Le General de Division Kellermann*, Germinal, Year VII *de la Republique Français.*
5. SHDDT: Xaa3 *Inspection de la Garde Constitutionnalle du Directoir-Executif faite par Le General de Division Kellermann*, Germinal, Year VII *de la Republique Français.*
6. SHDDT: Xaa3 *Inspection de la Garde Constitutionnalle du Directoir-Executif faite par Le General de Division Kellermann*, Germinal, Year VII *de la Republique Français.*
7. SHDDT: Xaa3 *Inspection de la Garde Constitutionnalle du Directoir-Executif faite par Le General de Division Kellermann*, Germinal, Year VII *de la Republique Français.*
8. SHDDT: Xaa3 *Inspection de la Garde Constitutionnalle du Directoir-Executif faite par Le General de Division Kellermann*, Germinal, Year VII *de la Republique Français.*
9. SHDDT: Xaa3 *Inspection de la Garde Constitutionnalle du Directoir-Executif faite par Le General de Division Kellermann*, Germinal, Year VII *de la Republique Français.*
10. SHDDT: Xaa3 *Inspection de la Garde Constitutionnalle du Directoir-Executif faite par Le General de Division Kellermann*, Germinal, Year VII *de la Republique Français.*
11. AN: AFIV/ 1170 *Garde Des Consuls Decompte.*
12. AN: AFIV 1382 *Inventaire* 1 Vend., Year XII.
13. AN: AFIV 1382 *Inventaire* 1 Vend., Year XII.
14. AN: AFIV 1382 *Inventaire* 20 Vend., Year XIII.
15. AN: AFIV 1382 *Inventaire* 20 Vend., Year XIII.

16. AN: AFIV 1382 *Inventaire* 20 Vend., Year XIII.
17. AN: AFIV 1382 *Inventaire* 20 Vend., Year XIII.
18. SHDDT: Xab 34 *Marché 24 Fevrier 1807.*
19. SHDDT: Xab 34 *Garde Impériale Habillement 5 Janvier 1807.*
20. SHDDT: Xab 34 *Lettre 8 Fevrier 1808.*
21. SHDDT: Xab 34 *Garde Impériale. Grenadiers-à-Cheval Habillement.*
22. SHDDT: Xab 34 *Garde Impériale. Grenadiers-à-Cheval Habillement.*
23. SHDDT: Xab 34 *Garde Impériale. Grenadiers-à-Cheval Habillement.*
24. SHDDT: Xab 34 *Garde Impériale. Grenadiers-à-Cheval Habillement.*
25. SHDDT: Xab 34 *Inventaire 1 Janvier 1809.*
26. SHDDT: Xab 34 *Marché 27 Octobre 1809.*
27. SHDDT: Xab 34 *Marché 27 Octobre 1809.*
28. SHDDT: Xab 34 *Marché 27 Octobre 1809.*
29. SHDDT: Xab 34 *Marché 15 Octobre 1811.*
30. SHDDT: Xab 34 *Marché 26 Janvier 1811.*
31. SHDDT: Xab 34 *Marché 26 Janvier 1811.*
32. SHDDT: Xab 34 *Marché 10 Octobre 1811.*
33. SHDDT: Xab 34 *Marché 10 Octobre 1811.*
34. SHDDT: Xab 34 *Marché 26 Janvier 1811.*
35. SHDDT: Xab 34 *Marché 26 Janvier 1811.*
36. SHDDT: Xab 34 *Garde Impériale. Grenadiers-à-Cheval Habillement.*
37. SHDDT: Xab 34 *Garde Impériale. Grenadiers-à-Cheval Habillement.*
38. Vanson, '*Grenadiers-à-Cheval de la Garde des Consuls*' in *Carnet de la Sabretache*, 1895, p. 224.
39. AN: AFIV 1170.
40. SHDDT: Xab 74.
41. SHDDT: IX 285.
42. SHDDT: Xab 34 *Garde Impériale. Grenadiers-à-Cheval Habillement.*
43. SHDDT: Xab 34 *Garde Impériale. Grenadiers-à-Cheval Habillement.*
44. Anon, '*Les Grenadiers-à-Cheval*' in *Carnet de la Sabretache*, 1972, p. 120.
45. SHDDT: Xab 33 271.
46. Vanson, p. 224.
47. Vanson, pp. 221 and 245.
48. www.Napoleon-online.de/html/augsburgerbilderserie.html (accessed 17 May 2008). Of note the plate shows the *aiguillette* on the left shoulder rather than the right, *soubise* pockets on the tails of the coat, as well as long pockets, a white cross to the bearskin and what may be the bearskin cords passing under the plume.
49. J. B. Gassendi, *Aide Memoire Chez Magimel*, Vol. 2, Paris, 1809, p. 569.
50. Napoleon to minister of war, 14 April 1803.
51. Napoleon to Bourcier, 7 June 1803.
52. Rousselot, 1966. *Planche 23 Garde Impériale- Grenadier-à-Cheval 1804-15.*
53. SHDDT: Xab 33 271. See also: SHDDT: Xab 34 62.
54. Gassendi, Vol. 2, pp. 567-73.
55. SHDDT: Xab 34 *Etat des effects d'harnachement 5 Janvier 1807.*
56. SHDDT: Xab 34 *Marché 13 Avril 1813.*
57. SHDDT: Xac 4.
58. SHDDT: YC 20 137.
59. SHDDT: YC 20 137.

60. Anon, '*Les Grenadiers-à-Cheval*' in *Carnet de la Sabretache*, 1972, p. 125.
61. Anon, '*Les Grenadiers-à-Cheval*' in *Carnet de la Sabretache*, 1972, p. 125.
62. AN: AFIV 1170.
63. SHDDT: Xab 33 271. See also: SHDDT: Xab 34 62.
64. SHDDT: Xab 34 *Garde Impériale. Grenadiers-à-Cheval Habillement.*
65. SHDDT: Xab 34 *Marché 27 Octobre 1809.*
66. Musée de l'Armee: MV6354.
67. SHDDT: Xab 33 271. See also: SHDDT: Xab 34 62.
68. G. Dempsey, *Napoleon's Soldiers. The Grande Armee of 1807 as depicted in the painting of the Otto Manuscript*, Arms and Armour Press, London, 1994, p. 48.
69. Musée de l'Armee: 2747.
70. M. Stein personal communication, 21 May 2008.
71. Y. Martin, '*Tables de la Garde Impériale presents au sacre du 2 Décembre 1804, par Nicholas Hoffman*' in *Soldats Napoleonienne*, 2004, pp. 9-22.
72. SHDDT: Xab 33 271. See also: SHDDT: Xab 34 62.
73. SHDDT: Xab 34 *Etat des effects d'harnachement 5 Janvier 1807.*
74. SHDDT: Xab 33 271. See also: SHDDT: Xab 34 62.
75. SHDDT: Xab 33 271. See also: SHDDT: Xab 34 62.
76. SHDDT: Xab 33 271. See also: SHDDT: Xab 34 62.
77. Musée de l'Armée: 2747 B4 79.
78. Dempsey, p. 48.
79. Dempsey, p. 48.
80. SHDDT: Xac 4.
81. Dempsey, p. 48.
82. Musée de l'Armée: 2747 B4 79.
83. Y. Martin, pp. 9-22.
84. AN: AFIC 1170 *Garde Des Consuls Decompte.*
85. SHDDT: GR 20 YC 135 13 Nivôse, Year VIII *(2 Janvier 1800)-11 Juillet 1807, (matricules: 1 à 1,875)*. See also: SHDDT: GR 20 YC 137 *1 Avril 1815-25 Novembre 1815 (matricules : 1 à 1,083)*.
86. SHDDT: Xab 33 271. See also: SHDDT: Xab 34 62.
87. SHDDT: Xab 73 *Depense Avril a Juillet 1815.*
88. SHDDT: Xab 33 271. See also: SHDDT: Xab 34 62.
89. Musée de l'Armee: MV6354.
90. Musée de l'Armee: 2747 B1/111.
91. Musée de l'Armee: 2747 B1/110. See also: Musée de l'Armee: 2747 B2/54. See also: Musée de l'Armee: 2747 B2/51.
92. SHDDT: Xab 33 271. See also: SHDDT: Xab 34 62.
93. Vanson, '*Tenues Oubilees*' in *Carnet de La Sabretache*, 1896, p. 577.

Chapter 3

1. AN: AFIV 1170 *Garde Des Consuls Decompte.*
2. AN: AFIV 1170 *Garde Des Consuls Decompte.*
3. AN: AFIV 1382 *Inventaire* 20 Vend., Year XII.
4. AN: AFIV 1382 *Inventaire* 20 Vend., Year XIII.
5. AN: AFIV 1382 *Inventaire* 20 Vend., Year XIII.
6. AN: AFIV 1382 *Inventaire 1 Janvier 1807.*
7. AN: AFIV 1382 *Inventaire 1 Janvier 1808.*

8. AN: AFIV 1382 *Inventaire 1 Janvier 1808.*
9. SHDDT: Xab 32 *Garde Impériale Chasseurs-à-Cheval.*
10. SHDDT: Xab 32 *Garde Impériale Chasseurs-à-Cheval.*
11. SHDDT: Xab 32 *Garde Impériale Chasseurs-à-Cheval.*
12. SHDDT: Xab 35 *Marché 28 Aout 1809.*
13. SHDDT: Xab 35 *releve de l'etat des effects d'habillement.*
14. SHDDT: Xab 35 *releve de l'etat des effects d'habillement.*
15. SHDDT: Xab 35 *Marché 17 Mai 1809.*
16. SHDDT: Xab 35 *Marché 29 Aout 1809.*
17. SHDDT: Xab 15 *Marché 25 Aout 1809.*
18. SHDDT: Xab 15 *Marché 25 Aout 1809.*
19. SHDDT: Xab 15 *Marché 25 Aout 1809.*
20. SHDDT: Xab 32 *Ex Garde Impériale, Chasseurs-à-Cheval, Compte de Habillement.*
21. SHDDT: Xab 35 *tariff effects d'habillement.*
22. SHDDT: Xab 35 *tariff effects d'habillement.*
23. SHDDT: Xab 35 *tariff effects d'habillement.*
24. J. B. Du Vergier, *Collection Complet des Lois, Décrets, Ordonnances, Reglements et Avis du Conseil*, Paris, Guyot et Scribe, 1827, p. 50. See also: Du Vergier pp. 58 and 110-5.
25. Le Dernier, '*Registre Correspondence du General Pully*' in *Carnet de la Sabretache*, Vol. 1, 1893, p. 118.
26. SHDDT: Xac 3.
27. Du Vergier, p. 50. See also: Du Vergier, pp. 58 and 110-5.
28. Du Vergier, p. 50. See also: Du Vergier, pp. 58 and 110-5.
29. SHDDT: Xac 3.
30. SHDDT: GR 20 YC 145 *bis corps royal des Chasseurs-à-Cheval organise le 29 Juillet 1814 et devenu le 1er Regiment de Chasseurs-à-Cheval et mamelukes le 26 Avril 1815.*
31. SHDDT: GR 20 YC 145 *bis corps royal des Chasseurs-à-Cheval organise le 29 Juillet 1814 et devenu le 1er Regiment de Chasseurs-à-Cheval et mamelukes le 26 Avril 1815.*
32. SHDDT: GR 20 YC 145 *bis corps royal des Chasseurs-à-Cheval organise le 29 Juillet 1814 et devenu le 1er Regiment de Chasseurs-à-Cheval et mamelukes le 26 Avril 1815.*
33. SHDDT: GR 20 YC 145 *bis corps royal des Chasseurs-à-Cheval organise le 29 Juillet 1814 et devenu le 1er Regiment de Chasseurs-à-Cheval et mamelukes le 26 Avril 1815.*
34. SHDDT: GR 20 YC 145 *bis corps royal des Chasseurs-à-Cheval organise le 29 Juillet 1814 et devenu le 1er Regiment de Chasseurs-à-Cheval et mamelukes le 26 Avril 1815.*
35. SHDDT: Xac 3.
36. SHDDT: Xac 3.
37. SHDDT: Xac 3.
38. SHDDT: Xac 3.
39. SHDDT: Xab 35 *tariff effects d'habillement.*
40. SHDDT: Xab 35 *tariff effects d'habillement.*
41. SHDDT: Xab 35 *tariff effects d'habillement.*
42. SHDDT: Xab 35 *tariff effects d'habillement.*
43. SHDDT: Xab35 *Garde Imperiale Chasseurs-à-Cheval Tarif des matiers.*
44. SHDDT: Xab 35 *Marché 25 Aout 1809.*
45. SHDDT: Xab35 *Garde Imperiale Chasseurs à Cheval Tarif des matiers.*
46. SHDDT: Xab35 *Garde Imperiale Chasseurs à Cheval Tarif des matiers.*
47. SHDDT: Xab35 *Garde Imperiale Chasseurs à Cheval Tarif des matiers.*
48. SHDDT: Xab35 *Garde Imperiale Chasseurs à Cheval Tarif des matiers.*

49. SHDDT: Xab 35 Krettly to Beauharnais Fructidor, Year XI.
50. SHDDT: Xab 35 *Marché* 24 Thermidor, Year XI.
51. SHDDT: Xab 35 *Rapport au minister*, no date Year XII.
52. SHDDT: Xab 35 Minister of war to Beauharnais *Rapport* 14 Ventôse, Year XII.
53. SHDDT: Xab 35 *Rapport faut au minister* Vendémiaire, Year XII.
54. SHDDT: Xab 35 *Rapport* 2 Vendémiaire, Year XII.
55. SHDDT: Xab 35 *Marché* 12 Vendémiaire, Year XII.
56. SHDDT: GR 20 YC 142 13 Nivôse, Year VIII-8 Nivôse, Year XII *(2 Janvier 1800-30 Décembre 1803) (matricules : 1 à 1,085).*

Chapter 4

1. AN: AFIV 1382 *Inventaire* 20 Vend., Year XII.
2. AN: AFIV 1382 *Inventaire* 20 Vend., Year XIII.
3. AN: AFIV 1382 *Inventaire* 20 Vend., Year XII.
4. AN: AFIV 1382 *Inventaire* 20 Vend., Year XII.
5. AN: AFIV 1382 *Inventaire* 20 Vend., Year XII.
6. AN: AFIV 1382 *Inventaire 1 Janvier 1807.*
7. AN: AFIV 1382 *Inventaire 1 Janvier 1808.*
8. SHDDT: Xab 32 *Garde Impériale Chasseurs-à-Cheval.*
9. SHDDT: Xab 32 *Garde Impériale Chasseurs-à-Cheval.*
10. SHDDT: Xab 35 *releve de l'etat des effects d'habillement.*
11. SHDDT: Xab 35 *releve de l'etat des effects d'habillement.*
12. SHDDT: Xab 35 *Marché 3 Novembre 1813.*
13. SHDDT: Xab 35 *Marché 3 Novembre 1813.*
14. SHDDT: Xab 36 *Ex Garde Impériale, Chasseurs-à-Cheval, Compte de Habillement.*
15. SHDDT: Xab 36 *Ex Garde Impériale, Chasseurs-à-Cheval, Compte de Habillement.*
16. SHDDT: Xab 36 *Ex Garde Impériale, Chasseurs-à-Cheval, Compte de Habillement.*
17. SHDDT: Xab 36 *Ex Garde Impériale, Chasseurs-à-Cheval, Compte de Habillement.*
18. SHDDT: Xab 36 *Ex Garde Impériale, Chasseurs-à-Cheval, Compte de Habillement.*
19. SHDDT: Xab 36.
20. SHDDT: Xab 36 *Inventaire 30 Mars 1814.*

Chapter 5

1. SHDDT: Xab 38 Napoleon to Clarke, 15 April 1806.
2. SHDDT: Xab 38 Clarke to Napoleon, 13 November 1806.
3. SHDDT: Xab 38 Napoleon to Clarke, 8 July 1807.
4. SHDDT: Xab 38 Napoleon to Clarke, 8 July 1807.
5. SHDDT: Xab 38 *Etat des Objects des Harnachment 10 Aout 1811.*
6. SHDDT: Xab 38 *Marché 13 Septembre 1806.*
7. SHDDT: Xab 38 *Marché 13 Septembre 1806.*
8. SHDDT: Xab 38 *Marché 13 Septembre 1806.*
9. AN: AFIV 1382 *Inventaire 1 Janvier 1807.*
10. AN: AFIV 1382 *Inventaire 1 Janvier 1807.*
11. AN: AFIV 1382 *Inventaire 1 Janvier 1808.*
12. AN: AFIV 1382 *Inventaire 1 Janvier 1807.*
13. AN: AFIV 1382 *Inventaire 1 Janvier 1807.*
14. SHDDT: Xab 38 *Marché 10 Aout 1811.*

15. SHDDT: Xab 38 *Marché 10 Aout 1811.*
16. SHDDT: Xab 38 *Marché 3 Septembre 1811.*
17. SHDDT: Xab 38 *Marché 28 Mai 1812.*
18. SHDDT: Xab 38 *Marché 28 Mai 1812.*
19. SHDDT: Xab 38 *Marché 28 Mars 1812.*
20. SHDDT: Xab 38 *Marché 28 Mars 1812.*
21. SHDDT: Xab 38 *Marché 1 Décembre 1812.*
22. SHDDT: Xab *Marché 10 Fevrier 1813.*
23. SHDDT: Xab 38 *Marché 13 Fevrier 1813.*
24. SHDDT: Xab *Marché 10 Fevrier 1813.*
25. SHDDT: Xab 38 *Marché 30 Juin 1813.*
26. SHDDT: Xab 38 *Marché 27 Octobre 1813.*
27. SHDDT: Xab *Marché 10 Fevrier 1813.*
28. SHDDT: Xab 38 *Marché 28 Mars 1812.*
29. SHDDT: Xab 38 *Marché 1 Décembre 1812.*
30. SHDDT: Xab 38 *Minute de la letter ećrit 5 Juillet 1813.*
31. SHDDT: Xab 38 *Marché 4 Juin 1812.*
32. SHDDT: Xab 38 *Marché 4 Juin 1812.*
33. SHDDT: Xab 38 *Etat des Objects des Harnachment 10 Aout 1811.*
34. SHDDT: Xab 38 *Marché 28 Mars 1812.*
35. SHDDT: Xac 4.
36. SHDDT: Xac 4.
37. SHDDT: Xac 4.
38. SHDDT: Xab 73.
39. SHDDT: Xab 38 *Marché 1 July 1806.*
40. SHDDT: Xab 38 *Marché 13 September 1806.*
41. SHDDT: Xab 38 *Marché 13 September 1806.*
42. Rousselot, *Planche 13 Dragons de la Garde Impériale.*
43. Rousselot, *Planche 13 Dragons de la Garde Impériale.*
44. Rousselot, *Planche 13 Dragons de la Garde Impériale.*
45. SHDDT: Xab 38 *Marché 1 April 1813.*
46. Rousselot, *Planche 13 Dragons de la Garde Impériale.*

Chapter 6

1. I am grateful to Mr George Lubomski for providing the text for this chapter on the history of the regiment and the discussion of the uniform. The commentary upon archive documents at Vincennes is my own.
2. SHDDT: Xab 51 *Marché 2 Fevrier 1809.*
3. I am grateful to Mr George Lubomski for providing the text for this section.
4. I am grateful to Mr George Lubomski for providing the text for this section.
5. SHDDT: Xab 41 *remplacement 1811.*
6. SHDDT: Xab 41 *remplacement 1811.*
7. SHDDT: Xab 41 *remplacement 1811.*
8. SHDDT: Xab 41 *remplacement 1811.*
9. SHDDT: Xab 41 *remplacement 1811.*
10. SHDDT: Xab 41 *fournissier de draps 2 Fevrier 1809.*
11. SHDDT: Xab 41 *remplacement 1811.*
12. SHDDT: Xab 41 *remplacement 1811.*

13. SHDDT: Xab 41 *remplacement 1811.*
14. SHDDT: Xab 41 *remplacement 1811.*
15. SHDDT: Xab 41 *remplacement 1811.*
16. SHDDT: Xab 41 *remplacement 1811.*
17. SHDDT: Xab 41 *remplacement 1811.*
18. SHDDT: Xab 41 *remplacement 1811.*
19. SHDDT: Xab 41 *remplacement 1811.*
20. SHDDT: Xab 41 *Marché 1e trimester 1812.*
21. SHDDT: Xab 41 *Marché 1e trimester 1812.*
22. SHDDT: Xab 41 *Marché 1e trimester 1812.*
23. SHDDT: Xab 41 *Marché 1e trimester 1812 Czapka.*
24. SHDDT: Xab 41 *dates de expiration.*
25. SHDDT: Xab 41 *Marché 1e Trimestre 1814.*
26. SHDDT: Xab 41 *Marché 1e Trimestre 1814.*
27. SHDDT: Xab 41 *Marché 3e Trimestre 1813.*
28. SHDDT: Xab 41 *Marché 1e Trimestre 1814.*
29. SHDDT: Xab 41 *Marché 1e Trimestre 1814.*
30. SHDDT: Xab 41 *Remplacements 1813.*
31. SHDDT: Xab 41 *Marché 1e Trimestre 1814.*
32. SHDDT: Xab 41 *Remplacements 1813.*
33. SHDDT: Xab 41 *Marché 1e Trimestre 1814.*
34. SHDDT: Xab 41 *Marché 1e Trimestre 1814.*
35. SHDDT: Xab 41 *Marché 1e Trimestre 1814.*
36. SHDDT: Xab 41 *Marché 1e Trimestre 1814.*
37. SHDDT: Xab 41 *Marché 1e Trimestre 1814.*
38. SHDDT: Xab 41 *Marché 1e Trimestre 1814.*
39. SHDDT: Xab 41 *Marché 1e Trimestre 1814.*
40. SHDDT: Xab 41 *Marché 1e Trimestre 1814.*
41. SHDDT: Xab 41 *Marché 1e Trimestre 1814.*
42. SHDDT: Xab 41 *Marché 1e Trimestre 1814.*
43. SHDDT: Xab 41 *Remplacements 1813.*
44. SHDDT: Xab 41 *Marché 1e Trimestre 1814.*
45. SHDDT: Xab 41 *Marché 1e Trimestre 1814.*
46. SHDDT: Xab 41 *Marché 1e Trimestre 1814.*
47. SHDDT: Xab 41 *Marché 1e Trimestre 1814.*
48. SHDDT: Xab 41 *Marché 1e Trimestre 1814.*
49. SHDDT: Xab 41 *Remplacements 1813.*
50. SHDDT: Xab 41 *Marché 1e Trimestre 1814.*
51. I am grateful to Mr George Lubomski for providing the text for this section.
52. I am grateful to Mr George Lubomski for providing the text for this section.

Chapter 7

1. SHDDT: 20 YC 165 *register matricule du Corps Royal de chevau leger lanciers de France, 21 Juin 1814-20 Mars 1815.*
2. SHDDT: Xab 42 *Marché 24 Mai 1811.*
3. SHDDT: Xab 42 *Marché 24 Mai 1811.*
4. SHDDT: Xab 42 *Marché 24 Mai 1811.*
5. SHDDT: Xab 42 *Marché 5 Juillet 1811.*

6. SHDDT: Xab 42 *Marché 24 Mai 1811.*
7. SHDDT: Xab 42 *Marché 5 Juillet 1811.*
8. SHDDT: Xab 42 *Marché 24 Mai 1811.*
9. SHDDT: Xab 42 *Marché 21 Mars 1812.*
10. SHDDT: Xab 42 *Marché 21 Mars 1812.*
11. SHDDT: Xab 42 *Marché 21 Mars 1812.*
12. SHDDT: Xab 42 *Marché 21 Mars 1812.*
13. SHDDT: Xab 42 *Marché 21 Mars 1812.*
14. SHDDT: Xab 42 *Marché 21 Mars 1812.*
15. SHDDT: Xab 42 *Marché 21 Mars 1812.*
16. SHDDT: Xab 42 *Marché 21 Mars 1812.*
17. SHDDT: Xab 42 *Marché 21 Mars 1812.*
18. SHDDT: Xab 42 *Marché 5 Juillet 1811.*
19. SHDDT: Xab 42 *Marché 21 Mars 1812.*
20. SHDDT: Xab 42 *Marché 1 Fevrier 1813.*
21. SHDDT: Xab 42 *Marché 30 Juin 1812.*
22. SHDDT: Xab 42 *Marché 1 Fevrier 1813.*
23. SHDDT: Xab 42 *Marché 1e Trimestre 1814.*
24. SHDDT: Xab 42 *Marché 1e Trimestre 1814.*
25. SHDDT: Xab 42 *Marché 1 Mai 1813.*
26. SHDDT: Xab 42 *Marché 1e Trimestre 1814.*
27. SHDDT: Xab 42 *Marché 1e Trimestre 1814.*
28. SHDDT: Xab 42 *Marché 1e Trimestre 1814.*
29. SHDDT: Xab 42 *Marché 3 Janvier 1814*. See also: SHDDT: *Marché 15 Janvier 1814.*
30. SHDDT: Xab 42 *Marché 1e Trimestre 1814.*
31. SHDDT: Xab 42 *Marché 1e Trimestre 1814.*
32. SHDDT: Xab 42 *Marché 1e Trimestre 1814.*
33. Du Vergier, p. 50. See also: Du Vergier, pp. 58 and 110-5.
34. Du Vergier, p. 50. See also: Du Vergier, pp. 58 and 110-5.
35. SHDDT: 2 YB 87 *2e régiment de chevau-legers lancers de la Garde Impériale*. See also: SHDDT: 2 YB 87 *2e régiment de chevau-legers lancers de la Garde Impériale.*
36. SHDDT: 2 YB 87 *2e régiment de chevau-legers lancers de la Garde Impériale*. See also: SHDDT: 2 YB 87 *2e régiment de chevau-legers lancers de la Garde Impériale.*
37. SHDDT: Xc 264 Correspondence General Pully, report 25 August 1814.
38. SHDDT: Xc 264 Correspondence General Pully, report 25 August 1814.
39. Le Dernier, p. 119.
40. Le Dernier, p. 118.
41. SHDDT: Xc 264 Correspondence General Pully, report 25 August 1814.
42. SHDDT: Xac 3 report Marshall Ney, 2 August 1814.
43. SHDDT: 2 YB 87 *2e régiment de chevau-legers lancers de la Garde Impériale*. See also: SHDDT: 2 YB 87 *2e régiment de chevau-legers lancers de la Garde Impériale.*
44. SHDDT: 2 YB 87 *2e régiment de chevau-legers lancers de la Garde Impériale*. See also: SHDDT: 2 YB 87 *2e régiment de chevau-legers lancers de la Garde Impériale.*
45. Du Vergier, p. 50. See also: Du Vergier, pp. 58 and 110-5.
46. SHDDT: 20 YC 165 *register matricule du Corps Royal de chevau leger lanciers de France, 21 Juin 1814-20 Mars 1815.*
47. SHDDT: Xac 3.
48. SHDDT: Xac 3.

Chapter 8

1. I am grateful to Mr George Lubomski for providing the text for this section.
2. I am grateful to Mr George Lubomski for providing the text for this section.
3. SHDDT: Xab 43 *Dossier 3e Lanciers. Lettre 2 Janvier 1813.*
4. SHDDT: Xab 43 Dossier *3e Lanciers. Décret 22 Mars 1813.*
5. I am grateful to Mr George Lubomski for providing the text for this section.
6. SHDDT: Xab 43 *Dossier 3e Lanciers. Lettre 2 Janvier 1813.*
7. SHDDT: Xab 43 *dossier Tatares. Letter 16 Avril 1813.*
8. I am grateful to Mr George Lubomski for providing the text for this section.
9. SHDDT: Xab 43 *dossier Tatares. Marché 1e trimester 1814.*
10. SHDDT: Xab 43 *dossier Tatares. Marché 1e trimester 1814.*
11. SHDDT: Xab 43 *dossier Tatares. Marché 1e trimester 1814.*
12. SHDDT: Xab 41 *Marché 1e trimester 1814.*

Chapter 9

1. SHDDT: Xab 44 *Dossier 1e Èclaireurs. Décret 9 Décembre 1813.*
2. SHDDT: Xab 44 *Dossier 1e Èclaireurs. Décret 9 Décembre 1813.*
3. SHDDT: GR 20 YC 140 *1er régiment d'éclaireurs, attaché au régiment de grenadiers à cheval., 1813-4 Intitulé de l'unité documentaire 27 Décembre 1813-27 Mai 1814 (matricules: 1 à 506).* See also: SHDDT: GR 20 YC 141 *1er régiment d'éclaireurs, attaché au régiment de grenadiers à cheval., 1813-4. 28 Décembre 1813-25 Mars 1814 (matricules: 1 à 608).*
4. SHDDT: GR YC 20 136. See also: SHDDT: GR YC 20 139. See also: SHDDT: GR YC 20 141.
5. SHDDT: GR YC 20 136. See also: SHDDT: GR YC 20 139. See also: SHDDT: GR YC 20 141.
6. SHDDT: Xab 44 *Dossier 1e Èclaireurs. Garde Impériale 1st regiment des Èclaireurs. Habillement.*
7. SHDDT: Xab 44 *Dossier 1e Èclaireurs. Garde Impériale 1st regiment des Èclaireurs. Habillement.*
8. SHDDT: Xab 44 *Dossier 1e Èclaireurs. Garde Impériale 1st regiment des Èclaireurs. Habillement.*
9. SHDDT: Xab 44 *Dossier 1e Èclaireurs. Marché 15 Fevrier 1814.*
10. SHDDT: Xab 44 *Dossier 1e Èclaireurs. Garde Impériale 1st regiment des Èclaireurs. Habillement.*
11. Du Vergier, p. 50. See also: Du Vergier, pp. 58 and 110-5.
12. SHDDT: GR YC 20 137.
13. SHDDT: Xac 4 *Corps Royale des Cuirassiers de France.*
14. SHDDT: Xac 4 *Corps Royale des Cuirassiers de France.*
15. SHDDT: Xac 4 *Corps Royale des Cuirassiers de France.*
16. AN: AFIV 1173 Drouot 7 *Décembre 1813.*
17. SHDDT: Xc 190 *3e Chasseurs. Dossier 1814.*
18. SHDDT: Xab 43 *dossier 3e Lanciers. Marché 1e trimester 1814.*
19. SHDDT: Xab 43 *dossier 3e Lanciers. Marché 1e trimester 1814.*
20. SHDDT: Xab 41.
21. SHDDT: Xab 43 *dossier 3e Lanciers. Marché 1e trimester 1814.*
22. SHDDT: Xab 44 *Dossier 3e Èclaireurs.*
23. SHDDT: Xab 43 *dossier 3e Lanciers. Marché 1e trimester 1814.*
24. SHDDT: Xab 43 *dossier 3e Lanciers. Marché 1e trimester 1814.*
25. SHDDT: Xab 43 *dossier 3e Lanciers. Marché 1e trimester 1814.*
26. SHDDT: Xab 43 *Dossier 3e Èclaireurs.*

Chapter 10

1. SHDDT: Xab 78, p. 24.
2. SHDDT: Xab 78, p. 38.
3. SHDDT: Xab 78, p. 86.
4. SHDDT: Xab 78, pp. 83-4.
5. SHDDT: GR 20 YC 133 *Gendarmes d'elite*, 1 Frimaire, Year X *22 Novembre 1801-2 Janvier 1808 (matricules 1 à 1,141).*
6. SHDDT: GR 20 YC 133 *bis Gendarmes d'elite*, Year X *Mars 1807 (matricules 1 à 480).*
7. SHDDT: GR 20 YC 4 *Gendarmerie d'elite de la garde des consuls, devenu impériale*, Year X *1802-14 (matricules 1 à 1,937).*
8. AN: AFIV 1170 *Garde des Consuls, Dossier Gendarmerie d'Elite, rapport* 28 Ventôse, Year X.
9. AN: AFIV 1170 *Garde des Consuls, Dossier Gendarmerie d'Elite, rapport* 28 Ventôse, Year X.
10. AN: AFIV 1170 *Garde des Consuls, Dossier Gendarmerie d'Elite, rapport* 28 Ventôse, Year X.
11. AN: AFIV 1170 *Garde des Consuls, Dossier Gendarmerie d'Elite, rapport* 1 Germinal, Year XI.
12. AN: AFIV 1170 *Garde des Consuls, Dossier Gendarmerie d'Elite, rapport* 1 Germinal, Year XI.
13. AN: AFIV 1170 *Garde des Consuls, Dossier Gendarmerie d'Elite, rapport* 1 Germinal, Year XI.
14. AN: AFIV 1170 *Garde des Consuls, Dossier Gendarmerie d'Elite, rapport* 1 Germinal, Year XI.
15. AN: AFIV 1170 *Garde des Consuls, Dossier Gendarmerie d'Elite, rapport* 1 Germinal, Year XI.
16. AN: AFIV 1382 *Inventaire* 1 Vend., Year XII.
17. AN: AFIV 1382 *Inventaire* 1 Vend., Year XII.
18. AN: AFIV 1382 *Inventaire* 1 Vend., Year XII.
19. AN: AFIV 1382 *Inventaire* 1 Vend., Year XIII.
20. SHDDT: Xab 37 *Rapport fait au minister 28 Aout 1809.*
21. SHDDT: Xab 37 *Marché, 1e Trimestre de 1812.*
22. AN: AFIV 1382 *Inventaire* 1 Vend., Year XIV.
23. AN: AFIV 1382 *Inventaire* 1 Vend., Year XIV.
24. AN: AFIV 1382 *Inventaire* 1 January 1807.
25. AN: AFIV 1382 *Inventaire* 1 January 1807.
26. AN: AFIV 1382 *Inventaire* 1 January 1808.
27. SHDDT: Xab 37 *Etat de prix des effets d'habillement 3 Juillet 1807.*
28. SHDDT: Xab 37 *Etat de prix des effets d'habillement 3 Juillet 1807.*
29. SHDDT: Xab 37 *Etat de prix des effets d'habillement 3 Juillet 1807.*
30. SHDDT: Xab 37 *Etat de prix des effets d'habillement 3 Juillet 1807.*
31. SHDDT: Xab 37 *Etat de prix des effets d'habillement 3 Juillet 1807.*
32. AN: AFIV 1382 *Inventaire* 1 January 1808.
33. AN: AFIV 1382 *Inventaire* 1 January 1808.
34. SHDDT: Xab 15 *Habillement Grenadiers-à-Pied 1804 a 1814. Dossier 3e Grenadiers. Marché 3e Décembre 1811.*
35. SHDDT: Xab 37 *Dossier Habillement. March 3e Trimestre de 1813.*

SHDDT: Xab 37 *Dossier Habillement. March 3e Trimestre de 1813.*
36. SHDDT: Xab 37 *Dossier Habillement. March 3e Trimestre de 1813.*
37. SHDDT: Xab 37 *Dossier Habillement. March 3e Trimestre de 1813.*
38. SHDDT: Xab 37 *Dossier Habillement. March 3e Trimestre de 1813.*
39. SHDDT: Xab 37 *Dossier Habillement. March 3e Trimestre de 1813.*
40. AN: AFIV 1170 *Garde des Consuls, Dossier Gendarmerie d'Elite Rapport* 1 Germinal, Year XI.
41. AN: AFIV 1170 *Garde des Consuls, Dossier Gendarmerie d'Elite Rapport* 28 Ventose, Year X.
42. SHDDT: Xab 37 *Etat de prix des effets d'habillement 3 Juillet 1807.*
43. SHDDT: Xab 37 *Dossier Habillement. Marché 3e Trimestre de 1813.*
44. AN: AFIV 1170 *Garde des Consuls, Dossier Gendarmerie d'Elite Rapport* 1 Germinal, Year XI.
45. SHDDT: Xab 37 *Dossier Habillement. Marché 3e Trimestre de 1813.*
46. SHDDT: GR 20 YC 133 *bis Gendarmes d'elite*, Year X Mars 1807 (*matricules 1 à 480*).
47. SHDDT: GR 20 YC 133 *Gendarmes d'elite,* 1 Frimaire, Year X *22 Novembre 1801-2 Janvier 1808 (matricules 1 à 1,141).*
48. SHDDT: GR 20 YC 4 *Gendarmerie d'elite de la garde des consuls, devenue impériale,* Year X 1802-1814 (*matricules 1 à 1,937*).
49. SHDDT: GR 20 YC 4 *Gendarmerie d'elite de la garde des consuls, devenue impériale,* Year X 1802-1814 (*matricules 1 à 1,937*).
50. SHDDT: GR 20 YC 133 *bis Gendarmes d'elite*, Year X Mars 1807 (*matricules 1 à 480*).

Chapter 11

1. AN: AFIV 1170 *Garde Des Consuls Decompte.*
2. AN: AFIV 1382 *Inventaire* 20 Vend., Year XIII.
3. AN: AFIV 1382 *Inventaire* 20 Vend., Year XIII.
4. AN: AFIV 1382 *Inventaire* 20 Vend., Year XIII.
5. AN: AFIV 1382 *Inventaire* 1 Vend., Year XII.
6. AN: AFIV 1382 *Inventaire* 20 Vend., Year XIII.
7. AN: AFIV 1382 *Inventaire* 20 Vend., Year XIII.
8. SHDDT: Xab 59 *Artillerie. Garde Impériale. Etat detaille de prix de chaque effects d'habillement.*
9. SHDDT: Xab59 *Ex Garde Impériale, Artillerie, Compte de Habillment 1811.*
10. SHDDT: Xab59 *Ex Garde Impériale, Artillerie, Compte de Habillment 1811.*
11. SHDDT: Xab 59 *Ex Garde Impériale, Artillerie, Compte de Habillment 1811.*
12. SHDDT: Xab 59 *Ex Garde Impériale. Releve Sommaire 1 Janvier 1812 a 1 Janvier 1814.*
13. SHDDT: Xab 29 *Artillerie. Garde Impériale. Etat detaille de prix de chaque effects d'habillement.*
14. SHDDT: Xab 59 *Ex Garde Impériale. Releve Sommaire 1 Janvier 1812 a 1 Janvier 1814.*
15. SHDDT: Xab 59 *Ex Garde Impériale, Artillerie, Compte de Habillement 1811.*
16. Rousselot, *Planche 074 Artillerie-à-Cheval de la Garde Impériale, Officers et Trompette.*
17. SHDDT: Xab 29 *Artillerie. Garde Impériale. Etat detaille de prix de chaque effects d'habillement.*

Chapter 12

1. SHDDT: Xab 60. See also: *ordre* 21 Fructidor, Year VIII.
2. AN: AFIV 1380 *Arête* 11 Brumaire, Year XII.
3. Marco de Saint Hilaire, available at www.Napoleon-series.org (accessed 6 September 2006).
4. L. Fallou, *'Train d'artillerie de la Garde Imperiale 1806-1815'* in *Le Passepoil*, Vol. 14, 1934, p. 29.
5. Fallou, p. 29.
6. SHDDT: Xab 78/126.
7. SHDDT: Xab 78/126.
8. SHDDT: Xab 78/206.
9. Napoleon, Correspondence no. 15,723, 31: 328-9 to Clarke, minister for war, 29 May 1809.
10. SHDDT: Xab 78 182.
11. AN: AFIV 170 *Garde Des Consuls Decompte.*
12. AN: AFIV 170 *Garde Des Consuls Decompte.*
13. AN: AFIV 1382 *Inventaire* 1 Vend., Year XII.
14. AN: AFIV 1382 *Inventaire* 20 Vend., Year XIII.
15. AN: AFIV 1382 *Inventaire* 20 Vend., Year XIII.
16. Thomas Hemmann, *Die Bilderhandschrift des Samuel Hahlo aus den Jahren 1807-1808*, Noderstedt, Books on Demand, 2010, pp. 44-5, Plate 9.
17. SHDDT: Xab 60 *Exercise 1e Trimestre 1807.*
18. SHDDT: Xab 60 *Exercise 1e Trimestre 1807.*
19. SHDDT: Xab 60 *Exercise 1e Trimestre 1808.*
20. SHDDT: Xab 60 *Marché 26 Avril 1809.*
21. SHDDT: Xab 60 *Marché 8 Avril 1809.*
22. SHDDT: Xab 60 *Marché 8 Avril 1809.*
23. SHDDT: Xab 60 *Marché 11 Avril 1809.*
24. SHDDT: Xab 60 *Marché 11 Avril 1809.*
25. SHDDT: Xab 60 *Marché 2 Juin 1809.*
26. SHDDT: Xab 60 *Marché 7 Aout 1809.*
27. SHDDT: Xab 60 *Marché 25 Aout 1809.*
28. SHDDT: Xab 29 *Artillerie. Garde Impériale. Etat detaille de prix de chaque effects d'habillement.*
29. SHDDT: Xab 29 *Artillerie. Garde Impériale. Etat detaille de prix de chaque effects d'habillement.*
30. SHDDT: Xab 29 *Artillerie. Garde Impériale. Etat detaille de prix de chaque effects d'habillement.*
31. SHDDT: Xab 29 *Artillerie. Garde Impériale. Etat detaille de prix de chaque effects d'habillement.*
32. SHDDT: Xab 29 *Artillerie. Garde Impériale. Etat detaille de prix de chaque effects d'habillement.*
33. SHDDT: Xab 60 *Marché 5 Avril 1811.*
34. SHDDT: Xab 60 *Marché 7 Mai 1811.*
35. SHDDT: Xab 60 *Marché 27 Mai 1811.*
36. SHDDT: Xab 60 *Marché 27 Mai 1811.*
37. SHDDT: Xab 60 *Marché 27 Mai 1811.*
38. SHDDT: Xab 60 *Marché 27 Mai 1811.*
39. SHDDT: Xab 60 *Marché 29 Juillet 1811.*
40. SHDDT: Xab 15 *Dossier 3e Grenadiers-à-Pied. Marché 3 Décembre 1811.*